# Prague

## THE ROUGH GUIDE

D0067927

**Rough Guide Credits**

| | |
|---|---|
| Series editor: | Mark Ellingham |
| Text editors: | John Fisher and Kate Berens |
| Editorial: | Martin Dunford, Jonathan Buckley, Greg Ward, Jules Brown, Graham Parker |
| Production: | Susanne Hillen, Andy Hilliard, Gail Jammy, Vivien Antwi, Melissa Flack, Alan Spicer |
| Publicity: | Richard Trillo |
| Finance: | Celia Crowley |

### Acknowledgements

**Special thanks** to David Charap, for taking an interest in, and trekking around, the city's more obscure corners (here's to the Nuselské schody), Mira for her Serbian cakes and hospitality, Laďa for loan of his flat but not his stereo, Petr, Pavla and Zdeněk for Brno breaks, Kate, Louise, Nat, Nancy, Stan, Gren, Juliet, Jan and Andy, as ever, and the old folks in Wetherby.

Thanks also to the following people who contributed to the production of this book with their letters and comments: Yvonne Marascalchi, Lorin Jay Cowell, Christopher White, Judy Stone, R. A. Blackie, David Charter and Briony Harrison, Pavel Horák, Mark Nelson and Caroline Edwards, Ron Farquhar, H. Downey, Huw Owen-Reece, M. Lindsay, Mary Millar, John Marrone, Glenda Hemken, D. S. Cox, Georgina M. Prince, Paul Smyth, Jo Plant, John Perowne, Alan Robinson, Noël Werle, Michael Fedor, Rupert R. Gonsalves, Marg Hodder, M. Holman, Mark C. Graham, John Randall, Judy Hague, Richard Dowthwaite, H. Hagan, Matthew Searle, Nicholas Thompson, Maurice Walshe, John Phillimore, Martin Spafford, Rene Cox, Robert and Pamela Smith, Mr & Mrs C. George, Helen Davies, Paddy Tucker, Penny Shackleton and Steve Cox, Bedřich Vohryzek, Dr Paddy O' Sullivan, Sylvia Forrest, Christine Eida, Chris and Angela Kenny, Tracy Young, Pat Yale, Georgina Bevan, Tony Gordon, Jon Wilson, Iain Forbes and Barbara Wright, Simon Gill and Lucy Nias.

And thanks to all those at **Rough Guides**, in particular Kate Berens and John Fisher (this time round), Jack Holland and Jules Brown (last time round), Ralph Mepham, Andy Hilliard, Gail Jammy, Susanne Hillen and Vivien Antwi (for the fastest turn around ever).

**Typography** and **original design** by Jonathan Dear and The Crowd Roars.
**Illustrations** throughout by Edward Briant.
**Maps** by Judit Ladik.

The publishers and authors have done their best to ensure the accuracy and currency of all information in *The Rough Guide to Prague*; however, they can accept no responsibility for any loss, injury, or inconvenience sustained by any traveller as a result of information or advice contained in the guide.

Published 1992 by Rough Guides Ltd, 1 Mercer Street, London WC2H 9QJ. Reprinted 1993.
Distributed by The Penguin Group:

Penguin Books Ltd, 27 Wrights Lane, London W8 5TZ.
Penguin Books USA Inc., 375 Hudson Street, New York 10014, USA
Penguin Books Australia Ltd, 487 Maroondah Highway, PO Box 257, Ringwood, Victoria 3134, Australia
Penguin Books Canada Ltd, 10 Alcorn Avenue, Toronto, Ontario, Canada M4V 1E4
Penguin Books (NZ) Ltd, 182–190 Wairau Road, Auckland 10, New Zealand

Previously published in the United States and Canada as *The Real Guide Prague*.

Printed in the United Kingdom by Cox & Wyman Ltd (Reading).

A catalogue record for this book is available from the British Library
ISBN 1-85828-015-X

# Prague

## THE ROUGH GUIDE

Written and researched by
Rob Humphreys

With additional contributions by
David Charap and Bronwyn Brady

THE ROUGH GUIDES

# The Contents

To Roztok

Baba

DEJVICE

BU

Šárka valley

Džbán

VOKOVICE

STŘEŠOVICE

HRADČANY

Prague
Castle

MALÁ
STRANA

LIBOC

Hvězda

Bílá hora
▲
380 m

BŘEVNOV

To the Airport

MOTOL

KOŠÍŘE

SMÍCHOV

To Plzeň

JINONICE

N

1 km

Prokop valley

HLUBOČEPY

To Zbraslav

**Help us update**

We've gone to a lot of effort to ensure that this first edition of *The Rough Guide to Prague* is accurate and up-to-date. However, things are changing at an extraordinary speed in Prague – every hotel, restaurant and bar in the country has changed hands since 1989 and the current economic instability means that many will do so again in the future. Any suggestions, comments or corrections would be much appreciated.

We'll credit all contributions, and send a copy of the next edition (or any other Rough Guide if you prefer) for the best letters. Send them to:
Rob Humphreys, The Rough Guides, 1 Mercer Street, London WC2H 9QJ.

# Introduction

Prague is one of the least "Eastern" European cities you could imagine. Architecturally, and in terms of city sights, it is a revelation: few other cities, anywhere in Europe, look so good – and no other European capital can present six hundred years of architecture so completely untouched by natural disaster or war. Culturally, it is closer in many ways to Paris than Moscow, and after four decades of Soviet-imposed isolation the city is now keen to re-establish its position as the political and cultural centre of *Mitteleuropa*.

One of Prague's most appealing characteristics is that its artistic wealth is not hidden away inside grand museums and galleries, but displayed in the streets and squares. Its town-planning took place in medieval times, its palaces and churches were decorated with a rich mantle of Baroque, and the whole lot has escaped the vanities and excesses of postwar redevelopment. Prague's unique compactness allows you to walk from the grandeur of the city's castle district, via a series of intimate Baroque lanes, across a medieval stone bridge, through one of the most alluring central squares on the continent, and end up sipping coffee on Wenceslas Square, the modern hub of the city, in under half an hour.

Yet despite Prague's museum-like qualities, Czechs have been at the forefront of European culture for much of the modern era. Before the first world war, Prague boasted a Cubist movement second only to Paris, and between the wars, a modernist architectural flowering to rival Bauhaus. Today, its writers, artists and film directors continue to exert a profound influence on European culture, out of all proportion to their numbers.

The city's recent history has attracted the attention of the west like no other capital in the former eastern bloc. The 1968 **Prague Spring** captured the imagination of a generation, with an explosion of cultural energy which, for a moment, made the "third way" between communism and capitalism seem a real possibility. Then, in the messy, sometimes bloody, upheavals of 1989, Czechoslovakia, and in particular Prague, outshone the rest with its unequivocably positive

"Velvet Revolution". True to its pacifist past, the country shrugged off forty years of Communism without so much as a shot being fired.

The exhilarating popular unity of that period, and the feeling of participating in history itself have now gone, perhaps forever. Few Czechs continue to talk about the events of 1989 as a "revolution". Frustration at the slow pace of change, the re-emergence of separatist nationalism in Slovakia, and the first real taste of western vices in the capital have taken their toll. Economically, too, the country is going through some seriously hard times. The West's refusal to cancel the foreign debt totted up by the Communists, and the lack of anything like the aid the Marshall Plan provided for the western democracies after World War II have made the transition to capitalism all the more difficult.

Walking the streets of the city centre, you'd be forgiven for thinking otherwise. But then Prague is in a privileged position vis-a-vis the rest of the country – as the place where the majority of the country's new businesses and corporations have made their head offices, and, of course, thanks to its potential for attracting western tourists. The feeling in much of the rest of the country is that Prague has prospered at the expense of other cities and regions. Which is not surprising, given that it is something like seven times the size of any other city in Bohemia, all the government ministries are based here, and it's where all the big decisions are made.

That's not to say that Prague doesn't have more than its fair share of problems. Its recent mini-boom may have brought crowds of tourists, but it has done little to improve life for much of the city's population. The westernised shops and restaurants in the centre, with their glitzy window dressing, are out of reach for most Praguers. Racial tensions, suppressed under the police state, have surfaced once more, with a spate of skinhead attacks on the city's considerable Romany and Vietnamese communities, which the police seem powerless and/or unwilling to prevent. Prostitution is endemic in Prague, thanks to the large number of western businessmen visiting the capital and the drastic drop in living standards. The lifestyle gulf between Party and non-Party members has been replaced by the western malaise of rich and poor. There's nothing new in this, but it does serve as a sobering footnote to the city's glowing image in the west.

Prague is also trying to come to terms with its more distant past. The forced, and frequently violent, removal of the German minority, and the virtual extinction of the Jewish population, both had a marked effect on the city, but were never discussed openly under the previous regime. Much of the current retrospection is positive, a cultural rediscovery of the cosmopolitan interwar period, when the city was ethnically far more diverse. There is also the extremely sensitive matter of the events of the last war: the degree of collaboration with the Nazis and of acquiescence in the fate of the Jews. These are issues that need to be addressed if the city is to break free from the monocultural straitjacket which makes it stand out amongst the multicultural capitals of the west.

## When to go

Lying at the heart of central Europe, Prague has a continental climate: winters can be bitterly cold, summers correspondingly scorching. The best times to visit, in terms of weather, are late spring and early autumn. Summer in the city can be pretty stifling, but the real reason for avoiding the peak season is that it can get uncomfortably crowded in the city centre – finding a place to eat in the evening, let alone securing a room, can become fraught with difficulties. If you're looking for good weather, April is the earliest you can expect at least some sunny days, October the last warm month. If you don't mind the cold, the city looks beautiful in the snowy winter months.

**Prague average daily temperature & rainfall**

|        | Jan | Feb | Mar | April | May | June | July | Aug | Sept | Oct | Nov | Dec |
|--------|-----|-----|-----|-------|-----|------|------|-----|------|-----|-----|-----|
| Min °C | -5  | -4  | -1  | 3     | 8   | 11   | 13   | 13  | 9    | 5   | 1   | -3  |
| Max °C | 0   | 1   | 7   | 12    | 18  | 21   | 23   | 22  | 18   | 12  | 5   | 1   |
| mm     | 18  | 18  | 18  | 27    | 48  | 54   | 68   | 55  | 31   | 33  | 20  | 21  |

# The Basics

# Getting There From North America

The quickest and easiest way to reach Prague from the US or Canada is to fly. In summer, the Czechoslovak national airline, ČSA, has four non-stop flights every week out of New York, two a week from Montréal, and dozens of one- and two-stop flights from other North American cities via major European cities.

However, because Prague is only now becoming well established as a tourist destination, flights there from North America are still comparatively expensive, and you may be better off buying a transatlantic flight to Paris, London or Frankfurt and making your way to Prague overland. Furthermore, because the tourist infrastructure is not as efficient as that of western Europe, even the most independent-minded traveller may want to consider some form of package tour. Names and addresses of agents specialising in travel to Prague, and details of all the various options are given below. Unless specified otherwise, prices quoted are for round-trip tickets and include all applicable taxes.

## Flights from the US

If you're flying out of New York, the **non-stop** service offered by ČSA, which costs under $800 in low season and rises to $948 in summer, is

probably your best bet. Starting from other US cities, airlines offering **flights to Prague** include *Delta* (via Frankfurt and Vienna), *Lufthansa* (via Frankfurt), *SAS* (via Copenhagen), *TWA* (via Amsterdam) and *American* (via London or Zurich). **Apex fares**, almost all of which allow a maximum stay of 21 days, are pretty much identical, with low-season rates starting at around $800 from New York, $1100 from West Coast cities; in summer fares rise to $1000 from the eastern US, $1200 from the west. If you want to stay longer than three weeks, the next level of ticket is good for visits of up to six months but costs around $150 more.

Full-time students and anyone under 26 can take advantage of the excellent deals offered by *Council Travel*, *STA* and other **student/youth travel agencies**. These fares are for flights on major carriers like *British Airways* or *Air France*, and even in the peak, summer season cost as little as $700 from the East Coast and $950 from the West Coast. For example, *Council Travel* offers round-trip tickets to Prague on the Belgian-run *Sabena Airways*, flying from New York via Brussels, for $636. A further advantage to these student fares is that they allow you to **stop over en route** for little or no extra charge, something you can't do on an Apex ticket. If you don't meet the student/youth agents' requirements, you can still save some money by buying your tickets

| Airlines serving Prague | |
|---|---|
| *Air France* | ☎ 1-800/237-2747 |
| *American* | ☎ 1-800/433-7300 |
| *British Airways* | ☎ 1-800/247-9297 |
| *ČSA* | ☎ 212/682-5833 |
| *Delta* | ☎ 1-800/241-4141 |
| *KLM* | ☎ 1-800/777-5553 |
| *Lufthansa* | ☎ 1-800/645-3880 |
| *SAS* | ☎ 1-800/221-2350 |
| *Sabena* | ☎ 1-800/955-2000 |
| *TWA* | ☎ 1-800/892-4141 |
| *United* | ☎ 1-800/538-2929 |

## Council Travel in the US ~~open 930-500~~

*Head Office:*

205 E 42nd St,
New York, NY 10017;  ☎212/661-1450

12 Park Place South,
Atlanta, GA 30303  ☎404/577-1678

2486 Channing Way,
Berkeley, CA 94704  ☎415/848-8604

729 Boylston St, Suite 201,
Boston, MA 02116  ☎617/266-1926

1384 Massachusetts Ave, Suite 206,
Cambridge, MA 02138  ☎617/497-1497

1153 N Dearborn St,
Chicago, IL 60610  ☎312/951-0585

1093 Broxton Ave, Suite 220,
Los Angeles, CA 90024  ☎213/208-3551

35 West 8th St,
New York, NY 10011  ☎212/254-2525

1138 13th St,
Boulder, CO 80302  ☎818/905-5777

312 Sutter St, Suite 407,
San Francisco, CA 94108  ☎415/421-3473

1501 University Ave SE, Room 300,
Minneapolis, MN 55414  ☎612/379-2323

2000 Guadalupe St, Suite 6,
Austin, TX 78705  ☎515/472-4931

1314 Northeast 43rd St, Suite 210,
Seattle, WA 98105  ☎206/632-2448

1210 Potomac St,
NW Washington, DC 20007  ☎202/337-6464

### STA in the US

273 Newbury St.,
Boston, MA 02116  ☎617/266-6014

7202 Melrose Ave,
Los Angeles, CA 90046  ☎213/937-5781

82 Shattock Sq,
Berkeley, CA 94704  ☎510/841-1037

48 E 11th St, Suite 805,
New York, NY 10003  ☎212/986-9470

166 Geary St, Suite 702,
San Francisco, CA 94108  ☎415/391-8407

### Travel Cuts in Canada

*Head Office:*

187 College St,
Toronto, Ontario M5T 1P7  ☎416/979-2406

12304 Jasper Ave,
Edmonton, AL T5N 3K5  ☎403/488-8487

1516 Duranleau St,
Granville Island,
Vancouver V6H 3S4  ☎604/687-6033

Student Union Building,
University of British Columbia,
Vancouver V6T 1W5  ☎604/228-6890

60 Laurier Ave E,
Ottawa K1N 6N4  ☎613/238-8222

96 Gerrard St E,
Toronto M5B 1G7  ☎416/977-0441

Université McGill,
3480 rue McTavish,
Montréal H3A 1X9  ☎514/398-0647

1613 rue St Denis,
Montréal H2X 3K3  ☎514/843-8511

### Nouvelles Frontières

**In the United States**

12 E 33rd St,
New York, NY 10016  ☎212/779-0600

6363 Wilshire Blvd, Suite 200,
Los Angeles, CA 90048  ☎213/658-8955

209 Post St., Suite 1121,
San Francisco, CA 94108  ☎415/781-4480

**In Canada**

800 bd de Maison Neuve Est,
Montréal, Québec H2L 4L8  ☎514/288-9942

176 Grande Allée Ouest,
Québec, G1R 2G9  ☎418/525-5255

---

through **discount agencies** like *Travel Avenue* (formerly *McTravel*), 180 N Jefferson Street, Chicago, IL (☎1-800/333-3335).

If you're flexible about your travel plans, or have waited until the last minute to buy your ticket, the best deals are available through **seat consolidators** like *TFI Tours*, 34 W 32nd St, New York, NY (☎212/736-1140 or ☎1-800/825-3834). For the best prices, scan the ads in the back pages of the Sunday travel sections of *The New York Times* or your local paper, and phone around. Because these tickets are basically impossible to change once you've paid for them, be sure about your dates and ask about the routing of the flight – many involve lengthy layovers and multiple changes of plane. They can be excellent value, however, with peak-season fares starting as low as $650 from New York, $850 from Los Angeles or Seattle.

## Flights from Canada

In contrast to the usual story, getting **flights from Canada to Prague** is no problem. *ČSA* fly nonstop twice a week from Montréal for under CDN$1000, though it can be difficult to arrange an inexpensive connection from elsewhere in the country. Outside Montréal, your best bet is *Lufthansa*, who fly direct from major Canadian airports to Prague via Frankfurt. Fares start at CDN$1000 from Toronto, CDN$1250 from Vancouver in low season, rising to CDN$1200/1550 in summer. **Students** and those under 26 can sometimes find cheap flights through *Travel Cuts*.

## Package Tours

Since the situation regarding tourism is still very changeable, along with everything else in the former Eastern Bloc, **travel agencies specialising in Eastern Europe**, such as *Travel Travel*, 10 E 39th Street, New York, NY (☎212/545-0737) and *Sir Bentley*, 17280 Newhope Street, Fountain Valley, CA (☎714/559-6946 or ☎1-800/675-0559) are excellent sources of up-to-date advice, as well as being the best way to find out about any other cheap flight deals that might be available. They can also arrange for accommodation and travel to other parts of Czechoslovakia, as can **package tour** companies like *Fugazy International*, 770 US-1, North Brunswick, NJ (☎1-800/828-4488) and *ČEDOK*, 10 E 40th St, New York, NY (☎212/689-9720), the old Czechoslovak state tourist monopoly, which still offers the broadest range of all-inclusive (and generally quite expensive) tours. Many of the airlines also offer flight-and-accommodation deals: *KLM* (☎1-800/777-1668), for example, gives you four nights in Prague at the deluxe *Intercontinental Hotel* for $1309 from New York, $1489 from Los Angeles.

## Via Europe

Since direct flights to Prague are more expensive than flights to other European cities, it may be worth your while to fly to another country and make your way overland from there. Munich, Berlin, Frankfurt and Vienna are the closest major European citie: you can reach Prague by train in well under twelve hours. Paris (21 hours by train) and London (27 hours by ferry and train) are equally cheap but more distant gateways.

"**Open-jaw**" fares, which enable you to fly into one city and out of another, usually split the difference between standard Apex round-trip fares. For example, you can fly from San Francisco into Berlin, then fly out of Prague two weeks later, for around $1200 in peak season. A similar flight from New York could cost well under $1000. See "Getting There From Britain", overleaf, for a more complete rundown of trans-European options.

# Getting There From Britain

By far the most convenient way to get to Prague is by plane. It takes just under two hours (compared with over 24hr by train), and there are direct flights from London daily throughout the year.

## By Plane

*Czechoslovak Airlines (ČSA)* and *British Airways (BA)* between them run daily **scheduled flights** from London to Prague. Prices are identical for both airlines, and the cheapest ticket is an **Apex** return, which currently costs £235 between April and September; £10 more for a weekend flight, £30 less over the winter period. The usual Apex fare restrictions apply: reservations must be made at least fourteen days in advance and there's a refund of fifty percent on tickets cancelled before the fourteen-day deadline. Tickets are valid for three months and can be booked direct from either airline or through most high-street travel agents.

Charter flights to Prague have always been thin on the ground, only occasionally making it into the "bucket shop" adverts of the various London freebie magazines, *Time Out, The Evening Standard* and the quality Sunday papers. There is a new charter flight, however, available

through *Campus Travel*, with one-ways from £59 and return flights from £99. Otherwise, you'll be hard pushed to find a return fare of much less than £150, and in peak season flights are booked up weeks in advance. It might be worth considering flying to a neighbouring European city like Berlin, Munich or Vienna, for which return fares can be under £100, though of course you'll have to add on the cost of travel from these places into Czechoslovakia.

### Package Deals and City Breaks

The only tour operator which specialises in simple flight and accommodation **package deals** to Czechoslovakia is *ČEDOK* (see box opposite for address), whose all-inclusive packages are much better value than their fairly exorbitant accommodation-only deals. The cheapest deal is the City Break, with a return flight from London and two nights' accommodation for around £100; better value are the six-night deals at around £300 per person. With either of these packages, there's no compulsion to go on any organised tours once you're there, but, should you wish to, each activity will cost extra.

Other companies which do packages to Prague tend to be either accommodation-only or specialist operators. A list of the main agents can be found in the box opposite.

### By Train

**From London to Prague** takes just over 24 hours by train. Departures are from Victoria station, daily at around 8–11am, arriving in Prague the following morning. There are two main routes, with a couple of minor variations, but all involve changing at least once to get to Prague.

### The Routes

The main route is **via the ferry to Ostend**, Brussels, Cologne, Frankfurt and Nuremberg, entering Czechoslovakia by the Schirnding/Cheb border crossing. You can opt for an hour-long wait at Nuremberg from 11pm to midnight; two very quick changes at Cologne and Frankfurt

## Airlines

**British Airways**
156 Regent St,
London W1     ☎ 081/897 4000

**Czechoslovak Airlines (ČSA)**
12a Margaret St,
London W1    Information ☎ 071/255 1366
          Reservations ☎ 071/255 1898

## Agents and Operators

**Campus Travel/Eurotrain**
52 Grosvenor Gardens,
London SW1     ☎ 071/730 3402
*Youth/student specialist.*

**ČEDOK**
17–18 Old Bond St,
London W1     ☎ 071/493 7841
*Official Czechoslovak travel agents; flights, accommodation and package deals.*

**Czech Travel Ltd**
21 Leighlands Rd,
South Woodham Ferrers,
Essex CM3 5XN     ☎ 0245/3286 47
*Rooms and flats for rent in Prague.*

**Czechbook Agency**
52 St John's Park,
London EC1     ☎ 081/853 1168
*Cheap private and self-catering accommodation in Prague.*

**Czech-in Ltd**
63 Market St,
Heywood,
Rochdale OL10 1HZ     ☎ 0706/620 999
*Self-catering flats and houses for rent in Prague.*

**Czechscene**
63 Falkland Rd,
Evesham,
Worcs WR11 6XS     ☎ 0386/442782
*B&B and self-catering flats available in Prague.*

**Martin Randal Travel**
10 Barley Mow Passage,
London W4 4PH     ☎ 081/994 6477
*Specialist cultural guided tours of Prague.*

**STA Travel**
86 Old Brompton Rd,
London SW7     ☎ 071/937 9921
117 Euston Rd,
London NW1
25 Queen's Rd,
Bristol
33 Sidney St,
Cambridge
36 George St,
Oxford
75 Deansgate,
Manchester
*Independent travel specialists; discount flights.*

**TK Travel**
14 Buckstone Close,
London SE23     ☎ 081/699 8065
*B&B and self-catering apartments for rent in Prague.*

**Travelscene**
11–15 St Ann's Rd,
Harrow,
Middlesex HA1     ☎ 081/427 4445
*Three- and five-night holidays in Prague.*

earlier in the evening (and a 7DM supplement for the German portion); or taking the *Jetfoil to Ostend* (an extra £6–9), with an hour at both Cologne and Stuttgart (a slightly longer, but, in fact, faster route).

Another option (though one that takes eight hours longer) is to travel **via Paris**, which means changing stations in Paris from the Gare du Nord to the Gare de l'Est (one stop on metro line 4 or 5). The advantage is that, thereafter, it's direct from Paris to Prague.

All the above routes are fairly comfortable provided you've reserved a seat; it's a good idea to do so well in advance in summer. You may also want to reserve a **couchette** for the final, overnight leg of the journey (around £9 one way).

## Tickets and Passes

A **standard rail ticket** from London (bookable through some high-street travel agents or at London's Victoria Station) will currently set you back £223 return (via Ostend) or £216 return (via Paris): tickets are valid for two months and allow one stopoff en route. If you're under 26, however, or plan to travel extensively by train, there are other options than simply buying a return ticket.

The best-known is the **InterRail pass** (currently £175 a month, £145 for fifteen days if you're under 26 or over 65; £235 a month, £175 for fifteen days if you're not). InterRail passes are available from British Rail or travel agents; the only restriction is that you must have been resident in Europe for at least six months. The pass entitles you to free travel on all European railways (including Turkey and Morocco), as well as half-price discounts in Britain and on the Channel ferries. If you're just headed for Prague this isn't necessarily a good deal (flights are about the same price); and even if you intend to visit places around Prague, the possibilities for rail travel in the immediate vicinity are fairly limited, and extremely cheap, so you may not really get your money's worth.

The alternative for under-26s is a discounted **BIJ** ticket from *Eurotrain* (through *Campus Travel/USIT*) or *Wasteels*. These can be booked for journeys from any British station to any major European station; they're valid for two months and allow unlimited stopovers along a pre-specified route (which can be different going out and coming home). The current return fare to Prague is £147 (via Ostend), £155 (via the Hook of Holland), or £179 (via Paris). If you travel overnight on the Hook of Holland ferry you'll pay £12 extra each way and get some lousy connections.

## By Coach

The cheapest way to get to Prague is by **coach**. There's a direct service from London to Prague every Wednesday and Saturday, leaving from Victoria Coach Station at 7pm and arriving around 24 hours later at Praha-Florenc bus terminal. It is operated by *Kingscourt Express*, who have offices in London and Prague; tickets currently cost £83.50 return, £45 one way. *Eurolines* also run coaches to Prague, leaving London at 7pm every Friday and Monday and arriving at the inconvenient hour of 10.30pm the following day; tickets currently cost £65 single and £109 return. Times and frequencies are liable to change, so always check first.

The journey is long but quite bearable – just make sure you take along enough to eat, drink and read, and a small amount of Belgian and German currency for coffee, etc. There are stops

for around fifteen minutes every three hours or so, and the routine is broken by the Dover–Ostend ferry (included in the cost of the ticket).

## By Car – The Ferries

**Driving** to Prague is not the most relaxing option – even if you're into non-stop rally motoring, it'll take the best part of two days – but with two or more passengers it can work out relatively inexpensive. The cheapest and quickest Channel crossings en route to Prague are the **ferry** or **hovercraft** links between **Dover** and Calais, and **Ramsgate** and Dunkirk. **Fares** vary with the time of year, and the size of your car. The Dover–Calais run, for example, starts at about £70 one way for a car, two adults and two kids, but roughly doubles in high season. Foot passengers should be able to cross for just under £25 single.

The most direct route from Calais/Dunkirk to Prague is via Brussels, Cologne, Frankfurt and Nuremberg, entering the country at the **Waidhaus–Rozvadov** border crossing: a distance of over 1000km. Another possibility is to head east from Cologne through Hessen via Erfurt and Chemnitz (formerly Karl Marx Stadt), and enter at the **Reitzenhain/Pohraniční** border crossing.

## Hitching

If you're **hitching** to Prague, your best bet is to catch the ferry to Ostend and follow the busier route via Cologne and Nuremberg. Buying a train/ferry ticket as far as Ostend will save you the hassle of hitching out of London and onto the Belgian autoroutes. At all events, you should organise a lift while you're still on the ferry. Hitching in Belgium, Germany and Czechoslovakia will seem like a doddle compared to anywhere in Britain, but again don't bank on getting there in less than two days. For all trips overland you should take a few Belgian francs and some Deutschmarks for the journey.

| **Train Information** | | **Coach Information** | |
|---|---|---|---|
| **British Rail European Travel Centre** | | **Eurolines** | |
| Victoria Station, | | *National Express*, | |
| London SW1 | ☎071/834 2345 | 164 Buckingham Palace Rd, | |
| | | London SW1 | ☎071/730 0202 |
| **Eurotrain** | | | |
| 52 Grosvenor Gardens, | | **Kingscourt Express** | |
| London SW1 | ☎071/730 3402 | 35 Kingscourt Rd, | |
| | | London SW16 | ☎081/769 9229 |
| **Wasteels** | | | |
| 121 Wilton Rd, | | | |
| London SW1 | ☎071/834 7066 | | |

# Red Tape and Visas

If you need to stay longer than three months, you'll have to fill in the application form known as *povolení k pobytu*, attach six photos and pay a fee of 100kčs. It's best to try this at the head passport office at Olšanská 2, Žižkov, Prague. Many people avoid this bureaucratic nightmare by simply leaving the country for a few days when their time runs out and getting a new date upon re-entry, but the legality of this is somewhat doubtful. If you cross over into Germany for this purpose, make sure that your passport gets stamped (which isn't done routinely) and come back into Czechoslovakia at least a couple of days later by a different border post.

## Customs and Allowances

Since the events of 1989, **border controls** have relaxed considerably. Export controls, however, are still quite restrictive, if infrequently enforced. Officially you're only allowed to export 600kčs worth of taxable goods (just over £10/$18 at the current exchange rate) duty-free, after which you're supposed to pay taxes; gifts worth up to 1000kčs (around £20/$34) can also be exported duty-free. In practice, you'll rarely have problems unless you're found exporting large amounts of high-quality Bohemian crystal and glassware. If you pay for goods in hard currency, and keep receipts, you'll avoid any possible hassle.

British, Irish, US and most EC nationals need only a full passport to enter Czechoslovakia for up to three months. New Zealand and Australian citizens still need a visa (valid for thirty days), available from a Czechoslovak embassy or consulate – usually on the day – or at border crossings with Germany and Austria. At the time of writing, Canadians were required to obtain a visa; check with your embassy for the latest information. There is no longer a minimum exchange requirement. If you need an extension, the local police office will issue one without too much fuss for around 100kčs.

---

### Czechoslovak Embassies and Consulates

**UK and Eire**
28 Kensington Palace Gardens,
London W8 4OX                    ☎071/727 3966
(Mon–Fri 10am–1pm)

**Australia**
169 Military Rd,
Dover Heights,
Sydney, NSW 2030                 ☎02-371 8878

**Austria**
Penzinger Strasse 11–13,
1140 Vienna                      ☎1-894 3741

**Belgium**
152 Avenue A. Buyl,
1050 Brussels                    ☎02-647 5898

**Canada**
50 Rideau Terrace,
Ottawa,
Ontario K1M 2A1                  ☎514/849-495

**France**
15 avenue Charles Floquet,
75 007 Paris                     ☎47 34 29 10

**New Zealand**
12 Anne St,
Wadesdown,
PO Box 2843,
Wellington                       ☎04-723 142

**USA**
3900 Linnean Ave NW,
Washington DC 20008              ☎202/363-6315

---

**Duty-free allowances** from Czechoslovakia into EC countries are different from the normal EC allowances: you can export 250 cigarettes, 2 litres of wine and 1 litre of spirits. These allowances may change in the future, though, so check with customs before you leave for Prague.

## Foreign Embassies in Prague

**Belgium**
Valdštejnská 6
Mala Strana ☎ 54 40 51

**Britain**
Thunovská 14,
Malá Strana ☎ 53 33 47

**Canada**
Mickiewiczova 6,
Hradčany ☎ 32 69 41

**Commonwealth of Independent States**
(formerly the Soviet embassy)
Pod kaštany 1,
Bubeneč ☎ 38 19 40

**Denmark**
U Havlíčkových sadů,
Vinohrady ☎ 25 47 15

**France**
Velkopřevorské náměstí 2,
Malá Strana ☎ 53 30 42

**Finland**
Dřevná 2,
Smíchov ☎ 20 55 41

**Germany**
Vlašská 19
Mala Strana ☎ 53 23 51

**Hungary**
I. V. Mičurinova 1,
Hradčany ☎ 36 50 41

**Italy**
Nerudova 20,
Malá Strana ☎ 53 06 66

**Norway**
Na Ořechovce,
Dejvice ☎ 35 66 51

**Poland**
Valdštejnská 8,
Malá Strana ☎ 53 69 51

**Sweden**
Úvoz 13,
Malá Strana ☎ 53 33 44

**USA**
Tržiště 15,
Malá Strana ☎ 53 66 41

# Insurance

On production of a passport all foreign nationals can get free emergency medical care, with a nominal charge for certain drugs or medicines. If it's not an emergency but you can't hold out until you return home, you're going to have to pay, and, depending on the treatment necessary, you might find yourself running up a considerable bill.

Some form of **travel insurance** is therefore essential, enabling you to claim back the cost of any treatment and drugs and covering your baggage/tickets in case of theft. **In Britain**, travel insurance schemes (from around £20 a month) are sold by all travel agents: *ISIS* policies, from any of the youth/student travel companies listed in "Getting There", or from branches of *Endsleigh Insurance* (in London at 97 Southampton Row, WC1; ☎071/436 4451) are among the cheapest.

## US and Canadian Citizens

In the **US and Canada**, insurance tends to be much more expensive, and may be medical cover only. Before buying a policy, check that you're not already covered by existing insurance plans. **Canadians** are usually covered by their provincial health plans; holders of **ISIC cards** and some other student/teacher/youth cards are entitled to $3000 worth of accident coverage and sixty days ($100 per diem) of hospital in-patient benefits for the period during which the card is

valid. **Students** will often find that their student health coverage extends through the vacations and for one term beyond the date of last enrollment. Bank and charge **accounts** (particularly *American Express*) often have certain levels of medical or other insurance included, and travel insurance may also be included if you use a major credit or charge card to pay for your trip. **Homeowners' or renters'** insurance often covers theft or loss of documents, money and valuables while overseas, though conditions and maximum amounts vary from company to company.

Only after exhausting the possibilities above might you want to contact a specialist travel insurance company; your travel agent can usually recommend one. Travel insurance policies are quite comprehensive, anticipating everything from charter companies going bankrupt to delayed or lost baggage, by way of sundry illnesses and accidents. **Premiums** vary widely, from the very reasonable ones offered primarily through student/youth agencies (*STA*'s policies range from about $50–70 for 15 days to $500–700 for a year, depending on the amount of financial cover), to those so expensive that the cost for anything more than two months of cover will probably equal the cost of the worst possible combination of disasters. Note also that very few insurers can make on-the-spot payments in the event of a major expense or loss; you will usually be reimbursed only after going home.

None of these policies insures against **theft** of anything while overseas. (Americans have been easy pickings for foreign thieves – a combination of naivety on the part of the former, and an all-Americans-are-rich attitude among the latter – and companies were going broke paying claims.) North American travel policies apply only to items **lost** from, or **damaged** in, the custody of an identifiable, responsible third party – hotel porter, airline, luggage consignment, etc. Even in these cases you will have to contact the local police to have a complete report made out for your insurer. If you are travelling via London it might be better to take out a British policy (though making the claim may prove more complicated).

# Points of Arrival

The major points of arrival are all fairly central, with the obvious exception of the airport. The public transport system is excellent, and from even the most obscure terminals there are fast city transport connections to the centre.

You'll also find some details about **leaving Prague** in this section, along with useful lists of airline addresses.

## Airport

Prague's **airport**, Ruzyně (☎36 77 60 or 36 78 14), is 15km northwest of the city, and pretty unimpressive, with few of the facilities you'd expect from a European capital's main point of entry. There are 24-hour exchange facilities (see "Costs, Money and Banks") and, should you need them, accommodation agencies (see "Finding a Place to Stay", Chapter 10), and car rental outlets (see "Driving and Vehicle Rental", p.17).

The airport is linked to the city by a regular, cheap and direct **bus service** (every 20–30min, 7.30am–7pm; journey time 10min), run by ČSA, which drops you at the ČSA offices on Revoluční, on the edge of Staré and Nové Město; to obtain a ticket simply pay the driver. There's a city bus connection, too: bus #119 (every 15–20min, 4.30am–11.30pm; journey time 20min), which ends its journey outside the Dejvická metro station at the end of metro line A.

**Taxis** from the airport into the centre cost roughly 250kčs to Hradčany, 350kčs to somewhere more central; make sure the driver turns on the meter, or, if in doubt, agree on a price before getting in.

When leaving, always allow plenty of time to **get to the airport**. Don't get off the city bus until the last stop – the first building saying *Praha letiště* (Prague Airport) is an outbuilding, and a good 2km from the international terminal. There's an airport restaurant in which to fritter away your surplus time and crowns.

## Train Stations

Arriving by **train** from the west, you're most likely to end up at the old Art-Nouveau **Praha hlavní nádraží**, on the edge of Nové Město and Vinohrady. Downstairs in the modern bit, there are exchange and information offices (a branch of the *PIS*), as well as a 24-hour left luggage office and hotel booking services (see "Finding a Place to Stay", p.197). It's only a five-minute walk into the centre from here, or there's a metro station inside the railway station.

| **Airlines** | |
|---|---|
| **Aeroflot** | |
| Pařížská 5, | |
| Staré Město | ☎26 08 62 |
| **Air France** | |
| Václavské náměstí 10, | |
| Nové Město | ☎26 01 55 |
| **Alitalia** | |
| Revoluční 5, | |
| Nové Město | ☎231 05 35 |
| **British Airways** | |
| Štěpánská 63, | |
| Nové Město | ☎236 03 53 |
| **ČSA** | |
| Revoluční 1, | |
| Nové Město | ☎21 46 |
| **Lufthansa** | |
| Pařížská 5, | |
| Staré Město | ☎232 74 40 |
| **Pan Am** | |
| Pařížská 11, | |
| Staré Město | ☎26 67 47 |
| **SAS** | |
| Štěpánská 61, | |
| Nové Město | ☎22 81 41 |

International expresses passing through from Berlin/Warsaw to Budapest/Vienna often stop only at **Praha-Holešovice**, in an industrial suburb north of the city centre, at the end of metro line C. Domestic trains may wind up at the central **Masarykovo nádraží** (previously known as Praha střed) on Hybernská, a couple of blocks east of náměstí Republiky.

Other possible arrival points for slow, (*osobný*) trains are **Praha-Smíchov** (trains from the south-west), connected to the centre by metro line B; **Praha-Vysočany** (trains from the east) – take tram #3 to Masarykovo nádraží; **Praha Dejvice** (trains from the west), close to Hradčanská metro station; and **Praha-Vršovice** (trains from the south) – take tram #24 to Wenceslas Square.

If you're catching a **train out of Prague**, don't leave buying your ticket – and *místenka* (seat reservation), should you need one – until the last minute, as the queues can be long and slow. You can buy international train tickets at either Praha hlavní nádraží (currently at windows 26, 28, 30 or 32 on the first floor) and Praha-Holešovice, or from *ČEDOK*, Na příkopě 22.

## Bus Terminals

Prague's main **bus terminal** is **Praha-Florenc**, on the eastern edge of Nové Město (Florenc metro station), where virtually all long-distance international and domestic services terminate. For destinations around Prague, you'll be directed to a variety of obscure bus terminals, listed opposite, most of which are easy to reach by metro. To find out which one you want, ask at any of the *PIS* offices in town, or check the comprehensive (and extremely complex) timetables at Praha-Florenc.

For day trips around Prague, you can simply pay the driver as you get on. But if you're travelling long-distance, it's a good idea to reserve a seat in advance, especially if you're departing early in the morning or at the weekend; the day before is usually fine.

---

### Bus Terminals

**Praha-Florenc**
Křižíkova,
Karlín (metro Florenc).
*For London and the rest of Europe, and to Lány, Rakovník, Louny, Terezín, Mladá Boleslav, Přerov nad Labem and Plzeň.*

**Praha-Holešovice**
Vrbenského,
Holešovice (metro Nádraží Holešovice).
*For Kralupy nad Vltavou, Veltrusy, Terezín, Mělník, Kokořín and Litoměřice.*

**Praha-Pankrác**
Na Pankráci,
Nusle (metro Pankrác).
*For Český Šternberk, Lipnice nad Sázavou and Benešov.*

**Praha-Smíchov**
Nádražní,
Smíchov (metro Anděl).
*For Zbraslav, Beroun and Příbram.*

**Praha-Strašnice**
Vinohradská,
Vinohrady (metro Želivského).
*For Kutná Hora, Kouřím, Sázava and Čáslav.*

**Praha-Vysočany**
Sokolovská,
Vysočany (metro Českomoravská).
*For Brandýs nad Labem and Stará Boleslav.*

---

# Getting Around

## City Transport

The centre of Prague, where most of the city's sights are concentrated, is reasonably small and best explored on foot. At some point, however, in order to cross the city quickly or reach some of the more widely dispersed attractions, you'll need to use the city's cheap and efficient public transport system, which comprises the metro and a network of trams and buses. To sort it all out, pick up a **city map** (*plán města*), available at most information offices, kiosks and bookshops around the city; the map marks all the tram, bus and metro lines.

On all the city's public transport, a single **ticket** (*lístek*) currently costs 4kčs for an adult; 1kčs for those aged 10–16; under-10s travel free. Tickets, which are standard for all forms of public transport, must be bought beforehand either from one of the yellow ticket machines found inside metro stations and at some bus and tram stops, or from a *tabák*, street kiosk or newsagent.

Except when changing lines on the metro, you must use a separate ticket each time you change tram or bus, punching it in one of the archaic little devices at hand. Buy as many tickets in advance as you think you'll need, to avoid the problem of trying to hoard change for the machines, or finding a machine that actually works.

To avoid any hassle, and to save money, most Praguers buy monthly or quarterly **passes** (which is why you see so few of them punching tickets). To do this, present ID and a passport-sized photo to the DP windows at major metro stations at the beginning of the month, and ask for a *měsíční jízdenka*. After the first week of the month, only I.P. Pavlova metro station will issue them. Monthly passes currently cost 120kčs.

Alternatively, if you're here for just a few days, it's worth getting hold of a **tourist pass** (*turistická síťová jízdenka*), valid from one to five days and currently costing 25–70kčs; no photos or ID are needed. There's nothing to stop people from freeloading on the system, since there are no barriers. However, plain-clothes inspectors make spot checks and will issue an on-the-spot fine of 100kčs and upwards to anyone caught without a valid ticket or pass.

### Metro

The futuristic Soviet-built **metro** is fast, smooth and ultra-clean, running daily from 5am to midnight with trains every two minutes during peak hours, slowing down to every six minutes by late in the evening. Its three lines (with a fourth planned) intersect at various points in the city centre and the route plans are easy to follow. The stations are fairly discreetly marked above ground with the logo as on the map opposite, in green (line A), yellow (line B) or red (line C). The constant bleeping at metro entrances is to enable blind people to locate the escalators.

In contrast to the trams and buses, you don't have to use a fresh ticket each time you change lines, though you must complete your journey within an hour (it would be difficult not to). Few people are in a hurry, though, and the escalators are a free-for-all, with no fast lane. Once inside the metro, it's worth knowing that *výstup* means exit and *přestup* means connection.

### Trams

The **tram** system, in operation since 1891, negotiates Prague's hills and cobbles with remarkable dexterity – the present Škoda trams were

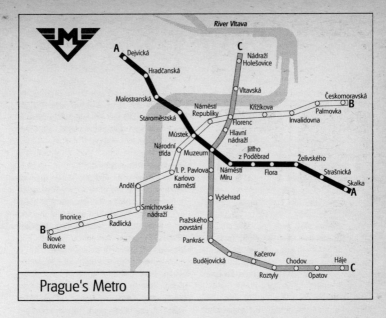

**Prague's Metro**

designed in the 1950s, but are due to be replaced soon. After the metro, trams are the fastest and most efficient way of getting around, running every ten to twenty minutes throughout the day – check the timetables posted at every stop (*zastávka*), which list only the departures times from that specific stop.

Some lines operate only during rush hour (Mon–Fri 5–8am & 1–3pm), while others run seven days a week (5am–midnight). Night trams (see box below) all pass by Lazarská in Nové Město. Tram #22, which runs from Vinohrady to Hradčany, is a good way to get to grips with the lie of the land, and is a cheap way of sightseeing.

---

### Night trams

The following trams leave roughly every 40min from 11.30pm to 4.30am.

**#51**
**Radošovická**, metro želivského, metro Flora, nám. Míru, nám. I. P. Pavlova, Lazarská, Národní, metro Staroměstská, nábř. kpt. Jaroše, metro Hradčanská, metro Dejvická, Evropská, **Divoká Šárka**.

**#52**
**Hlubočepy**, metro Anděl, Lazarská, Masarykovo nádraží, metro Florenc, metro Křižíkova, metro Palmovka, **Lehovec**.

**#53**
metro **Pankrác**, Lazarská, Masarykovo nádraží, nábř. kpt Jaroše, nádraží Holešovice, Trojská, **Vozovna Kobylisy**.

**#54**
**nádraží Braník**, Lazarská, Národní, metro Staroměstská, nábř. kpt Jaroše, nádraží Holešovice, metro Palmovka, **sídliště Ďáblice**.

**#55**
**Ústřední dílny ňž**, metro Strašnická, Vršovická, Lazarská, Masarykovo nádraží, metro Florenc, metro Křižíkova, metro Palmovka, **Lehovec**.

**#56**
**Spořilov**, Nuselská, Bělehradská, Lazarská, Masarykovo nádraží, metro Florenc, metro Hradčanská, **Petřiny**.

**#57**
**nádraží Hostivař**, Radošovická, nám. Míru, Lazarská, Národní, metro Malostranská, metro Hradčanská, **Bílá hora**.

**#58**
**Spojovací**, metro želivského, metro Flora, Olšanské nám., Lazarská, Národní, metro Anděl, **sídliště Řepy**.

---

## Buses

You'll rarely need to use Prague's **buses**, which for the most part keep well out of the centre of town. If you're intent upon visiting some of the more obscure suburbs, though, you may need to use them: their hours of operation are similar to those of the trams, and route numbers are given in the text where appropriate.

## Taxis

**Taxis**, which come in all shapes and sizes, are cheap and plentiful. There's a minimum charge of 6kčs, and after that it's currently 8kčs or more per kilometre, depending on the time of day. Supply far exceeds demand at the moment, so competition is fierce. There are numerous taxi ranks in the centre of town, notably on Wenceslas Square, Národní and outside the Obecní dům.

Tourists are seen as easy prey by some taxi drivers; if the meter isn't switched on, ask the driver to do so – *zapněte taxametr, prosím*; and if you suspect you've been overcharged, asking for a receipt – *prosím, dejte mi potrzení* – should have the desired effect. Watch out for cabs which display signs like *TAXL* or *FAXI* – as long as it isn't *TAXI*, they can legally set their own rates.

---

**Cabs can be called on the following numbers:**
☎35 03 20          ☎35 04 91
☎20 29 51          ☎20 39 41

---

# Transport Out of the City

Most of the places mentioned in Chapter 9, *Out of the City*, are accessible by public transport. The system is extremely cheap, but often very slow, so if you're short on time it might be worth considering hiring a car. All the transport terminals for **routes out of Prague** are described in "Points of Arrival", above.

## Trains

The most relaxing way to day-trip from Prague is by **train**. The antiquated rolling stock is a pleasure to travel in, and the restaurant cars (usually only on long-distance trains) are still relatively cheap, run with a shabby semblance of Austrian formality. However, the system, which has changed little since it was bequeathed to the country by the Habsburgs in 1918, is slightly more expensive and a lot slower than the buses – though still extremely cheap compared with western Europe.

Czechoslovak State Railways, *Československé státní dráhy (ČSD)*, run two main **types of train**: *rychlík* trains are the faster ones which stop only at major towns. They cost very little, but still almost twice as much as an *osobný vlak* or local train, which stops at every station on the line and averages about 30km an hour. Other fast trains go by the name of *expres* or *spěšný*. It's better to avoid the international expresses which, although theoretically faster, often get delayed at border crossings.

### Tickets and reservations

**Tickets** can be bought at the station (*nádraží*) before or on the day of departure. Write down all the relevant information on a piece of paper and hand it to the clerk to avoid any linguistic misunderstandings – rectifying any mistakes involves a lengthy bureaucratic process and costs you ten percent of the ticket price.

If you simply say the destination, it will be assumed that you want a second-class single (*jednoduchá*) on an *osobný vlak* (the ticket most Czechs buy). If you want a return ticket (*zpátečni*), you must say so. First-class carriages (*první třída*) exist on all fast trains; tickets are fifty percent more expensive but should guarantee you a seat on a busy train if you've forgotten to buy a reservation or *místenka* (see below). If you end up in the wrong carriage, you'll be fined upwards of 100kčs on the spot.

There are half-price **discount fares** for children under twelve, and you can take two children under five for free (providing they don't take up more than one seat). There are even some "crèche carriages" on the slower trains, for the exclusive use of mothers with children under five.

All international through-trains, and any other services marked with an "R" surrounded by a box, require a **seat reservation** or *místenka*. For those marked with an "R" but without a box, reservations are recommended but not obligatory: it's advisable to get one if you're travelling at the weekend on one of the main routes. The *místenka* costs very little, but you must get it at least an hour before your train leaves, and after you've purchased your ticket.

### Information and timetables

With very few English-speakers employed on the railways, it can be difficult getting **train information**. The larger stations have a simple airport-style flip-over arrivals and departures board,

> The state train system is currently in deep financial crisis, and, at the time of going to print, there was much talk in the press of drastically reduced services, including the axing of anything up to one hundred and fifty lines as of June 1992. Check the timetables displayed in all stations for the current state of play.

which includes information on delays under the heading *zpoždění*. Many stations have poster-style displays of arrivals and departures, the former on white paper, the latter on yellow, with fast trains printed in red.

In addition to the above, all but the smallest stations have a comprehensive display of **timings and route information** on rollers. These timetables may seem daunting at first, but with a little practice they should become increasingly decipherable. First find the route you need to take on the diagrammatic map and make a note of the number printed beside it; then follow the timetable rollers through until you come to the appropriate number. The only problem now is language since everything will be written in Czech. Arrivals are *příjezd* (*příj.* in short form) and departures are *odjezd* (*odj.* in short form). A platform or *nástupiště* is usually divided into two *kolej* on either side. Some of the more common notes at the side of the timetable are *jezdí jen v* (only running on), or *nejezdí v* or *nechodí v* (not running on), followed by a date or a symbol: a cross or an "N" for a Sunday; a big "S" for a Saturday; two crossed hammers for a workday; "A" for a Friday and so on. Small stations may simply have a board with a list of departures under the title *směr* (direction) followed by a town.

If you're going to be travelling by train a lot, it's a good idea to invest in a *ČSD* **timetable** (*jízdní řád*), which comes out every May (and often sells out soon afterwards). There's one for each region – *Středočeský kraj* is the one for the region around Prague – and a bumper national edition, available from bookshops and tobacconists.

### Buses

Since the reduction of state subsidies on the railways, **buses** (*autobus*) have become an even more attractive alternative to the trains. Most routes are still run by the state bus company, *Československá státní automobilová doprava*

(*ČSAD*). Private companies do exist but, for the time being, are confined to the more popular, long-distance routes such as Prague–Brno–Bratislava. *ČSAD* buses go almost everywhere, and from town to town they're nearly always faster (and cheaper) than the train. Bear in mind, though, that in rural areas timetables are often designed with the working and/or school day in mind. That means up and out at 6am and back at around 3pm during the week, and completely different services at weekends.

In places outside Prague, the **bus station** is often adjacent to the train station, though you may be able to pick up the bus from the centre of town, too. The bigger terminals in Prague, like Praha-Florenc, are run with train-like efficiency. Often you can book your ticket in advance, and it's absolutely essential to do so if you're travelling at the weekend or early in the morning on one of the main routes. For most minor routes, simply buy your ticket from the driver.

Bus **timetables** are even more difficult to figure out than train ones, as there are no maps at any of the stations. Each service is listed separately, so you may have to scour several timetables before you discover when the next bus is. Make sure you check on which day the service runs, since many run only on Mondays, Fridays or at the weekend (see the "Trains" section for key phrases).

Minor bus stops are marked with a rusty metal sign saying *zastávka*. If you want to get off, ask *já chci vystoupit?*; "the next stop" is *příští zastávka*. It's probably not worth buying any of the *ČSAD* regional bus timetables, (*jízdní řád*) though you might feel the urge to buy volume 1, which covers the area around Prague, or volume 11, which details the international and long-distance services (*medzinárodné a diaľkové linky*).

### Driving and Vehicle Rental

Although traffic in Prague is relatively light, you really don't need a **car**, since much of the city centre is pedestrianised and there's a cheap and efficient public transport system. You may, however, want to rent one if you're planning a lot of day trips. With just one in five Czechs owning a vehicle and most of those used only at the weekend, traffic outside the city is sparse, and road conditions are generally not bad. The price of petrol is cheaper than in much of Europe, currently around 18kčs a litre (£0.36/$0.60).

Most foreign driver's licences are honoured in Czechoslovakia – including all EC, US and Canadian ones – but an **International Driver's Licence** (available from the AA or RAC) is an easy way to set your mind at rest. If you're bringing your own car, you'll need the vehicle's registration document. If it's not in your name, you must have a letter of permission signed by the owner and authorised by the AA, RAC or another official body. Check with your insurance company before leaving home whether you need a **green card**, as without one you may only get third party cover. You're also required to carry a red warning triangle, a first-aid kit and a set of replacement bulbs, and to display a national identification sticker.

## Rules of the Road

**Rules and regulations** on Czech roads are pretty stringent – a legacy of the police state – though less strictly adhered to by Czechs nowadays. On-the-spot fines are still regularly handed out, ranging from a pathetic 20kčs to over 200kčs. The basic rules are driving on the right; compulsory wearing of seatbelts outside built-up areas; and children under twelve must travel in the back. It's against the law to have any alcohol in your blood when you're driving. Also, don't overtake a tram when passengers are getting on and off if there's no safety island for them. As in other continental countries, a yellow triangle means you have right of way; a black line through it means you don't.

**Speed limits** are 110kph on motorways (and if you travel any faster you *will* be fined), 90kph on other roads and 60kph in all cities, towns and villages between 5am and 11pm; after that you can, theoretically, tear through town at 90kph. In addition, there's a special speed limit of 30kph for **level crossings** (you'll soon realise why if you try ignoring it). A large number of Czech level crossings have no barriers, simply a sign saying *pozor* and a series of lights: a single flashing light means that the line is live; two red flashing lights mean there's a train coming.

## Fuel and garages

**Petrol** (*benzín*) comes in two types: *super* (96 octane) and *special* (90 octane); diesel (*nafta*) is also available but two-stroke fuel (*mix*), which powers the old east German Trabants and Wartburgs, is being phased out. Remember that petrol stations aren't as frequent as in western Europe and many are closed at lunchtimes and after 6pm (though 24-hour ones can be found in

Prague). **Lead-free** petrol (*natural* or *bezolovnatý*) is available from most petrol stations in and around Prague (*ČEDOK* publish a list of them).

If you have **car trouble**, dial ☎154 at the nearest phone and wait for assistance. For peace of mind it might be worth taking out an insurance policy such as the AA Five-Star scheme, which will pay for any on-the-spot repairs and, in the case of emergencies, ship you and all your passengers back home free of charge.

Since every other car in Czechoslovakia is a Škoda, and most of the rest are Ladas and Trabants, obtaining **spare parts** for any other vehicles can be a tricky business. Small Fiats, Renault 12s and German models are probably slightly better catered for than most, but there are still only a few western-marque garages in Prague and none in the countryside (see the box opposite for details). If it's simply a case of a flat tyre, however, go to the nearest *pneuservis*.

## Driving in Prague

If you do end up driving in Prague, beware that there are **on-the-spot fines** for driving in restricted streets, most notably Wenceslas Square, plus other obstacles like careering trams and buses, treacherous cobbled streets, and a fiendish one-way system. Incidentally, Prague's rush hour – in so far as there is one – can begin as early as 2pm. Also, **vehicle crime** is on the increase and western cars are a favourite target – never leave anything visible or valuable in the car.

The other big nightmare is **parking**. Spaces in the centre are expensive and few and far between, and illegally parked cars are quickly towed away. If this happens, you'll find the car pound on Černokostelecká, way out in Prague 10 (tram #11). If you're staying in a private room outside the centre, you'll have no problems; if you're at a hotel, they will probably have a few parking spaces reserved for guests in the neighbouring streets, though whether you'll find one vacant is another matter. Otherwise, your best option is to park at a big hotel near a metro station out of the centre – try the *Hotel Forum* (metro Vyšehrad) or *Panorama* (metro Pankrác).

## Car Rental

There's a list of **car rental companies** in Prague below. You'll need to be 21 and have been driving for at least a year, and, if you book from abroad, you're looking at over £15/$25 per day for a small car (cheaper by the week, and with special rates at the weekend). The big companies all have offices in Prague, but you'll get a better deal if you go to a local agent like *Escucar*.

## Motorbikes

Czechoslovakia would be a great country for **motorcycling**. If it weren't for the prohibitive **speed limits** for bikes – devised with domestic machines in mind, the biggest of which are the Jawa 350s that the police still ride. In towns and villages the limit is 60kph but out on the open roads, and even on motorways, the limit is 80kph. Unless you ride a Jawa, or an MZ, be prepared for crowds of curious onlookers to surround your bike in every town and village. Helmets are compulsory, as is some form of eye protection (goggles or visor) for the driver; you should use dipped headlights at all times. At the time of writing, it was still not possible to rent motorbikes or mopeds in Prague.

## Hitching, Cycling and Walking

**Hitching** is widely practised in Czechoslovakia. Despite the low cost of public transport, it's still too much for many people and there's usually a long line of hitchers on the roads out of Prague. The main problem is the scarcity of vehicles, so to hit what rush hour there is, you'll have to set out early – and that means 6–8am. Although many Czech women hitch, usually in pairs, women travelling alone should still exercise the usual caution about which lifts to accept. "Where are you heading?" is *kam jdete?* and if you want to get out of the car, just say *já chci vystoupit.*

**Cycling** is no fun in Prague, and very few Czechs do it. The combination of cobbled streets and tram lines, not to mention sulphurous air, are enough to put most people off. Outside Prague, the rolling hills of Bohemia are hard work on the legs, but rewarding. Facilities for **bike rental** are now quite common in Prague. We've given a couple of outlets in the box below but there are plenty of others around Wenceslas Square and Staroměstské náměstí. If you're serious about cycling, though, it is, of course, best to bring your own machine (and plenty of spare parts).

**Walking**, however (curiously enough *tramping* in Czech), is a very popular pastime. Young, old or indolent, they all spend their weekends following the dense network of paths that covers not just the hills and mountains but the whole countryside – some within the city boundaries of Prague itself. All the trails are colour-coded with clear markers every 200m or so, and signs indicating how long it'll take you to reach your destination. The walks around Prague are usually fairly easygoing, but it can be wet and muddy underfoot even in summer. There are no hiking guides in English, but it's a good idea to get hold of a *soubor turistických map,* which details all the marked paths in the area (see "Information and Maps").

| **Car repairs in Prague** | | **Budget** | |
|---|---|---|---|
| **24-hour breakdown** | | Národní 17, | |
| Limuzská 12, | | Nové Město | ☎ 232 29 16 |
| Malešice | ☎ 77 34 55 | **Escucar** | |
| **Austin Rover** | | Husitská 58, | |
| Jeseniova 56, | | Žižkov | ☎ 691 22 44 |
| Žižkov | ☎ 27 23 20 | **Europcar** | |
| **BMW, Ford, Mercedes & VW** | | Pařížská 26, | |
| Severní XI, | | Nové Město | ☎ 231 02 78 |
| Spořilov | ☎ 76 67 52 | **Hertz** | |
| **Fiat,** | | *Hotel Palace,* | |
| Na stráži, | | Panská 12, | |
| Krč | ☎ 42 66 14 | Nové Město | ☎ 236 16 37 |
| **Renault** | | | |
| Ďablická 2, | | **Bike hire** | |
| Kobylisy | ☎ 88 82 57 | **Cyklo Centrum** | |
| | | 27–29 Karlovo náměstí, | |
| **Car rental firms in Prague** | | Nové Město | |
| **Avis/Pragocar** | | **Půjčovna kol** | |
| Opletalova 33, | | Národní 38, | |
| Nové Město | ☎ 34 10 97 | Nové Město | |

# Information and Maps

The Czechoslovak Travel Bureau, ČEDOK, produces and gives away various maps, pamphlets and special interest leaflets. Visit one of their offices before you leave and stock up, especially on the lists of campsites, hotels etc, and to check details of the latest regulations and changes likely to affect travellers.

## Information Offices

Once in Prague, the main tourist office is the **Prague Information Service** or **PIS** (*Pražská informačni služba*), whose main branch is at Na příkopě 20, Nové Město (Mon–Fri 8am–7/8pm, Sat 8am–3.30pm). The staff speak at least four languages between them, including English, and will be able to answer most enquiries, except on the subject of accommodation (for which see "Finding a Place to Stay", Chapter 10). PIS also distributes some useful free publications, worth picking up while you're there: *The Month in Prague*, an English-language leaflet listing the major events, concerts and exhibitions; a separate broadsheet of cinema listings; and a fairly basic orientation map (they sell more comprehensive ones, too). There are additional offices at the PIS in the main train station, Praha hlavní nádraží, and on Staroměstské náměstí.

ČEDOK was originally conceived as an agency for Czechs to book their organised tours

round the former Eastern Bloc, and many of Prague's numerous ČEDOK offices – like the most visible one on Wenceslas Square – still just handle foreign travel for Czechs. Really, the only reason for going to ČEDOK is to book a hotel room – and even then they only deal with the upper end of the market and, for the most part, won't touch private rooms. A nominal fee is charged for this service. The only offices you may need to use are the ones at Na příkopě 18, Nové Město (June–Sept Mon–Fri 8.15am–4.15pm, Sat 8.15am–2pm; Oct–May Mon–Fri 8.15am–4.15pm; ☎212 71 11), which sells international train, bus and boat tickets, and organises guided tours; and at Panská 5, Nové Město (Mon–Fri 9am–8pm; Sat & Sun 8.20am–2pm), which can book hotel accommodation.

**Outside Prague**, ČEDOK has branches in most sizeable towns, generally open Monday to Friday 9am to noon and 1 to 5pm, plus Saturday mornings in larger places. They're most useful, again, for booking accommodation; only occasionally do they have any useful maps, brochures or information about the town you're in, and, in addition, the staff are notoriously underpaid, unmotivated and unhelpful. The lack

## ČEDOK offices abroad

**UK and Eire**
17–18 Old Bond St,
London W1     ☎071/629 6058

**USA and Canada**
10 East 40th St,
New York, NY 10157     ☎212/689-9720

**Netherlands**
Leidsestraat 4,
Amsterdam     ☎20-220 101

**Germany**
Kaiserstrasse 54,
6000 Frankfurt-am-Main     ☎69-232 975

**Denmark**
Vester Farimagsgade 6,
1606 Copenhagen V     ☎01-120121

**Sweden**
Sveavägen 9–11,
11157 Stockholm     ☎8-207290

## Addresses

The street name is always written before the number in **addresses**. The word for street (*ulice*) is either abbreviated to *ul.* or missed out altogether – Celetná ulice, for instance, is commonly known as Celetná. Other terms often abbreviated are *náměstí* (square), *třída* (avenue), and *nábřeží* (embankment), which become *nám.*, *tř.* and *nábř.* respectively.

In this guide, we have used the names of districts as they appear on street signs, for example Hradčany, Smíchov etc. Prague's numbered **postal districts**, as listed below, are too large to be any help in orientation but are usually found in addresses.

### Praha 1
Hradčany, Malá Strana, Staré Město, Josefov, and the northern half of Nové Město.

### Praha 2
Southern Nové Město, Vyšehrad, and the western half of Vinohrady.

### Praha 3
Eastern Vinohrady and Žižkov.

### Praha 4
Nusle, Michle, Podolí, Braník, Krč, Chodov, Háje, Hodkovičky, Lhotka, Kunratice, Šeberov, Újezd, Modřany, Libuš, Komořany, Cholupice, Točná and Písnice.

### Praha 5
Smíchov, Motol, Košíře, Radlice, Jinonice, Stodůlky, Zličín, Sobín, Hlubočepy, Malá Chuchle, Slivenec, Holyně, Řeporyje, Velká Chuchle, Lochkov, Zadní Kopanina, Lahovice, Radotín, Zbraslav and Lipence.

### Praha 6
Western Bubeneč, Dejvice, Vokovice, Střešovice, Břevnov, Veleslavín, Liboc, Ruzyně, Řepy Nebušice, Lysolaje, Sedlec and Suchdol.

### Praha 7
Eastern Bubeneč, Holešovice and Troja.

### Praha 8
Karlín, Libeň, Kobylisy, western Střížkov, Bohnice, Čimice, Dáblice, Dolní Chabry and Březiněves.

### Praha 9
Vysočany, Hloubětín, Hrdlořezy, Kyje, Hostavice, Černý most, Prosek, eastern Střížkov, Letňany, Kbely, Satalice, Dolní Počernice, Horní Počernice, Klánovice, Běchovice, Koloděje and Újezd nad lesy.

### Praha 10
Vršovice, Strašnice, Malešice, Štěrboholy, Dubeč, Hájek, Královice, Uhříněves, Dolní and Horní Měcholupy, Záběhlice, Hostivař, Petrovice, Křeslice, Pitkovice, Benice, Kolovraty, Lipany and Nedvězí.

---

of basic tourist information outside Prague is one of the most glaring (and deliberate) omissions of the previous regime as regards tourism. Foreigners were effectively discouraged from embarking on individual travel in the country and instead rounded up into organised tours. Hopefully, this will change in the near future as locally organised tourist offices start to emerge, and the country wakes up to the income to be derived from tourism – and tourists.

## Maps

The city maps in this guide should be fine for most purposes, but if you crave a bit more detail, or are staying out of the centre, it's worthwhile investing in a detailed **street plan** of Prague (*plán města*). *Kartografie Praha* produce the cheapest and most comprehensive one: 1:20,000, covering not only the city centre but also many of the suburbs, with a full street index, and the metro, tram and bus routes marked on. They also produce a smaller 1:15,000 *plán středu města* covering just the historic centre, again with a street index and

local transport routes marked. You can get hold of either, and any other maps you may want, from the map suppliers listed in the box over the page Once in Prague, you can buy the same maps for about a quarter of the price, from *PIS* offices, most bookshops (*knihkupectví*) and some hotels.

For a **road map** of the country, the new 1:200,000 *Autoatlas Československa* is the best, written in four languages including English, and marking all campsites and petrol stations. You can get portions of the same map in the *Poznáváme Československo* series of seventeen fold-out maps, which mark all castles, museums and other sights (though not campsites), as well as giving a brief, dry, four-language account of the major places of interest.

If you're planning to do any **walking** in the hills around Prague, get hold of the relevant map from the *Soubor turistických map* series, which marks the complex network of coloured footpaths that weave their way across the countryside – the *Praha okolí* map covers Prague's immediate environs.

## Map Suppliers

BRITAIN

**Stanford's**
12–14 Long Acre,
London WC2E 9LP ☎ 071/836 1321
*Excellent specialist map and
general travel shop.*

**The Map Shop**
15 High St,
Upton-on-Severn,
Worcs WR8 0HJ ☎ 06846/31 46
*Mail order service.*

USA

**The Complete Traveler**
199 Madison Ave,
New York, NY 10016 ☎ 212/685-9007

**Rand McNally Mapstore**
150 East 52nd St,
New York, NY 10022 ☎ 212/758-7488

**French and European Publications**
115 Fifth Ave,
Now York, NY 10003 ☎ 212/673-7400

**Map Link**
529 State St,
Santa Barbara, CA 93101 ☎ 805/963-4438

# Costs, Money and Banks

Right now, Prague is still incredibly cheap for westerners. The only exception is accommodation, which is comparable with the rest of Europe. That said, prices are rising much faster than wages, and for most Czechs many of the newly privatised shops and restaurants appear extremely expensive.

You'll find exact costs for accommodation, food and drink in the relevant sections of the book: see Chapter 10, "Finding a Place to Stay", and Chapter 11, "Eating and Drinking". On average, though, if you stay in hostels and stick to *pivnice* for your eating, you could get by on as little as £5–10/$9–18 a day. If you intend to stay in private accommodation or hotels, and eat fancier meals, then you'll need more like £15–20/$26–35 a day. In fact, you'd be hard pushed to spend over £20/$35 a day even if you set your mind to it.

**Accommodation** will be your largest daily expense, with hostels and private accommodation both costing at least £10/$18 a night. All other basic costs like **food**, **drink** and **transport** remain very cheap, a good meal washed down with a couple of beers in a local *pivnice* or restaurant still costs as little as £2–3/$3–5 a head – and even in the top-class establishments prices rarely go much over £10–15/$18–26 a head.

## Money and the Exchange Rate

The **currency** in Czechoslovakia is the crown or *koruna* (indicated in this book as kčs), which is divided into one hundred heller or *haléř* (indicated as h). Coins come in the denominations 5h, 10h, 20h, 50h, 1kčs, 2kčs and 5kčs; notes as 10kčs, 20kčs, 50kčs, 100kčs, 500kčs and 1000kčs. A whole new series of notes replacing the old workerist ones is being gradually introduced, so any 1000kčs notes issued before 1985 are now invalid. Production has also stopped on the new bile-green 100kčs note, introduced as recently as the summer of 1989 and sporting a picture of Klement Gottwald, Czechoslovakia's first Communist president.

In January 1991, the Czechoslovak crown was drastically devalued by around 100 percent. Since then, it has remained pretty steady against the major western currencies, though it still can't be bought or sold entirely freely on the foreign exchange markets. The **exchange rate** is currently around 50kčs to the pound sterling, 30kčs to the US dollar. It is still technically illegal to import or export Czechoslovak crowns, though if you keep your exchange receipts, you can convert any surplus crowns back into western currency.

## Travellers' Cheques and Credit Cards

Probably the safest and easiest way to carry your funds is in **travellers' cheques**; sterling, US dollars or Deutschmarks are all equally acceptable. If you hold an account with a British bank you can apply for Eurocheques and a Eurocheque card. With this you can write cheques in crowns in some shops and hotels, as well as withdraw cash from most banks or exchange outlets. You pay a small commission plus a flat fee every time you write a cheque, and perhaps a set charge for the cheque card.

**Credit cards** like *Visa*, *Master Card* (*Access*) and *Amex* are accepted in most hotels, upmarket restaurants and some of the flashier shops. You can also get cash on your plastic at downtown banks and five-star hotels, subject to withdrawing a minimum of the equivalent of £50/$100. It's a good idea to keep at least some hard currency in **cash** for emergencies, as it will be accepted almost anywhere. If you lose your credit card, ring the Prague credit card hotline ☎ 236 66 88.

## Changing Money

Most Czech **banks** should be prepared to change travellers' cheques (albeit with reluctance for certain less well-known brands), accept Eurocheques, and give cash advances on credit cards – look for the window marked *směnárna*. Commissions at banks are fairly reasonable, but the queues and the bureaucracy can mean a long wait. Quicker, but more of a ripoff in terms of commission, are the exchange outlets which seem to be a feature of every street corner in the old town.

**Banking hours** are Mon–Fri 7.30am–noon & 1.30–3.30pm. Outside of these times you may find the odd bank open, but will otherwise have to rely on the exchange outlets and the international hotels. There's a 24-hour exchange desk at the airport.

With the banks offering virtually the same rates as the streets, the attraction of the **black market** is pretty slim for westerners. Before the currency reform, it was a universal and fairly harmless pursuit, occasionally interrupted by a plain-clothes policeman, but nowadays it really doesn't seem worth the risk – you'll have to change a large amount to make any great profit out of the deal, and the likelihood of receiving dodgy notes is high.

# Health Matters

No inoculations are required for Czechoslovakia. Health standards are coming under increasing criticism, however. With much of the country blighted by decades of ecological abuse, there have been well-founded criticisms about the quality of the water, milk, meat and vegetables. More specifically, if you have respiratory problems, avoid coming to Prague during the winter months when sulphur dioxide levels in the city centre regularly reach three or four times

World Health Organisation safety levels (see box below).

## Pharmacies, Doctors and Hospitals

If you should become ill, it's easiest to go to a *lekárna*. Pharmacists are willing to give advice (though language may well be a problem), and able to dispense many drugs available only on prescription in other western countries. They usually keep normal shopping hours (ie 8am–1pm & 2–5pm), but several are open 24 hours: the most central is at Na příkopě 7.

If the pharmacist can't help you, or it's a more serious case, and you wish to see an **English-speaking doctor**, you should go to the *Fakultní poliklinika* on the second floor at Karlovo náměstí, Nové Město, or the private *Diplomatic Health Centre for Foreigners*, Na homolce 724, Smíchov. Take your passport and at least 1000kčs to put down as a deposit. If you do have to pay for any medication, keep the receipts for claiming on your insurance once you're home.

---

### Pollution in Prague

Don't be fooled by the outward beauty of Prague's buildings. The city is sick, suffering some of the highest levels of sulphur dioxide of any European capital. And the worst place to be is the old town itself: in 1991 Staré Město recorded a winter average of 207 micrograms of pollutants per cubic metre of air (the *WHO* safety maximum is 150 micrograms). On about ten days over the winter of 1991–92, pollution levels rose to 400 micrograms, forcing the municipal authorities to introduce a total ban on non-essential traffic within the city – domestic and foreign – unless fitted with catalytic converters.

Between October and March, Prague is plagued by a lethal cocktail of winter weather, the city's basin-like topography, and the brown coal which provides energy for industry and most of the city's heating. The heavy, cold air sits in the basin, trapped in by the warmer air above, and thus preventing the sulphur dioxide and carbon monoxide from dispersing. Car ownership looks set to rise dramatically over the next decade, and a year-round ban on cars in the city centre is now being considered.

---

### Emergencies

| | |
|---|---|
| **Ambulance** | ☎333 |
| **Dentist** | |
| Emergency service (7pm–7am) at | |
| Vladislavova 22, | |
| Nové Město | ☎26 13 74 |
| **Doctor** | ☎155 |
| **Hospital** | |
| *Záchranná služba*, | |
| Dukelských hrdinů 21, | |
| Holešovice | |
| **24hr chemist** | |
| Na příkopě 7, | |
| Nové Město | ☎22 00 81 |

# Communications: Post, Phones and Media

## Post

The **main post office** (*pošta*) in Prague is at Jindřišská 14 (☎26 48 41), just off Wenceslas Square. Certain services, such as parcels, telegrams and telephones, operate 24 hours a day. Make sure you queue at the right counter (there are 53 to choose from): *známky* (stamps) are currently sold from windows 8–15; the new phone cards (*telecarty*) are available from windows 20–22; *balky* (parcels) are dealt with at windows 6–7. Each postal district in Prague has several post offices, though these have far less comprehensive hours and services.

In Prague, **poste restante** (pronounced as five syllables in Czech) letters will arrive at the main post office mentioned above; go to window 28 (open Mon–Fri 6.30am–8pm, Sat 6.30am–1pm). Alternatively, *American Express*, at Václavské náměstí 54 (Mon–Fri 9am–6pm, Sat 9am–noon), will hold mail for a month for card and/or cheque holders.

**Outbound post** is reasonably reliable, with letters or cards taking around five working days to the UK, a week to ten days to North America. You can buy **stamps** from newsagents, tobacconists and kiosks, as well as at the post offices. If you want to send a **parcel over 1kg**, you must go to the special parcel office at the junction of Plzeňská and Vrchlického in Prague 5.

## Phones

Public **phones** in Czechoslovakia are far from reliable. Although there are usually instructions in English, you may still encounter technical problems. The yellow phones take only 1kčs coins, and are only good for **local calls**. Theoretically, you simply pick up the receiver and dial the number with your crown poised in the slot. To call outside the local area code, you must find one of the elusive grey phone boxes which take 1, 2 and 5kčs coins. When you run out of money, you'll hear a recorded message berating you in Czech to put more in.

More sophisticated phones that give back any unused coins are beginning to appear in Prague, as are **card phones**. Phonecards (*telecarty*), currently available in 50 and 150kčs denominations, can be bought at post offices. The **dialling tone** is a short followed by a long pulse; the **ringing tone** is long and regular; **engaged** is short and rapid; the standard Czech response is *prosím*; the word for extension is *linka*. If you have any problems, ring ☎0135 and ask for an English-speaking operator.

It's also theoretically possible to make **international calls** from the grey phone boxes, but few people do. It's a lot less hassle to seek out one of the new card phones, or simply go to the

| Dialling codes | |
|---|---|
| **To Prague** | |
| From Britain | ☎010 42 2 |
| From USA & Canada | ☎011 42 2 |
| From Australia & New Zealand | ☎0011 42 2 |
| | |
| Phoning from elsewhere in Czechoslovakia, the Prague city code is ☎02 | |
| | |
| **From Prague** | |
| UK | ☎0044 |
| Eire | ☎00353 |
| Australia | ☎0061 |
| New Zealand | ☎0064 |
| USA and Canada | ☎001 |

telephone exchanges situated in most major post offices. Write down the town and number you want, leave a deposit of around 200kčs and wait for your name to be called out. Keep a close watch on the time since international calls are extremely expensive at whatever time of the day or night you ring. You can also make calls from most hotels, although their surcharge is usually pretty hefty. It might be easier in the long run to ask for a **collect call** – which will cost the recipient less than it would cost you. Dial ☎0132 and ask for an English speaker or say in Czech *na účet voleného*.

## The Media

For years, **foreign newspapers** were restricted to old copies of the *Morning Star*, and its fraternal equivalents. All that has changed, and it's now possible to get most of the quality British papers, and the *International Herald Tribune*, from several stalls around the centre of Prague. They're generally a day old, though one that you can buy on the day of issue is the European edition of *The Guardian*, printed in Frankfurt (it arrives on the streets of Prague around mid-morning).

By far the most respected **Czech newspaper** is *Lidové noviny*, which started life as a monthly *samizdat* under the Communists. It is generally considered to be "close to the Castle", that is to say pro-Havel; many of its regular contributors, like Havel, were involved in the human rights organisation Charter 77. The other positive independent political voice is the weekly *Respekt*. The slickly produced centre-right *Telegraf* is the latest of the "independents" to be launched; most of the rest of the press is run along party political lines. *Rudé právo*, once the official mouthpiece of the Communist Party, with a guaranteed readership of around one million, has survived against all odds, though it now describes itself as a "left-wing daily".

Two **English-language** papers to look out for are *The Prague Post*, a quality weekly with a useful **listings** section at the back, and *Prognosis*, a more youthful fortnightly paper, with a separate listings section specifically designed for first-time visitors. And with just a little Czech, there's the monthly listings magazine *Přehled*, and the much more comprehensive weekly listings broadsheet *Program*, both easily decipherable.

As far as **magazines** go, western glossies grab the attention of most of the nation more effectively than their domestic competitors, with

the exception of the Czech edition of *Playboy*, whose success has taken place against the background of a huge nationwide increase in **porn** magazines and books.

### TV and Radio

Until recently, the only good thing to be said about Czechoslovak state television was that, since federalisation in 1969, it had consistently broadcast in Czech *and* Slovak. This commitment to **bilingual broadcasting** was so strictly adhered to that, in the course of an ice hockey match, the first half would be commentated in Czech, the second in Slovak. For the last twenty years this, more than anything else, has helped nurture a generation for whom the differences between the two nations, at least linguistically, are irrelevant.

Since 1989, the Slovaks and Czechs have begun to dismantle the old system. Both sides now have programmes almost exclusively in their own language, linking up nationwide solely for things like the news. Both state-run channels are pretty bland, with keep-fit classes and classical concerts still taking up much of peak-time viewing. All foreign films and serials are dubbed and everything shuts down well before midnight. A third channel, *OK3*, has recently joined in: a seemingly arbitrary mix of *CNN* and sundry satellite channels of varying quality. *CNN* is currently broadcast from midnight to 8am, from 9 to 10am and again from noon to 2pm.

As far as **radio** goes, most cafés and bars tune into one of the new FM music stations that have recently appeared. The most popular is *Europe II*, on 88.2MHz, which dishes out bland Euro-pop; followed by *Radio Czechoslovakia*, on 102.5MHz, which is a mixture of news, classical and folk music (Havel does his presidential chat every Sunday at 2.15pm). Other new favourites are *Radio 1*, on 91.9MHz, which plays a wide range of rock from east and west, and has a short English-language bulletin at 10am and 3.30pm on weekdays; *Radio Bonton*, on 99.7MHz, featuring yet more western pop; and the most recent arrival, *Radio Golem*, on 90.3MHz, which doles out everything from rap to heavy metal.

You can pick up the *BBC World Service* fairly easily now, on 101.1m. *Radio Prague International* broadcasts news and features on a variety of medium and short-wave frequencies from 7.30am to 10.30pm. Be warned: most FM stations give out pretty weak signals, so don't expect to get much once you've left the city.

# Sleeping

Except in high season, finding a place to stay in Prague is no longer a problem. Although the city still suffers from a chronic shortage of hotels, the number of private rooms available has alleviated most of the difficulties visitors used to encounter. That said, accommodation is still likely to be by far the largest chunk of your daily expenditure, with most private rooms starting at around 250–350kčs per person. Either side of that figure, the cheapest youth hostel beds in the city go for around 50–150kčs per person; and you can comfortably spend 2000kčs and upwards in the various hotels with three or more stars – some are very firmly in the super-luxury class. For full lists of accommodation in Prague, turn to "Finding a Place to Stay", p.197.

If you're going to Prague at a time when demand for beds will be great (from Easter to September, and over the Christmas holidays), it's sensible to arrange accommodation before you arrive. ČEDOK (see box on p.20) are the only outfit at present who can book hotel rooms from abroad – except as an all-inclusive package – but their selection starts at £45/$77 a double. A much better bet is to book private accommodation through one of the cheaper specialist agencies listed on p.7.

## Hotels

Prague's **hotels** are in a state of flux at the moment. For a start, there's still an extreme shortage of hotel beds in the city. The new hotels that are being built are almost exclusively in the luxury category, often joint-ventures with

western firms. The cheaper hotels have been sold off in the recent state auctions, and the vast majority are currently undergoing modernisation; a handful have been returned to their former owners under the "restitution" law.

Previously classified from A to C, according to the facilities they provided and the price they charged, most hotels have now started using the star system. Whichever scale is used, it should be taken with a large pinch of salt, since conditions and prices can vary greatly within each category. For the moment, at least, hotels are still charging foreigners two to three times what Czechs pay, in an effort to reflect the real disparity between Czech and non-Czech incomes.

For the most part, Prague's hotels tend to be drab, concrete affairs. There are, of course, exceptions, but the interiors of even the older buildings have often been routinely modernised. Most hotel rooms are sparsely furnished, with just a washbasin and the obligatory *Tesla* radio permanently tuned to the state radio station. Hot water and heating can be erratic – it's either boiling and you can't turn the thing off, or else it's unremittingly cold. In the top hotels, of course, you can be fairly certain of pristine service and consistently overheated rooms.

**Breakfast** isn't normally included unless you're paying a lot for your room. If it is, you'll be given a voucher covering a specific amount of money, which you hand in to the waiter as payment. Almost without fail, hotels also have a restaurant and/or a bar.

---

### Accommodation Prices

Hotels listed in the guide are given a symbol which corresponds to one of **five price categories:**

① Under 250kčs.
② 250–500kčs
③ 500–1000kčs
④ 1000–2000kčs
⑤ 2000kčs and upwards

For more information, see "Finding a Place to Stay", Chapter 10.

---

## Private Rooms

Since 1989, there has been a huge increase in the number of **private rooms** available, making them by far the most common choice of accommodation for the moment. Most Czechs keep their places very tidy and clean, but before agreeing to part with any money, be sure you know exactly where you're staying and check about transport to the centre – some places can be a long way out of town. It's also worth asking about whether you'll be sharing bathroom, cooking facilities etc with the family or not – Czech hospitality can be somewhat overwhelming, although meals other than breakfast are not generally included in the price. It's quite possible to rent a self-contained flat, if you so wish, though it will cost a lot more.

For **people travelling alone**, private rooms are definitely the best bet, since prices are invariably charged per person. Single rooms can be hard to find in hotels, and are generally only slightly less than the price of a double.

## Youth Hostels and Campsites

There are a handful of **youth hostels** in Prague, which are useful if you're travelling alone, or are looking for a very cheap bed. Although some will rent out blankets and sheets, it's as well to bring your own sleeping bag. A couple of official hostels-cum-hotels are run by *Cestovní kancelář*

*mládeže* (*CKM*), which is affiliated to the *International Youth Hostel Federation* (*IYHF*). It's not necessary to have a card to stay there but at 1000kčs a double, they're no great bargain – and the reductions for members are significant (if you can get a place). In addition to the *CKM* hostels, there are a number of other unofficial hostels, listed in full in Chapter 10. Standards and prices vary, but you can pay as little as 50kčs per night.

*CKM* also organise **student accommodation**, which is let out on the cheap in July and August. The beds, usually in dormitories, cost about 50kčs per person for students, double that for anyone else. They're often heavily booked up in advance by groups, but will try their best to squeeze you in. **Curfews** operate in many hostels and they tend to be quite early (around 10pm–midnight). Addresses change from year to year, so to check out the current locations, go to the *CKM* head office in Prague, at Žitná 12, Nové Město (☎ 29 45 87).

There's a wide choice of **campsites** in Prague, though few have anything but the most basic facilities, and some lack even those. Very few sites are open all year round, and most don't get going until May at the earliest, closing towards October. Costs are reasonable, though not devastatingly cheap: two people plus car and tent weigh in at around 100–150kčs. Again, details are in Chapter 10.

# Eating and Drinking

There are several ways of eating out in Prague: you can go to a *restaurace* or *vináma* and have a full meal; you can have something cheaper, more basic (though equally filling) and in less formal surroundings at a *pivnice*, *hostinec* or *hospoda*; or, at the budget end of the scale, you can eat very cheaply indeed at one of the stand-up *bufets* or fast-food places.

## Breakfast, Snacks and Takeaways

Most Czechs get up so early in the morning (often around 5 or 6am) that they don't have time to start the day with anything more than a quick cup of coffee. As a result, the whole concept of **breakfast** as such is alien to the Czechs. Most hotels will serve the "continental" basics, but it's cheaper and more enjoyable to go hunting for your own.

**Pastries** (*pečivo*) are available from Prague's bakeries (*pekářství* or *pekárna*), but rarely in bars and cafés, so you'll most likely have to eat them on the go. Traditional Czech pastry (*koláč*) is more like sweet bread, dry and fairly dense with only a little condiment to flavour it, such as almonds (*oříškový*), poppy seed jam (*mákový*), plum jam (*povidlový*) or a kind of sour-sweet Slovak curd cheese (*tvarohový*). Recently, French- and Viennese-style bakeries have started to appear in Prague, selling croissants (*loupáky*) and lighter cream cakes.

Czech **bread** (*chléb*) is some of the tastiest around when fresh. The standard loaf is *šumava*, a dense mixture of wheat and rye, which you can buy whole, in halves (*půl*) or quarters (*čtvrtina*). *Český chléb* is a mixture of rye, wheat and whey, with distinctive slashes across the top; *kmínový chléb* is the same loaf packed full of caraway seeds. *Moskva* is a national favourite, despite the name – a moist, heavy, sour dough loaf that lasts for days. Rolls come in two varieties: *rohlík*, a plain white finger roll, and *houska*, a rougher, tastier round bun.

The ubiquitous Czech street **takeaway** is the hot dog or *párek*, a dubious-looking frankfurter (traditionally two – *párek* means a pair), dipped in mustard and served with a white roll (*v rohlíku*). A Czech speciality all year round is *smažený sýr* – a slab of melted cheese (and, more often than not, ham) fried in breadcrumbs and served with a roll (*v housce*). If it's *plněný* or *se šunkou*, then you can be certain it's got ham in it, and it generally comes with a large dose of Czech tartare sauce – a lot less piquant than its western counterpart. The greasiest option of the lot is *bramborák*, a thin potato pancake with little flecks of bacon or salami in it. Finally, there's *langoše*; a Hungarian invention – a deep-fried doughy base smothered in garlic. In the autumn, you'll find freshly cooked corn on the cob (*kukuřice*) sold on the streets.

## Bufets and Fast Food

Prague's stand-up *bufets* are open from as early as 6am and offer everything from light snacks to full meals. They're usually self-service (*samoobsluha*) and non-smoking, and occasionally have rudimentary seats. The cheapest of the tired-looking meat sausages on offer is *sekaná*, bits of old meat and bread squashed together to form a meat loaf – for connoisseurs only. *Guláš* is popular – stew that may bear little relation to the original of that name – usually *Szegedinský* (pork with sauerkraut) but sometimes *special* (with better meat and a creamier sauce). If you're prepared to risk it, you could try some roast chicken.

Less substantial fare boils down to *chlebíčky* – artistically presented **open sandwiches** with combinations of gherkins, cheese, salami, ham and aspic – and mountains of **salad**, bought by weight (200 grammes is a medium-sized portion). *Feferonkový salát* is a mildly hot pepper and pea salad, while *vajíčkový salát* is a rich egg and mayonnaise dish. Others, like *vlašský* or *taliánský* (Italian) or *francouský* (French) *salát*, are, in reality, Czech affairs with varying amounts of salami, ham, potato and mayonnaise.

**Western-style fast food** has yet to hit Prague in a really big way, but *McDonalds* are set to reverse that trend, with the first of six outlets recently opened just off Wenceslas Square. In the meantime there are sort of cross-breed *bufets* serving Czech fare, plus *hamburgery* (as the Czechs call them), pizzas and other "international" dishes, most recently falafel. Other staple fast-food snacks include *hranolky* (chips/ French fries) or *krokety* (croquettes), served with tartare sauce. Czech crisps (*chips*) are lightly salted, greasy and generally stale.

## Coffee, Tea and Cakes

Like the Austrians who once ruled over them, the Czechs have a grotesquely sweet tooth, and the coffee-and-cake hit is part of the daily ritual. **Coffee** is drunk black and described rather hopefully as *turecká* (Turkish) – it's really just hot water poured over coffee grains. Downmarket *bufets* sell *ledová káva*, a weak, cold black coffee, while at the other end of the scale *Vídeňská káva* (Viennese coffee) is a favourite with the older generation, not quite as refined as the Austrian original, but still served with an adequate dollop of whipped cream. Espresso coffee (*presso*) is becoming trendy in Prague, though it rarely matches up to the Italian version. Whatever you do, avoid *kapucín*, which is normally nothing like the cappuccino it purports to be.

**Tea** is drunk weak and without milk, although you'll usually be given a glass of boiling water and a tea bag so you can do your own thing. **Milk** itself is rarely drunk on its own, though it can be bought in supermarkets – but bearing in mind that some seventy percent of it is unfit for human consumption, it might be wiser to buy UHT milk. The Czechs produce a delicious selection of **yoghurts** and sour milks, which you should buy in preference to the sugary western stuff that has flooded the market recently; *bílý jogurt* is natural yoghurt, but look

out for *kefír* or *biokys*, the thick and thin respectively of the sour milks.

The *cukrárna* is the place to go for cake-eating. There are two main types of cake: *dort*, like the German *tort*, consist of a series of custard cream, chocolate and sponge layers, while *řez* are lighter, square cakes, usually containing a bit of fruit. A *věneček*, filled with "cream", is the nearest you'll get to an eclair; a *větrník* is simply a larger version with a bit of fresh cream added. One speciality to look out for is *rakvička*, which literally means "Granny's little coffin", an extended piece of sugar with cream, moulded vaguely into the shape of a coffin.

Whatever the season, Czechs have to have their daily fix of **ice cream** (*zmrzlina*), dispensed from window kiosks in the sides of buildings. In a *cukrárna* there's generally more choice, but the outlets advertising *italská zmrzlina* (actually nothing like Italian ice cream) are the most popular.

## Full Meals

For a **full meal**, you can go anywhere from a local *pivnice* to a regular *restaurace* or late-night *vinárna*. It's as well to remember that Czechs eat their main meal of the day at lunchtime, between noon and 2pm. Traditionally, they only have cold meats and bread later on, but obviously the posher restaurants make more of the evening.

If your main concern is price, the local beer-swilling *pivnice*, *hospoda* or *hostinec* are the ones to go for. Nearly all of them will serve hot meals from mid-morning until 2 or 3pm, and some continue serving until 8 or 9pm. A *vinárna* (wine bar) – though not necessarily its kitchen – will sometimes stay open after 11pm.

Away from the big hotels, the **menu** (*jídelní lístek*), which should be displayed outside, is often in Czech only and deciphering it without a grounding in the language can be quite a feat. Just bear in mind that the general rule is for the right-hand column to list the prices, while the far left column usually gives you the estimated weight of every dish in grammes; if what you get weighs more or less, the price alters accordingly.

Most Prague restaurants insist, with varying degress of coercion, that you leave your coat and bags in the **cloakroom** (*šatna*). It's another leftover of Austrian airs and graces, but also provides a meagre employment for the pensioners who generally run them. A modest form of **tipping** exists, generally done by rounding up the bill to the nearest few crowns.

# A food and drink glossary

## Basics

| | |
|---|---|
| snídaně | Breakfast |
| oběd | Lunch |
| večeře | Supper/dinner |
| nůž | Knife |
| vidlička | Fork |
| ižice | Spoon |
| deska | Plate |
| šálek | Cup |
| pohár | Glass |
| předkrmy | Starters |
| polévka | Soup |
| zákusky | Dessert |
| chléb | Bread |
| maslo | Butter |
| houska | Round roll |
| rohlík | Finger roll |
| chlebíček | Open sandwich |
| med | Honey |
| mléko | Milk |
| vejce | Eggs |
| volské oko | Fried egg |
| pečivo | Pastry |
| maso | Meat |
| ryby | Fish |
| ovoce | Fruit |
| gukr | Sugar |
| sůl | Salt |
| pepř | Pepper |
| ocet | Vinegar |
| hořčice | Mustard |
| tartarská omáčka | Tartare sauce |
| křen | Horseradish |
| rýže | Rice |
| knedlíky | Dumplings |
| jidla na objednávku | Main dishes to order |
| zeleniny | Vegetables |

## Soups, fish and poultry

| | |
|---|---|
| boršč | Beetroot soup |
| bramborová | Potato soup |
| čočková | Lentil soup |
| fazolová | Bean soup |
| hovězí | Beef soup |
| hrachová | Pea soup |
| kapustnica | Sauerkraut, mushroom and meat soup |
| kachna | Duck |
| kapr | Carp |
| kuře | Chicken |
| kuřecí | Thin chicken soup |
| makrel | Mackerel |
| pstruh | Trout |
| rajská | Tomato soup |
| sardinka | Sardine |
| zavináč | Herring/rollmop |
| zeleninová | Vegetable soup |

## Meat dishes

| | |
|---|---|
| dršťky | Tripe |
| čevapčiči | Spicy meat balls |
| hovězí | Beef |
| játra | Liver |
| jazyk | Tongue |
| klobásy | Sausages |
| kotleta | Cutlet |
| kýta | Thigh |
| ledvinky | Kidneys |
| salám | Salami |
| sekaná | Meat loaf |
| skopové | Mutton |
| slanina | Bacon |
| svíčková | Sirloin |
| šunka | Ham |
| telecí | Veal |
| vepřové | Pork |
| vepřové řízek | Breaded pork cutlet or schnitzel |
| žebírko | Ribs |

## Vegetables

| | |
|---|---|
| brambory | Potatoes |
| cibule | Onion |
| česnek | Garlic |
| čočka | Lentils |
| fazole | Beans |
| houby | Mushrooms |
| hrášky | Peas |
| chřest | Asparagus |
| květák | Cauliflower |
| kyselá okurka | Pickled gherkin |
| kyselé zelí | Sauerkraut |
| lečo | Ratatouille |
| karot | Carrot |
| okurka | Cucumber |
| rajče | Tomato |
| ředkev | Radish |
| řepná bulva | Beetroot |
| hranolky | Chips, french fries |
| špenát | Spinach |
| zelí | Cabbage |
| žampiony | Mushrooms |

## Fruit and cheese

| | |
|---|---|
| banán | Banana |
| borůvky | Bilberries |
| broskev | Peach |
| bryndza | Goat's cheese in brine |
| citrón | Lemon |
| druh citrusu | Grapefruit |
| hrozni | Grapes |
| hruška | Pear |
| jablko | Apple |
| kompot | Stewed fruit |
| jahody | Strawberries |
| maliny | Raspberries |

| | | | |
|---|---|---|---|
| *mandle* | Almonds | *m.m.* | With butter |
| *meruňka* | Apricot | *na kmíně* | With caraway seeds |
| *hermelín* | Czech brie | *na roštu* | Grilled |
| *uzený sýr* | Smoked cheese | *nadivaný* | Stuffed |
| *niva* | Semi-soft, crumbly, blue cheese | *nakládaný* | Pickled |
| | | *(za)pečený* | Baked/roast |
| *oříšky* | Peanuts | *plněný* | Stuffed |
| *ostružiny* | Blackberries | *slatký* | Sweet |
| *ošťěpek* | Heavily smoked, curd cheese | *smažený* | Fried in breadcrumbs |
| | | *syrový* | Raw |
| *parenyica* | Rolled strips of lightly smoked, curd cheese | *udený* | Smoked |
| | | *vařený* | Boiled |
| *pomeranč* | Orange | *znojmský* | Served with gherkins |
| *pivný sýr* | Cheese flavoured with beer | | |
| | | **Drinks** | |
| *rozinky* | Raisins | *čaj* | Tea |
| *švestky* | Plums | *destiláty* | Spirits |
| *třešeň* | Cherry | *káva* | Coffee |
| *tvaroh* | Fresh, curd cheese | *koňak* | Brandy |
| *urda* | Soft, fresh, whey cheese | *láhev* | Bottle |
| | | *led* | Ice |
| *vlašské ořechy* | Walnuts | *minerální (voda)* | Mineral (water) |
| | | *mléko* | Milk |
| **Common Terms** | | *pivo* | Beer |
| *čerstvý* | Fresh | *suché víno* | Dry wine |
| *domáci* | Home-made | *svařené víno* | Mulled wine |
| *dušený* | Stew/casserole | *vinný střik* | White wine with soda |
| *grilovaný* | Roast on the spit | *víno* | Wine |
| *kyselý* | Sour | *na zdraví* | Cheers! |

## Czech Cuisine

Forty years of culinary isolation has meant that there have been few innovations to the Germanic-influenced **Czech cuisine**, with a predilection for big slabs of meat served with lashings of gravy, dumplings and pickled gherkins, not to mention a good helping of pickled cabbage. On the plus side, Prague ham is justly famous and Czech beer is among the best in the world*.

Most menus start with the **soups** (*polévky*), one of the country's culinary strong points, served mainly at lunchtimes. Posher joints will have a serious selection of starters such as *uzený jazyk* (smoked tongue), *tresčí játra* (cod's liver) or perhaps *kaviárové vejce* (a hard-boiled egg with caviar on top). *Šunková rolka* is another favourite, consisting of ham topped with whipped cream

---

*Even Hitler was tempted enough to break his lifelong vow of vegetarianism and teetotalism and tuck into some Prague ham and Pilsen beer when he and his troops marched into the capital in March 1939.

and horseradish, but you're more likely to find yourself skipping the starters, which are often little more than a selection of cold meats.

Main courses are overwhelmingly based on **meat** (*maso*), usually pork or beef. The Czechs are experts on these meats, and although the quality could often be better, the variety of sauces and preparative techniques beats traditional Anglo-American cooking hands down. The difficulty lies in decoding names such as *klašterny tajemství* ("mystery of the monastery") or even a common dish like *Moravský vrabec* (literally "Moravian sparrow", but actually just roast pork).

**Fish** (*ryby*) are generally listed, along with chicken and other fowl like duck, under a separate heading. Trout and carp (the traditional dish at Christmas) are cheap and widely available, and although their freshness may be questionable, they are usually served, grilled or roasted, in delicious buttery sauces.

Most main courses are served with potatoes, pickled cabbage and/or **dumplings** (*knedlíky*), which, though German in origin and name, are now the mainstay of Bohemian cooking. The term itself is misleading for English-speakers, since they resemble nothing like the English dumpling – more like a heavy white bread. *Houskové knedliky* come in large flour-based slices (four or five to a dish), while *bramborové knedliky* are smaller and made from potato and flour. Occasionally, you may be treated to *ovocné knedliky* (fruit dumplings), the king of Czech dumplings. **Fresh salads** are a new concept in Czech restaurants, and most rarely rise above lettuce, tomato or cucumber, often swimming in a slightly sweet, watery dressing.

With the exception of *palačinky* (pancakes) filled with chocolate or fruit and cream, **desserts**, where they exist at all, can be pretty unexciting. Even the ice cream in restaurants isn't up to the standards of the street stuff, so go to a *cukrárna* if you want a dose of sugar.

## Vegetarians

Czechoslovakia is no place for **vegetarians** or health freaks; its meat consumption is one of the highest in the world – around half a kilo a day per head. On top of that, most of the animals are factory-farmed and often seriously ill by the time they're slaughtered, rendering large parts of the carcass unfit for human consumption. Inefficiencies in agricultural production mean that, even in this rich and fecund land, you'll be offered few fresh vegetables as compensation.

If you eat fish but not meat you won't have too hard a time in Prague. Most Czech menus feature a fish dish, usually trout or carp. Many also have a section called *bezmasa* (literally "without meat") but this often simply means the dish is not entirely based around a slab of burnt flesh, for example *omeleta se šunkou* (ham omelette). Regular standbys are *knedliky s vejce* (dumplings and egg) or *omeleta s hrášem* (pea omelette), both of which most chefs will knock up for you without too much fuss. Another possibility is, of course, pizza, an approximation of which is becoming increasingly popular in Prague.

**Vegans** will have little or no choice in restaurants, aside from certain pizzas; even dishes like beans or lentils regularly turn up with an egg plonked in the middle. Falafel is beginning to appear in Prague, and, in addition, a number of health-food shops have opened which sell soya-based produce. The takeaways from *Country Life* on Melantrichova are mostly, if not exclusively, vegan.

### Vegetarian phrases

As a serious meat-eating nation, most Czechs simply can't conceive of anybody going through even a small portion of their life without eating meat (unless they're critically ill or clinically insane). So simply saying you're a vegetarian or that you don't eat meat or fish may instil panic and/or confusion in the waiter – it's often better to ask what's in a particular dish you think looks promising.

The phrases to remember are *"jsem vegetarián/vegeteriánka. máte nejaké bezmasa?"* (I'm a vegetarian. Is there anything without meat?); for emphasis, you could add *"nejím maso nebo ryby"* (I don't eat meat or fish).

## Alcoholic Drinks

**Alcohol** consumption in Czechoslovakia has always been high, and in the decade following the events of 1968 it doubled. A whole generation found solace in drinking, mostly beer. It's a problem which seldom spills out onto the streets; violence in pubs is uncommon and you won't see that many drunks in public. Nevertheless, it's not unusual to see someone legless in the afternoon, on their way home from work.

Czechoslovakia is currently second in the world league table of beer consumption, behind the Germans, its **beer** ranking among the best in the world. It may not boast the variety of its western neighbour, but it remains the true home of most of the lager drunk around the world today. It was in the Bohemian city of Plzeň (Pilsen) that the first **bottom-fermented** beer was introduced in 1842, after complaints from the citizens about the quality of the top-fermented predecessor. The new brewing style quickly spread to Germany, and is now blamed for the bland rubbish served up in the English-speaking world as lager or Pils.

Whether due to lack of technological know-how or through positive choice, brewing methods in Czechoslovakia have remained stuck in the old ways, eschewing chemical substitutes. The distinctive flavour of Czech beer comes from the famous Bohemian hops, Žatec (Saaz) Red, still hand-picked and then combined with the soft local water and served with a high content of absorbed carbon dioxide – hence the thick, creamy head. Even if you don't think you like lager, you must try at least a *malé pivo* (0.3 litre). The average jar is medium strength, usually about 1050 specific gravity or 4.2% alcohol (12° to the Czechs who use their own peculiar Balling scale).

The most famous Czech beer is **Pilsner Urquell**, know to the Czechs as *Plzeňský Prazdroj*, the original bottom-fermented Pils from Plzeň (Pilsen), a city 80km southwest of Prague. Plzeň also boasts the **Gambrinus** brewery, thus producing two out of the three main Czech export beers. The other big Bohemian brewing town is České Budějovice (Budweis), home to **Budvar**, a mild beer for Bohemia but still leagues ahead of *Budweiser*, the German name for *Budvar* that was adopted by an American brewer in 1876. All three Czech beers are available in Prague pubs.

The biggest brewery in the country, however, is in the Smíchov suburb of Prague where **Staropramen** is produced, a typical Bohemian brew with a mild hoppy flavour. Prague also produces some of the country's best strong, special beer: **Flek**, a dark caramel concoction brewed and served exclusively at a pub called *U Fleků* in Prague's Nové Město since 1399, and **Braník**, a light malty beer from south Prague, creamy even by smooth Bohemian standards. Other Bohemian beers worth sampling are the award-winning bitter **Velkopopovický kozel**, and the smooth, hoppy **Krušovice** beer.

Czechoslovakia's **wine** will never win over as many people as its beer, but since the import of French and German vines in the fourteenth century, it has produced a modest selection of medium-quality wines. Since few are exported, and labelling is notoriously imprecise – most wines are made by large farm co-ops and sold under brand names – it's difficult to give a very clear picture. The two main wine regions are along the hot southern edge of Slovakia and in the hills of South Moravia. Bohemia's wine-growing region consists of just 1000 acres around the town of Mělník, but it produces at least one good red, *Ludmila*, and a couple of passable whites.

Suffice it to say that most domestic wine is pretty drinkable – *Frankovka* is a perfectly respectable red; *Tramín* a good, dry white – and rarely more than about £1.50/$2.50 a bottle in shops, while the best stuff can only be had from the private wine cellars, hundreds of which still exist.

All the usual **spirits** are on sale and known by their generic names, with rum and vodka dominating the market. Domestic brands originate mostly from Slovakia and east Moravia: the home-production of brandies being a national pastime, which results in some almost terminally strong liquors.

The most renowned of the lot is *slivovice*, a plum brandy originally from the border hills between Moravia and Slovakia but now available just about everywhere. You'll probably also come across *borovička*, a popular firewater from the Slovak Spiš region, made from pine trees; *myslivec* is a rough brandy with a firm following.

There's also a fair selection of intoxicating herbal concoctions: *fernet* is a dark-brown bitter drink, known as *bavorák* (Bavarian beer) when it's mixed with tonic, while *becherovka* is a supposedly healthy herbal spirit from the Bohemian spa town of Karlovy Vary, with a very unusual taste.

## Soft Drinks

Unfortunately, aside from the country's plentiful mineral water, **soft drinks** in Czechoslovakia are rather nasty. As well as the ubiquitous *Coke* and *Pepsi*, there's *Perla*, a sugary lemon drink, and *Topic*, reputedly made with grapes and herbs; *Vinea* is a slightly subtler version. If you ask for a lemonade (*limonáda*), you're just as likely to get orangeade, and vice versa if you ask for *oranž*.

Unless you long for a cross between cherryade and dandelion and burdock, avoid the variety of vivid fizzy drinks that go under the promising name of *džus* (pronounced "juice"). Fresh fruit juice has only recently become available. The safest bet for those without a sweet tooth is to ask for *soda* or *tonic*. *Minerální voda* (mineral water) is everywhere, always carbonated, and a lot more "tasty" than western brands. Try *Mattoni* for a milder option.

## Where to Drink

Even the most simple *bufet* in the Czech Lands serves draught beer, but the **pivnice** or pub (which closes around 10 or 11pm) is the place where most heavy drinking goes on. It's common practice to share a table with other drinkers; *je tu volno?* (Is this seat free?) is the standard question. Waiter-service is the norm, so sit tight and a beer should come your way. When you want to leave, simply say *zaplatím, prosím* (literally "I'll pay, please"), and your tab will be totted up.

Since *pivnice* (and the more local *hospoda* or *hostinec*) are traditionally male preserves, women tend to head for the more mixed atmosphere of the country's restaurants or *vinárna* (wine bar). A *vinárna* generally stays open slightly later, often doubling as an upmarket restaurant or nightclub. The younger generation hangs out more in the **kavárna** (café) or ubiquitous continental bars.

# Opening Hours and Public Holidays

Shops in Prague are generally open Monday to Friday from 9am to 5pm, though most supermarkets stay open later. Smaller shops usually close for lunch for an hour sometime between noon and 2pm. Those shops that do open on Saturday are generally shut by noon or 1pm; and none open on Sunday. Pubs and restaurants tend to close between 10 and 11pm, with food often unobtainable beyond 9pm. Over the weekend, they close for one or two days out of Saturday, Sunday and Monday.

## Museums, Art Galleries and Churches

**Opening hours** for museums and galleries tend to be from 9 or 10am to 5 or 6pm every day except Monday, all year round. Full opening hours are detailed in the text. Ticket prices are still negligible (rarely more than 20kčs) – proof of student status will cut costs in half. As with hotels, some of the more touristy sights currently charge a special rate (anything up to five times as much) for foreigners, but, again, it's rarely more than 50kčs.

Getting into **churches** can present more of a problem. The really important ones operate in much the same way as museums and occasionally even have an entry charge, particularly for their crypts or cloisters. Other churches, though, are usually kept locked, opening only for worship in the early morning (around 7 or 8am) and/or the evening (around 6 or 7pm). Synagogues in Josefov follow museum hours, except that they close on Saturdays rather than Mondays.

**Outside Prague**, in the high season, castles and monasteries open from 8 or 9am to noon or 1pm, and again from 2pm to 4pm or later. On Mondays and from the end of October to the beginning of April, most places are closed. In April and October, opening hours are often restricted to weekends and public holidays only. Whatever the time of year, if you want to see the interior of a building, nine times out of ten you'll be forced to go on a **guided tour** (nearly always in Czech, occasionally in German) that can last for an hour or more. Ask for an *anglický text*, an often unintentionally hilarious English resumé of the castle's history.

Guided tours invariably set off on the hour, and the last one leaves an hour before the final closing time. Entrance tickets cost very little – hence no prices are quoted in the text – and no proof is needed to claim student status, which usually chops the price in half. More than likely you'll be asked to wear special furry overshoes which protect and polish the floors at the same time.

---

### Closed for technical reasons

On any one day, anything up to a quarter of Prague's museums and galleries can be temporarily "closed for technical reasons", or, more permanently, "closed for reconstruction". Notices are rarely more specific than that, but the widespread shortage of staff and funds is often behind the closure. It's impossible to predict what will be closed when, but it's a good idea to make alternative plans when visiting galleries and museums, just in case.

---

## National Holidays

**Official national holidays** were always a potential source of contention with the old regime. Even the final big **May Day** celebrations that took place in Prague in 1989 were marred by "anti-socialist elements", who unrolled banners calling for democracy and *glasnost*. For the moment at least, the 100-year tradition of the event, and the public holiday, look set to stay, as do the other *slavné májové dny* (Glorious May Days): **May 5**, the beginning of the Prague Uprising in 1945, and VE Day. From 1992 the Czechs have decided to break with the Soviet tradition of celebrating VE Day on May 9, one day later than the west, and join with their western allies on **May 8**. Apart from these, none of the former Communist national holidays remain.

---

**National Holidays**

January 1
Easter Monday
May 1
May 5
May 8
July 5 (Introduction of Christianity)
July 6 (Death of Jan Hus)
October 28 (Foundation of the Republic)
December 24
December 25
December 26

---

# Festivals and Celebrations

Prague's annual festive calendar is light compared to most European capitals, with just a couple of cultural events in addition to the usual religious festivities. To find out what's going on, check out one of the listings magazines mentioned on p.27.

Prague's most famous festival is the *Pražské jaro* (Prague Spring), not to be confused with the political events of 1968. It begins every year on May 12, the anniversary of Smetana's death, with a procession from Smetana's grave in Vyšehrad to the Obecní dům, where the composer's *Ma vlást* (My Country) is performed in the presence of the president. It ends three weeks later, on June 2, with Beethoven's Ninth Symphony.

During the summer, there are outdoor concerts in the gardens of Malá Strana, and theatrical and musical performances on the islands in the Vltava. In October, Prague puts on a surprisingly good **International Jazz Festival**, which attracts all the best names in Czech jazz as well as foreign artists (Winston Marselis appeared in 1991).

The rest of Prague's stirrings are mostly of a religious nature. At **Easter** (*Velikonoce*), the age-old sexist ritual of whipping girls' calves with braided birch twigs tied together with ribbons (*pomlázky*) is still practised. To prevent such a fate, the girls are supposed to offer the boys a coloured easter egg and pour a bucket of cold water over them. What may once have been an innocent bucolic frolic has now become another excuse for Czech men to harass any woman who dares to venture onto the street during this period.

As in the rest of Europe, **Christmas** (*Vánoce*) is a time for overconsumption and family gatherings and therefore a mostly private occasion. On December 4, the feast day of Saint Barbara, cherry tree branches are bought as decorations, the aim being to get them to blossom before Christmas.

On the eve of December 6, numerous trios, dressed up as *svaty Mikuláš* (Saint Nicholas), an angel and a devil, tour round the neighbourhoods, the angel handing out sweets and fruit to children who've been good, while the devil dishes out coal and potatoes to those who've been naughty. The Czech Saint Nicholas has white hair and a beard, and dresses not in red but in a white priest's outfit, with a bishop's mitre.

With a week or so to go, large barrels are set up in the streets from which huge quantities of live carp (*kapr*), the traditional Christmas dish, are sold. Christmas Eve (*štědrý večer*) is traditionally a day of fasting, broken only when the evening star appears, signalling the beginning of the Christmas feast of carp, potato salad, schnitzel and sweet breads. Only after the meal are the children allowed to open their presents.

Birthdays are much less important in Czechoslovakia than **saint's name days**, which fall on the same day each year. Thus popular names like Jan or Anna are practically national celebrations, and an excuse for everyone to get drunk since you're bound to know at least one person with those names.

# Popular Culture: sport, music and the arts

Freed from the straitjacket of Communist censorship, and state control of the arts, popular culture has diversified considerably in the last few years. Theatre, jazz and rock, in particular, are enjoying something of a renaissance. The position of sport and classical music – both actively encouraged and subsidised by the old regime – is slightly different.

## Sport

Czechoslovakia is probably most famous for its world-class tennis players and for its national ice hockey team. But the sport which actually pulls the biggest crowds is soccer. Getting tickets to watch a particular sport is easy (and cheap) enough on the day – even big matches rarely sell out. Taking part is more difficult – Czechs who do so all belong to local clubs and there are still remarkably few rental facilities for the general public; see p.220 for details.

### Soccer

Prague's top **soccer** team is **Sparta Praha**, who dominate the country's *první liga* or national league and the *Československý pohár* (the knock-out competition). They supplied five of the country's 1990 World Cup squad, including the competition's top goal-scorer Tomáš Skuhravý, who, like the rest, has since been lured to the west. They play every Sunday at the Sparta Stadium, opposite the Letná park (the season runs Sept–Dec & March–June); tickets cost less than £1/$2.

Prague is also home to three other clubs: **Slavia Praha** and **Bohemians**, who both play in the southern suburb of Vršovice, the former just south of Vršovické náměstí, the latter further out on Vladivostocká (tram #4 or #22 for both from metro Náměstí Míru); and the army side, **Dukla Praha**, who play in Dejvice (bus #125 from Švermův most).

### Ice Hockey

**Ice hockey** runs soccer a close second as the nation's most popular sport. It's not uncommon to see kids playing their own form of the game in the street, rather than kicking a football around. As in soccer, the best ice hockey team is *Sparta Praha* and the stadium is next door to the soccer stadium.

Games are fast and physical, cold but compelling viewing, taking place on Tuesday and Friday at around 6pm. The season starts at the end of September and culminates in the annual World Championships the following summer, when the fortunes of the national side are subject to close scrutiny, especially if pitched against the former Soviet Union. A double victory against them in 1969 precipitated riots in towns across the country, culminating in the torching of the Soviet airline *Aeroflot's* offices in Prague.

### Tennis

**Tennis** has been one of Czechoslovakia's most successful exports of the 1980s, although the country holds no major international events and its national Davis Cup team rarely gets anywhere. Martina Navrátilová, now approaching retirement, has been the most consistent Czech player on the circuit, although she became a naturalised American some years ago.

On the men's side, Ivan Lendl has been a towering figure in world tennis since the mid-1980s, even though a Wimbledon title has consistently eluded him. He, too, has had his day, and despite the efforts of the now-retired Miroslav Mečíř and Hana Mandlíková, the country badly lacks a young generation of players to take their place. Any home-grown talent there is will be on display in the Czechoslovak Open, held every August in Prague.

## Music

**Folk songs** lie at the heart of Czech music: people strike up traditional songs and contemporary folk tunes at the slightest excuse, especially in the countryside. A living tradition still exists only in the more remote mountain regions of Slovakia: elsewhere professional and amateur groups keep the music alive. Styles of music vary from the more familiar Bohemian dances to the Carpathian shepherd songs of Slovakia. In Prague, your only hope of hearing any of the country's traditional music is at the one-off concerts of the various national touring companies; look out for posters advertising lídová skupina.

The nation's great wealth of folk tunes have found their way into much of the country's **classical music**, of which the Czechs are justifiably proud, having produced four composers of considerable stature – Dvořák, Janáček, Smetana and Martinů – and, a fifth, Mahler, was born in Bohemia. The country has also produced a host of singers, like the late Ema Destinová, and virtuoso violinists, the latest of whom play with the prestigious Suk Quartet. For details of where to hear classical music, see p.215.

Nowadays, if you turn on your radio in Prague, you'll be inundated by **rock and pop music**. The majority of the indigenous product is divided evenly between western muzak and heavy metal, but there's a more interesting side to Czech music – the protest songs that grew out of the 1960s and the punk-influenced sound of *The Plastic People of the Universe* and their various imitators. This stuff is only just beginning to appear on disc, but check out the fly-posters and media listings for up-and-coming gigs, which cover the whole spectrum from highly accomplished folk/jazz performers to crass derivations of Motorhead. Some bands to look out for are *Půlnoc* (the leftovers of the Plastic People), thrash-band *Gaáž* and the *Yo Yo Band* (Prague's version of reggae).

**Jazz** (or *džez* as it is sometimes written) has a well-established tradition in Prague, and, despite the best efforts of the Nazis and the Communists to suppress it, has enjoyed something of a renaissance since 1989. For full details of where to go to hear Prague's jazz and rock offerings, see p.212.

## Theatre and Cinema

**Theatre**, for so long heavily subsidised – and censored – by the authorities, is going through a difficult patch at the moment. Czech audiences have dropped considerably and tourists have become a lucrative source of income at a time when money is desperately needed. The serious stuff goes on in the opulent *kamenná divadla* or "stone theatres", where tickets – for certain productions, at least – are approaching western prices .

Prague has a strong tradition of **mime** and **"black theatre"**, ranging from the classical style of the late Ladislav Fialka and his troupe to the more experimental work of Boris Polívka. Czechs and foreigners alike turn up to see these shows, whereas Prague's long-running multimedia company, *Laterna magika*, deliberately gears its programme towards tourists.

**Puppet theatre** (*loutkové divadlo*) also has a long folk tradition in Czechoslovakia, but nowadays only Prague's *Divadlo Spejbla a Hurvínka* maintains the traditional puppets-only set-up; the rest have introduced live actors into their repertoire, making the shows less accessible if you don't speak the language.

The **cinema** (*kino*) is still a cheap and popular form of entertainment, though since 1989 the majority of films on show have tended to be the standard Hollywood blockbusters. Most foreign films are dubbed into Czech (indicated by a small white square on the poster), but a fair few are shown with subtitles (*The Prague Post* and *Prognosis* both list the relevant ones). Titles are always translated into Czech, so you'll need to have your wits about you to identify films such as *Umělcova smlouva* as *The Draughtsman's Contract*. The film's country of origin is always indicated – *VB* means it's British, *USA*, American.

For more on the current state of Czech cinema, see *Contexts*; for full details of all Prague's theatres and cinemas, see p.216.

# Trouble and the Police

Despite their recent change of name, the national police force – the former Communist police (*Veřejná bezpečnost* or *VB*), now known simply as *Policie* – are still extremely unpopular, certainly among the younger generation, and they know it. Their participation in the November 17 *masakr* destroyed what little credibility they had managed to hold on to over the last forty years of Communist control.

Public confidence in their competence has also suffered a severe blow due to the dramatic rise in the level of **crime** since 1989. The murder rate has quadrupled, and prostitution is rife in Prague. However, you shouldn't be unduly paranoid: the crime rate is still very low, especially when compared with other western European or North American cities.

There are just two main types of police nowadays: the *Policie* and the municipal police. The *Policie*, in khaki-green uniforms (hence their nickname – *žáby* or "frogs") with red lapels and a red band on their caps are the national force, with the power of arrest, and are under the control of the Ministry of Interior. They drive around in clapped-out green and white Škodas and Ladas. If you do need the police, though – and above all if you're reporting a serious crime – you should always go to the municipal police, run by the Prague city authorities, and known as *Černé šerif* (Black Sheriffs) because of their all-black uniforms.

In addition, there are various private police forces, most notably supplied by the American firm *Pinkertons*, employed mostly by hotels and banks. They are often very officious, though in reality they are little more than glorified security guards. They are allowed to carry guns, but have no powers of arrest, and you are not legally obliged to show them your ID.

## Avoiding Trouble

Almost all the problems encountered by tourists in Prague are to do with **petty crime** – mostly theft from cars and hotel rooms – rather than more serious physical confrontations. Sensible precautions include making photocopies of your passport, and leaving passport and tickets in the hotel safe; and noting down travellers' cheque and credit card numbers. If you have a car, don't leave anything in view when you park it; take the radio with you if you can. Vehicles are rarely stolen, but luggage and valuables left in cars do make a tempting target and rental cars are easy to spot.

In theory, you're supposed to carry some form of **identification** at all times, and the police can stop you in the street and demand it. In practice, they're rarely bothered if you're clearly a foreigner (unless you're driving). In any case, the police are now so deferential that they tend to confine themselves to socially acceptable activities like traffic control and harassing Romanies.

## What to do if you're robbed

If you are unlucky enough to have something stolen, you will need to **go to the police** to report it, not least because your insurance company will require a police report. It's unlikely that there'll be anyone there who speaks English, and even less likely that your belongings will be retrieved but, at the very least, you should get a statement detailing what you've lost for your insurance claim. Try the phrase *pravě mi ukradl někdo* – "I have just been robbed". The main **police station** in Prague is at Konviktská 14, Staré Město.

# Disabled Travellers

In the past, very little attention has been paid to the needs of the disabled anywhere in Czechoslovakia. Attitudes are slowly changing, but there is still a long way to go, and the chronic shortage of funds for almost anything is not helping matters.

*ČEDOK* claims to be able to book holidays which cater for the disabled, but most people's experiences have proved otherwise. A shortlist of hotels with wheelchair access to at least a handful of rooms appears in the box below; inevitably, most of these are expensive. **Transport** is a major problem, since buses and trams are virtually impossible for wheelchairs and trains only slightly better (though there are special carriages designed to take wheelchairs on certain trains). At the time of writing, none of the car rental companies could offer vehicles with hand controls in Prague. If you're driving to Prague, most cross-Channel ferries now have adequate facilities, as do *British Airways* for those who are flying.

## Accessible Hotels

**Atlantic**
Na poříčí 9,
Nové Město     ☎ 231 85 12

**Atrium**
Rohanské nábřeží,
Karlín     ☎ 284 11 11

**Belvedere**
Milady Horákové 19,
Holešovice     ☎ 37 03 51

**Diplomat**
Evropská 15,
Dejvice     ☎ 331 41 11

**Forum**
Kongresová 1,
Nusle     ☎ 41 02 38

**Olympik**
Sokolovská 138,
Karlín     ☎ 684 55 01

**Palace**
Panská 12,
Nové Město     ☎ 236 00 08

## Contacts for Disabled Travellers

**Holiday Care Service**
2 Old Bank Chambers, Station Road, Horley, Surrey RH6 9HW ☎ 0293/774 535.
*Information on all aspects of travel.*

**Jewish Rehabilitation Hospital**
3205 Place Alton Goldbloom, Québec H7V 1R2 ☎ 514/688-9550.
*Guidebooks and travel information.*

**Kéroul**
4545 ave. Pierre de Coubertin, CP 1000, Montréal, Québec H1V 3R2 ☎ 512/252-3104.
*Travel for mobility-impaired people.*

**Metatur**
Štefaniková 48, Smíchov, Prague ☎ 55 10 64.
*Only organisation in Prague which campaigns for the disabled. English-speakers available, and can arrange trips in Czechoslovakia.*

**Mobility International USA**
PO Box 3551, Eugene, OR 97403 ☎ 503/343-1248.
*Information, access guides, tours and exchange programmes.*

**RADAR** (*The Royal Association for Disability and Rehabilitation*)
25 Mortimer Street, London W1N 8AB ☎ 071/637 5400.
*Information on all aspects of travel.*

**Travel Information Center**
Moss Rehabilitation Hospital, 1200 West Tabor Road, Philadelphia, PA 19141 ☎ 215/329-5715, x2233.
*Write for access information.*

# Women in Prague

Despite the sloganeering of the Communist regime, women are still treated as second-class citizens in Czechoslovakia, and not even a vaguely feminist women's movement exists. Ironically, part of the reason for this is the adverse effect of the official campaigns for women's equality, which forced women to take jobs, usually at the bottom of the pay ladder. What women's organisations there are tend to focus on single issues such as the environment. For more on women in Prague, see *Contexts*.

As far as **sexual harassment** is concerned, things are, if anything, marginally less intimidating than in western Europe, although without the familiar linguistic and cultural signs, it's easier to misinterpret situations. Attitudes in Prague are much more liberal than in most of rural Czechoslovakia, where women travelling alone can still expect to encounter stares and comments. Single women should nonetheless avoid going to the nightclubs on Wenceslas Square, where it will be assumed by many men that you are a prostitute. Hitchhiking is a risk, as it is anywhere, and although it's quite common to see Czech women hitching, they at least have the advantage of a common language.

# Finding Work

Unless you've some particular skill and have applied for a job advertised in your home country, the only real chance of long-term work in Prague is teaching English, either privately or in one of the many language schools. With English having replaced Russian on most school syllabuses, and a chronic shortage of English teachers, it's a good time to try your luck.

Obviously it's best to have a TEFL (Teaching English as a Foreign Language) or ESL (English as a Second Language) certificate, but you may find that even without the qualification many language schools will still be prepared to take you on.

Finding a teaching job is mainly a question of perusing the English-language papers, and walking the streets asking about vacancies. The city's cultural institutes (see "Directory", below) will give you a list of schools. Other options are to try advertising private lessons (better paid, but harder to make a living at) on the university notice boards, or in the weekly advertising paper, *Annonce*. With unemployment rocketing, finding temporary work of any kind is extremely unlikely.

If you have a legitimate job, getting a **work permit** should be easy, but getting a **residence permit** is a lengthy and bureaucratic process which, unless your employers are prepared to do it on your behalf, it's not worth the hassle.

# Directory

**BOTTLES** Czechoslovakia has yet to become a fully paid-up member of the throw-away culture and most drinks still come in bottles which have a deposit on them. Shops and supermarkets will refund bottles bought elsewhere providing they stock the relevant type. Otherwise, there are now numerous bottle banks scattered around Prague.

**CIGARETTES** Loosely packed and lethal, their only virtue is their cheapness. The poseurs smoke the top of the domestic range, *sparta* – paradoxically named after the country's leading soccer! team. President Havel smokes *petra*, as do countless million others, while the workers smoke *mars* or the filterless *start*. Marlboro lead the western brands, with *Peter Stuyvesant* running a close second – all at standard continental prices. Domestic rolling tobacco, and cigarette papers, are worth avoiding, especially now that *Duma* is fairly widely available. Matches are *círky* or *zápalky*.

**CONTRACEPTIVES** Condoms (*preservativ*) are now available in metro stations in the centre of Prague from the machines marked *Men's Shop*, *Easy Shop* or some such euphemism. They're also on sale from pharmacies.

**CULTURAL INSTITUTES** The *British Council*, at Národní 10, Nové Město (Mon–Fri 8am–noon & 1–4pm; ☎22 45 50), has a cinema and an English language library, but there's a waiting list to gain borrowing rights. The *American Library*, Vlasská 11, Malá Strana (Mon–Fri 10am–5pm; closed Aug), has lectures and discussions on American history and culture throughout the week, plus a wide-ranging selection of newspapers, magazines and reference books. Other institutes worth checking out for their cultural programmes are: *Francouzský institut* (French institute), Štěpánská 35, Nové Město; *Italský kulturní institut* (Italian cultural institute), Šporkova 14, Malá Strana; *Maďarské kulturní středisko* (Hungarian cultural centre), Rytířská 25, Staré Město; and *Polské kulturní a informační středisko*, (Polish cultural and information centre) Václavské náměstí 19, Nové Město.

**ELECTRICITY** is the standard continental 220 volts AC: most European appliances should work as long as you have an adaptor for European-style two-pin round plugs. North Americans will need this plus a transformer.

**FILM** Western brands of colour film are now widely available. Prague is also a very cheap and quick place to get your black-and-white film developed and printed.

**GAY AND LESBIAN** Homosexuality isn't illegal in Czechoslovakia, and the situation in Prague is better than in the rest of the country, where attitudes remain conservative. There is no great "scene" in Prague as such, but there are a few bars and clubs that have become an established part of Prague nightlife. All the details are on p.213. Since 1989, an organisation for gays and lesbians has started up, *Lambda Praha*, c/o Jan Lány, Pod Kotlářkou 14, Smíchov, Prague. They publish a monthly paper called *Lambda*, and run a gay/lesbian helpline (evenings only; ☎57 73 88) usually with at least one English-speaker on call.

**KIDS/BABIES** Being a Catholic country, the attitude towards kids and babies is much more positive than in the UK and North America. Hotels and private landlords are generally very accommodating, but you'll rarely see any children in restaurants. Kids under ten travel free on public transport within Prague, while those under five go free on trains; five- to ten-year olds pay half-fare. Disposable nappies are not widely available, nor is convenience food for babies. Some private landlords will baby-sit by prior arrangement. For a list of specific places to take children in Prague, see p.219.

**LANGUAGE SCHOOLS** A number of month-long beginners' courses in Czech are held regularly in Prague. Average cost is £300/$500 for the month, which includes half-board accommodation. For further details (and possible financial assistance), contact the British Council in Prague.

**LAUNDRIES** The first self-service launderette in Prague opened as recently as 1991. Most Czechs still wash by hand or leave their clothes for a few days at a *čistírna*, where your clothes are washed, dried, ironed and folded neatly for you. Prague's self-service launderette is *Laundry Kings*, Dejvická 16; ☎312 37 43; metro Hradčanská. Open daily 8am–10pm.

**LEFT LUGGAGE** Most bus and train stations have lockers and/or a 24-hour left luggage office, which officially only take bags under 15kg. If your bag is very heavy, say *promiňte, je těšký* and offer to carry it yourself – *já to vezmo*. To work the lockers, find an open one, put a crown in the slot on the inside of the door and set the code (choose a number you can easily remember and make a note of it), then shut the door and make a note of the locker number. To re-open it, set the code on the outside and wait a few seconds before trying the door. The lockers are usually checked every night, and the contents of any still occupied are taken to the 24-hour left luggage office.

**LOST PROPERTY** Bolzanova 5, Nové Město; ☎24 84 30.

**RACISM** It is a sad fact that racism in Czechoslovakia is a casual and common phenomenon. The country's half-million Romanies and much smaller Vietnamese communities bear the brunt of the nation's ignorance and prejudice. Another alarming development is the rise of right-wing extremism and the skinhead movement. There are now an estimated 2000 skinheads in Prague, and attacks on Romanies, Vietnamese and foreign black tourists are on the increase. Consequently, anyone even remotely dark-skinned can expect to arouse, at the very least, a great deal of curiosity.

**TAMPONS** Tampons (*tampóny*) and sanitary towels (*vložky*) are cheap and easy to get hold of, though if you prefer something a bit more subtle, it's best to bring your own.

**TIME** Czechoslovakia is generally one hour ahead of Britain and nine hours ahead of EST, with the clocks going forward as late as May and back again some time in September – the exact date changes from year to year.

**TOILETS** Public toilets (*záchod* or *WC*) are few and far between, although automatic ones are beginning to appear in central Prague. In most, you can buy toilet paper (by the sheet) from the attendant, whom you will usually have to pay as you enter, the amount depending on the purpose of your visit. It's generally acceptable to use the toilets in state-run restaurants and hotels; other places worth trying are any of the metro stations. Standards of hygiene are generally low.

### Metric Weights and Measures

| | |
|---|---|
| 1 ounce = 28.3 grammes | 1 inch = 2.54 centimetres (cm) |
| 1 pound = 454 grammes | 1 foot = 0.3 metres (m) |
| 2.2 pounds = 1 kilogramme | 1 yard = 0.91 m |
| 1 pint = 0.47 litres | 1.09 yards = 1m |
| 1 quart = 0.94 litres | 1 mile = 1.61 kilometres (km) |
| 1 gallon = 3.78 litres | 0.62 miles = 1km |

# The City

# Chapter 1

# Introducing the City

With a population of just one and a quarter million, **Prague** is one of the smallest capital cities in Europe. It originally developed as four separate, self-governing towns and a walled ghetto, whose individual identities and medieval street plans have been preserved, more or less intact, to this day. Almost everything of any historical interest lies within these central districts, the majority of which are easy to master quickly on foot. Only in the last hundred years has Prague spread beyond its ancient perimeter, and its suburbs now stretch across the hills for miles on every side. There's a cheap and efficient transport system on which to explore them – a decent map is all you need to find your way around.

The castle district or **Hradčany** (Chapter 2) spreads across the hill on the left bank of the River Vltava where the first Slavs settled in the seventh or eighth century. At its eastern end is **Prague Castle** (known simply as the *Hrad* in Czech), which contains a whole series of important historical buildings, including the cathedral, the seat of the president, and the royal palace and gardens, as well as a cluster of museums and galleries. The rest of Hradčany lies to the west of the castle: a sleepy district ranging in scale from the miniature cottages of Nový Svět to the gargantuan facade of the Černín Palace. One art gallery you won't want to miss in Hradčany is the **Šternberk Palace**, housing the city's main European art collection.

Squeezed between the castle hill and the river are the Baroque palaces and houses of the "Little Quarter" or **Malá Strana** (Chapter 3) – around 150 acres of twisting cobbled streets and secret walled gardens – home to most of the city's embassies and dominated by one of the landmarks of the left bank, the green dome and tower of the church of sv Mikuláš. At the southern end of Malá Strana, a funicular railway carries you out of the cramped streets to the top of **Petřín Hill**, the city's most central leafy escape, with a wonderful view across the river.

The twisting matrix of streets is at its most confusing in the original medieval hub of the city, **Staré Město** (Chapter 4) – literally, the "Old Town" – on the right bank of the Vltava. The **Charles Bridge**, its main link with the opposite bank, is easily the city's most popular

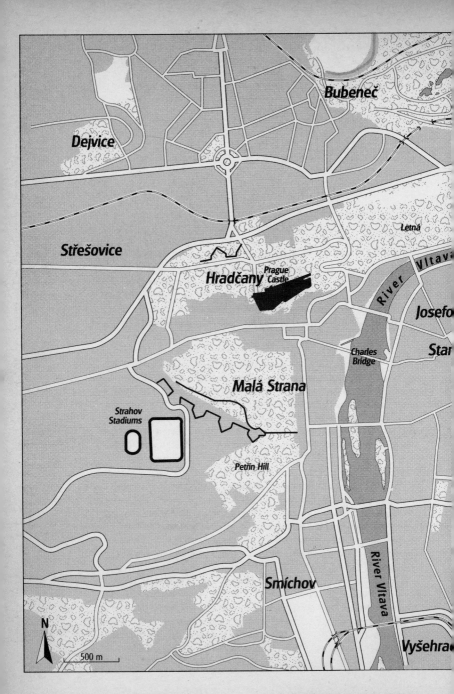

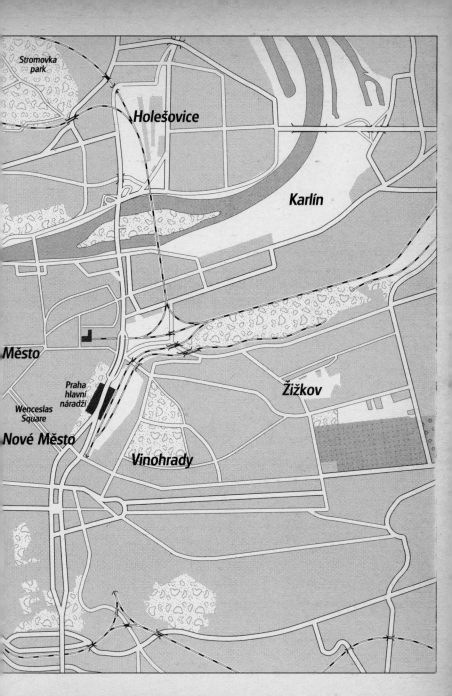

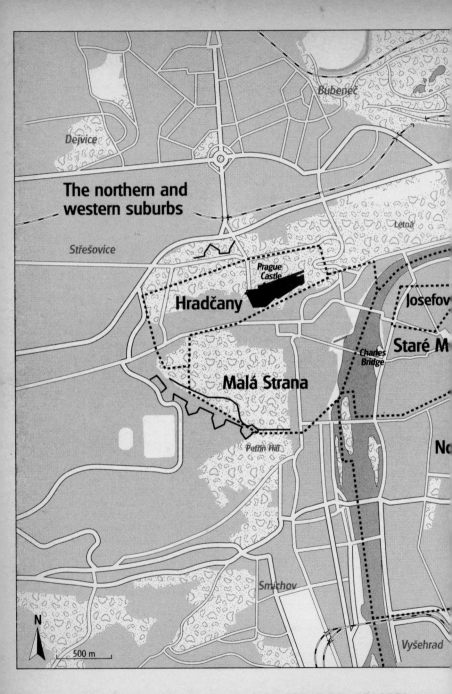

The northern and
western suburbs

Bubeneč

Dejvice

Letná

Střešovice

Prague
Castle

Hradčany

Josefov

Staré M

Charles
Bridge

Malá Strana

Petřín Hill

No

Smíchov

Vyšehrad

N

500 m

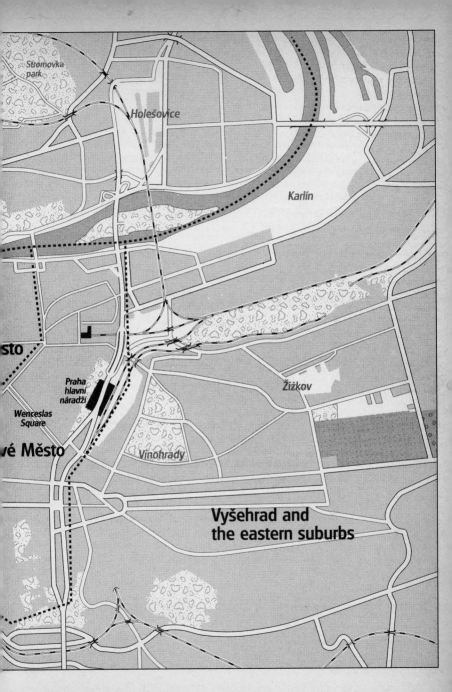

Stromovka
park

Holešovice

Karlín

sto

Praha
hlavní
náradží

Žižkov

Wenceslas
Square

vé Město

Vinohrady

Vyšehrad and
the eastern suburbs

historical monument, bristling with Baroque statuary and one of the most beautiful places from which to view the city. Staré Město's other great showpiece is its main square, **Staroměstské náměstí**, somewhere it's easy to sit for hours, just soaking up the sights – the astronomical clock, the Hus monument and the spiky towers of the Týn church.

Nothing else in Staré Město can quite match these two spots, but it's worth spending at least an afternoon exploring the quarter's backstreets and alleyways, and in the process losing the crowds. Enclosed within the boundaries of Staré Město, to the northwest of the main square, is the Jewish quarter, or **Josefov** (Chapter 5). The ghetto walls have long since gone, and the whole area was remodelled at the turn of the century, but six synagogues, a medieval cemetery and a town hall survive as powerful reminders of a community which has existed here for over a millennium.

South and east of the old town is the large sprawling district of **Nové Město** (Chapter 6), whose main arteries make up the city's commercial and business centre. Despite its name – literally, "New Town" – Nové Město was founded back in the fourteenth century, and even its outer reaches are worth taking the trouble to explore. The main rail station, Praha hlavní nádraží, is here, a short walk away from **Wenceslas Square**, focus of the political upheavals of the modern-day republic and a showcase of modern architecture. The district also contains numerous potent symbols of the Czech struggle for nationhood, such as the National Theatre, the Obecní dům and the National Museum.

Further afield lie various **suburbs**, most of which developed only in the last hundred years or so. The single exception is **Vyšehrad**, one of the original fortress settlements of the newly arrived Slavs in the last millennium. Nowadays, it's a peaceful escape from the city, and its cemetery is the final resting place for leading Czech artists of the modern age, including Smetana and Dvořák. To the east is the once wealthy residential suburb of **Vinohrady**, peppered with parks and squares; and **Žižkov**, traditionally a working-class district, whose two landmarks – the Žižkov monument and the futuristic television tower – are visible for miles around. All of these areas are covered in Chapter 7.

Nineteenth-century suburbs also sprang up to the north of the city centre in **Holešovice**, which boasts two huge swathes of greenery: the Letná plain, overlooking the city; and the Stromovka park, beyond which lie the city chateau of **Troja** and the zoo. Further west, leafy interwar suburbs like **Dejvice** and **Střešovice**, dotted with modernist family villas, give an entirely different angle on Prague. At the very edge of the city limits, the chateaux of **Hvězda** and **Zbraslav** are easily visited in an afternoon, given their good transport links. All these places are covered in Chapter 8.

If you're keen to head **out of the city** entirely, there's a wide choice of destinations within an hour or so's journey from Prague. The royal hideaway of **Karlštejn** is an obvious day trip, though the surrounding woods, and those of nearby Křivoklát, are equally enticing. The medieval mining town of **Kutná Hora**, east of Prague, boasts one of central Europe's most stunning pieces of ecclesiastical architecture, plus a host of other attractions. The legacy of the last war hangs over two places to the northwest: **Lidice**, which was razed to the ground by the Nazis; and the ghetto town of **Terezín**, through which most of the country's Jews passed, en route to the extermination camps. Finally, devotees of (and converts to) Bohemian beer might consider making a pilgrimage to **Plzeň**, home of *Pilsner Urquell, Gambrinus* and, technically speaking, the birthplace of all the world's lager. The above destinations, and many more, are covered in Chapter 9.

## City transport; food, drink and entertainment

**Transport** details – tram numbers and metro stations – are given throughout the following chapters, but for a full rundown of how to use the city and regional transport systems (and a metro map) see p.14.

You're never more than a few blocks from a restaurant or pub in Prague, and you'll find full **listings** of recommended places to eat and drink on p.202; out of the city, details are given in the text. Also in the listings section are details of clubs and venues, the arts, activities for kids, sports and shopping.

# Chapter 2

# Hradčany

**H**RADČANY's *raison d'être* is its castle, or **Hrad**, built on the site of one of the original hill settlements of the Slav tribes who migrated here in the seventh or eighth century AD. The Přemyslid prince, Bořivoj I, erected the first castle here sometime in the late ninth century, and, since then, whoever has occupied the Hrad

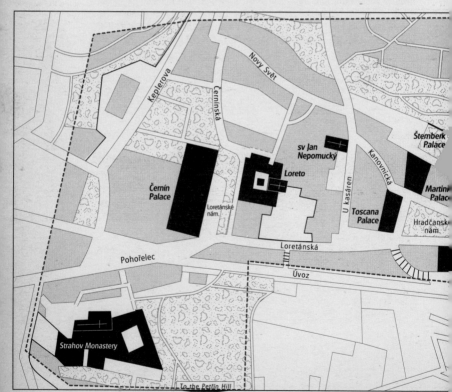

has exercised authority over the Czech Lands. Consequently, unlike the city's other districts, Hradčany has never had a real identity of its own – it became a royal town only in 1598 – existing instead as a mere appendage, its inhabitants serving and working for their masters in the Hrad. The same is still true now. For although the odd café or *pivnice* survives in amongst the palaces (and even in the Hrad itself), there's very little real life here beyond the stream of tourists who trek through the castle and the civil servants who work either for the president or in the multifarious ministries whose departmental tentacles spread right across Hradčany.

Stretched out along a high spur above the River Vltava, Hradčany shows a suitable disdain for the public transport system. There's a choice of **approaches** from Malá Strana, all of which involve at least some walking. From Malostranská metro station, most people take the steep short cut up the Staré zámecké schody, but there are more opportunities for stopping and admiring the view along the stately Zámecké schody, which leaves you gasping at the castle gates. The alternative to all this climbing is to take tram #18 or #22 from

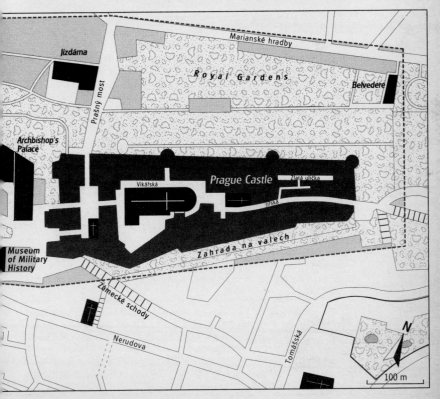

Malostranská metro, which tackle the hairpin bends of Chotkova with ease, and deposit you either outside the Royal Gardens to the north of the Hrad, or, if you prefer, outside the gates of the Strahov monastery, at the far western edge of Hradčany.

# Prague Castle (Pražský hrad)

Viewed from the Charles Bridge, PRAGUE CASTLE (popularly known as the Hrad) stands aloof from the rest of the city, protected, not by bastions and castellated towers, but by its palatial Neoclassical facade – an "immense unbroken sheer blank wall", as Hilaire Belloc described it – breached only by the great mass of St Vitus Cathedral. It's *the* picture-postcard image of Prague, though for the Czechs the castle has been an object of disdain as much as admiration, its alternating fortunes mirroring the shifts in the nation's history. The golden age and the dark ages, Masaryk's liberalism and Gottwald's terror – all emanated from the Hrad. When the first posters appeared in December 1989 demanding "*HAVEL NA HRAD*" (Havel to the Castle), they weren't asking for his reincarceration. Havel's occupancy of the Hrad was the sign that the reins of government had finally been wrested from the Communist regime.

The site has been successively built on since the first castle was erected here in the ninth century, but two **architects** in particular bear responsibility for the present outward appearance of the Hrad. The first is **Nicolo Pacassi**, court architect to Empress Maria Theresa, whose austere restorations went hand in hand with the deliberate run-down of the Hrad until it was little more than an administrative barracks. For the Czechs, his grey-green eighteenth-century cover-up, which hides a variety of much older buildings, is unforgivable. Less apparent, though no less controversial, is the hand of **Josip Plečnik**, the Slovene architect who was commissioned by T. G. Masaryk, president of the newly founded Czechoslovak Republic, to restore and modernise the castle in the 1920s (for more on Plečnik, see box opposite).

## The first and second courtyards

The **first courtyard** (první nádvoří), which opens on to Hradčanské náměstí, is guarded by Ignaz Platzer's *Battling Titans* – two gargantuan figures, one on each of the gate piers, wielding club and

---

*Unless otherwise stated, the opening hours for sights within* Prague Castle *are April–Oct Tues–Sun 9am–5pm; Nov–March Tues–Sun 9am–4pm; you have to buy a separate entry ticket for each one. Entry to St Vitus Cathedral is free; the castle courtyards and streets are open until late in the evening. There's an information office on the north of the cathedral at Vikářská 37 (opening hours as above), and a post office in the third courtyard, open daily 8am–8pm.*

## Josip Plečnik: post-modernist in the making

Born in Ljubljana, Josip Plečnik (1872–1957) studied under the great Viennese architect Otto Wagner at the turn of the century, and was appointed the chief architect to Prague Castle shortly after the foundation of the First Republic. Despite having the backing of the leading Czech architect Jan Kotěra, and President Masaryk himself, controversy surrounded him as soon as the appointment was announced; his non-Czech background and, moreover, his quirky, eclectic style placed him at odds with the architectural establishment of the day. He remained so until his rediscovery in the 1980s by the newly ascendant post-modernist movement. The darlings of post-modernism, Robert Venturi and Denise Scott-Brown, made special trips to Prague to see Plečnik's work, which, like their own, borrows elements from any number of genres from classical to Assyrian architecture.

Plečnik's most conspicuous contributions to the castle – the fir-tree flag poles in the first courtyard and the granite obelisk in the third courtyard – are only a small sample of the work he carried out, which included the President's apartments, the Zahrada na valech, and several halls in the west wing of the second courtyard. Much of his work, though, is currently either under reconstruction or closed to the public. One of his most influential contemporary admirers is Havel himself, and a special exhibition on Plečnik's work within the Hrad is planned for the summer of 1993, by which time much of the restoration work should be complete.

*Plečnik went on to work on the President's summer palace at Lány (see p.188), and to build one of Prague's most unusual churches, in Vinohrady (see p.147)*

dagger and about to inflict fatal blows on their respective victims. Below them stand a couple of impassive presidential sentries, no longer kitted out in the paramilitary khaki of the last regime, but sporting new blue uniforms that deliberately recall those of the First Republic. They were designed by the Oscar-winning costume designer for Miloš Forman's film *Amadeus*, and chosen by Havel himself. The hourly changing of the guard is a fairly subdued affair, but every Sunday at noon there's a much more elaborate parade, accompanied by a brass ensemble which appears at the first-floor windows to play local rock star Michal Kocáb's gentle, slightly comical, modern fanfare.

To reach the **second courtyard** (druhé nádvoří), you must pass through the early Baroque Matthias Gate, originally a freestanding triumphal arch, now set into one of Pacassi's blank walls. Grand stairways on either side lead to the presidential apartments in the south wing, and to the **Spanish Hall** (Španělský sál) and **Rudolf Gallery** (Rudofova galerie) in the north wing – two of the most stunning rooms in the entire complex, sadly used only for state occasions (and, of course, the filming of *Amadeus*). Once you've entered the rectangular courtyard, there's no escape from the monotonous onslaught of Pacassi's plastering and the smooth granite paving added in the 1960s. It's an unwelcoming and impersonal space, relieved only by Anselmo Lurago's Chapel of the Holy Cross, which cowers in one corner. Its richly painted interior used to house the treasury (klenotnice), a macabre selection of medieval reliquaries, but recently it's been rather brutally converted into a dull private gallery.

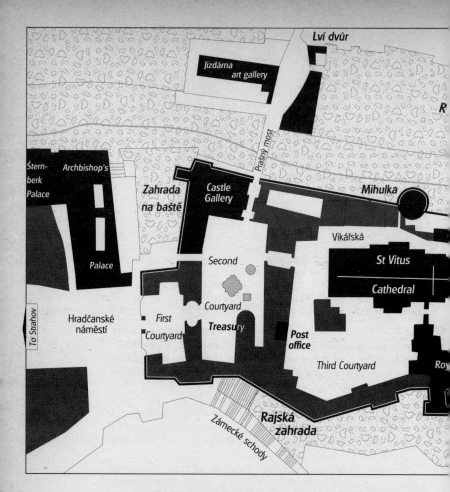

In the north wing, the **Castle Gallery** (Obrazárna Pražského hradu; Tues–Sun 10am–6pm) occupies what were once the royal stables and contains European paintings from the sixteenth to the eighteenth centuries. The collection was begun by Rudolf II, the Habsburgs' most avid art collector, but, sadly, the best of what he amassed was either taken as booty by the marauding Saxons and Swedes, or sold off by Rudolf's successors – a fact which explains the bizarre inclusion of photographs of much better paintings from other European galleries. The best of what's left includes *The Assembly of the Olympian Gods*, a vast, crowded canvas of portly naked figures by Rubens, a couple of fine paintings by Veronese, and a *Flagellation* by Tintoretto. There's a bust of Rudolf by his court sculptor, Adriaen de Vries, and works by one of his court painters, Hans von Aachen, but only photographs of the

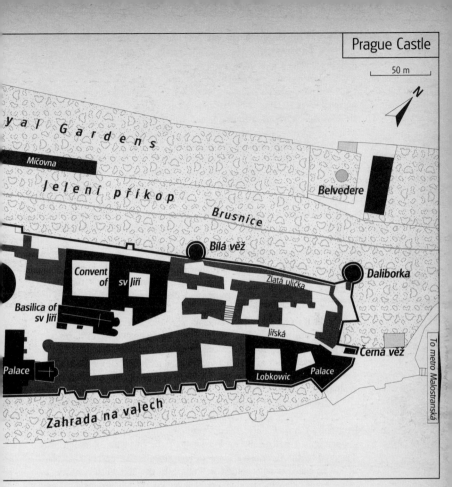

work of the most unusual painter in Rudolf's employ, Giuseppe Arcimboldo, whose portrait of Rudolf is a surrealist collage of fruit, with his eyes as cherries, cheeks as apples and hair as grapes.

## Across the Prašný most

From the second courtyard, it's worth making a short detour beyond the official limits of the castle walls. Passing through the north gate, you come to the **Prašný most** (Powder Bridge), first erected in the sixteenth century to connect the newly established Royal Gardens with the Hrad, though the original wooden structure has long since been replaced. Below lies the wooded **Jelení příkop** (Stag Moat), once used by the Habsburgs for growing figs and lemons, and storing game for the royal hunts, but now populated only by bored castle guards.

Beyond the bridge, to the left, Jean-Baptiste Mathey's plain French Baroque **Jízdárna** (Riding School) has been converted into an open-plan art gallery (Tues–Sun 10am–6pm), which currently serves as the city's main exhibition space for twentieth-century Czech art. The temporary installations are consistently impressive, but any hopes of a permanent collection will have to wait until the new premises in Holešovice are up and running (see p.155).

### The Royal Gardens and Belvedere

Opposite the Jízdárna is the entrance to the **Royal Gardens** (Královská zahrada; May–Sept), founded by Emperor Ferdinand I on the site of a former vineyard. Burned down by the Saxons and Swedes, and blown up by the Prussians, the gardens were only saved from French attack by the payment of thirty pineapples. Today, this is one of the best-kept gardens in the capital, with fully functioning fountains and immaculately cropped lawns. Consequently, it's a very popular spot, though more a place for admiring the azaleas and almond trees than lounging around on the grass. It was here that tulips brought from Turkey were first acclimatised to Europe, before being exported to the Netherlands, and every spring there's an impressive, disciplined crop.

At the entrance to the gardens is the **Lví dvůr** (Lion's Court), built by Rudolf II to house his private zoo, which included leopards, lynxes, bears and wolves, as well as lions, all housed in heated cages to protect them from the Prague winter. Rudolf was also responsible for the real-tennis court, known as the **Míčovna** (closed to the public), built into the south terrace and tattooed with sgraffito by his court architect Bonifaz Wolmut.

At the end of the gardens is Prague's most celebrated Renaissance legacy, the **Belvedere** or Royal Summer Palace (Belvedér or Královské letohrádek), a delicately arcaded summerhouse topped by an inverted copper ship's hull, built by Ferdinand I for his wife, Anne. It was designed by the Genoese architect Paolo della Stella, one of a number of Italian masons who settled in Prague in the sixteenth century; to inspect it at close quarters, you must leave the Royal Gardens and head down Mariánské hradby. Unlike the gardens, the Belvedere is open all year (Tues–Sun 10am–6pm) and is now used for contemporary exhibitions, the artists chosen by the president himself. At the centre of the palace's miniature formal garden is the **Singing Fountain** (Zpívající fontána), built shortly after the palace and named for the musical sound of the drops of water falling in the metal bowls below. From the garden terrace, you have an unrivalled view of Prague Castle's finest treasure – the cathedral.

*The Chotkovy sady, beyond Belvedere, are covered in Chapter 8, see p.152*

## St Vitus Cathedral

**St Vitus Cathedral** (katedrála svatého Víta) takes up so much of the third courtyard that it's difficult to get an overall impression of this chaotic Gothic edifice. Its asymmetrical appearance is the product of a long and chequered history, for although the foundation stone was laid in 1344, the cathedral was not completed until 1929 – exactly 1000 years after the foundation of the first church within the Hrad.

The site of the present cathedral was originally a sacrificial altar to the heathen god **Svantovit**, which partly explains why the first church, founded in 929 by Prince Václav, was dedicated to Saint Vitus (*svatý Vít* in Czech), patron saint of epilepsy and the convulsive disorder chorea (popularly known as St Vitus' Dance). The inspiration for the medieval cathedral came from Charles IV, who, while still only heir to the throne, not only wangled an independent archbishopric for Prague, but also managed to gather together the relics of Saint Vitus.

Inspired by the cathedral at Narbonne, Charles commissioned the Frenchman **Matthias of Arras** to start work on a similar structure. Matthias died eight years into the job in 1352, with the cathedral barely started, and Charles summoned **Peter Parler**, a precocious 23-year-old from a family of great German masons, to continue the work. For the next 46 years, Parler imprinted his slightly flashier, more inventive *SonderGotik* ("Unusual Gothic") style on the city, but the cathedral got no further than the construction of the choir and the south transept before his death in 1399.

Little significant work was carried out during the next four centuries and the half-built cathedral became a symbol of the Czechs' frustrated aspirations to nationhood. Not until the Czech national revival or *národní obrození* of the nineteenth century did building begin again in earnest, with the foundation, in 1861, of the **Union for the Completion of the Cathedral**. A succession of architects, including Josef Mocker and Kamil Hilbert, oversaw the completion of the entire west end, and, with the help of countless other Czech artists and sculptors, the building was transformed into a treasure-house of Czech art. The cathedral was finally given an official opening ceremony in 1929, though work, in fact, continued right up to World War II.

### The exterior

The sooty Prague air has made it hard now to differentiate between the two building periods. Close inspection, however, reveals that the **western facade**, including the twin spires, is the rigorous if unimaginative work of the neo-Gothic restorers (their besuited portraits can be found below the rose window), while the **eastern section** – best viewed from the Belvedere – shows the building's authentic Gothic roots. The south door (see Zlatá brána, below) is also pure Parler. Oddly then, it's above the south door that the cathedral's tallest steeple reveals the most conspicuous stylistic join: Pacassi's Baroque topping resting absurdly on a Renaissance parapet of light stone, which is itself glued onto the blackened body of the original Gothic tower.

### The Chapel of sv Václav

The cathedral is the country's largest church and once **inside**, it's difficult not to be impressed by the sheer height of the nave. Of the 22 side chapels, the grand **Chapel of sv Václav** (St Wenceslas, patron saint of Czechoslovakia), by the south door, is easily the main attraction. Although officially dedicated to Saint Vitus, spiritually the cathedral belongs as much to the Přemyslid prince, Václav (of "Good King" fame, see box below), who was killed by his pagan brother, Boleslav the Cruel. Ten years later, in 939, Boleslav repented, converted, and apparently transferred his brother's remains to this very spot. Charles, who was keen to promote the cult of Wenceslas in order to cement his own Luxembourgeois dynasty's rather tenuous claim to the Bohemian throne, had Peter Parler build the present chapel on top of the original grave; the lion's head **door-ring** set into the north door is said to be the one to which Václav clung before being killed. The chapel's rich, almost Byzantine decoration is like the inside of a jewel casket: the gilded walls are inlaid with over 1372 semiprecious Bohemian stones (corresponding to the year of its creation), set around ethereal four-teenth-century frescoes of the *New Heavenly Jerusalem*, while the tragedy of Wenceslas unfolds above in the later paintings of the Litoměřice school.

Though a dazzling testament to the golden age of Charles IV's reign, it's not just the chapel's artistic merit which draws visitors. A door in the south wall gives access to a staircase leading to the corona-tion chamber (only rarely open to the public) which houses the **Bohemian crown jewels**, including the gold crown of Saint Wenceslas, studded with some of the largest sapphires in the world. The door is secured by seven different locks, the keys kept by seven different people, starting with the president himself – like the seven seals of the holy scroll from *Revelations*. The tight security is partly to prevent any pretenders to the throne trying on the headgear, an alleg-edly fatal act: the Nazi *Reichsprotektor* Reinhard Heydrich tried it, only to suffer the inevitable consequences (see p.135).

---

**Good King Wenceslas**

As it turns out, there's very little substance to the story related in the nine-teenth-century Christmas carol, *Good King Wenceslas*, by J. M. Neale. For a start, Václav was only a duke, and never a king (though he did become a saint); the St Agnes fountain, by which "yonder peasant dwelt" wasn't built until the thirteenth century; in fact, he wasn't even that "good", except in comparison with the rest of his family.

Born in 907, Václav inherited his title at the tender age of thirteen. His Christian grandmother, Ludmilla, was appointed regent in preference to Dragomíra, his pagan mother, who murdered Ludmilla in a fit of jealousy the following year. On coming of age in 925, Václav became duke in his own right, and took a vow of celibacy, intent on promoting Christianity throughout the dukedom. Even so, the local Christians didn't take to him, and when he began making conciliatory overtures to the neighbouring Germans, they persuaded his pagan younger brother, Boleslav the Cruel, to do away with him. On December 28, 929, two days after the Feast of Stephen, Václav was stabbed to death by Boleslav at the entrance to a church just outside Prague.

# The Tomb of St John of Nepomuk

The perfect Baroque answer to the medieval chapel of sv Václav is the Tomb of St John of Nepomuk, plonked in the middle of the ambulatory in 1736. It's a work of grotesque excess, designed by Fischer von Erlach's son, and sculpted entirely in silver with free-flying angels holding up the heavy drapery of the baldachin. Where Charles sought to promote Wenceslas as the nation's preferred saint, the Jesuits, with Habsburg backing, replaced him with the Czech martyr, John of Nepomuk (Jan Nepomucký), who had been arrested, tortured, and then thrown – bound and gagged – off the Charles Bridge in 1393 on the orders of Václav IV, allegedly for refusing to divulge the secrets of the queen's confession. A cluster of stars was said to have appeared over the spot where he drowned, hence the halo of stars on every subsequent portrayal of the saint.

The Jesuits, in their efforts to get him canonised, exhumed his corpse and produced what they claimed to be his tongue – alive and licking, so to speak (it was in fact his very dead brain). In 1729, he duly became a saint, and, on the lid of the tomb, back-to-back with the martyr himself, a cherub points to his severed tongue, sadly no longer the "real" thing. In fact, the reason for John of Nepomuk's death was simply that he was caught up in a dispute between the archbishop and the king over the appointment of the abbot of Kladruby, and backed the wrong side. Tortured along with several other priests, only John was physically unable to sign a document denying he had been tortured. The Vatican finally admitted this in 1961, some 232 years after his canonisation.

# The Royal Oratory and the tombs of the kings

Between the chapel of sv Václav and the tomb of St John of Nepomuk, Bohemia's one and only Polish ruler, Vladislav Jagiello, built a **Royal Oratory**, connected to his bedroom in the Royal Palace by a covered bridge. The balustrade sports heraldic shields from Bohemia's (at the time) quite considerable lands, while the hanging vault is smothered in an unusual branch-like decoration, courtesy of Benedict Ried. To the left, the statue of a miner is a reminder of just how important Kutná Hora's silver mines were in funding such artistic ventures.

At the centre of the choir, within a fine Renaissance grill, cherubs irreverently lark about on the sixteenth-century marble **Imperial Mausoleum**, commissioned by Rudolf II and containing his grandfather Ferdinand I, his Polish grandmother, and his father Maximilian II, the first Habsburgs to wear the Bohemian crown. Rudolf himself rests beneath them, in one of the two pewter coffins in the somewhat cramped **Royal Crypt** (the entrance is beside the Royal Oratory; there's a small entry charge). A good number of other Czech kings and queens are buried here, too, reinterred this century in incongruously modern 1930s sarcophagi, among them the Hussite King George of Poděbrady, Charles IV and, sharing a single sarcophagus, all four of his wives.

There are more dead royals (from the Přemyslid dynasty), plus Rudolf's internal organs, in the chapels of the ambulatory (temporarily closed to the public). Directly behind the main altar, the obscure location of the **Tomb of St Vitus** only confirms the inferior status of the church's patron saint when compared with his usurpers, Saint Wenceslas and Saint John of Nepomuk.

### The modern additions

Of the later additions to the church, the most striking is František Bílek's **wooden crucifix**, on the north side of the transept, which breaks free of the neo-Gothic strictures that hamper other contemporary works inside. Also worth some attention are the cathedral's modern **stained-glass** windows, which on sunny days send shafts of rainbow light into the nave. Beautiful though the effect is, it's entirely out of keeping with Parler's original concept, which was to have almost exclusively clear glass windows. The most unusual windows are those by František Kysela, which look as though they have been shattered into hundreds of tiny pieces, a technique used to greatest effect in the rose window over the west door with its kaleidoscopic *Creation of the World* (1921).

In keeping with its secular nature, two of the works from the time of the First Republic were paid for by financial institutions: the *Cyril and Methodius* window, in the third chapel in the north wall, was commissioned from Alfons Mucha by the *Banka Slavie*; while on the opposite side of the nave, the window on the theme *Those Who Sow in Tears Shall Reap in Joy* was sponsored by a Prague insurance company.

## The third courtyard and Royal Palace

The rest of the **third courtyard** (třetí nádvoří) reveals yet more Pacassi plasterwork, the monotony broken by just a couple of distractions. A fourteenth-century **bronze statue**, executed by a couple of Transylvanian Saxon sculptors, depicts a rather diminutive Saint George astride a disturbingly large horse (actually two hundred years younger than the rest of the ensemble), slaying an extremely puny dragon; the original is in the Convent of sv Jiří (see below). Apart from Plečnik's polished granite **obelisk**, commemorating those who died in World War I, the only other reason for hanging about in the third courtyard is to admire Parler's **Zlatá brána** (Golden Gate), decorated with a multicoloured fourteenth-century mosaic of the *Last Judgement*, which was, at the time of writing, chronically overdue for its regular five-year cleanup operation.

### The Royal Palace

Across the courtyard from the Zlatá brána, the **Royal Palace** (Královský palác) was home to the princes and kings of Bohemia from the eleventh to the sixteenth centuries. It's a sandwich of royal apartments, built one on top of the other by successive generations, but left largely unfurnished and unused for the last three hundred years. The original Romanesque palace of Soběslav I now forms the cellars of the present building, above which Charles IV built his own Gothic chambers; these days you enter at the third and top floor, built at the end of the fifteenth century.

Immediately past the antechamber (which now serves as the ticket office) is the bare expanse of the massive **Vladislav Hall** (Vladislavský sál), the work of Benedikt Ried, the German mason appointed by Vladislav Jagiello as his court architect. It displays some remarkable, sweeping rib-vaulting which forms floral patterns on the ceiling, the petals reaching almost to the floor. It was here that the early Bohemian kings were elected, and since Masaryk in 1918 every president has been sworn into office in the hall – the last ceremony to take place was on December 29, 1989, when Václav Havel took office. In medieval times, the hall was also used for banquets and jousting tournaments, which explains the ramp-like **Riders' Staircase** in the north wing.

From the southwest corner of the hall, you can gain access to the Ludvík Wing. The rooms themselves are pretty uninspiring but the furthest one, the **Bohemian Chancellery**, was the scene of Prague's second defenestration. After almost two centuries of uneasy coexistence between Catholics and Protestants, matters came to a head over the succession to the throne of the Habsburg archduke Ferdinand, a notoriously intolerant Catholic. On May 23, 1618, a posse of over 100 Protestant nobles, led by Count Thurn, marched to the Chancellery for a showdown with Jaroslav Martinic and Wilhelm Slavata, the two Catholic governors appointed by Ferdinand I. After a "stormy discussion", the two councillors (and their personal secretary, Philipp Fabricius) were thrown out of the window. As a contemporary historian recounted: "No mercy was granted them and they were both thrown dressed in their cloaks with their rapiers and decoration headfirst out of the western window into a moat beneath the palace. They loudly screamed *ach, ach, oweh!* and attempted to hold on to the narrow window-ledge, but Thurn beat their knuckles with the hilt of his sword until they were both obliged to let go." There's some controversy about the exact window from which they were ejected, although it's agreed that they survived to tell the tale, landing in a medieval dung heap below, and – so the story goes – precipitating the Thirty Years' War.

*Details of the first defenestration are on p.134*

At the far end of the hall, to the right, there's a **viewing platform**, from which you can contemplate the councillors' trajectory, and enjoy a magnificent view of Prague (at its best in the late afternoon). On the opposite side of the hall, to the right of the Riders' Staircase, is the **Diet**, laid out as if for a seventeenth-century session: the king on his throne, the archbishop to his right, the judiciary to his left, the nobility facing him – and just one representative from the townsfolk (with just one vote), confined to the gallery by the window.

The bare and basically rather dull rooms up a stairwell to the left of the Riders' Staircase are hardly worth the effort. Instead, a quick canter down the Riders' Staircase takes you to the **Gothic and Romanesque chambers** of the palace, equally bare, but containing a couple of interesting models showing the castle at various stages in its development, plus copies of busts by Peter Parler's workshop, including the architect's remarkable self-portrait; the originals are hidden from view in the triforium of the cathedral.

## The Basilica and Convent of sv Jiří

The only exit from the Royal Palace is via the Riders' Staircase, which deposits you in Jiřské náměstí. Don't be fooled by the uninspiring red Baroque facade of the **Basilica of sv Jiří** (St George) which dominates the square; inside it is Prague's most beautiful Romanesque building, meticulously scrubbed clean and restored to recreate something like the honey-coloured stone basilica that replaced the original tenth-century church in 1173. The double staircase to the chancel is a remarkably harmonious late Baroque addition and now provides a perfect stage for chamber music concerts. The choir vault contains a rare Romanesque painting of the *New Heavenly Jerusalem*, while to the right of the chancel, only partially visible, are thirteenth-century frescoes of the **burial chapel of sv Ludmila** (St Ludmilla), grandmother of Saint Wenceslas, who was killed by her own daughter in 921 (see box on p.64), thus becoming Bohemia's first Christian martyr and saint.

*There are a number of other, equally atmospheric concert venues in Prague; see Chapter 13 for a complete list*

Next door is Bohemia's first monastery, the **Convent of sv Jiří**, founded in 973 by Mlada, sister of the Přemyslid prince Boleslav the Pious, who became its first abbess. Like most of the country's religious institutions, it was closed down and turned into a barracks by Joseph II in 1782, and now houses the National Gallery's **Old Bohemian Art Collection** (Tues–Sun 10am–6pm). The exhibition is arranged chronologically, starting in the crypt with a remarkable collection of Gothic art, which first flourished here under the patronage of Charles IV. A half-century after Giotto in Italy had made a decisive break from the Byzantine tradition of stylised icons, Bohemian artists were developing a nostalgic style that has become known as International Gothic, usually referred to in Bohemia as the "Beautiful Style".

The **earliest works** are almost exclusively symbolical depictions of the Madonna and Child, the artists known only by their works and locations, not by name. Here you'll find – among other things – the monumental tympanum from the church of Panna Marie Sněžná in Prague and the nine-panelled altarpiece from the Cistercian monastery at Vyšší Brod. The first named artist is **Master Theodoric**, who painted over 100 panels for Charles IV's castle at Karlštejn (see p.184); just six are on display here, their larger-than-life portraits overflowing onto the edges of the panels.

On the next floor, the first work is the tympanum from the Týn church (see p.100) – originally coloured and gilded – by Peter Parler's workshop, whose mastery of composition and depth heralded a new stage in the development of Bohemian art. The following room contains mostly paintings by the **Master of Třeboň**, whose work shows even greater variety of balance and depth, moving ever closer to outright portraiture. The last room on this floor is devoted to a series of superb woodcuts by **Master I. P.**, including an incredibly detailed scene with Christ, Mary and Death, whose entrails are in the process of being devoured by some creature.

The transition from this to the next floor, where you are immediately thrown into the overtly sensual and erotic **Mannerist paintings** of Rudolf II's reign, is something of a shock. Soon, however, the restraining influence of Baroque is felt, and the collection begins to wane under the sheer volume and mediocrity of the likes of Bohemia's Karel Skréta and Petr Brandl, whose paintings and sculptures fill chapels and churches across the Czech Lands. Aside from the works of Jan Kupecký and the statues of Matthias Bernhard Braun, this might well be the moment to head for the gallery's little coffee bar on the ground floor.

## Zlatá ulička and the Lobkovic Palace

Around the corner from the convent is the **Zlatá ulička** (Golden Lane), a blind alley of miniature sixteenth-century cottages in dolly-mixture colours, built for the 24 members of Rudolf II's castle guard, though the lane takes its name from the goldsmiths who followed (and modified the buildings) a century later. By the nineteenth century, it had become a kind of palace slum, attracting artists and craftsmen, its two most famous inhabitants being Jaroslav Seifert, Czechoslovakia's Nobel prize-winning poet, and Franz Kafka. Kafka's youngest sister, Ottla, rented no. 22, and during a creative period in the winter of 1916 he came here in the evenings to write short stories. Finally, in 1951, the Communists kicked out the last residents and turned most of the houses into souvenir shops for tourists.

The tower at the far end of the lane, **Daliborka** (April–Oct 9am–5pm), is dedicated to its first prisoner, the young Czech noble, Dalibor, accused of supporting a peasants' revolt at the beginning of the fifteenth century. According to Prague legend, he learnt to play the violin while imprisoned here, and his playing could be heard all over the castle – a tale that provided material for Smetana's opera, *Dalibor*. **Bílá věž**, the tower at the opposite end of the lane, was the city's main prison from Rudolf's reign onwards. Edward Kelley, the English alchemist, poisoned himself here, having been locked up by Rudolf for failing to make quite enough gold, while the emperor's treasurer hanged himself by his chain of office, after being accused of embezzlement. If you're keen to see the inside of one of the castle towers, you'll have to backtrack to **Mihulka**, the tower just off Vikářská, which runs along the north side of the cathedral. Its name comes from the lamprey (*mihule*), an eel-like fish supposedly bred here for royal consumption, though it's actually more noteworthy as the place where Rudolf's team of alchemists (including Kelley) were put to work trying to discover the philosopher's stone.

### The Lobkovic Palace

If your grounding in Czech history is still a bit sketchy, the hotchpotch historical collection in the **Lobkovic Palace** (Tues–Sun 9am–5pm), towards the bottom of Jiřská, is a good introduction to the subject. The exhibition actually begins on the top floor, but by no means all the objects on display deserve attention; the following is a quick rundown of some of the more memorable exhibits. The first cabinet worth more than a passing nod is in the second room, and contains copies of the Bohemian crown jewels (the originals are hidden away above the Chapel of sv Václav in the cathedral). Next door, in the Hussite room, there's an interesting sixteenth-century carving of *The Last Supper*, originally an altarpiece from the Bethlehem Chapel, while, further on, Petr Vok's splendid funereal shield hangs on the wall, constructed out of wood covered with cloth shot through with gold.

All things post-1620 and pre-1848 are displayed in the six rooms downstairs, starting with the sword of the famous Prague executioner, Jan Mydlář, who could lop a man's head off with just one chop, a skill he demonstrated on 24 of the 27 Protestant leaders who were executed on Staroměstské náměstí in 1621; Mydlář's invoice covering labour and expenses is displayed beside the sword. Several rooms on are some more unusual exhibits – three contemporary scaled-down models of eighteenth-century altars, and further on still, three carved marionettes from later that century, among the oldest surviving in Bohemia.

# From Hradčanské náměstí to the Strahov Monastery

The monumental scale and appearance of the rest of Hradčany, outside the castle, is a direct result of the **great fire of 1541**, which swept up from Malá Strana and wiped out most of the old dwelling places belonging to the serfs, tradesmen, clergy and masons who had settled here in the Middle Ages. With the Turks at the gates of Vienna, the Habsburg nobility were more inclined to pursue their major building projects in Prague instead, and, following the Battle of Bílá hora in 1620, the palaces of the exiled (or executed) Protestant nobility were up for grabs too. The newly ensconced Catholic aristocrats were keen to spend some of their expropriated wealth, and over the next two centuries, they turned Hradčany into a grand architectural showpiece. As the Turkish threat subsided, the political focus of the empire gradually shifted back to Vienna and the building spree stopped. For the last two hundred years, Hradčany has been frozen in time, and, two world wars on, its buildings have survived better than those of any other central European capital.

# Hradčanské náměstí

Hradčanské náměstí fans out from the castle gates, surrounded by the oversized palaces of the old Catholic nobility. For the most part, it's a tranquil space that's overlooked by the tour groups marching through, intent on the Hrad. The one spot everyone does head for is the ramparts in the southeastern corner, which allow an unrivalled view over the reddish-brown rooftops of Malá Strana, past the famous dome and tower of the church of sv Mikuláš and beyond, to the spires of Staré Město. Only the occasional bookish Praguer or tired traveller makes use of the square's central green patch, which is marked by a giant green wrought-iron lamppost decked with eight separate lamps – one of two such lampposts in Hradčany.

Until the great fire of 1541, the square was the hub of Hradčany, lined with medieval shops and stalls but with no real market as such. After the fire, the developers moved in; the **Martinic Palace** at no. 8 was one of the more modest newcomers, built in 1620 by one of the councillors who survived the second defenestration. Its rich sgraffito decoration, which continues in the inner courtyard, was only discovered during restoration work in the 1970s, and was part of the reason it was featured as Mozart's house in the film *Amadeus*. Mathey's rather cold, formal **Toscana Palace** was built on a more ambitious scale, replacing the row of butchers' shops that once filled the west end of the square.

The powerful Lobkovic family replaced seven houses on the south side of the square with the over-the-top sgraffitoed pile at no. 2, known as the **Schwarzenberg Palace** after its last aristocratic owners (the present-day count, Karl, is one of Havel's closest advisers). For a brief period, it belonged to the Rožmberks, whose last in line, Petr Vok, held the infamous banquet at which the Danish astronomer Tycho de Brahe overdrank his fill, and staggered off with a burst bladder to his house in Nový Svět, where he died five days later. All of which makes the **Museum of Military History** (Vojenské muzeum; May–Oct Tues–Sun 9.30am–4.30pm), which now occupies the palace, seem considerably less gruesome. Czechoslovakia has a long history of supplying top-class weaponry to world powers (most recently in the form of Semtex to the Libyans and tanks to the Syrians). It's no coincidence that one of the two Czech words to have made it into the English language is pistol (*pistole* in Czech). Among the endless uniforms and instruments of death – all of which are pre-1914 – you'll find an early Colt 45 and the world's largest mortar (courtesy of Škoda).

On the opposite side of the square, just outside the castle gates, stands the sumptuous **Archbishop's Palace** (Archbiskupský palác), seat of the archbishop of Prague since the beginning of the Roman Catholic church's suzerainty over the Czechs, following the Battle of Bílá hora. The Rococo exterior only hints at the even more extravagant furnishings inside. The elusive interior (open to the public only

From Hradčanské náměstí to the Strahov Monastery

You'll find Prague's modern military collections at the Military Museum, covered on p.150

on Maundy Thursday – the Thursday before Easter) is presently enjoyed by Archbishop Tomášek (known affectionately as "Frantši"), who is now in his nineties.

## Šternberk Palace – the European Art Collection

A passage down the side of the Archbishop's Palace leads to the early eighteenth-century Šternberk Palace (Tues–Sun 10am–6pm), now the main building of the National Gallery, housing its European Art Collection (ie non-Czech) – which, though rich enough for most tastes, is relatively modest in comparison with those of other European capitals. The collection is divided into three sections: the first floor contains icons and Italian, German, Dutch and Flemish masters from the fourteenth to the sixteenth centuries; the second floor covers the rest of European art up to the twentieth century; and the final, most popular section is the "French Art" collection on the ground floor of the north wing, across the courtyard from the entrance.

The **first floor** kicks off with Florentine religious art, most notably a series of exquisite miniature triptychs by Bernardo Daddi. Also worth checking out are the side rooms containing Orthodox icons from the Balkans to northern Russia. The section ends with a series of canvases by Breughel the Younger, and *Haymaking* by Breughel the Elder.

The **second floor** contains one of the most prized paintings in the whole collection, the *Festival of the Rose Garlands* by Albrecht Dürer, depicting, among others, the Virgin Mary, the Pope, the Holy Roman Emperor, and even a self-portrait of Dürer himself (top right). This was one of Rudolf's many aquisitions (he was an avid Dürer fan), which was transported on foot across the Alps to Prague (he didn't trust wheeled transport with such a precious object). There are other outstanding works here, too: a whole series of portraits by the Saxon master, Lucas Cranach – including the striking, almost minimalist *Portrait of an Old Man* – and a mesmerising *Head of Christ* by El Greco. Rubens' colossal *Murder of St Thomas* is difficult to miss, with its pink-buttocked cherubs hovering over the bloody scene, and a couple of dogs clearing up the mess. Nearby, there's a wonderful portrait of an arrogant "young gun" named Jasper by Frans Hals, followed by various Dutch masters from the eighteenth century.

At this point, you are suddenly propelled straight into the world of **twentieth-century art**, beginning with Klimt's mischievous *Virgins*, a mass of naked bodies and tangled limbs painted out in psychedelic colours. Although none of the artists here is Czech, many of them had close connections with Bohemia: Egon Schiele's mother came from Český Krumlov, the subject of a tiny autumnal canvas; and the handful of works by Oskar Kokoschka date from his brief stay here in the 1930s, when the political temperature got too hot in Vienna. Perhaps the most influential artist on show is Edvard Munch, whose one canvas, *Dance at the Seaside*, hardly does justice to the considerable effect he had on a generation of Czech artists after his celebrated exhibition in Prague in 1905.

By far the most popular section of the gallery is the "**French**" **art** section across the courtyard on the ground floor, featuring anyone of note who hovered around Paris in the fifty years from 1880 onwards. There are few of the artists' famous masterpieces here, but it's all high quality stuff. Among those represented are Gauguin, Monet, Pissarro, Seurat, Van Gogh, Cézanne, Toulouse-Lautrec, Dufy and Matisse. Several works by Rodin are scattered around the room, particularly appropriate given his ecstatic reception by Czech sculptors at the beginning of this century, following his Prague exhibition in 1902. And there's a surprisingly good collection of Picassos, including several paintings and sculptures from his crucial early Cubist period (1907–08). Four of his works – worth an estimated 30 million dollars – were stolen in the summer of 1991 and only recently recovered, illustrating a problem common to all east European galleries since the opening up of the borders. At the end of this section there's a shop selling postcards, posters, books and coffee.

## Nový Svět to the Loreto Chapel

At the other end of Hradčanské náměstí, Kanovnická heads off towards the northwest corner of Hradčany. Nestling in this shallow dip, Nový Svět (meaning "New World", though not Dvořák's) provides a glimpse of life on a totally different scale from Hradčanské náměstí. Similar in many ways to the Zlatá ulička in the Hrad, this cluster of brightly coloured cottages, which curls around the corner into Černínská, is all that's left of Hradčany's medieval slums, painted up and sanitised in the eighteenth and nineteenth centuries. Despite having all the same ingredients for mass tourist appeal as Zlatá ulička, it remains remarkably undisturbed, save for a few kitsch ateliers, swish wine bars, and the studio of the renowned Czech animator, Jan Švankmajer.

Up the hill from Nový Svět, Loretánské náměstí is dominated by the phenomenal 150-metre-long facade of the **Černín Palace** (Černínský palác), decorated with thirty Palladian half-pillars and supported by a swathe of diamond-pointed rustication. For all its grandeur – it's the largest palace in Prague, for the sake of which two whole streets were demolished – it's a miserable, brutal building, commissioned in the 1660s by Count Jan Humprecht Černín, one-time imperial ambassador to Venice and a man of monumental self-importance. After quarrelling with the master of Italian Baroque, Gianlorenzo Bernini, and disagreeing with Prague's own Carlo Lurago, Count Černín settled on Francesco Caratti as his architect, only to have the finished building panned by critics as a tasteless mass of stone. The grandiose plans, which were nowhere near completion when the count died, nearly bankrupted future generations of Černíns, who were eventually forced to sell the palace in 1851 to the Austrian state, which converted it into military barracks.

Since the First Republic, the palace has housed the Ministry of Foreign Affairs, and during the war it was the Nazi *Reichsprotektor*'s residence. On March 10, 1948, it was the scene of Prague's third – and most widely mourned – defenestration. Only days after the Communist coup, **Jan Masaryk**, the only son of the founder of the Republic, and the last non-Communist in Gottwald's cabinet, plunged forty-five feet to his death from the top-floor bathroom window of the palace. Whether it was suicide (he had been suffering from bouts of depression, partly induced by the country's political path) or murder will probably never be satisfactorily resolved, but for most people Masaryk's death cast a dark shadow over the newly established regime.

## The Loreto

The facade of the **Loreto** (Loreta; Tues–Sun 9am–noon & 1–5pm), immediately opposite the Černín Palace, was built by the Dientzenhofers, a Bavarian family of architects, in the early part of the eighteenth century, and is the perfect antidote to Caratti's humourless monster: all hot flourishes and twirls, topped by a tower which lights up like a Chinese lantern at night – and by day clanks out the hymn *We Greet Thee a Thousand Times* on its 27 Dutch bells.

The facade and the cloisters, which were provided a century earlier to shelter pilgrims from the elements, are, in fact, just the outer casing for the focus of the complex, the **Santa Casa**, founded by Kateřina Lobkovic in 1626 and smothered in a mantle of stucco depicting the building's miraculous transportation from the Holy Land. Legend has it that the Santa Casa (Mary's home in Nazareth), under threat from the heathen Turks, was transported by a host of angels to a small village in Dalmatia and from there, via a number of brief stop-offs, to a small laurel grove (*lauretum* in Latin, hence *Loreto*) in northern Italy. News of the miracle spread across the Catholic lands, prompting a spate of copy-cat shrines, and during the Counter-Reformation, the cult was actively encouraged in an attempt to broaden the popular appeal of Catholicism. The Prague Loreto is one of fifty to be built in the Czech Lands, each of the shrines following an identical design, with pride of place given to a lime-wood statue of the *Black Madonna and Child*, encased in silver.

*The Lobkovic family gave Prague its other famous pilgrimage shrine, the pražské Jezulátko, see p.85*

Behind the Santa Casa, the Dientzenhofers built the much larger **Church of the Nativity** (Kostel Narození Páně), packed with some fairly gruesome Baroque kitsch. On either side of the main altar are glass cabinets containing the (fully clothed) skeletons of Saint Felicissimus and Saint Marcia, and next to them, paintings of Saint Apolena – who had her teeth smashed in during her martyrdom and is now invoked for toothache – and Saint Agatha, carrying her severed breasts on a dish. Last but not least of the weird and wonderful saints in Loreto is Saint Wilgefortis, a painting of whom is in the final chapel of the cloisters. Daughter of the King of Portugal, she was due to marry the King of Sicily, despite having taken a vow of virginity. God intervened and she grew a beard, whereupon the King of Sicily broke off the marriage and her father had her crucified. Wilgefortis thus became the patron saint of unhappily married women, and is traditionally depicted bearded on the cross.

You can get some idea of the Santa Casa's serious financial backing in the **treasury** (situated on the first floor of the west wing), much ransacked over the years but still stuffed full of gold. The padded ceilings and low lighting create a kind of giant jewellery box for the master exhibit, a tasteless Viennese silver monstrance studded with 6222 diamonds, standing over three feet high and weighing nearly two stone. It was constructed in 1699 to a design by Fischer von Erlach, on the posthumous orders of one of the Kolovrat family who had made the Loreto sole heir to her fortune.

## The Strahov Monastery

West of Loretánské náměstí, Pohořelec, an arcaded street-cum-square, leads to the chunky remnants of the zigzag eighteenth-century fortifications that mark the edge of the old city, as defined by Charles IV back in the fourteenth century. Close by, to the left, is the **Strahov Monastery** (Strahovský klášter), founded in 1140 by the Premonstratensian order. Strahov was one of the lucky few to escape Joseph II's 1783 dissolution of the monasteries, a feat it managed by declaring itself a scholarly institution – the monks had, in fact, amassed one of the finest libraries in Bohemia. It continued to function until shortly after the Communists took power, when, along with all other religious establishments, it was closed down and most of its inmates thrown into prison. Following the events of 1989, the monks have returned, so the future of the monastery as a tourist sight is now somewhat uncertain.

The Baroque entrance to the monastery is topped by a statue of Saint Norbert, founder of the Premonstratensian order, whose relics were brought here in 1627. Just inside the main cobbled courtyard is a tiny deconsecrated church built by Rudolf II and dedicated to Saint Roch, protector against plagues, one of which had very nearly rampaged through Prague in 1599; it's now used for art exhibitions. The other church in this peaceful little courtyard is the still functioning monastery church, first built back in the twelfth century, and given its last remodelling in Baroque times by Jean-Baptiste Mathey. The ticket office is beside the church, under the arch that leads to the **Museum of Czech Literature** (Památník národního písemnictví; Tues–Sun 9am–5pm). Since the return of the monks, the museum has forsaken its permanent collection and now only puts on temporary literary exhibitions, of limited interest to non-Czech speakers.

It's the monastery's two **libraries** that are the real reason for visiting Strahov; the entrance for both is back in the main courtyard to the left. The first room you come to is the later of the two, the Philosophical Hall (Filosofický sál), built in some haste in the 1780s, in order to accommodate the books and bookcases from Louka, a Premonstratensian monastery in Moravia that failed to escape Joseph's decree. The walnut bookcases are so tall they touch the library's lofty ceiling, which is busily decorated with frescoes by the Viennese painter Franz Maulpertsch on *The Struggle of Mankind to Know Real Wisdom*. The other main room is the low-ceilinged Theological Hall (Teologický sál), its wedding-cake stucco framing frescoes on a similar theme, executed by one of the monks seventy years earlier.

If you leave the monastery through the narrow doorway in the eastern wall, you enter the gardens and orchards of the **Strahovská zahrada**, from where you can see the whole city in perspective. The gardens form part of Petřín Hill, and the path to the right contours round to the miniature Eiffel Tower (see p.87).

# Chapter 3

# Malá Strana

More than anywhere else, MALÁ STRANA, the "Little Quarter", conforms to the image of Prague as the ultimate Baroque city. It was here that Miloš Forman chose to shoot many of the street scenes in *Amadeus*, judging that its picturesque alleyways resembled Mozart's Vienna more than Vienna itself. And it's true; the streets have changed very little since Mozart walked them, as he often did on his frequent visits to Prague between 1787 and 1791. Unlike Hradčany, its main arteries are filled with city life during the day; while around practically every corner, narrow cobbled streets lead to some quiet walled garden, the perfect inner-city escape.

Many visitors never stray from the well-trodden paths that link the Charles Bridge with Hradčany, thus bypassing most of Malá Strana. This is easy to do, given that the whole town takes up a mere 150 acres of land squeezed in between the river and the Hrad, but means missing out on one of the greatest pleasures of Malá Strana – casually exploring its hilly eighteenth-century backstreets.

*Some of the city's best restaurants, jazz clubs and most exclusive vinárna are located within Malá Strana, see Chapters 11 and 12 for details*

Long before the Přemyslid king, Otakar II, decided to establish a German community here in 1257, a mixture of Jews, merchants and monks had settled on the slopes below the castle. But, as with Hradčany, it was the fire of 1541 – which devastated the entire left bank of the Vltava – and the expulsion of the Protestants after 1620, that together had the greatest impact on the visual and social make-up of the quarter. In place of the old Gothic town, the newly ascendant Catholic nobility built numerous palaces here, though generally without quite the same destructive glee as up in Hradčany. In 1918, the majority of these buildings became the foreign embassies of the newly established First Republic, and after 1948 the rest of the real estate was turned into flats to alleviate the postwar housing shortage. The cycle has come full circle again since 1989, and property in Malá Strana – much of it in an extremely bad state of repair – is now among the most sought after in Prague. For the moment, the cash-strapped city authorities seem to be shying away from a wholesale sell-out to foreign companies, but the restitution law has brought back many former owners, and the face of Malá Strana looks set to change once more.

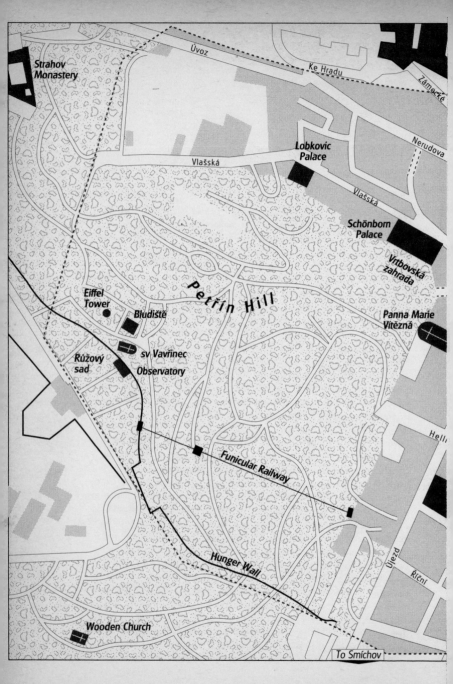

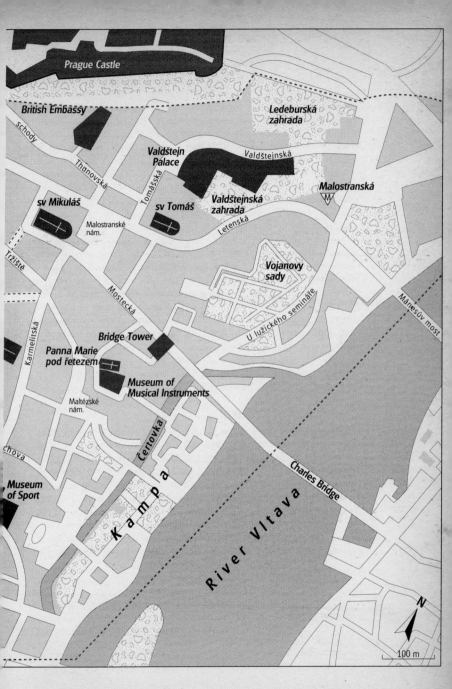

Prague Castle

British Embassy

Ledeburská zahrada

schody

Thunovská

Valdštejn Palace

Valdštejnská

sv Mikuláš

Tomášská

sv Tomáš

Valdštejnská zahrada

Malostranská
Ⓜ

Malostranské nám.

Letenská

Tržiště

Mostecká

Vojanovy sady

Karmelitská

U lužického semináře

Mánesův most

Bridge Tower

Panna Marie pod řetezem

Museum of Musical Instruments

Maltézské nám.

Čertovka

chova

K  a  m  p  a

Museum of Sport

Charles Bridge

River Vltava

N

100 m

# Malostranské náměstí and around

The main focus of Malá Strana has always been the sloping, cobbled Malostranské náměstí, across which hurtle trams and cars, as well as a procession of people – some heading up the hill to the Hrad, others pausing for coffee and cakes at the *Malostranská kavárna*, whose tables and chairs spill out on to the square. This has remained one of the most popular cafés in Malá Strana since it was first established back in 1874, and in the 1920s was a regular haunt of Kafka, Brod, Werfel and friends.

On every side, musty Neoclassical facades line the square, none boasting the colour or grandeur of those of Hradčanské or Staroměstské náměstí. To the south, the original Gothic houses survive, several of their vaulted cellars now occupied by *vinárna*. The largest of the developments that replaced the old town houses, the Liechtenstein Palace, takes up the square's entire west side\*. Its pleasing frontage (currently being restored to its former glory for the university's arts faculty) hides a history linked to repression: first as the home of Karl von Liechtenstein, the man who pronounced the death sentence on the 27 Protestant leaders in 1621; then as headquarters for the Swedes during the 1648 siege; and later as home to the Austrian conservative Windischgrätz, scourge of the 1848 revolution. On the north side, the Smiřický Palace, distinguished by its two little turrets, was where the Protestant posse met up to decide how to get rid of Emperor Ferdinand's Catholic governors: whether to attack them with daggers, or, as they eventually attempted to do, kill them by chucking them out of the window (see p.67).

## The church of sv Mikuláš

Dominating and dividing the square, as it does the whole of Malá Strana, is the church of sv Mikuláš (St Nicholas), easily the most magnificent Baroque building in the city, and one of the last great structures to be built on the left bank, begun in 1702. For Christoph Dientzenhofer, a German immigrant from a dynasty of Bavarian architects, this was his most prestigious commission and is, without doubt, his finest work. For the Jesuits, it was their most ambitious project yet in Bohemia, the ultimate symbol of their stranglehold on the country. When Christoph died in 1722, it was left to his son Kilian Ignaz Dientzenhofer, along with Kilian's son-in-law, Anselmo Lurago, to

---

\*Under the law of *restituce* (restitution), all property confiscated by the Communists from 1948 onwards is automatically returned to its former owners. This has dismayed the hundreds whose property was appropriated much earlier, either in 1945, 1938 or, as in the much publicised case of the Liechtensteins, 1918. The Grand Duchy has officially requested that the Czechoslovak government hand back at least some of the Liechtensteins' former properties, which comprise something like 1600 square kilometres of land – ten times the area of present-day Liechtenstein. Negotiations look likely to continue for some time.

> **Mozart in Prague**
>
> Mozart made the first of several visits to Prague in 1787, staying with his friend and patron Count Thun in what is now the British Embassy (Thunovská 14). A year earlier, his opera *The Marriage of Figaro*, which had failed dismally to please the opera snobs in Vienna, had been given a rapturous reception at Prague's *Nostitz Theater* (now the Stavovské divadlo, see p.103); and on his arrival in 1787, Mozart was already flavour of the month, as he wrote in his diary: "Here they talk about nothing but Figaro. Nothing is played, sung or whistled but Figaro. Nothing, nothing but Figaro. Certainly a great honour for me!". Encouraged by this, he chose to premiere his next opera, *Don Giovanni*, later that year, in Prague rather than Vienna. He arrived with an incomplete score in hand, and wrote the overture at the Dušeks' Bertramka Villa in Smíchov (see p.161), dedicating it to the "good people of Prague". In 1791, the year of his death, *La Clemenza di Tito*, commissioned for the coronation of Leopold II as King of Bohemia – and apparently written on the coach from Vienna to Prague – was premiered here. Although Mozart was buried in Vienna as a little-known pauper, in Prague 4000 people turned out for his memorial service, held in Malá Strana's church of sv Mikuláš to the strains of his *Requiem Mass*.

finish the project, which they did with a masterful flourish, adding the giant green dome and tower – now among the most characteristic landmarks on Prague's left bank. Sadly for the Jesuits, they were able to enjoy the finished product for just twenty years, before they were banished from the Habsburg Empire in 1773.

Nothing about the relatively plain west facade prepares you for the overwhelming High Baroque **interior**. The fresco in the nave, by Jan Lukáš Kracker, is one of the largest paintings in Europe, covering an area of over 1500 square metres and portraying some of the more fanciful miraculous feats of Saint Nicholas. Apart from his role as Santa Claus, he is depicted here rescuing sailors in distress, saving women from prostitution by throwing them bags of gold, and reprieving from death three unjustly condemned men. Even given the overwhelming proportions of the nave, the dome at the far end of the church, built by the younger Dientzenhofer, remains impressive, thanks, more than anything, to its sheer height. Leering over you as you gaze up at the dome are Ignaz Platzer's two terrifyingly oversized and stern Church Fathers, leaving no doubt as to the gravity of the Jesuit message.

## Nerudova

The most important of the various streets leading up to the Hrad from Malostranské náměstí is **Nerudova**, named after the Czech journalist and writer Jan Neruda (1834–91), who lived for a while at *U dvou sluncū* (The Two Suns), a former inn at the top of the street. His tales of Malá Strana immortalised bohemian life on Prague's left bank, and inspired countless other writers, not least the Chilean Nobel prize-winner, Pablo Neruda, who took his pen name from the lesser-known

*Nerudova was once famous for its pubs, sadly now there's just one left, U kocoura, see p.205*

There are more
house signs in
Nerudova than in
any other street in
Prague; see box
opposite

Czech. Historically, this is Prague's artists' quarter, and although few of the present inhabitants are names to conjure with, the various private galleries and craft shops that have sprouted up over the last few years continue the tradition.

The houses that line the steep climb up to the Hrad are typically restrained, many retaining their medieval barn doors, and most adorned with their own peculiar house signs. A short way up the hill, you'll pass two of the street's fancier buildings: at no. 5 is the **Morzin Palace**, now the Romanian Embassy, its doorway supported by two moors (a pun on the owner's name); diagonally opposite, two giant eagles hold up the portal of the **Thun-Hohenstein Palace**, now the Italian Embassy. Further up the street, Casanova and Mozart shared lodgings at no. 33, the Bretfeld Palace, in 1791, while the latter was in town for the premiere of *La Clemenza di Tito* (see box above).

Halfway up the hill, Nerudova halts at a crossroads; the cobbled hairpin of Ke Hradu is the path the royal coronation procession used to take; continuing west along Úvoz (The Cutting) takes you to the Strahov Monastery. On the south side of Úvoz, the houses come to an end, and a view opens up over Malá Strana's red Baroque roofs, while to the north, narrow stairways squeeze between the towering buildings of Hradčany, emerging on the path to the Loreto chapel.

## Tržiště and Vlašská

Running (very) roughly parallel to Nerudova is **Tržiště**, which sets off from the south side of Malostranské náměstí. Halfway up on the left is the **Schönborn Palace**, now the American Embassy, whose present incumbent is none other than Shirley Temple-Black, of *Good Ship Lollipop* fame. The entrance, and the renowned gardens, are nowadays watched over by closed-circuit TV and machine-gun toting GIs – a far cry from the dilapidated palace in which Kafka rented an apartment in March 1917, and where he suffered his first bout of tuberculosis.

As Tržiště swings to the right, bear left up **Vlašská**, home to yet another **Lobkovic Palace**, now the (united) German Embassy, which witnessed the first rumblings of the 1989 revolutions. In the summer of that year, several thousand East Germans (a mere fraction of the six million or so who used to visit Czechoslovakia each year) climbed over the garden wall and entered the embassy compound to demand West German citizenship, which had been every German's right since partition. The neighbouring streets were jam-packed with abandoned Trabants, while the beautiful palace gardens became a muddy home to the refugees. Finally, the Czechoslovak government gave in and organised special trains to take the East Germans over the Federal border, cheered on their way by thousands of Praguers, and thus prompted the exodus that eventually brought about *Die Wende*.

The palace itself is a particularly refined building, best viewed from the **gardens** around the back, which were laid out in the early nineteenth century by Václav Skalník, who went on to landscape the

### House Signs

As well as preserving their Gothic or Romanesque foundations, many houses throughout Prague retain their ancient **house signs**, which you'll see carved into the gables, on hanging wooden signs, or inscribed on the facade. The system originated in the fourteenth century, and still survives today, though it's now used predominantly by *pivnice*, restaurants and *vinárna*.

Some signs were deliberately chosen to draw custom to the business of the house, like *U zeleného hroznu* (The Green Bunch of Grapes), a wine shop in the Malá Strana; others, like *U železných dveří* (The Iron Door), simply referred to some distinguishing feature of the house, often long gone. The pervasive use of *zlatý* (gold) in the house names derives from the city's popular epithet, *Zlatá Praha* (Golden Prague), referring either to the halcyon days of Charles IV, when the new Gothic copper roofing shone like gold, or the period of alchemy under Rudolf II, depending on your viewpoint. Religious names, like *U Černé Matky boží* (The Black Madonna), were popular, too, especially during the Counter-Reformation.

In the 1770s, the Habsburgs, in their rationalising fashion, introduced a numerical system, with each house in the city entered onto a register according to a strict chronology, and later, the conventional system of progressive street numbering was introduced; so don't be surprised if seventeenth-century pubs like *U medvídků* (The Little Bears) have, in addition to a house sign, two numbers: in this case 7 and 345; the former, Habsburg number, written on a red background, the latter, modern number, on blue.

spa at Mariánské Lázně. They're usually open to the public but, given the hammering they took in 1989, are likely still to be undergoing major botanical surgery; if they're accessible, you should be able to get a look at David Černý's sculpture, *Quo Vadis?*, a gold Trabant on legs, erected in memory of the fleeing East Germans.

# The Valdštejn Palace and gardens

To the north of Malostranské náměstí, the **Valdštejn Palace** takes up the whole of the eastern side of Valdštejnské náměstí, as well as the entire length of Valdštejnská. As early as 1621, Albrecht von Waldstein (known to the English as Wallenstein, and to the Czechs as Albrecht z Valdštejna) started to build a palace which would reflect his status as commander of the Imperial Catholic armies. By buying, confiscating, and then destroying twenty-five houses around the square, he succeeded in ripping apart a densely populated area of Malá Strana to make way for one of the largest and, quite frankly, most unappealing Baroque palaces in the city – at least from the outside.

The Ministry of Culture is now firmly ensconced in the palace, with just one wing, containing, ironically enough, the **Comenius Museum** (Pedagogické muzeum; Tues–Sun 10am–noon & 1–5pm), accessible to the public. This is a small and none too exciting exhibition on Czech education and, in particular, the influential teachings of Jan Amos Komenský (1592–1670) – often anglicised to John Comenius – who

**The Valdštejn Palace and gardens**

was forced to leave his homeland after the victory of the Catholic armies under Valdštejn, eventually settling in Protestant England. To get to the exhibition, go through the main gateway and continue straight across the first courtyard; the museum is on your right.

If you've no interest in pedagogical matters, the formal **Valdštejnská zahrada** (Valdštejn gardens; May–Sept daily 9am–7pm) are a good place to take a breather from the city streets. The focus of the gardens is the gigantic Italianate *sala terrena*, a monumental arch which stands at the end of an avenue of sculptures, the originals of which were taken off as booty by the Swedes in 1648. On the opposite side of the gardens, the palace's former riding school has been converted into a gallery, which puts on exhibitions of fine art and photography. Access to the gardens is via a concealed entrance on Letenská; you can get to the riding school from the courtyard of the nearby Malostranská metro station.

### More palaces and gardens

There are a number of other Baroque palace gardens on the slopes below the castle, and all except the Polish Embassy's Fürstenberská zahrada are, theoretically at least, open to the public. The **Černínská zahrada** is the best-loved – a jumble of balustrades, terraces and (dried-up) fountains – closely followed by the **Ledeburská zahrada**. You may find that in practice you can't get into any of them – if you're thwarted, try instead the **Vojanovy sady**, securely concealed behind a ring of high walls off U lužického semináře. It's a public park rather than a palace garden, with sleeping babies, weeping willows and the occasional open-air art happening.

# From Karmelitská to Kampa

**Karmelitská** is the busy cobbled street that runs south from Malostranské náměstí along the base of Petřín Hill towards the industrial suburb of Smíchov (see p.160), becoming Újezd at roughly the halfway point. Between here and the River Vltava are some of Malá Strana's most picturesque and secluded streets. Although there are no major sights around here, the island of **Kampa**, in particular, makes up one of the most peaceful stretches of riverfront in Prague.

### Karmelitská and Újezd

On the corner of Karmelitská and Tržiště, at no. 25, is the entrance to one of the most elusive of Malá Strana's many Baroque gardens, the **Vrtbovská zahrada**, founded on the site of the former vineyards of the Vrtba Palace. Laid out on Tuscan-style terraces, dotted with ornamental urns and statues of the gods by Matthias Bernhard Braun, the gardens twist their way up the lower slopes of Petřín Hill to an observation terrace, from where there's a spectacular rooftop perspective on the city.

Further down, on the same side of the street, is the rather plain church of **Panna Marie Vítězná**, which was begun in early Baroque style by German Lutherans in 1611, and later handed over to the Carmelites after the Battle of Bílá hora. The main reason for coming here is to see the *pražské Jezulátko* or *Bambino di Praga*, a high-kitsch wax effigy of the infant Jesus enthroned in a glass case illuminated with strip-lights, donated by one of the Lobkovic family's Spanish brides in 1628. Attributed with miraculous powers, the *pražské Jezulátko* became an object of international pilgrimage equal in stature to the Santa Casa in Loreto, similarly inspiring a whole series of replicas. It continues to attract visitors (as the multilingual prayer cards attest) and boasts a vast personal wardrobe of expensive swaddling clothes, regularly changed by the local prelate.

A block or so further south, Karmelitská becomes Újezd, site of another former nunnery, this time Dominican, at no. 40. The Kinský family later built a Renaissance palace here, but from 1787 it fell into disrepair and remained so until the *Sokol* nationalist sports movement bought it in 1921. The sports faculty of the Karolinum and the **Museum of Physical Culture and Sport** (Muzeum tělesné výchovy a sportu; Tues–Sun 9am–5pm) are now housed here. Sport played an important part in the Czech *národní obrození* through *Sokol*, the extremely popular nationalist organisation set up in 1862, in direct answer to the German *Turnverband* physical education movement. The Communists continued the tradition with the *Spartakiáda*, extravaganzas of synchronised gymnastics held every five years in the Strahov stadium, behind Petřín Hill. Even the *Spartakiáda* were popular, but, indelibly tainted by their political past, the last one, due to have been held in 1990, was cancelled. The museum fails to mention the *Spartakiáda*, and instead traces the history of *Sokol*, and focuses on the postwar Olympic successes of the likes of the Czech long-distance runner, Emil Zátopek.

## Maltézské náměstí and around

From the trams and traffic fumes of Karmelitská, it's a relief to cut across to the calm restraint of **Maltézské náměstí**, one of a number of delightful little squares between here and the river. It takes its name from the Order of the Knights of St John of Jerusalem (better known by their later title, the Maltese Knights), who founded the nearby church of **Panna Marie pod řetězem** (Saint Mary below-the-chain) in 1160. The original Romanesque church was pulled down by the Knights themselves in the fourteenth century, but only the chancel and towers were successfully rebuilt by the time of the Hussite Wars. The two severe Gothic towers are still standing and the chancel is now thoroughly Baroque, but the nave remains unfinished, an open, grassy, and generally inaccessible space.

Just to the south, music wafts across Velkopřevorské náměstí, another pretty little square where the Prague Conservatoire and the **Museum of Musical Instruments** (April–Oct Tues–Sun 10am–6pm) occupy what used to be the Knights' Grand Priory. The museum faces an uncertain future, and its mixed bag of exhibits – including a quarter-tone piano, designed by the microtonal Czech composer Alois Hába – may well be locked away until a new home is found for them. Around the corner, on the opposite side of the square, sitting pretty in pink, is the **Buquoy Palace**, built for a French family and appropriately enough now the French Embassy.

In these unlikely surroundings, along the garden wall of the Grand Priory, Prague's youth set up what has become known as **John Lennon's mock-grave**. Following the violent death of the Beatle and lifelong pacifist in 1980, graffiti from the inane to the profound was scrawled on the wall in honour of Lennon. Inevitably the wall also developed into a forum for grievances against the state; and a running battle between the police and the graffiti artists still continues despite the events of 1989.

## Kampa

The two or three streets that make up **Kampa**, the largest of the central islands, contain no notable palaces or museums; just a couple of old mills, an exquisite main square, and a serene riverside park – in other words, plenty enough diversion for a lazy summer afternoon. The island is separated from the left bank by Prague's "Little Venice", a thin strip of water called **Čertovka** (Devil's Stream), which used to power several mill-wheels until the last one ceased to function in 1936. In contrast to the rest of the left bank, the fire of 1541 had a positive effect on Kampa, since the flotsam from the blaze effectively stabilised the island's shifting shoreline. Nevertheless, Kampa was still subject to frequent flooding right up until the Vltava was dammed in the 1950s.

For much of its history, the island was the city's main wash house, a fact commemorated by the church of sv Jan Na Prádle (St John at the Wash House) on Říční, near the southernmost tip of the island. It wasn't until the sixteenth and seventeenth centuries that the Nostitz family, who owned Kampa, began to develop the northern half of the island; the southern half was left untouched, and today is laid out as a public park. To the north, the oval main square, **Na Kampě**, once a pottery market, is studded with slender trees and cut through by the Charles Bridge, to which it is connected by a double flight of steps.

# Petřín Hill

The scaled-down version of the Eiffel Tower is the most obvious landmark on **Petřín Hill**, the largest green space in the city centre. The tower is just one of the exhibits built for the 1891 Prague Exhibition, whose modest legacy includes the **funicular railway** (lanová dráha) which climbs up from a station just off Újezd. The original funicular was powered by a simple but ingenious system whereby two carriages, one at either end of the steep track, were fitted with large watertanks

that were alternately filled at the top and emptied at the bottom. The
new electric system, built in the 1960s, runs every ten to fifteen
minutes until around 11.30pm – tickets are the same as for the rest of
the public transport system. As the carriages pass each other at the
halfway station of Nebozízek, you can get out and visit the restaurant
of the same name, where the food and views are spectacular day and
night.

## Along the Hunger Wall

At the top of the hill, it's possible to trace the southernmost perimeter
wall of the old city – popularly known as the **Hunger Wall** (Hladová
zeď) – as it creeps eastwards back down to Újezd, and northwestwards
to the Strahov Monastery. Instigated in the 1460s by Charles IV, it has
been much lauded (especially by the Communists) as a great public
work which provided employment for the burgeoning ranks of the
city's destitute (hence its name); in fact, much of the wall's construction was paid for by the expropriation of Jewish property.

Follow the wall northwest and you come to the aromatic **Růžový
sad** (rose garden), laid out in front of Petřín's **observatory**
(Hvězdárna; hours vary enormously month by month), which offers a
range of telescopes for use by the city's amateur astronomers. On the
other side of the wall is Palliardi's twin-towered church of **sv Vavřinec**
(St Lawrence), from which derives the German name for Petřín Hill –
Laurenziberg. Dotted along the nearby paths are the Stations of the
Cross, culminating in the sgraffitoed Calvary Chapel, just beyond the
church.

Opposite the church are a series of buildings from the 1891
Exhibition, starting with the diminutive **Eiffel Tower** (Rozhledna; daily
11am–11pm), a hexagonal interpretation – though a mere fifth of the
size – of the tower which shocked Paris in 1889, and a tribute to the
city's strong cultural and political links with Paris at the time; naturally, the view from the public gallery is terrific in fine weather. The
next building along is an idealised neo-Gothic bastion, its interior
converted into a **Maze** (Bludiště; April–Oct daily 9am–6pm), a stroke
of infantile genius by the exhibition organisers. The humour of the
convex and concave mirrors inside is so simple, it has both adults and
kids giggling away. The maze also contains an action-packed, life-sized
diorama of the Prague students' and Jews' victory over the Swedes on
the Charles Bridge in 1648.

From the tower, the path contours round to the northwest, giving
great views over Petřín's palatial orchards and a sea of red tiles until it
ducks under the perimeter wall of the Strahov Monastery (see p.75). In
the opposite direction, south of the Hunger Wall, the woods of Petřín
continue into Smíchov (see p.160).

# Chapter 4

# Staré Město

S TARÉ MĚSTO, literally the "Old Town", is Prague's most central, vital ingredient. People live, work and sleep here; many of the capital's best markets, shops, restaurants and pubs are located in the area; and during the day a gaggle of shoppers and tourists fills its narrow streets. The district is bounded on one side by the river, on the other by the arc of Národní, Na příkopě and Revoluční, and at its heart is **Staroměstské náměstí**, Prague's showpiece main square, easily the most magnificent in central Europe.

Merchants and craftsmen began settling in what is now Staré Město as early as the tenth century, and in the mid-thirteenth century it was granted town status, with jurisdiction over its own affairs. The fire of 1541, which ripped through the quarters on the other side of the river, never reached Staré Město, though the 1689 conflagration made up for it. Nevertheless, fewer houses were built and destroyed here than by the nobles who colonised the left bank, and apart from the Jesuits' power-house, the Klementinum, and the largely reconstructed Jewish Quarter that sits within the old town (see Chapter 5), the medieval street plan remains intact. But like so much of Prague, Staré Město is still, on the surface, overwhelmingly Baroque, built literally on top of its Gothic predecessor to guard against the floods which plagued the town.

## From the Charles Bridge to Celetná

In their explorations of Staré Město, most people unknowingly retrace the **králová cesta**, the traditional route of the coronation procession from the Prašná brána to the Hrad, established by the Přemyslids, and followed, with a few minor variations, by every king until the Emperor Ferdinand IV in 1836, the last of the Habsburgs to bother having himself crowned in Prague. It's also the most direct route from the Charles Bridge to the main square, Staroměstské náměstí, and therefore a natural choice. However, many of the real treasures of Staré Město lie away from the *králová cesta*, so if you want to escape the crowds, it's worth heading off into the quarter's silent, twisted matrix of streets, and simply follow your nose.

# The Charles Bridge (Karlův most)

The Charles Bridge – which for over four hundred years was the only link between the two halves of Prague – is by far the city's most familiar monument. It's an impressive piece of medieval engineering, aligned slightly askew between two mighty Gothic gateways, but its fame is due almost entirely to the magnificent Baroque statues, additions to the original structure, that punctuate its length. Individually, only a few of the works are outstanding, but taken collectively, set against the backdrop of the Hrad, the effect is breathtaking.

The bridge was begun in 1357 to replace an earlier structure after this was swept away by one of the Vltava's frequent floods in 1342. Charles IV commissioned his young German court architect, Peter Parler, to carry out the work, which was finally completed in the early fifteenth century. For four hundred years thereafter it was known simply as the Prague or Stone Bridge – only in 1870 was it officially named after its patron. Since 1950, the bridge has been closed to vehicles, and is now one of the most popular places to hang out, day and night; apart from the steady stream of sightseers, the niches created by the bridge-piers provide space for souvenir hawkers, buskers, punks and politicos.

A bronze crucifix has stood on the bridge since its construction, but the first sculpture wasn't added until 1683, when St John of Nepomuk appeared. His statue was such a success with the church authorities that another 21 were added between 1698 and 1713. These included works by Prague's leading Baroque sculptors, led by Matthias Bernhard Braun and Maximilian Brokoff; the Max brothers unimaginatively filled in the remaining piers in the mid-nineteenth century. The original sculptures, mostly crafted in sandstone, have weathered badly over the years and are gradually being replaced by copies.

The following account of the statuary starts from the Malá Strana side, where two unequal **bridge towers**, connected by a castellated arch, form the entrance to the bridge. The smaller, stumpy tower was once part of the original Judith Bridge (named after the wife of Vladislav I, who built the twelfth-century original); the taller of the two, crowned by one of the pinnacled wedge-spires more commonly associated with Prague's right bank, can be climbed for a bird's-eye view (daily 10am–5/6pm).

---

**Building the bridge**

There are countless legends regarding the bridge's initial construction: the most persistent is that the builders mixed eggs (and, in some versions, wine) with the mortar to strengthen it. Having quickly depleted the city's egg supply, orders were sent out for contributions from the surrounding villages: the villagers of Velvary, who were worried that raw eggs wouldn't have quite the right consistency, hard-boiled theirs, and from Unhošť were sent curd, cheese and milk to bond the bricks even harder.

---

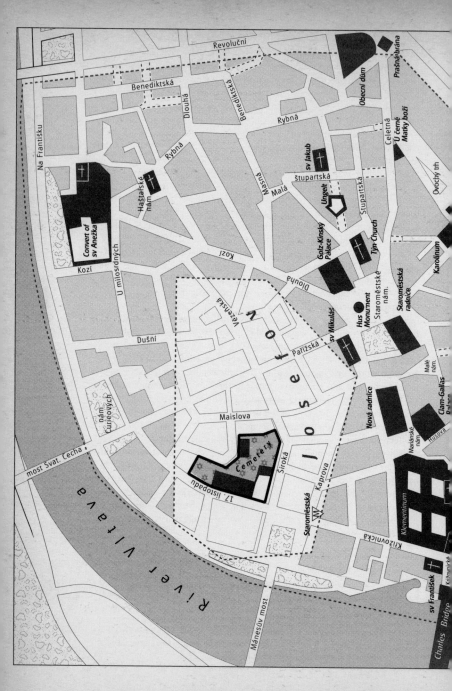

Revoluční

Benediktská

Na Františku

Dlouhá

Benediktská

Rybná

Rybná

Obecní dům

Prašná brána

Celetná

Ú černé Matky boží

Masná

Malá

štupartská

sv Jakub

štupartská

Stupartská

Ovocný trh

Haštalské nám.

Ungelt

Convent of sv Anežka

Golz-Kinsky Palace

Týn Church

Karolinum

Kozí

Kozí

U milosrdných

Dlouhá

Staroměstské nám.

Staroměstská radnice

Hus Monument

Dušní

Věžeňská

sv Mikuláš

Pařížská

Maislova

Nová radnice

Malé nám.

Clam-Gallas Palace

Mariánské nám.

Husova

nám. Curieových

Cemetery

Josefov

most Svat. Čecha

Široká

17. listopadu

Klementinum

Staroměstská

Kaprova

Křížovnická

River Vltava

sv František

Křížovnická

Mánesův most

Charles Bridge

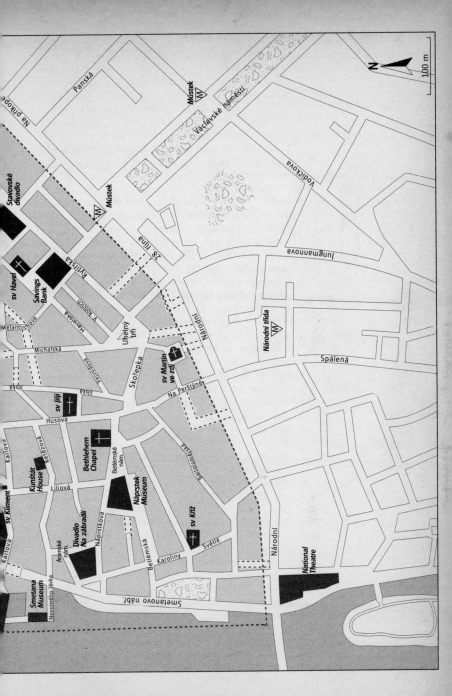

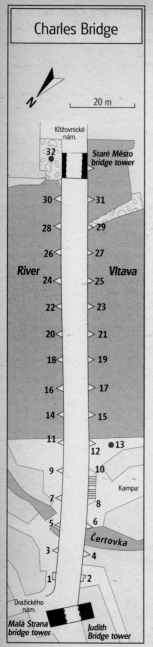

## Charles Bridge

N

20 m

Křížovnické nám.

32

Staré Město bridge tower

30 — >31

28 — >29

26 — >27

**River**

24 — >25

**Vltava**

22 — >23

20 — >21

18 — >19

16 — >17

14 — >15

11

12 ● 13

9 — 10

Kampa

7 — 8

5 — 6

Čertovka

3 — >4

1 — ?2

Dražického nám.

**Malá Strana bridge tower**

**Judith Bridge tower**

## The statues

In the first statue group on the left, paid for by the university medical faculty, Jesus is flanked by **Saint Cosmas and Saint Damian (1)**, both dressed in medieval doctors' garb – they were renowned for offering their medical services free of charge to the poor. Opposite stands **Saint Wenceslas (2)**, added by Czech nationalists in the nineteenth century. On the next pier, Brokoff's **Saint Vitus (3)** is depicted as a Roman legionary, his foot being gently nibbled by one of the lions that went on to devour him in a Roman amphitheatre. Facing him is one of the most striking sculptural groups **(4)**, again by Brokoff: Saints John of Matha, Ivan, Felix of Valois and his pet stag, founders of the **Trinitarian Order**, whose good works included ransoming persecuted Christians – three petrified souls can be seen through the prison bars below – from the infidels, represented by a bored Turkish jailor and his rabid dog.

Amid all the blackened sandstone, the lightly coloured figure of the (at the time) only recently canonised Servite friar, **Saint Philip Benizi (5)**, stands out as the only marble statue on the bridge. At his feet sits the papal crown, which he refused to accept when it was offered to him in 1268. Opposite stands Prague's second bishop, the youthful **Saint Adalbert (6)**, who was hounded out of the city on more than one occasion by the blissfully pagan citizens of Prague. Another recently canonised saint is **Cajetan (7)**, founder of the Theatine Order (and of a whole chain of non-profit-making pawnshops in Naples), who stands in front of a column of cherubs sporting a sacred heart.

One of the most successful statues is that of the blind Cistercian nun, **Saint Lutgard (8)**, sculpted by Braun when he was just twenty-six years old. She is depicted here in the middle of her celebrated vision, in which Christ appeared to show off his wounds. The Augustinians sponsored the next duo: **Saint Augustine (9)**, and one his later followers, **Saint Nicholas of Tolentino (10)**, who is dishing out bread to the poor. On the top-floor balcony of the house immediately behind Saint Nicholas of Tolentino is a strange collection of objects – a Madonna, a mangle and a lantern. The story goes that the Madonna was retrieved from the river during a particularly bad flood, and saved the house from further inundation; she went on to save a washerwoman whose sleeves got caught in the mangle; as for the lantern, if it goes out while you're passing by, it means you'll die within the year.

Next pier along, the apostle **Saint Jude Thaddaeus (11)**, patron saint of those in dire straits, holds the club with which the pagans beat him to death. On the opposite side, the Dominican friar **Saint Vincent Ferrer (12)** stands over one of his converts to self-flagellation, while the inscription below lists his final conversion total – 8000 Muslims and 25,000 Jews, not to mention countless demons. He is joined on his pedestal, somewhat inexplicably, by Bohemia's best-loved hermit, **Saint Procopius**. If you look over the side of the bridge at this point, you'll see a nineteenth-century sculpture of **Roland (13)** – known as *Bruncvík* in Czech – brandishing his miraculous golden sword.

The Franciscan pier – **Saint Anthony of Padua (14)**, and a lifeless nineteenth-century figure of **Saint Francis of Assisi**, accompanied by two angels **(15)** – is worth passing over to reach the bridge's earliest and most popular sculpture, **Saint John of Nepomuk (16)**. The only bronze statue on the bridge, it's now green with age, the gold-leaf halo of stars and palm branch gently blowing in the breeze. Saint John's appearance in 1683, on the bridge from which he was thrown to his death, was part of the Jesuits' persistent campaign to have him canonised; the statue later inspired hundreds of copies, which adorn bridges throughout central Europe. On the base, there's a bronze relief depicting his martyrdom, the figure of John now extremely worn through years of being touched for good luck. Facing Saint John is Bohemia's first martyr, a rather androgenous version of **Saint Ludmilla (17)**, holding the veil with which she was smothered and standing alongside her grandson, Saint Wenceslas, here depicted as a young child; his future martyrdom is recounted in the base relief (for more on Wenceslas and co, see p.64).

*For the story of Saint John of Nepomuk's martyrdom, see p.65*

With the exception of the Jesuit general **Saint Francis Borgia (19)**, the next two piers are glum nineteenth-century space-fillers: a trio of Bohemian saints – **Norbert**, **Sigismund** and, for the third time, **Wenceslas (18)** – followed by **John the Baptist (20)** and **Saint Christopher (21)**. Between the piers, on the left, a small bronze cross is set into the wall, marking the spot where John of Nepomuk was dumped in the river (see above). In 1890, the two Jesuit statues on the next pier were swept away by a flood: the statue of the founder of the order, Saint Ignatius Loyola, was replaced with the most recent additions to the bridge (completed in 1938), **saints Cyril and Methodius (22)**, the ninth-century missionaries who first introduced Christianity to the Slavs; the other, the Jesuit missionary **Saint Francis Xavier (23)**, survived the order's unpopularity and was replaced by a copy. This is one of the more unusual sculptural groups on the bridge: the saint, who worked in India and the Far East, is held aloft by three Moorish and two "Oriental" converts; Brokoff placed himself on the saint's left side.

Next in line are **Jesus**, **Mary**, and Mary's mother, **Saint Anne (24)**, and, facing them, **Joseph (25)**, a nineteenth-century replacement for another Brokoff, this time destroyed by gunfire during the 1848 revolution. The **Crucifixion** scene **(26)** is where the original fourteenth-century crucifix stood alone on the bridge for two hundred years. The gold-leaf, Hebrew inscription, "Holy, Holy, Holy Lord", was added in 1696, paid for by a Prague Jew who was ordered to do so by the city court, having been found guilty of blasphemy before the cross. Apart from Christ himself, all the figures, and the **Pietà** opposite (27), were added by the Max brothers.

On the penultimate pier, the Dominicans placed their founder, **Saint Dominic**, and their other leading light, **Saint Thomas Aquinas**, beside the **Madonna** (28); in amongst the cherubs is the order's emblem, a dog with a burning torch in his mouth. Opposite, **Saint Barbara**, the patron saint of miners, whose beautifully sculpted hands so impressed Kafka, is accompanied by **Saint Margaret** and **Saint Elizabeth** (29). There's one final Madonna (30), this time presiding over the kneeling figure of Saint Bernard, and a bubbling mass of cherubs mucking about with the instruments of the Passion – the cock, the dice and the centurion's gauntlet. Lastly, **Saint Ivo** (31), patron saint of lawyers, stands with an outstretched hand, into which Prague law students traditionally place a glass of beer after their finals.

### The Staré Město bridge tower

On the Staré Město side is arguably the finest **bridge tower** of the lot, its eastern facade still encrusted in Gothic cake-like decorations from Peter Parler's workshop, plus a series of mini-sculptures: the central figures are Saint Vitus, flanked by Charles IV on the right and his son, Václav IV, on the left; above stand two of Bohemia's patron saints, Adalbert and Sigismund. The severed heads of ten of the Protestant leaders were displayed here following the executions on Staroměstské náměstí in 1621, and, in 1648, it was the site of the last battle of the Thirty Years' War, fought between the besieging Swedes and an ad hoc army of Prague's students and Jews, which trashed the western facade of the bridge tower.

## Křižovnické náměstí to Malé náměstí

Pass under the Staré Město bridge tower and you're in **Křižovnické náměstí**, an awkward space hemmed in by its constituent buildings, and a dangerous spot for unwary pedestrians. Hard by the bridge tower is a nineteenth-century cast-iron statue of **Charles IV** (32), erected on the 500th anniversary of his founding of the university, and designed by a German, Ernst Julius Hähnel, in the days before the reawakening of Czech sculpture. To his left is an unusual plaque commemorating a Czech who was shot by mistake by the Red Army during the battles of May 1945.

The two churches on the square are both quite striking. The half-brick church of **sv František** (St Francis) was built by Jean-Baptiste Mathey for the Order of Knights of the Cross with a Red Star, the original gatekeepers of the old Judith Bridge, who were at the zenith of their power in the seventeenth century, when they supplied most of the archbishops of Prague. The single dome plan and rich marble furnishings inside are both untypical in Prague. Over the road is the church of **sv Salvátor**, its facade prickling with blackened saints which are lit up enticingly at night. Built between 1578 and 1602, sv Salvátor marks the beginning of the Jesuits' rise to power and, like many of their churches, is designed along the lines of the Gesù church in Rome. It's worth a quick look, if only for the frothy stucco work and delicate ironwork in its triple-naved interior.

## Along Karlova

Running from Křižovnické náměstí all the way to Malé náměstí is the narrow street of **Karlova**, packed with people winding their way towards Staroměstské náměstí, their attention divided between checking out the waffle stalls and souvenir shops, and not losing their way. At the first wiggle in Karlova, you come to the **Vlašská kaple** (Italian Chapel), which served the community of Italian masons, sculptors and painters who settled in Prague during the Renaissance period, and is still, strictly speaking, the property of the Italian state. Further down, at the junction with Liliová, is U **zlatého hada** (The Golden Serpent), where the Armenian Deomatus Damajan opened the city's first coffee house in 1708. According to legend, the café was always full, not least because Damajan had a red-wine fountain inside. It's still a café now, though sadly minus the fountain and its original furnishings.

## The Klementinum

As they stroll down Karlova, few people notice the **Klementinum**, the former Jesuit College on the north side of the street, which covers an area second in size only to the Hrad. In 1556, Ferdinand I summoned the Jesuits to Prague to help bolster the Catholic cause in Bohemia, giving them the church of sv Kliment (see below), which Dientzenhofer later rebuilt for them. Initially, the Jesuits proceeded with caution, but once the Counter-Reformation set in, they were put in control of the whole university and provincial education system. From their secure base at sv Kliment, they began to establish space for a great Catholic seat of learning in the city by buying up the surrounding land, demolishing over 32 old town houses, and, over the next two hundred years, gradually building themselves a palatial headquarters. In 1773, soon after it was completed, the Jesuits were turfed out of the country and the Klementinum handed over to the university authorities.

Nowadays the Klementinum houses the National Library's collection of over five million volumes, but much of the original building has been left intact. The **entrance** is inconspicuously placed just past the church of sv Kliment; it's easy enough just to walk past the caretakers – they'll probably allow you in anyway, but are unlikely to speak anything but Czech. Once inside, there are several ornate corridors worth checking out, but the chief attraction is the old **Music Library**

(Hudební oddělení) on the first floor, filled with leather tomes, ancient globes and lovely frescoes. In the same wing there are temporary exhibitions of some of the library's prize possessions, which include the world's largest collection of works by the early English reformer, Yorkshireman John Wycliffe, whose writings had an enormous impact on the fourteenth-century Czech religious community, inspiring preachers like Hus to speak out against the social conditions of the time.

At roughly the centre of the Klementinum complex is the **observatory tower** from where seventeenth-century Prague's most illustrious visiting scientist, Johannes Kepler, did his planet-gazing. A religious exile from his native Germany, Kepler succeeded Tycho de Brahe as court astronomer to Rudolf II, and lived at no. 4 Karlova for a number of years, during which time he drew up the first laws on the movement of the planets.

The church of **sv Kliment** (St Clement) itself can also be visited: its opening hours are erratic – the entrance is alongside the Vlašská kaple – but if you do get in, you'll find a spectacular set of frescoes depicting the life of Saint Clement (whose fate was to be lashed to an anchor and hurled into the Black Sea), and an unusual modern screen added by its new owners, the eastern rites Uniate Church (*Řecko-katolický*).

## Mariánské náměstí and around
Where the Klementinum ends, the corner house **U zlaté studné** (The Golden Well), now a flashy wine bar, stands out like a wedge of cheese; its thick stucco reliefs of assorted saints were commissioned by the owner in gratitude for having been spared the plague.

A short diversion here, left down Seminářská, brings you out onto **Mariánské náměstí**, generally fairly deserted compared to Karlova. It's hard to believe that the **Nová radnice** (New Town Hall), on the east side of the square, was built by Osvald Polívka, architect of the exuberant Art-Nouveau Obecní dům (see p.130). Its most striking features are the two gargantuan figures which stand guard at either corner, by the sculptor of the Hus Monument, Ladislav Šaloun. The one on the left, looking like Darth Vader, is the "Iron Knight", mascot of the armourers' guild; to the right is the somewhat grotesquely caricatured sixteenth-century Jewish sage and scholar, Rabbi Löw, who was visited by Death on several occasions, but allowed to live to the ripe old age of ninety-six, provided he did not stray from his religious studies – here, a naked woman tries unsuccessfully to attract his attentions. To get back to Karlova, head down Husova, and try not to miss the Baroque **Clam-Gallas Palace** (Clam-Gallasův palác), which, despite its size – it takes up a good five or six old houses – is easy to overlook in this narrow space. Although it's a typically lavish affair by the Viennese architect Fischer von Erlach, only the big and burly *Atlantes* supporting the portals generally attract the attention of passers-by.

*For the full story of Rabbi Löw, see p.113*

### Malé náměstí

After a couple more boutiques, hole-in-the-wall bars and a final twist in Karlova, you emerge onto **Malé náměstí**, a square originally settled by French merchants in the twelfth century. The square was also home to the first pharmacy in Prague, opened by a Florentine in 1353, and the tradition is continued today by the *lékárna* at no. 13, which boasts chandeliers and a restored Baroque interior. Two doors up, there's no fear of missing the *American Hospitality Centre*, set up within months of the Velvet Revolution. The square's best known building, though, is the russet-red, neo-Renaissance **Rott Haus**, previously an ironmongers' shop belonging to the Rott family – a building which immediately catches the eye, smothered in agricultural scenes and motifs inspired by the Czech artist Mikuláš Aleš. The original house sign of three white roses has been preserved on the central gable.

From the
Charles Bridge
to Celetná

## Staroměstské náměstí

East of Malé náměstí is **Staroměstské náměstí** (Old Town Square), easily the most spectacular square in Prague, and the traditional heart of the city. Most of the brightly coloured houses look solidly eighteenth-century, but their Baroque facades hide considerably older buildings. From the eleventh century onwards, this was the city's main marketplace, known simply as Velké náměstí (Great Square), to which all roads in Bohemia led, and where merchants from all over Europe gathered. When the five towns that made up Prague were united in 1784, it was the square's town hall that was made the seat of the new city council, and for the next two hundred years the square was the scene of the country's most violent demonstrations and battles. For a long time now, the whole place has been closed to traffic, the cafés have spread out their tables and the tourists have poured in to watch the town hall clock chime, to sit on the steps of the Hus Monument, and to drink in this historic showpiece.

### The Hus Monument

The most recent arrival in the square is the colossal **Jan Hus Monument**, a turbulent sea of blackened bodies – the oppressed to his right, the defiant to his left – out of which rises the majestic moral authority of Hus himself, gazing into the horizon. For the sculptor Ladislav Šaloun, a maverick who received no formal training, the monument was his life's work, commissioned in 1900 when the Viennese Secession was at its peak, but strangely old-fashioned by the time it was completed in 1915. It would be difficult to claim that it blends in with its Baroque surroundings, yet this has never mattered to the Czechs, for whom its significance goes far beyond aesthetic merit.

Its unveiling on July 6, 1915, the 500th anniversary of the death of Hus, was accompanied by boisterous nationalist outbursts. Draped in swastikas by the invading Nazis in March 1939, and in black by Praguers in August 1968, when the Soviets marched in, it has always

*For a brief
biography of Jan
Hus, see p.106*

been a powerful symbol of the Czech nation. The inscription along the base is a quote from *The Will of Comenius*, one of his later followers, and includes Hus' most famous dictum, *Pravda vítězí* (Truth Prevails), which has been the motto of just about every Czech revolution since then.

### The Staroměstská radnice

It wasn't until the reign of King John of Luxembourg (1310–46) that Staré Město was allowed to build its own town hall, the **Staroměstská radnice**. Short of funds, the citizens decided against an entirely new structure, buying a corner house on the square instead and simply adding an extra floor; later on, they added the east wing, with its graceful Gothic oriel and obligatory wedge-tower. Gradually, over the centuries, the neighbouring merchants' houses to the west were incorporated into the building, so that now it stretches all the way across to the richly sgraffitoed **Dům U minuty**, which juts out into the square.

On May 8, 1945, on the final day of the Prague Uprising, the Nazis still held on to Staroměstské náměstí, and in a last desperate act set fire to the town hall – one of the few buildings to be irrevocably damaged in the last war. The tower was rebuilt immediately, but of the rest of the neo-Gothic east wing, which stretched almost to the church of sv Mikuláš, only a crumbling fragment remains; the rest of it is marked by a small stretch of grass. Embedded in the wall of the tower is a plaque marked "Dukla", and a case containing a handful of earth from the Slovak pass where some 80,000 Soviet and Czechoslovak soldiers lost their lives in the first battle to liberate the country in October 1944. Below, set into the paving, are 27 **white crosses** commemorating the Protestant leaders who were condemned to death on the orders of the Emperor Ferdinand II, following the Battle of Bílá hora. They were publicly executed in the square on June 21, 1621: twenty-four enjoyed the nobleman's privilege and had their heads lopped off; the three remaining commoners were hung, drawn and quartered.

Today, the town hall's most popular feature is its *orloj* or **Astronomical Clock** – every hour, a crowd of tourists and Praguers gather in front of the tower to watch a mechanical performance by the clock's assorted figures. The Apostles shuffle past the top two windows, bowing to the audience, while perched on pinnacles below are the four threats to the city as perceived by the medieval mind: Death carrying his hourglass and tolling his bell, the Jew with his moneybags, Vanity admiring his reflection, and a turbaned Turk shaking his head. Beneath the moving figures, four characters representing virtues stand motionless throughout the performance. Finally, a cockerel pops out and flaps its wings to signal that the show's over; the clock then chimes the hour.

The clock itself has been here since the beginning of the fifteenth century; the working figures were added in 1490 by a **Master Hanuš** who, legend has it, was then blinded with a red-hot poker by the town councillors, to make sure he couldn't repeat the job for anyone else. In retaliation, he groped his way around the clock, succeeded in stopping it, and then promptly died of a heart attack – the clock stayed broken for over eighty years.

The powder-pink facade on the south side of the town hall now forms the **entrance** to the whole complex (daily March–Oct 8am–6pm; Nov–Feb 8am–5pm). As long as at least five people turn up, a thirty-minute guided tour of the four rooms that survived the last war sets off every hour, when the clock has finished striking. It was in these rooms that the Bohemian kings were elected until the Habsburgs established hereditary rule and in 1422 Jan Želivský, the fiery Hussite preacher and inspiration behind Prague's first defenestration (see p.134), was executed here. Despite being steeped in history, there's not much of interest here, apart from a few decorated ceilings, striped with chunky beams, and a couple of Renaissance portals. You'll probably get more enjoyment from climbing the tower – with access for the disabled – for the panoramic sweep across Prague's spires.

### The church of sv Mikuláš
The destruction of the east wing of the town hall in 1945 rudely exposed Kilian Ignaz Dientzenhofer's church of **sv Mikuláš** (Tues, Wed & Fri 10am–1pm, Thurs 2–5pm), built in just three years between 1732 and 1735. The original church was founded by German merchants in the thirteenth century, and served as Staré Město's parish church until the Týn Church (see below) was completed. Later, it was handed over to the Benedictines, who commissioned Dientzenhofer to replace it with the present building. His hand is obvious: the south front is decidedly luscious – painted in brilliant white, with Braun's blackened statuary popping up at every cornice – promising an interior to surpass even its sister church of sv Mikuláš in Malá Strana, which Dientzenhofer built with his father immediately afterwards (see p.80).

Inside, however, it's a curious mixture. Although caked in the usual mixture of stucco and fresco, the church has been stripped over the years of much of its ornament and lacks the sumptuousness of its namesake on the left bank. This is partly due to the fact that Joseph II closed down the monastery and turned the church into a storehouse, and partly because it's now owned by the very "low", modern, Czechoslovak Hussite Church.

### The rest of the square
The largest secular building on the square is the Rococo **Golz-Kinský Palace**, designed by Kilian Ignaz Dientzenhofer and built by his son-in-law Anselmo Lurago. In the nineteenth century it became a German *Gymnasium*, which was attended by Kafka (whose father ran a haberdashery shop on the ground floor). The palace is perhaps most notorious, however, as the venue for the fateful speech by the Communist

prime minister, Klement Gottwald, who walked out on to the grey stone balcony one snowy February morning in 1948, flanked by his Party henchmen, to address the thousands of enthusiastic supporters who packed the square below. It was the beginning of *Vitězná února* (Victorious February), the bloodless coup which brought the Communists to power and sealed the fate of the country for the next forty-one years. The top floor now houses the National Gallery's specialist exhibitions of graphic art, but the entire palace was recently purchased by the Kafka Society who plan to turn it eventually into a vast museum and library dedicated to Kafka.

*Gottwald's
appearance forms
the opening to
Milan Kundera's
novel* The Book of
Laughter and
Forgetting; *see
Books, p.258*

Until recently, the Dům U kamenného zvonu (House at the Stone Bell) was much like any other of the merchant houses that line Staroměstské náměstí – covered in a thick icing of Baroque plaster-work and topped by a undistinguished roof gable. In the 1970s, however, it was stripped down to its Gothic core, uncovering the original honey-coloured stonework and simple wedge roof, and it now serves as a superb central venue for modern art exhibitions, lectures and concerts.

The south side of the square boasts a fine array of facades, mostly Baroque, with the notable exception of the neo-Renaissance **Storch House**, adorned with a sgraffito painting by Mikuláš Aleš. Next door, **U bílého jednorožce** (The White Unicorn) is the site of Prague's famous *salon*, run by Berta Fanta. An illustrious membership, including Kafka, Max Brod and Franz Werfel, came here to attend talks given by, among others, Albert Einstein and Rudolf Steiner.

### The Týn Church and Ungelt

Staré Město's most impressive Gothic structure, the mighty **Týn Church** (Panna Marie před Týnem), whose two irregular towers rise like giant antennae above the arcaded houses which otherwise obscure its facade, is a building of far more confidence than sv Mikuláš. Like the nearby Hus monument, the Týn Church, begun in the fourteenth century, is a source of Czech national pride. In an act of proud defiance, George of Poděbrady, the last Czech and the only Hussite King of Bohemia, adorned the high stone gable with a statue of himself and a giant gilded *kalich* (chalice), the mascot of all Hussite sects. The church remained a hotbed of Hussitism until the Protestants' crushing defeat at the Battle of Bílá hora, after which the chalice was melted down to provide a newly ensconced statue of the Virgin Mary with a golden halo, sceptre and crown.

Despite being one of the main landmarks of Staré Město, it's well-nigh impossible to appreciate the church from anything but a consider-able distance, since it's boxed in by the houses around it, some of which are actually built right against the walls. At the moment, its opening hours are restricted to the evening mass around 6pm, so you may well find it closed; to reach the entrance, take the third arch on the left, which passes under the Venetian gables of the former Týn School.

Given the church's significance, it's sad that the interior is mostly dingy, unwelcoming and in need of repair, with little of the feel of the original Gothic structure surviving the church's ferocious Catholicisation. One exception is the fine north portal and canopy, which bears the hallmark of Peter Parler's workshop; the fifteenth-century pulpit also stands out from the dark morass of black and gold Baroque altarpieces, its panels enhanced by some sensitive nineteenth-century icons. The pillar on the right of the chancel steps contains the marble tomb of Tycho de Brahe, the famous Danish astronomer who arrived in Prague wearing a silver and gold false nose, having lost his own in a duel in Denmark. Court astronomer to Rudolf II for just two years, Brahe laid much of the groundwork for Johannes Kepler's later discoveries – Kepler getting his chance of employment when Brahe died of a burst bladder after one of Petr Vok's notorious binges in 1601.

Behind the Týn Church lies the Týn Court or Ungelt, which, as the trading base of eastern merchants, was one of the first settlements on the Vltava. A hospice, church and hostel were built for the use of the merchants, and by the fourteenth century the area had become an extremely successful international marketplace; soon afterwards the traders moved up to the Hrad, and the court was transformed into a palace. At the time of writing it is undergoing restoration work, and rumour has it that a large part of the complex is destined to become a hotel.

## Celetná and around

Celetná, whose name comes from the bakers who used to bake a particular type of small loaf (*calty*) here in the Middle Ages, leads east from Staroměstské náměstí direct to the Prašná brána, one of the original gateways of the old town. It's one of the oldest streets in Prague, lying along the former trade route from the old town market square, as well as on the *králová cesta*. Its buildings were smartly refaced in the Baroque period, and their pastel shades are now crisply maintained. Most of Celetná's shops veer towards the chic end of the Czech market, making it a popular place for a bit of window-shopping, but the spruced-up surroundings are only skin-deep. Dive down one of the covered passages to the left and you're soon in Staré Město's more usual, dilapidated backstreets.

Two-thirds of the way along Celetná, at the junction with Ovocný trh, is the Dům U černé Matky boží (House at the Black Madonna), one of the best examples of Czech Cubist architecture, built in 1911–12 by Josef Gočár. It was a short-lived style, whose most surprising attribute, in this instance, is its ability to adapt existing Baroque motifs: Gočár's house sits much more happily amongst its eighteenth-century neighbours than, for example, the functionalist Baťa shoe-shop opposite – one of Gočár's later designs from the 1930s.

*There are a number of other Cubist houses in Prague, see Chapter 7*

Celetná ends at the fourteenth-century Prašná brána, beyond
which is náměstí Republiky (see Chapter 6), at which point, strictly
speaking, you've left Staré Město behind. Sticking to the old town for
the moment, head north into the backstreets which conceal the
bubbling, stucco facade of the Franciscan church of sv Jakub, on Malá
Štupartská. Its massive Gothic proportions – it has the longest nave in
Prague after the cathedral – make it a favourite venue for organ recitals, Mozart masses and other concerts. After the great fire of 1689,
Prague's Baroque artists remodelled the entire interior, adding huge
pillasters, a series of colourful frescoes and over twenty side altars.
The most famous of these is the tomb of the Count of Mitrovice, in the
northern aisle, designed by Fischer von Erlach and Prague's own
Maximilian Brokoff.

The church has close historical links with the butchers of Prague,
who were given the first chapel on the left in gratitude for their
defence of the city in 1611 and 1648. Hanging from the west wall,
close to the chapel, is a thoroughly decomposed human forearm. It has
been there for over four hundred years now, ever since a thief tried to
steal the jewels of the Madonna from the high altar. As the thief
reached out, the Virgin supposedly grabbed his arm and refused to let
go. The next day the congregation of butchers had no option but to
lop it off, and it has hung there as a warning ever since.

## The Convent of sv Anežka

Further north through the backstreets, the Convent of sv Anežka (St
Agnes), Prague's oldest surviving Gothic building, stands within a
stone's throw of the river as it loops around to the east. It was founded
in 1233 as a convent for the Order of the Poor Clares, and named after
Agnes, youngest sister of King Václav I, who left her life of regal privilege to become the convent's first abbess. Agnes herself was beatified
in 1874 to try and combat the spread of Hussitism amongst the
Czechs, and there was much speculation about the wonders that would
occur when she was officially canonised, an event which finally took
place on November 12, 1989, when Czech Catholics were invited to a
special mass at St Peter's in Rome. Four days later the Velvet
Revolution began: a happy coincidence, even for agnostic Czechs.

The convent itself was closed down in 1782, and fell into rack and
ruin. It was squatted for most of the next century, and though saved
from demolition by the Czech nationalist lobby, its restoration only
took place in the 1980s. The convent now houses the National
Gallery's nineteenth-century Czech art collection (Tues–Sun 10am–
6pm), and if the art inside is not always of the highest quality, it is at
least interesting in terms of the Czech *národní obrození*, while the
building itself is also worth inspecting.

The well-preserved cloisters are filled with unremarkable
Bohemian glass, porcelain and pewter dating from the nineteenth
century; the fine art is housed in the three remaining chapels and

continues on the first floor. The predominant trend in Czech painting at this time was the depiction of events of national significance: favourite themes – on display in several works here – ranged from legendary figures such as Břetislav and Jitka to the real-life tragedy of the Battle of Bílá hora. Far superior to these in technique is the work of Josef Václav Myslbek, the grand master of Czech sculpture, whose simple statue of Saint Agnes from his *Monument to St Wenceslas* (see p.124) is the gallery's outstanding exhibit.

Upstairs, the rooms are dominated by the Romantic landscapes of Antonín Mánes, Josef Navrátil and Antonín Chittussi, which lovingly recreate the rolling hills of Bohemia. In the same vein, though they were to be more influential on later generations of Czech artists, are the portraits and landscapes of Josef Mánes, who took an active part in the 1848 disturbances in Prague and consistently espoused the nationalist cause in his paintings. The final room is given over to the graphics of Mikuláš Aleš, whose designs can be seen in the sgraffito on many of the city's nineteenth-century buildings.

*There's a much
more impressive
collection of
nineteenth- and
twentieth-century
sculpture in
Zbraslav, see
p.161*

# Southern Staré Město

The southern half of Staré Město is a triangular wedge bounded by the *králová cesta* and the curve of Národní and Na příkopě, which follow the course of the old fortifications. There are no showpiece squares like Staroměstské náměstí here, but the complex web of narrow lanes and hidden passageways, many of which have changed little since medieval times, make this an intriguing quarter to explore.

## From Ovocný trh to Uhelný trh

Heading southwest from the Dům U černé Matky boží on Celetná, you enter **Ovocný trh**, site of the old fruit market, its cobbles recently restored along with the lime-green and white **Stavovské divadlo** (Estates Theatre), which lies at the end of the marketplace. Built in the early 1780s by Prague's large and powerful German community, the theatre is one of the finest Neoclassical buildings in Prague, reflecting the enormous self-confidence of its patrons. It is also something of a mecca for Mozart fans, since it was here rather than in the hostile climate of Vienna that the composer chose to premiere both *Don Giovanni* and *La Clemenza di Tito*. This is, in fact, the only opera house in Europe which remains intact from Mozart's time, a major factor in Miloš Forman's decision to film the concert scenes for his Oscar-laden *Amadeus* here.

*For more on
Mozart's time in
Prague, see p.81*

On the north side of the Stavovské divadlo is the **Karolinum** or Charles University, named for its founder Charles IV, who established it in 1348 as the first university in this part of Europe. Although it was open to all nationalities, with instruction in Latin, it wasn't long before differences arose between the German-speaking students, who were in the majority, and the Czechs, who, with Jan Hus as their rector,

## The former Gottwald Museum

One block west of the Stavovské divadlo, at no. 29 Rytířská, is the former **Prague Savings Bank**, a large, pompous neo-Renaissance building designed in the 1890s by Osvald Polívka, before he went on to erect some of Prague's most flamboyant Art-Nouveau structures.

For over thirty years it housed the museum all Praguers loved to hate – dedicated to **Klement Gottwald**, the country's first Communist president. A joiner by trade, a notorious drunkard and womaniser by repute, he led the Party with unswerving faith from the beginnings of Stalinism in 1929 right through to the show trials of the early 1950s. He died shortly after attending Stalin's funeral in 1953 – either from grief or, more plausibly, from drink.

Remarkably, his reputation survived longer than that of any other East European leader. While those whom he had wrongfully sent to their deaths were posthumously rehabilitated, and the figure of Stalin denigrated, Gottwald remained sacred, his statue gracing every town in the country for the last forty-odd years. As recently as October 1989, the Communists were happily issuing brand new 100kčs notes emblazoned with his bloated face, only to have them withdrawn from circulation a month later, when the regime toppled.

Not surprisingly, the museum has closed and the building is once again a savings bank. It's worth a peek inside; go upstairs to the left and check out the main hall.

---

successfully persuaded Václav IV to curtail the privileges of the Germans. In protest, the Germans upped and left for Leipzig, the first of many ethnic problems which continued to bubble away throughout the university's six-hundred-year history until the forced expulsion of Germans after World War II.

To begin with, the university had no fixed abode; it wasn't until 1383 that Václav IV bought the present site. All that's left of the original fourteenth-century building is the Gothic oriel window which emerges from the south wall; the rest was trashed by the Nazis in 1945. The new main entrance is a peculiarly ugly red-brick curtain wall by Jaroslav Fragner, set back from the street and inscribed with the original Latin name *Universitas Karolina*. Only a couple of small departments and the rectorate are now housed here, with the rest spread over the length and breadth of the city. The heavily restored Gothic vaults of the south wing are now used as a public **art gallery** for contemporary Czech art.

### Around sv Havel

The junction of Melantrichova and Rytířská is always teeming with people pouring out of Staroměstské náměstí and heading for Wenceslas Square. Clearly visible from Melantrichova is the undulating Baroque facade of the church of **sv Havel**, sadly no relation to the playwright-president but named after the Irish monk, Saint Gall. It was built in the thirteenth century to serve the local German community who had been invited to Prague partly to replace the Jewish traders killed in the city's 1098 pogrom. After the expulsion of the

Protestants, the church was handed over to the Carmelites who rede-signed the interior, now only visible through an iron grille.

Straight ahead of you as you leave sv Havel is Prague's last surviv-ing open-air market – a poor relation of its Germanic predecessor, which stretched all the way from Ovocný trh to Uhelný trh. Traditionally a flower and vegetable market, it runs the full length of the arcaded Havelská, and sells everything from celery to CDs. The stalls on V kotcích, the narrow street parallel to Havelská, sell mainly clothes.

### Uhelný trh, sv Martin ve zdi and Bartolomějská

Both markets run west into Uhelný trh, which gets its name from the *uhlí* (coal) that was sold here in medieval times. South of Uhelný trh, down Martinská, the street miraculously opens out to make room for the twelfth-century church of sv Martin ve zdi (St Martin-in-the-Walls), originally built to serve the Czech community of sv Martin, until it found itself the wrong side of the Gothic fortifications when they were erected in the fourteenth century. It's still essentially a Romanesque structure, adapted to suit Gothic tastes a century later, and thoroughly restored at the beginning of this century by its present owners, the Czech Brethren, who added the creamy neo-Renaissance tower. For them, it has a special significance as the place where communion "in both kinds" (ie bread and wine), one of the fundamental demands of the Hussites, was first administered to the whole congregation, in 1414.

Around the corner from sv Martin ve zdi is the gloomy lifeless street of **Bartolomějská**, dominated by a tall, grim-looking building on its south side, which served as the main interrogation centre of the universally detested secret police, the *Státní bezpečnost*, or *StB*. Although now officially disbanded, the *StB* continues to be one of the most controversial issues of the post-revolutionary period. As in the rest of Eastern Europe, the accusations and revelations of who exactly collaborated with the *StB* have caused the downfall of a number of leading politicians right across the political spectrum. Up until the 1950s, the building was occupied by Franciscan nuns, a small number of whom have recently returned to try and exorcise the building, in order to continue where they left off some forty years ago.

## Betlémské náměstí

After leaving the dark shadows of Bartolomějská, the calm of Betlémské náměstí comes as a welcome relief. The square is named after the **Bethlehem Chapel** (Betlémská kaple), whose high wooden gables face on to the square. This was founded in 1391 by the leading Czech reformists of the day, who were denied the right to build a church, so proceeded instead to build the largest chapel in Bohemia, with a total capacity of 3000. Sermons were delivered not in the custo-mary Latin, but in the language of the masses – Czech. From 1402 to 1413, **Jan Hus** preached here (see below), regularly pulling in more

Southern Staré Město

STARÉ MĚSTO    105

than enough commoners to fill the chapel. Hus was eventually excommunicated for his outspokenness, found guilty of heresy and burnt at the stake at the Council of Constance in 1415.

The chapel continued to attract reformists from all over Europe for another two centuries – the leader of the German Peasants' Revolt, **Thomas Müntzer**, preached here in the sixteenth century – until the advent of the Counter-Reformation in Bohemia. Inevitably, the chapel was handed over to the Jesuits, who completely altered the original building, only for it to be demolished after they were expelled by the Habsburgs in 1773. What you see now (when it finally reopens after its most recent renovation) is a scrupulous reconstruction of the fourteenth-century building by Jaroslav Fragner, using the original plans and a fair amount of imaginative guesswork. The reconstruction work was carried out after the war by the Communists, who were keen to portray Hus as a Czech nationalist and social critic as much as a religious reformer, and, of course, to dwell on the revolutionary Müntzer's later appearances here.

*Náprstek's Asian
and Oriental
collections are
housed in the
chateau at
Liběchov, see
p.167*

At the western end of the square stands the **Náprstek Museum** (Náprstkovo muzeum; Tues–Sun 10am–noon & 1–6pm), whose founder, Vojta Náprstek, was inspired by the great Victorian museums of London while in exile following the 1848 revolution. On his return, he turned the family brewery into a museum, initially intending it to concentrate on the virtues of industrial progress. Náprstek's interests gradually shifted, however, and the museum now displays just his American, Australian and African collections; the original exhibits are now in the Technical Museum (see p.155).

---

### Jan Hus

The legendary preacher – and Czech national hero – **Jan Hus** (often anglicised to John Huss) was born in a small village in South Bohemia around 1369. From a childhood of poverty, he enjoyed a meteoric rise through the education system to become rector of Charles University in 1403. He was a controversial choice of candidate, since his radical sermons criticising the social conditions of the time had already caused a scandal in Prague the previous year.

Hus was not the first to draw attention to the plight of the city's poor, nor did he ever actually advocate many of the more famous tenets of the heretical religious movement that took his name – Hussitism. For example, he never advocated giving communion "in both kinds" – bread and wine – to the general congregation, nor did he ever denounce his Catholicism. In fact, it was his outspokenness against the sale of indulgences to fund papal wars that prompted his unofficial trial at the Council of Constance in 1415. He refused to renounce his beliefs and was burnt at the stake as a heretic, despite having been guaranteed safe conduct by Emperor Sigismund himself. The Czechs were outraged, and Hus became a national hero overnight, inspiring thousands to rebel against the authorities of the day. In 1965, the Vatican finally overturned the sentence, and the anniversary of his death is now a national holiday.

---

# Husova and around

Between Betlémské náměstí and Staroměstské náměstí lies a confusing maze of streets, passageways and backyards, containing few sights as such, but nevertheless a joy to explore. One building that might catch your eye is the church of **sv Jiljí** (St Giles), on Husova, whose outward appearance suggests another Gothic masterpiece, but whose interior is decked out in the familiar white and gold excess of the eighteenth century. The frescoes by Václav Vavřinec Reiner (who's buried in the church) are full of praise for his patrons, the Dominicans, who took over the church after the Protestant defeat of 1620. They were expelled, in turn, after the Communists took power, only to return following the events of 1989.

Reiner's paintings also depict the unhappy story of Giles himself, a ninth-century hermit who is thought to have lived somewhere in Provence. Out one day with his pet deer, Giles and his companion were chased by the hounds of King Wanda of the Visigoths. The hounds were rooted to the spot by an invisible power, while the arrow from the hunters struck Giles as he defended his pet – the hermit was later looked upon as the patron saint of cripples.

A short step away, just off Husova on Řetězová, is the **House of the Lords of Kunštát and Poděbrady** (Dům pánů z Konštátu a Poděbrad; Tues–Sun 10am–noon & 1–6pm), the home of George of Poděbrady before he became the Czechs' first and last Hussite king in 1458. It's not exactly gripping, but it does give you a clear impression of the antiquity of the houses in this area, and illustrates the way in which the new Gothic town was built on top of the old Romanesque one. Thus the floor on which you enter was originally the first floor of a twelfth-century palace, whose ground floor has been excavated in the cellars.

## To the waterfront

Continuing west along Řetězová and Anenská brings you eventually to the waterfront. On Anenské náměstí, just before you reach the river, is the **Divadlo na zábradlí** (Theatre at the Balustrade). In the 1960s, this became the centre of Prague's absurdist theatre scene, with Havel himself working first as a stagehand and later as resident playwright.

The gaily decorated neo-Renaissance building at the very end of Novotného lávka, on the riverfront itself, was once the city's waterworks but now houses a café-theatre and, on the first floor, the **Smetana Museum** (10am–5pm; closed Tues), of specialist interest only. Smetana, despite being a German-speaker, was without doubt the most nationalist of all the great Czech composers, taking an active part in the 1848 revolution and much of the later *narodní obrození*. Towards the end of his life he went deaf, and eventually died of syphilis in a mental asylum. Outside, beneath the large weeping willow that droops over the embankment, the statue of the seated Smetana is rather unfortunately placed, with his back towards one of his most famous sources of inspiration, the River Vltava (Moldau in German).

# Chapter 5

# Josefov

*It is crowded with horses; traversed by narrow streets not
remarkable for cleanliness, and has altogether an uninviting aspect.
Your sanitary reformer would here find a strong case of
overcrowding.*

Walter White,
"A July Holiday in Saxony, Bohemia and Silesia" (1857)

L ess than half a century after Walter White's comments, all that
was left of the former ghetto of **JOSEFOV** were six synagogues,
the town hall and the medieval cemetery. At the end of the nineteenth century, a period of great economic growth for the Empire, it
was decided that Prague should be turned into a beautiful bourgeois
city, modelled on Paris. The key to this transformation was the "sanitisation" of the ghetto, a process, begun in 1893, which reduced the
notorious malodorous backstreets and alleyways of Josefov to rubble
and replaced them with block after block of luxurious five-storey
mansions. The Jews, gypsies and prostitutes were cleared out and the
area became a desirable residential quarter, rich in Art-Nouveau buildings festooned with decorative murals, doorways and sculpturing – the
beginning of the end for a community which had existed in Prague for
almost a millennium.

In any other European city occupied by the Nazis in World War II,
what little was left of the old ghetto would have been demolished. But
although Prague's Jews were transported to the new ghetto in Terezín,
by a grotesque twist of fate Hitler chose to preserve the ghetto itself as
the site for his planned "Exotic Museum of an Extinct Race". With this
in mind, Jewish artefacts from all over central Europe were gathered
here, and now make up one of the richest collections of Judaica in
Europe – and one of the most fascinating sights in Prague.

### A history of Jewish settlement in Prague
Jews probably settled in Prague as early as the tenth century in what is
now Malá Strana. From the outset they were subjected to violent
pogroms, and harsh, often arbitrary persecution, through laws restrict-

ing their choice of profession, their movements and dress. The first dress codes were introduced under Vratislav II (1061–92) and required Jews to wear a yellow cloak; later, it was enough to wear a yellow circle, but some form of visible identification remained a constant feature of ghetto life.

In 1096, at the time of the first crusade, the first recorded pogrom took place, though it wasn't until the thirteenth century (300 years before the word "ghetto" was coined in Venice) that Jews were actually herded into a **walled ghetto** within Staré Město, cut off from the rest of the town and subject to a curfew. Prague's Jews effectively became the personal property of the king, protected by him when the moment suited, used as scapegoats when times were hard. During one of the worst pogroms, in 1389, 3000 Jews were massacred over Easter, some while sheltering in the Old-New Synagogue – an event which is still commemorated there every year on Yom Kippur. In 1541, following a wave of expulsions right across central Europe, Emperor Ferdinand I ordered Prague's Jews to leave. In the end he relented, and a small number of families were allowed to remain.

By contrast, the reign of Rudolf II (1576–1612) was a time of economic and cultural prosperity for the community. The Jewish mayor, **Mordecai Maisl**, Rudolf's minister of finance, became one of

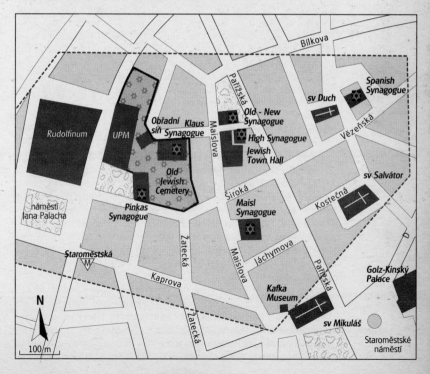

the richest men in Bohemia and the success symbol of a generation; his money bought the Jewish quarter a town hall, a bath house, pavements and several synagogues. This was the golden age of the ghetto: the time of **Rabbi Löw**, who, according to Jewish legend, created the famous "golem" (see box on p.113), and David Gans, the Jewish chronicler, both of whom are buried in the old cemetery.

In 1648, the Jews, along with the city's students, repelled the marauding Swedes on the Charles Bridge, for which they won the lasting respect of Ferdinand III (1637–57). At this time the ghetto was considerably enlarged, and the population grew to around 11,500. Things went into reverse again during the eighteenth century, until in 1745, Empress Maria Theresa used the community as a scapegoat for her disastrous war against the Prussians, and ordered the expulsion of all Jews from Prague. She allowed them to return three years later, though only after much pressure from the guilds, who were missing Jewish custom. It was the enlightened **Emperor Joseph II** (1780–90) who did most to lift the restrictions on Jews. His 1781 Toleration Edict ended the dress codes, opened up education to all non-Catholics, and removed the gates from the ghetto. In 1850, the community paid him homage by officially naming the ghetto Josefov, or Josefstadt.

The downside to Joseph's reforms was that he was hellbent on assimilating the Jews into the rest of the population. The use of Hebrew or Yiddish in business transactions was banned, and Jews were ordered to Germanise their names (the list of permitted names comprised 109 male ones and 35 female). It wasn't until the social upheavals of 1848 that Jews were given equal status within the Empire and allowed officially to settle outside the confines of the ghetto – concessions which were accompanied by a number of violent anti-Semitic protests on the part of the Czechs.

## From 1848 to the present day

From 1848, the ghetto went into terminal decline. The more prosperous Jewish families began to move to other districts of Prague, leaving behind only the poorest Jews and strictly Orthodox families, who were rapidly joined by the underprivileged ranks of Prague society: gypsies, beggars, prostitutes and alcoholics. By 1890, only twenty percent of Josefov's population was Jewish, yet it was still the most densely populated area in Prague. The ghetto had become a carbuncle in the centre of bourgeois Prague, a source of disease and vice: in the words of Gustav Meyrink, a "demonic underworld, a place of anguish, a beggarly and phantasmagorical quarter whose eeriness seemed to have spread and led to paralysis".

The ending of restrictions, and the destruction of most of the old ghetto, increased the pressure on Jews to assimilate, a process which brought with it its own set of problems. Prague's Jews were predominantly German- or Yiddish-speaking, and therefore seen by the Czech nationalists as a Germanising influence. By 1900 two-thirds of Prague's German population were Jewish. Tensions between the country's

German-speaking minority and the Czechs grew steadily worse in the run-up to World War I, and the Jewish community found itself caught in the firing line – "like powerless stowaways attempting to steer a course through the storms of embattled nationalities", as one Prague Jew put it.

Despite several anti-Semitic riots in the first few years following the war, the foundation of the new republic in 1918, and, in particular, its founder and first president, T. G. Masaryk, whose liberal credentials were impeccable, were welcomed by most Jews. For the first time in their history, Jews were given equal rights as a recognised ethnic minority, though only a small number opted to be registered as Jewish. The interwar period was probably the nearest Prague's Jewish community came to a second golden age, a time most clearly expressed in the now famous flowering of its *Deutsche Prager Literatur*, led by writers such as Franz Werfel, Franz Kafka, Max Brod and Egon Erwin Kisch.

After Hitler occupied Prague on March 15, 1939, the city's Jews were subject to an increasingly harsh set of regulations, which saw them barred from most professions, placed under curfew, and compelled once more to wear the yellow Star of David. In November 1941, the first transport of Prague Jews set off for the new ghetto in Terezín, 60km northwest of Prague. Of the estimated 55,000 Jews in Prague at the time of the Nazi invasion, over 36,000 died in the camps. Many survivors emigrated to Israel and the USA. Of the 8000 who registered as Jewish in the Prague census of 1947, a significant number joined the Communist Party, only to find themselves victims of Stalinist anti-Semitic wrath during the 1950s. Nowadays, it's extremely difficult to estimate how many Jews remain in Prague: around 1000 are registered, and most of them belong to the older generation. Just two synagogues continue to function, and even they look unlikely to survive into the next millennium.

# The former ghetto

Geographically, Josefov lies to the northwest of Staroměstské náměstí, between the church of sv Mikuláš and the Vltava river. Through the heart of the old ghetto runs the ultimate bourgeois avenue, Pařížská, a riot of turn-of-the-century sculpturing, spikes and turrets. It's Josefov's main street, a lively stretch of international airline offices and glitzy boutiques; once you leave it, however, you're immediately in the former ghetto, now one of the most restful parts of the old town.

---

All the "sights" of Josefov are run by the **State Jewish Museum** and you need just one ticket, available from the main box office in the Klaus Synagogue, next door to the Old Jewish Cemetery on U starého hřbitova. Opening hours for all are April–Oct 9am–5pm; Nov–March 9am–noon & 1–4.30pm; closed Sat.

# The Old-New Synagogue and the Jewish Town Hall

Halfway down Pařížská, on the left, are the steep, jagged brick gables of the **Old-New Synagogue** (Staronová synagóga or Altneuschul), the oldest functioning synagogue in Europe. Begun in the second half of the thirteenth century, it's one of the earliest Gothic buildings in Prague and still the religious centre for Prague's Orthodox Jews. Since Jews were prevented by law from becoming architects, the synagogue was most probably constructed by the Franciscan builders working on the convent of sv Anežka. Its five-ribbed vaulting is unique for Bohemia; the extra rib was added to avoid any hint of a cross.

*Prague's other
working
synagogue is in
Nové Město, see
p.131*

To get to the **main hall**, you must pass through one of the two low vestibules from which women are allowed to watch the proceedings. Above the entrance is an elaborate tympanum covered in the twisting branches of a vine tree, its twelve bunches of grapes representing the tribes of Israel. The low glow from the chandeliers is the only light in the hall, which is mostly taken up with the elaborate wrought-iron cage enclosing the *bimah* in the centre. In 1357, Charles IV allowed the Jews to fly their own municipal standard, a moth-eaten remnant of which is still on show. The other flag – a tattered red banner – was a gift to the community from Emperor Ferdinand III for helping fend off the Swedes in 1648. On the west wall is a glass cabinet, shaped like Moses' two tablets of stone and filled with tiny personalised light bulbs, each one lighting up on the anniversary of a person's death (there's even one for Kafka).

Just south of the synagogue is the **Jewish Town Hall** (Židovnická radnice), one of the few such buildings to survive the Holocaust. Founded and funded by Maisl in the sixteenth century, it was later rebuilt as the creamy-pink Baroque house you now see, housing a kosher lunchtime restaurant. The belfry, permission for which was granted by Ferdinand III, has a clock on each of its four sides, plus a Hebrew one stuck on the north gable which, like the Hebrew script, goes "backwards". On the other side of the synagogue is one of the many statues in Prague that were hidden from the Nazis for the duration of the war: an anguished statue of Moses by František Bílek, himself a committed Protestant.

## The Old Jewish Cemetery

*The New Jewish
Cemetery, where
Kafka, among
others, is buried,
is in Žižkov, see
p.149*

The main reason most people visit Josefov is to see the **Old Jewish Cemetery** (Starý židovský hřbitov), called *Beth Chaim* in Hebrew, meaning "House of Life". Established in the fifteenth century, it was in use until 1787, by which time there were an estimated 100,000 buried here, one on top of the other, as many as twelve layers deep. The oldest grave, dating from 1439, belongs to the poet Avigdor Karo, who lived to tell the tale of the 1389 pogrom. Get there before the crowds, and the cemetery can be a poignant reminder of the ghetto, its inhabitants subjected to inhuman overcrowding even in death. The rest of Prague recedes beyond the sombre lime trees and cramped perimeter walls, the haphazard headstones and Hebrew inscriptions casting a powerful spell.

The former ghetto

Each headstone bears a symbol denoting the profession or tribe of the deceased: a pair of hands for the Cohens; a jug for the Levis; scissors for a tailor; a violin for a musician, etc. On many graves you'll see pebbles holding down small messages. According to Judaism, there is no afterlife, and the only way for the dead to continue is in the prayers of the living – when one scrap of paper is blown away by the wind, it's soon replaced by another. The greatest number of pebbles sits on the grave of Rabbi Löw, creator of the "golem", who is buried by the wall directly opposite the entrance; followed closely by the rich Renaissance tomb of Mordecai Maisl, some ten metres to the southeast.

Immediately on your left as you leave the cemetery is the **Obřadní síň**, a grim neo-Renaissance house that was the site of the original Jewish Museum, founded in 1906. It's now devoted to a harrowing exhibition of children's drawings from the Jewish ghetto in Terezín.

*For a full account of Terezín (Theresienstadt), see p.169*

---

## The Golem

Legends concerning the animation of unformed matter (which is what the Hebrew word *golem* means), using the mystical texts of the *Kabbala*, were around long before Frankenstein started playing around with corpses. Two hungry fifth-century rabbis may have made the most practical golem when they sculpted a clay calf, brought it to life and then ate it; but the most famous is undoubtedly **Rabbi Löw**'s giant servant made from the mud of the Vltava, who was brought to life when the rabbi placed a *shem* in its mouth, a tablet with a magic Hebrew inscription.

There are numerous versions of the tale: in some, Yossel, the golem, is a figure of fun, flooding the rabbi's kitchen rather in the manner of Disney's *Sorcerer's Apprentice*; others portray him as the guardian of the ghetto, helping Rabbi Löw in his struggle with the anti-Semites at Rudolf II's court. In almost all, however, the golem finally runs amok. One particularly appealing tale is that the golem's rebellion was because Löw forgot to allow his creature to rest on the sabbath. He was conducting the service when news of its frenzy arrived, and he immediately ran out to deal with it. The congregation, reluctant to continue without him, merely repeated the verse in the psalm the rabbi had been reciting until Löw returned. This explains the peculiarity at the Old-New Synagogue where a line in the sabbath service is repeated even today. In all the stories, the end finally comes when Löw removes the *shem* once and for all, and carries the remains of his creature to the attic of the Old-New Synagogue, where they have supposedly resided ever since (a fact disputed by the pedantic journalist Egon Erwin Kisch, who climbed in to check).

The legends are amended at each telling, and have proved an enduringly popular theme for generations of artists and writers. Paul Wegener's German expressionist film version and the dark psychological novel of Gustav Meyrink are probably two of the most powerful treatments. Meyrink's golem lives in a room which has no windows and no doors, emerging to haunt the streets of Prague every 33 years. By which reckoning, it should be back some time in the mid-1990s.

---

## The museum-synagogues

Opposite the entrance to the cemetery is the **Klaus Synagogue**
(Klausová synagóga), a late seventeenth-century building, originally
founded by Mordecai Maisl in what was then a notorious red-light
district of Josefov. The first floor is now used for the interesting
temporary exhibitions put on by the State Jewish Museum; the rest
contains a display of Jewish prints and manuscripts (the world's first
Jewish printing house was founded in Prague in 1512).

On the south side of the cemetery, the **Pinkas Synagogue**
(Pinkasova synagóga) juts out at an angle from the cemetery wall. It's
accessible only from Široká, that is if it's open at all – it's been closed
since 1968, allegedly due to problems with the masonry. It was built for
the powerful Pinkas family, and has undergone countless restorations
over the centuries. In 1958, a chilling memorial to the 77,297 Czech
and Slovak Jews killed during the Holocaust was unveiled inside – a
simple *menorah* (candelabra) set against the carved stone backdrop of
a complete list of the names of those who perished. It was destroyed at
some point in the last twenty years – by damp, according to the
Communists. Whatever the reason, there are plans now to reconstruct
the memorial, and to reopen the synagogue as a museum in 1993.

On the far side of the town hall it was once part of is the **High
Synagogue** (Vysoká synagóga), whose rich interior stands in complete
contrast to its dour, grey facade. The huge vaulted hall is now used to
display a mere fraction of the hundreds of Jewish textiles, dating from
the sixteenth to the early twentieth century, which were gathered here
by the Nazis for their infamous museum. Across Pařížská, on Dušní, is
the **Spanish Synagogue** (Španělská synagóga), closed "for electrical
rewiring" since 1980, and used for storage in the meantime. Which is a
great shame, since this is one of the most ornate synagogues in
Josefov, rebuilt at the turn of the century in a Moorish style recalling
its fifteenth-century roots, when it was founded by Sephardic Jews
fleeing the Spanish Inquisition.

The neo-Gothic **Maisl Synagogue** (Maislova synagóga), set back
from the neighbouring houses on Maislova, has recently reopened after
a lengthy restoration. Founded and paid for entirely by Mordecai Maisl,
in its day it was without doubt one of the most ornate synagogues in
Josefov. Nowadays, it is almost entirely bare apart from the rich offerings of its glass cabinets, which contain gold and silverwork, *hanuka*
candlesticks, *torah* scrolls and other religious paraphernalia.

## On Kafka's Trail

*Prague never lets go of you . . . this dear little mother has sharp claws*

**Franz Kafka** was born on July 3, 1883, above the *Batalion* schnapps
bar on the corner of Maislova and Kaprova (the original building has
long since been torn down). He spent most of his life in and around
Josefov. His father was an upwardly mobile small businessman from a
Czech-Jewish family of kosher butchers (Kafka himself was a vegetar-

ian), his mother from a wealthy German-Jewish family of merchants. The family owned a haberdashery shop, located at various premises on or near Staroměstské náměstí. In 1889, they moved out of Josefov and lived for the next seven years in the beautiful Renaissance Dům U minuty, next door to the Staroměstská radnice, during which time Kafka attended the *Volksschule* on Masná (now a Czech primary school), followed by a spell at an exceptionally strict German *Gymnasium*, located on the third floor of the Golz-Kinský Palace.

At eighteen, he began a law degree at the German half of Charles University, which was where he met his lifelong friend and posthumous biographer and editor, Max Brod. Kafka spent most of his working life as an insurance clerk, until he was forced to retire through ill health in 1922. Illness plagued him throughout his life and he spent many months as a patient at the innumerable spas in *Mitteleuropa*. He was engaged three times, twice to the same woman, but never married, finally leaving home at the age of thirty-one for bachelor digs on the corner of Dlouhá and Masná, where he wrote the bulk of his most famous work, *The Trial*. He died of tuberculosis in a Viennese sanatorium on June 3, 1924, at the age of forty, and is buried in the New Jewish Cemetery in Žižkov (see p.149).

### Kafka's legacy

As a German among Czechs, a Jew among Germans, and an agnostic among believers, Kafka had good reason to live in a constant state of fear, or *Angst*. Life was precarious for Prague's Jews, and the destruction of the Jewish quarter throughout his childhood – the so-called "sanitisation" – had a profound effect on his psyche, as he himself admitted. It comes as a surprise to many Kafka readers that anyone immersed in so beautiful a city could write such claustrophobic and paranoid texts; and that as a member of the café society of the time, he could write in a style so completely at odds with his verbose, artistic friends. It's also hard to accept that Kafka could find no publisher for *The Castle* or *The Trial* during his lifetime.

After his death, Kafka's works were published in Czech and German and enjoyed brief critical acclaim, before the Nazis banned them, first within Germany, then across Nazi-occupied Europe. Even after the war, Kafka, along with most German-Czech authors, was deliberately overlooked in his native Czechoslovakia, since he belonged to a community and a culture which had been exiled. In addition, his account of the terrifying brutality and power of bureaucracy over the individual, though not in fact directed at totalitarian systems as such, was too close to the bone for the Communists. The 1962 Writers' Union conference at Liblice finally broke the official silence on Kafka, and, for many people, marked the beginning of the Prague Spring. In the immediate aftermath of the 1968 Soviet invasion, the Kafka bust was removed from Josefov, and his books remained unpublished until 1990.

Nowadays, thanks to his popularity with western tourists, Kafka has become an extremely marketable commodity: his image is plastered across T-shirts, mugs and postcards all over the city centre. And cinema audiences can have the pleasure of seeing two recently released Kafka-inspired films, both shot in Prague: Steven Soderbergh's *Kafka*, starring Jeremy Irons, and the BBC's *The Trial*, with Anthony Hopkins.

Kafka's birthplace is commemorated by a gaunt-looking modern bust. Next door, there is now a small **Kafka Museum** (Tues–Sat 10am–6pm), which retells Kafka's life simply but effectively with pictures and quotes (in Czech, German and English). It's run by the Kafka Society, who are planning to open a much bigger museum and cultural centre in the Golz-Kinský Palace on Staroměstské náměstí, sometime in the future.

*Palach is also
honoured at the
martyrs' shrine
on Wenceslas
Square, see p.124*

# Around náměstí Jana Palacha

As Kaprova and Široká emerge from Josefov, they meet at the newly christened **náměstí Jana Palacha**, previously called náměstí Krasnoarmejců (Red Army Square) and embellished with a flowerbed in the shape of a red star, in memory of the Soviet dead who were temporarily buried here in May 1945. It was probably this, as much as the fact that the building on the east side of the square is the Faculty of Philosophy, where Palach was a student, that prompted the new authorities to make the first of the street name changes here in 1989 (there's a bust of Palach on the corner of the building). By a happy coincidence, the road which intersects the square from the north is called 17 listopadu (17 November), originally commemorating the students' anti-Nazi demonstration of 1939, but now equally good for more recent events.

The north side of the square is taken up by the **Rudolfinum** or Dům umělců (House of Artists), designed by Josef Zítek and Josef Schulz. One of the proud civic buildings of the nineteenth-century *národní obrození*, it was originally built to house an art gallery, museum and concert hall for the Czech-speaking community. In 1918, however, it became the seat of the new Czechoslovak parliament, only returning to its original artistic purpose in 1946; in the last couple of years it's been sandblasted back to its original woody-brown hue, and is now one of the capital's main art and concert venues.

### UPM – the Decorative Arts Museum

A short way down 17 listopadu from the square is the **UPM**, or Umělecko-průmyslové muzeum (Tues–Sun 10am–6pm), installed in another of Schulz's worthy nineteenth-century creations, richly decorated in mosaics, stained glass and sculptures. Literally translated, this is a "Museum of Decorative Arts", though the translation hardly does justice to what is one of the most fascinating museums in the capital. From its foundation in 1885 through to the end of the First Republic, the UPM received the best that the Czech modern movement had to offer – from Art Nouveau to the avant-garde – and judging from previous catalogues and the various short-term exhibitions mounted in the past, its collection is unrivalled.

Unfortunately, the permanent exhibition consists of just a sample from each of the main artistic periods from the Renaissance to the

1930s, giving only the vaguest hints at the wealth of exhibits stored away in the museum's vaults. Worse still, the top floor, which covers the period from the 1880s to the 1930s, had been closed for a number of years at the time of writing. As a consolation, the museum's ground and first floors are used for some of the best temporary exhibitions in Prague, mostly taken from its twentieth-century collections. There's also a **public library** in the building (Mon noon–6pm, Tues–Fri 10am–6pm; closed July & Aug), specialising in catalogues and material from previous exhibitions.

# Chapter 6

# Nové Město

A lthough it comes over as a sprawling late nineteenth-century bourgeois quarter, **NOVÉ MĚSTO** was actually founded in 1348 by Charles IV, as an entirely new town, intended to link the southern fortress of Vyšehrad with Staré Město to the north. Large market squares, wide streets, and a level of town-planning far ahead of its time were employed to transform Prague into the new capital city of the Holy Roman Empire. However, this quickly became the city's poorest quarter after Josefov, renowned as a hotbed of Hussitism and radicalism throughout the centuries. In the second half of the nineteenth century, the authorities set about a campaign of slum clearance similar to that inflicted on the Jewish quarter; only the churches and a few important historical buildings were left standing, but Charles' street layout survived pretty much intact. The leading architects of the day began to line the wide boulevards with ostentatious examples of their work, which were eagerly snapped up by the new class of status-conscious businessman – a process that has continued into this century, making Nové Město the most architecturally varied part of Prague.

Today, Nové Město remains the city's main commercial and business district, with most of the hotels, nightclubs, cafés, fast-food outlets and department stores. The obvious starting point, and probably the only place in Prague most visitors can put a name to, is

---

**An Art-Nouveau hit list**

Prague's Art Nouveau (the term is *secesní* in Czech) ranges from the vivacious floral motifs of Paris to the more restrained Secession of Vienna, with several shades in between. The following are some of the more striking examples covered in this chapter.

| | | | |
|---|---|---|---|
| Hotel Central | p.131 | Pojišťovna Praha | p.128 |
| Hlahol | p.136 | Praha hlavní nádraží | p.126 |
| Hotel Evropa | p.124 | Topičův dům | p.128 |
| Obecní dům | p.130 | U Dorflerů | p.129 |
| Peterkův dům | p.123 | U Nováků | p.133 |

Wenceslas Square, hub of the modern city, and somewhere you're bound to find yourself passing through again and again. The two principal streets which lead off it are **Národní** and **Na příkopě**, the latter pedestrianised and sporting benches, buskers, and a handful of convenient café terraces from which to watch the spectacle. Together, these streets also contain some of Prague's finest late nineteenth-century and Art-Nouveau architecture.

The rest of Nové Město, which spreads out northeast and southwest of the square, is much less explored, and for the most part solidly residential; unusually for Prague, using the tram and metro systems to get around here will save some unnecessary legwork. A few specific sights are worth singling out for attention – the **Dvořák Museum** on Ke Karlovu and the **Mánes Gallery** on the waterfront, for example – but the rest is decidedly less exciting than all that's gone before. However, if your ultimate destination is Vyšehrad (covered in Chapter 7), you can easily take in some of the more enjoyable bits of southern Nové Město en route.

# The Golden Cross

The so-called *zlatý kříž* or "**golden cross**", Prague's commercial centre and probably the most expensive slice of real estate in the capital, is made up of **Wenceslas Square**, Nové Město's main square, and **Národní** and **Na příkopě**, Prague's busiest shopping streets and promenades, lined with banks, boutiques and bookshops. Their boomerang curve – following the course of the old moat, which was finally filled in in 1760 – marks the border between Staré Město and Nové Město (strictly speaking, the dividing line runs down the middle of the street). Ranged around here are a variety of stylish edifices, including the city's most flamboyant Art-Nouveau buildings.

Even under the Communists this remained a relatively prosperous area of state-sponsored consumerism, with neon signs advertising a bizarre range of items from Bulgaria's Import-Export Company to Coca-Cola; now, under the free market, it's taking off once more, with the usual multinationals buying up the choicest properties, and the streets themselves taken up with impromptu stalls, soap-box speakers, hustlers and buskers.

## Wenceslas Square (Václavské náměstí)

The natural pivot around which modern Prague revolves, and the focus of the events of November 1989, is **Wenceslas Square**, more of a wide, gently sloping boulevard than a square as such. It's scarcely a conventional – or even convenient – space in which to hold mass demonstrations, yet night after night following the November 17 *masakr* (see p.127), over 250,000 people crammed into the square, often enduring subzero temperatures to call for the resignation of the Party leaders and demand free elections. On November 27, the whole

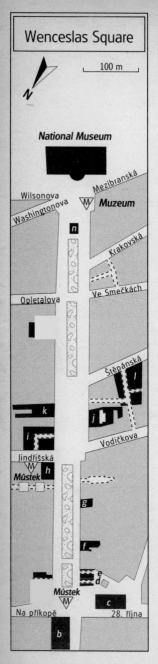

## Wenceslas Square

|___ 100 m ___|

N

**National Museum**

Wilsonova
Washingtonova
Mezibranská
Ⓦ **Muzeum**

n

Krakovská

Opletalova
Ve Smečkách

Štěpánská

l

k

i

Vodičkova

Jindřišská
Ⓦ
**Můstek**
h

g

f

e
d

**Můstek**
Ⓦ
c

Na příkopě
28. října

b

of Prague came to a standstill, a bigger crowd than ever converging on the square to show their support for the two-hour nationwide general strike called by the opposition umbrella group, Občanské fórum (Civic Forum). It was this last mass mobilisation that proved decisive – by noon the next day, the Communist old guard had thrown in the towel.

The square's history of protest goes back to the revolutionary events of 1848, which began with a large outdoor mass held here. On the crest of the nationalist disturbances, the square – which had been known as Koňský trh (Horse Market) since its foundation as such by Charles IV – was given its present name. It was only appropriate, then, that it was here that the First Republic was declared in 1918. In 1948, the square was filled to capacity once more, this time with Communist demonstrators in support of the February coup. In August 1968, it was the scene of some of the most violent confrontations between the Soviet invaders and the local Czechs, during which the National Museum came under fire (according to the Czechs, the Soviet officer in charge mistook it for the Parliament building). And, of course, it was here on January 19, 1969, that Jan Palach set fire to himself in protest at the invasion.

Despite the square's medieval origins, its oldest building dates from the eighteenth century, and the vast majority are much younger. As the city's money moved south of Staré Město during the industrial revolution, so the square became the architectural showpiece of the nation, and is now lined with self-important six- or seven-storey buildings, representing every artistic trend of the last hundred years, from neo-Renaissance to Socialist Realism. Even if you've no interest in modern architecture, there's plenty to keep you occupied in the shops, arcades, cinemas, theatres and general hubbub of the square.

Wenceslas Square has always been the place to be seen, and above all to parade the latest four-wheeled frivolity, from luxury coach to Lamborghini. Gone are the times when unfamiliarity with western vehicles meant that even a Vespa was looked on as if it were a recently landed intergalactic spaceship; these days, more than a little post-revolutionary cynicism accompanies the stares. This is also the one place in Prague where life goes on after midnight – the hotels and nightclubs buzzing, and the police playing cat-and-mouse with the pimps and prostitutes, while turning a blind eye to most of the nation's new-found vices.

## The bottom of the square

The northern end of the square, around Můstek, the city's most central
metro station, is a popular place to meet up before hitting town, and,
without doubt, the busiest part of the square. It's dominated by a hulk-
ing wedge of sculptured concrete and gold, the **Palác Koruna (a)**, built
in 1914 by one of Jan Kotěra's many pupils and employing a rare
mixture of heavy constructivism and gilded ornamentation. The rather
half-hearted post-modernism of the **ČKD dům (b)**, directly above the
main entrance/exit to Můstek, is no architectural match for it, though
it does contain no fewer than three cafés, including one on the roof
(under reconstruction at the time of writing) with an unbeatable view
straight up Wenceslas Square. For a street-level lookout, try the café
terrace on the ground floor of the old **Civic Forum headquarters (c)**,
which is, strictly speaking, on 28 října, the short street connecting
Wenceslas Square with Národní.

## Dům obuv to the Assicurazione Generali

On the same side of the square are two functionalist buildings
designed by Ludvík Kysela in the late 1920s, billed at the time as the
ultimate glass curtain-wall buildings. Along with the Hotel Juliš (see
below), they represent the perfect expression of the optimistic mood
of progress and modernism that permeated the interwar republic. The
building on the right **(d)** was erected by the chocolate firm, Lindt;
while the **Dům obuv** (House of Shoes; **e**), on the left, was built for the
Czech shoe magnate, Tomáš Baťa, one of the greatest patrons of
avant-garde Czech art. It was recently returned to the family, along
with a number of their shoe factories, and is due to reopen soon as a
Baťa shoe shop.

Twenty-five years earlier, Czech architecture was in the throes of
its own version of Art Nouveau, one of whose earliest practitioners was
Jan Kotěra. The **Peterkův dům (f)**, a slender essay in the new style,
was his first work, undertaken at the age of 28. Kotěra, a pupil of the
great Otto Wagner, came from the restrained Viennese school of
Secession, and very soon moved on to a much less flamboyant
constructivism. The square's earliest example of Czech functionalism,
a few doors further up at no. 22, is the **Hotel Juliš (g)**, designed by
Pavel Janák, who had already made his name as one of the leading
lights of the short-lived Czech Cubist (and later Rondo-Cubist) movement (see p.146). The young Kafka worked for a couple of years as an
insurance clerk in the neo-Baroque **Assicurazione Generali (h)**, on
the corner of Jindřišská, designed by Osvald Polívka and Bedřich
Ohmann, and now home to the Polish Cultural Institute.

## Around Hotel Evropa

One of the Communists' most miserable attempts to continue the
square's tradition of grand architecture was the **Hotel Družba (i)**,
which stands like a 1970s reject on the other side of Jindřišská.
Diagonally opposite is the **Melantrich** publishing house **(j)**, whose first

floor is occupied by the offices of the Socialist Party newspaper, *Svobodné slovo* (The Free Word). For forty years, the Socialist Party was a loyal puppet of the Communist government, but on the second night of the November 1989 demonstrations, the newspaper handed over its well-placed balcony to the opposition speakers of Občanské fórum (Civic Forum).

Melantrich House faces probably the most famous and most beautiful building on the entire square, the Art-Nouveau **Hotel Evropa (k)**, built in 1903–04 by Dryák and Bendelmajer, two of Ohmann's disciples. It represents everything the Czech modern movement stood against: chiefly, ornament for ornament's sake, not that this has in any way dented its popularity. The café terrace has always had a reputation for low-key cruising and a great deal of posing, but it's worth forgoing the sunlight for the interior, which is as sumptuous as it was when the hotel first opened.

Opposite the hotel is the vast **Lucerna Palace (l)**, designed in the early part of this century by, among others, Havel's grandfather. The main entrance, just up Štěpánská, gives access to one of the more appealing of the square's numerous dimly lit shopping arcades, as well as a cinema and a lavishly decorated main concert hall. Apart from a brief glance at the **Hotel Jalta (m)**, built in the Stalinist aesthetic of the 1950s, there's nothing more to stop for, architecturally speaking, until you get to the Wenceslas Monument.

## The Wenceslas Monument

A statue of Saint Wenceslas (sv Václav) has stood at the top of the square since 1680 but the present **Wenceslas Monument (n)**, by the father of Czech sculpture, Josef Václav Myslbek, was not finally unveiled until 1912, after thirty years on the drawing board. The Czech patron saint sits astride his mighty steed, surrounded by smaller-scale representations of four other Bohemian saints – his mother Ludmilla, Procopius, Adalbert and Agnes – added in the 1920s. It was at the foot of this monument that the new republic of Czechoslovakia was declared in 1918, while World War I was still raging on the western front. And in 1968, and again in 1989, the monument was used as a national political noticeboard, constantly festooned in posters, flags and slogans; even now, it remains the city's favourite soapbox venue.

*For a brief
biography of
Wenceslas, see
p.64*

A few metres below the statue, on January 19, 1969, the 21-year-old student Jan Palach set himself alight in protest against the continuing occupation of his country by the Soviets. His example was emulated four days later by another four people around the country, and, on February 25 – the anniversary of the Communist coup – by a fifth, Jan Zajíc. The spot is now occupied by the small, impromptu martyrs' shrine, with photos, candles and messages commemorating the deaths of all those who died at the hands of the Communist state. Another photo you might see is that of Miloslav Mareček, a Charter 77 signatory, who had just ended his second hunger strike at the time of going to press in 1992 (he lasted a record-breaking 96 days). His

protest is aimed at the decision of the present government not to pros-
ecute the legislators responsible for the 1989 baton law, which called
for harsh punishment for dissidents.

## The National Museum

At the top, southern, end of Wenceslas Square sits the broad, brooding
hulk of the National Museum (Mon & Fri 9am–4pm, Wed, Thurs, Sat
& Sun 9am–5pm), built by Josef Schulz. Deliberately modelled on the
great European museums of Paris and Vienna, it dominates the view
up the square like a giant golden eagle with outstretched wings. Along
with the National Theatre (see below), this is one of the great landmarks of the nineteenth-century Czech *národní obrození*, sporting a
monumental gilt-framed glass cupola, worthy clumps of sculptural
decoration and narrative frescoes from Czech history.

Unless you're a geologist or a zoologist, you're unlikely to be
excited by most of the exhibits – room after room of stuffed animals
and endless display cases full of rocks – but it's worth taking at least a
quick look at the ornate marble entrance hall, and the Pantheon of
Czech notables at the top of the main staircase. Arranged under the
glass-domed hall are some forty-eight busts and statues of distinguished Czech men (plus a couple of token women and Slovaks),
including the universally adored T. G. Masaryk, the country's founding
president, whose statue was removed by the Communists from every
other public place. Since the revolution, the appeal of the museum's
temporary exhibitions (on such themes as Masaryk himself) has
increased dramatically, so it's always worth checking to see what's on.

*There's a brief
A–Z of leading
Czechs, past and
present, on p.269*

# Wilsonova

At the southern end of Wenceslas Square is some of the worst blight
that Communist planners inflicted on Prague; above all, the six-lane
highway that now separates Nové Město from the residential suburb of
Vinohrady to the east and south, and effectively cuts off the National
Museum from Wenceslas Square. Previously known as Vítězného
února (Victorious February) after the 1948 Communist coup, the road
was renamed Wilsonova in honour of US President Woodrow Wilson
(a personal friend of the Masaryk family), who effectively gave the
country its independence from Austria-Hungary in 1918.

The Prague Stock Exchange building alongside the National
Museum, only completed in the 1930s but rendered entirely redundant
by the 1948 coup, was another victim of postwar "reconstruction". The
architect Karel Prager was given the task of designing a new "socialist"
Federal Assembly building on the same site, without destroying the
old bourse: he opted for a supremely unappealing bronze-tinted plate-
glass structure, supported by concrete stilts and sitting uncomfortably
on top of its diminutive predecessor. No longer the sham, rubber-
stamp body it was on completion in 1973, its main problem now is
taking any effective decisions at all, such is the fragmentation of the
present multi-party system.

Next to the Parliament building, the **Smetanovo divadlo** (Smetana Theatre), the grand opera house built by the Viennese duo Helmer and Fellner, looks stunted and deeply affronted by the traffic which now tears past its front entrance. It was opened in 1888 as the *Neues Deutsches Theater*, shortly after the Czechs had built their own National Theatre on the waterfront. Always second fiddle to the Tyl, though equally ornate inside, it was one of the last great building projects of Prague's once all-powerful German minority. The velvet and gold interior is still as fresh as it was when the Bohemian-born composer Gustav Mahler brought the traffic to a standstill, conducting the premiere of his Seventh Symphony.

The last building on this deafening freeway is **Praha hlavní nádraží**, Prague's main railway station, and one of the final glories of the dying Empire, designed by Josef Fanta and officially opened in 1909 as the *Franz Josefs Bahnhof* (though the emperor himself failed to attend). Trapped in the overpolished subterranean modern section, it's easy to miss the station's surviving Art-Nouveau parts. The original entrance on Wilsonova still exudes imperial confidence, with its wrought-iron canopy and naked figurines clinging to the sides of the towers; on the other side of the road, two great glass protrusions signal the new entrance in the Vrchlického sady.

## Jungmannovo náměstí

Back on the course of the old moat, heading west from the northern end of Wenceslas Square along 28 října (October 28 – the foundation of the republic), it's only a short way before you reach **Jungmannovo náměstí**. The square takes its name from Josef Jungmann (1772–1847), a prolific writer, translator and leading light of the *národní obrození*, whose pensive, seated statue was erected here in 1878.

The chunky charcoal-coloured **Adria Palace**, on the south side of the square, was designed in the 1920s by Pavel Janák and Josef Zasche. Janák was a leading figure in prewar Czech Cubism, but after the war attempted to create a national style of architecture appropriate for the new republic. The style was dubbed "Rondo-Cubism", though few of the projects actually got off the ground, and most of its protagonists soon moved on to embrace the international modern movement of the likes of Le Corbusier and Bauhaus.

*You'll find
another example
of Rondo-Cubism
in Prague covered
on p.131*

Originally built for the Italian insurance company *Reunione Adriatica di Sicurità*, the palace's basement was until very recently a studio theatre for the multimedia **Laterna magika** (Magic Lantern) company. In 1989, it became the underground nerve centre of the Velvet Revolution, when Civic Forum found temporary shelter here shortly after their inaugural meeting on the Sunday following the November 17 demonstration. Against a stage backdrop for Dürenmatt's *Minotaurus*, the Forum thrashed out tactics in the dressing rooms and gave daily press conferences in the auditorium during the crucial fortnight before the Communists relinquished power. Since

**The masakr – November 17, 1989**

On the night of Friday, November 17, 1989, a 50,000-strong, officially sanctioned student demonstration, organised by the students' union, *SSM* (League of Young Socialists), worked its way down Národní with the intention of reaching Wenceslas Square. Halfway down the street they were confronted by the *bílé přílby* (white helmets) and *červené barety* (red berets) of the hated riot-police. For what must have seemed like hours, there was a stalemate as the students sat down and refused to disperse, some of them handing flowers out to the police. Suddenly, without any warning, the police attacked and what became known as the **masakr** (massacre) began – no one was actually killed, though it wasn't for want of trying by the police. Under the arches of Kaňka's house (Národní 16), there's a small symbolic bronze relief of eight hands reaching out for help, a permanent shrine in memory of the hundreds who were hospitalised in the violence.

then, *Laterna magika* have moved to the much more spacious Nova scéna (see below) and the *Divadlo za branou II* is now based here instead. Upstairs, there's a good café-terrace from which to observe life on the square below.

On the other side of the Jungmann statue is one of Prague's most endearing Cubist legacies, Vlastislav Hofman's unique **Cubist streetlamp** (and seat) from 1912. Close by are the iron gates of the church of **Panna Marie Sněžná** (St Mary-of-the-Snows), once one of the great landmarks of Wenceslas Square, when it towered over the backs of the old two-storey houses that lined the square, but now barely visible from any of the surrounding streets. If the gates are shut, try going through the unpromising courtyard back near the Jungmann statue.

Like most of Nové Město's churches, the Panna Marie Sněžná was founded by Charles IV, who envisaged a vast coronation church on a scale comparable with the St Vitus Cathedral, on which work had just begun. Unfortunately, the money ran out shortly after completion of the chancel; the result is curious – a church which is short in length, but equal to the cathedral in height. The hundred-foot-high vaulting – which collapsed on the Franciscans who inherited the half-built building in the seventeenth century – does little to stave off claustrophobia, further compounded by an overbearing Baroque altar which touches the ceiling. To get an idea of the intended scale of the finished structure, take a stroll through the small gardens, to the south of the church.

## Národní

The eastern end of Národní is taken up with shops, galleries and clubs, all of which begin to peter out as you near the river. At the last crossroads before the waterfront is the new **British Council building**, which formerly belonged to the old GDR. On the outside, the original constructivist facade, designed in the 1930s by Osvald Polívka, has been kept intact, while the light interior has been thoroughly and imaginatively modernised in an interesting synthesis of central European and British architectural styles, using ample helpings of the country's surplus glass. Take a peek at the lobby as you pass.

Further down, on the right-hand side, is an eye-catching duo of much earlier Art-Nouveau buildings, designed by Polívka in 1907–08. The first, at no. 7, was built for the **pojišťovna Praha** (Prague Savings Bank), hence the beautiful mosaic lettering above the windows advertising *život* (life insurance) and *kapital* (loans), as well as help with your *důchod* (pension) and *věno* (dowry). Next door, the slightly more ostentatious **Topičův dům**, headquarters of *Československý spisovatel*, the official state publishers, provides the perfect accompaniment, with a similarly ornate wrought-iron and glass canopy.

Opposite, the convent and church of **sv Voršila** (St Ursula) are distinguished by the rare sight (in this part of town) of a tree sticking out of its white facade. When it was completed in 1678, this was one of the first truly flamboyant Baroque buildings in Prague, and its white stucco and frescoed interior have recently been restored to their original state. The Ursuline nuns were booted out by the Communists, but have returned post-1989 to found one of the first ecclesiastical schools in the country.

### The National Theatre

At the western end of Národní, overlooking the Vltava, is the gold-crested **National Theatre** (Národní divadlo), proud symbol of the Czech nation. Refused money by the Austrian state, Czechs of all classes dug deep into their pockets to raise funds for the venture themselves. The foundation stones, gathered from various historically significant sites in Bohemia and Moravia, were laid in 1868 by the historian and politician, František Palacký, and the composer, Bedřich Smetana; the architect, Josef Zítek, spent the next thirteen years on the project. In August 1881, just two months after the opening night, fire ripped through the building, destroying everything except the outer walls. But within two years the whole thing was rebuilt – even the emperor contributed this time – under the supervision of Josef Schulz (who went on to design the National Museum), and it opened once more to the strains of Smetana's opera *Libuše*. The grand portal on the north side of the theatre is embellished with suitably triumphant allegorical figures, and, inside, every square inch is taken up with paintings and sculptures by leading artists of the *národní obrození*. Tickets are relatively cheap but most productions are in Czech, so unless there's an opera or ballet on, content yourself with a quick peek at the decor.

See Chapter 13,
The Arts, for
details of Prague's
theatres and box
office

Standing behind the National Theatre, and in dramatic contrast with it, is the theatre's state-of-the-art extension, the ultra-modern glass box of the **Nová scéna**, designed by Karel Prager, the leading architect of the Communist era, and completed in 1983. It's one of those buildings most Praguers love to hate – it was described by one Czech as looking like "frozen piss" – not that this seems to put off the swarms of theatregoers who choose to eat in its restaurant before the show. Just for the record, the lump of molten rock in the courtyard is a symbolic evocation of *My Socialist Country*, by Malejovský.

The Golden Cross

The famous **Café Slavia**, opposite the theatre, has been a favourite haunt of the city's writers and artists (and, inevitably, actors) since the days of the First Republic. The Czech avant-garde movement, *Devětsil*, led by Karel Teige, used to hold its meetings here in the 1920s, recorded for posterity by another of its memners, the Nobel prize-winner Jaroslav Seifert, in his *Slavia Poems*. It's been carelessly modernised since those arcadian days but remains as popular as ever, with Czechs as much as tourists.

*For more on Jaroslav Seifert, see p.148*

## Na příkopě

Heading the other way from Wenceslas Square, you can join the crush of bodies ambling down **Na příkopě** (literally "On the moat"). The street was once lined on both sides with grandiose buildings, like the former *Haas* department store at no. 4, built in 1869–71 by Theophil von Hansen, the architect responsible for much of the redevelopment of the Ring in Vienna. Many of the finest buildings, though – like the *Café Corso* and the *Café Francais*, once the favourite haunts of Prague's German-Jewish literary set – were torn down and replaced during the enthusiastic construction boom of the interwar republic. The Art-Nouveau U **Dorflerů**, at no. 7, from 1905, is one of the few survivors along this stretch, its gilded floral curlicues gleaming in the midday sun.

Further along, there are another couple of interesting buildings at nos. 18 and 20, originally designed by Polívka for the *Zemská banka* and connected by a kind of Bridge of Sighs suspended over Panská. It's worth nipping inside the **Živnostenka banka**, on the left, built in the 1890s in neo-Renaissance style, to appreciate the financial might of Czech capital in the last decades of the Austro-Hungarian Empire. On the right is the **Státní banka**, built some twenty years later, an arresting blend of the competing styles of the day – Art Nouveau and nineteenth-century historicism. Yet more financial institutions, this time from the dour 1930s, line the far end of Na příkopě, as it opens up into náměstí Republiky.

# Northern Nové Město

Náměstí Republiky is worth pausing at, if only to admire the Obecní dům – Prague's most alluring Art-Nouveau structure – but this apart, there's nothing in the northern or eastern part of Nové Město that merits a special trip. Nevertheless, you may find yourself in this part of town by dint of its shops and hotels, or perhaps en route to Prague's main domestic train station, Masarykovo nádraží. Tourists rarely venture this far east, and for that reason alone, it makes an interesting diversion, revealing a side to Prague that few visitors see.

# Náměstí Republiky

Náměstí Republiky is an unruly space, made more so since the construction of its metro station and the ugly brown *Kotva* department store. The oldest structure on the square is the **Prašná brána** (Powder Tower), one of the eight medieval gate-towers that once guarded Staré Město. The present tower was begun by King Vladislav Jagiello in 1475, shortly after he'd moved into the royal court, which was situated next door at the time. Work stopped when he retreated to the Hrad to avoid the wrath of his subjects; later on, it was used to store gunpowder – hence the name. The small historical exhibition inside (April & Oct Sat, Sun & holidays 10am–5pm; May–Sept Sat, Sun & holidays 10am–6pm) traces the tower's architectural metamorphosis over the centuries, up to its present remodelling courtesy of the nineteenth-century restorer, Josef Mocker. Most people, though, ignore the displays, and climb straight up for the modest view from the top.

## The Obecní dům

Attached to the tower, and built on the ruins of the old royal court, the **Obecní dům** (Municipal House) is by far the most exciting Art-Nouveau building in Prague, one of the few places that still manages to conjure up the atmosphere of Prague's turn-of-the-century café society. Conceived as a cultural centre for the Czech community, it's probably the finest architectural achievement of the *národní obrození*, designed by Osvald Polívka and Antonín Balšánek, and extravagantly decorated inside and out with the help of almost every artist connected with the Czech Secession. From the lifts to the cloakrooms, just about all the furnishings remain as they were when the building was completed in 1911, and the simplest way of soaking up the cavernous interior – peppered with mosaics and pendulous brass chandeliers – is to have a beer and a bite to eat in the *restaurace*, or sit around the fountain at the far end of the equally spacious *kavárna*.

It's worth wandering upstairs, too, for a peek at the central **Smetanova síň**, the city's largest concert hall, where the opening salvo of the Prague Spring Festival – traditionally a rendition of Smetana's *Má vlast* (My Country) – takes place in the presence of the president. Recently, there have been **guided tours** of the building, showing off its abundant treasures (which include paintings by Alfons Mucha, Jan Preisler and Max Švabinský, among others); check at the *PIS* for the current times. Otherwise, the restaurant and café are open from 7am to 11pm, and there's a chance you may be able to just stroll into the other parts of the building.

## Hybernská and Senovážné náměstí

Large international art exhibitions – occasionally worth a look – are held in **U hybernů** (The Hibernians), an Empire building situated opposite the Obecní dům, which belonged to the order of Irish Franciscans in the seventeenth century (hence its name). If you walk

down **Hybernská** from here, you'll pass the Art-Nouveau **Hotel**
**Central** on the right. Dating from 1900, this is one of the few restored
buildings in the area, its gilded decoration all the more startling for it.

Opposite the hotel is the headquarters of the **Social Democratic Party**, which was forcibly amalgamated with the Communist Party shortly after the 1948 coup. Since 1989, the party has regained its independence, but unable to shake off the stigma of its past collaboration, it has yet to win any significant support in the polls. In January 1912, a small backroom was given over to a congress of the Russian Social Democratic Labour Party. The party was deeply divided, and the meeting poorly attended, with only fourteen voting delegates present (all but two of them were Bolsheviks), and **Lenin** himself in the chair. It was this meeting which pushed through the formal takeover of the party by the Bolsheviks, to the exclusion of the Mensheviks and others, and gave the Czech Communists the perfect excuse for turning the whole place into a vast museum dedicated to Lenin, of which there is now, not surprisingly, absolutely no trace.

A little further down, a wrought-iron canopy marks the entrance to Prague's first railway station, **Masarykovo nádraží**, opened in 1845 – a modest, almost provincial affair compared to the Art-Nouveau Praha hlavní nádraží. On the opposite side of Hybernská is the **Café Arco**, once a favourite of Kafka (who worked nearby), and the circle of writers known as the *Arconauts*. As yet, nothing is made of its literary associations, the interior is unremarkable, and most of the customers are here to kill time before their train leaves.

### Senovážné náměstí and around
A couple of blocks south of Hybernská, down Dlážděná, is the old hay market, **Senovážné náměstí** (formerly Gorkého náměstí), packed out with parked cars and a couple of market stalls. Its most distinguished feature is the freestanding fifteenth-century belfry of the church of sv **Jindřich** (St Henry); both have undergone several facelifts, most recently by the ubiquitous Gothic restorer, Josef Mocker. A short way up Jeruzalémská, you'll find the **Jubilee Synagogue** (Jubilejní synagóga), built in the early part of this century, in a colourful Moorish style similar to that of the Spanish Synagogue in Josefov. This and the Old-New Synagogue are the only synagogues in Prague that still hold regular sabbath services; at all other times, it's usually closed. *Prague's other synagogues are covered in Chapter 5*

# Na poříčí, Těšnov and a couple of museums
Running roughly parallel with Hybernská, to the north, is the much busier street of **Na poříčí**, an area that, like sv Havel in Staré Město, was originally settled by German merchants. Kafka spent most of his working life as a clerk for the *Arbeiter-Unfall-Versicherungs-Anstalt* (Workers' Accident Insurance Company), in the grand nineteenth-century building at no. 7. Further along on the right is a much more unusual piece of banking architecture, the **Banka legií**, one of Pavel Janák's rare Rondo-Cubist efforts from the early 1920s (for more on

Janák and the Cubists, see p.146). Set into the bold smoky-red moulding is a striking white marble frieze by Otto Gutfreund, depicting the
epic march of the Czechoslovak Legion from their embroilment in the
Russian Revolution. The glass curtain-walled **Bílá labuť** (White Swan)
department store, opposite, is a good example of the functionalist style
which Janák and others went on to embrace in late 1920s and 1930s.

As a lively shopping street, Na poříčí seems very much out on a
limb, as do the cluster of hotels at the end of the street, and around
the corner in Těšnov. The reason behind this is the now defunct
Těšnov train station, which was demolished in the 1960s to make way
for the Wilsonova flyover. The neo-Renaissance mansion housing the
**Prague Museum** (Muzeum hlavní města Prahy; Tues–Sun 10am–
12.30pm & 1.30–6pm), on the other side of the flyover to the south, is
the lone survivor of this redevelopment. Inside, there's an ad hoc
collection of the city's art, a number of antique bicycles, and usually
an intriguing temporary exhibition on some aspect of the city. The
museum's prize possession, though, is Langweil's model of Prague
from 1834. It's a fascinating insight into early nineteenth-century
Prague – predominantly Baroque, with the cathedral incomplete and
the Jewish quarter "unsanitised" – and, consequently, has served as
one of the most useful records for the city's restorers. The most
surprising thing, of course, is that so little has changed.

North of Na poříčí, towards the river, there's another museum
worth a look: the **Postage Museum** (Muzeum postovní známky; Tues–
Sun 9am–5pm), housed in the Vávra mill, near one of Prague's many
water towers. The first floor contains nineteenth-century wall paintings
of Austrian landscapes, and a series of drawings on postman themes.
The real stuff is on the ground floor – a vast international collection of
stamps arranged in vertical pull-out drawers. The Czechoslovak issues
are historically and artistically interesting, as well as of appeal to philat-
elists. Stamps became a useful tool in the propaganda wars of this
century; even such short-lived ventures as the Hungarian-backed
Slovak Socialist Republic of 1918–19 and the Slovak National Uprising
of autumn 1944 managed to print special issues. Under the First
Republic, the country's leading artists, notably Alfons Mucha and Max
Švabinský, were commissioned to design stamps, some of which are
exceptionally beautiful.

# Southern Nové Město

The streets south of Národní and Wenceslas Square still run along the
medieval lines of Charles IV's town plan, though they're now lined
with grand, nineteenth-century buildings. Such is their scale, however,
that some of these broad boulevards – like Žitná and Ječná – have
become the main arteries for Prague's steadily increasing traffic.
Together with the large distances involved, this makes southern Nové
Město one part of the city where trams can come in useful.

# South to Karlovo náměstí

Of the many roads which head down towards Karlovo náměstí,
**Vodičkova** is probably the most impressive, running southwest for half
a kilometre from Wenceslas Square. You can catch several trams (#3,
#14, #24) along this route, though there are a handful of buildings
worth checking out on the way. The first, **U Nováků**, is impossible to
miss, thanks to Jan Preisler's mosaic of bucolic frolicking (its actual
subject, *Trade and Industry*, is confined to edges of the picture), and
Polívka's curvilinear window frames and delicate, ivy-like ironwork.
Originally built for the *Novák* department store in the early 1900s, for
the last sixty years it has been a cabaret hall, restaurant and café all
rolled into one.

Halfway down the street, at no. 15, the *McDonald's* "restaurant",
opened in March 1992, must qualify as a landmark of sorts. Directly
opposite is an imposing neo-Renaissance school, covered in bright-red
sgraffito patterning, which was founded in 1866 as the **Minerva girls'
school**, the first in Prague. At the beginning of this century, the school

---

### Milena Jesenská

The most famous "Minervan" was **Milena Jesenská**, born in 1896 into a
Czech family whose ancestry stretched back to the sixteenth century. Shortly
after leaving school, she was confined to a mental asylum by her father when
he discovered that she was having an affair with a Jew. On her release, she
married him and moved to Vienna, where she took a job as a railway porter
to support the two of them. While living in Vienna, she sent a Czech translation of one of Kafka's short stories to his publisher; Kafka wrote back
himself, and so began their platonic, mostly epistolary, relationship. Kafka
described her later as "the only woman who ever understood me", and with
his encouragement she took up writing professionally. Tragically, by the time
Milena had extricated herself from her disastrous marriage, Kafka, still
smarting from three failed engagements with other women, had decided
never to commit himself to anyone else; his letters alone survived the war, as
a moving testament to their love.

Milena returned to Prague in 1925, and moved on from writing exclusively
fashion articles to critiques of avant-garde architecture, becoming one of the
leading journalists on the main centrist newspaper of the day. She married
again, this time to the prominent functionalist architect Jaromír Krejčar, but
later, a difficult pregnancy and childbirth left her addicted to morphine. She
overcame her dependency only after joining the Communist Party, but was to
quit after the first of Stalin's show trials in 1936. She continued to work as a
journalist in the late 1930s, and wrote a series of articles condemning the
rise of fascism in the Sudetenland.

When the Nazis rolled into Prague in 1939, Milena's Vinohrady flat had
already become a centre for resistance. For a while, she managed to hang on
to her job, but her independent intellectual stance and provocative gestures –
like wearing a yellow star – soon attracted the attention of the Gestapo, and
after a brief spell in the notorious Pankrác prison, she was sent to
Ravensbrück, the women's concentration camp near Berlin, where she died
of nephritis (inflammation of the kidneys) in May 1944.

---

became notorious for the antics of its pupils, the "Minervans", who shocked bourgeois Czech society with their experimentations with fashion, drugs and sexual freedom (see box above). As Vodičkova curves left towards Karlovo náměstí, Lazarská, meeting point of the city's night trams, leads off to the right. At the bottom of this street is **Diamant**, another of Prague's Cubist buildings, completed in 1912 by Emil Králíček. It's grubby with pollution now, but the geometric sculptural reliefs on the facade, the main portal on Spálená, and the frame enclosing a Baroque statue of St John of Nepomuk remain special nonetheless.

### Karlovo náměstí

Once Prague's biggest square, **Karlovo náměstí**'s impressive proportions are no longer so easy to appreciate, obscured by a tree-planted public garden and cut in two by the busy thoroughfare of Ječná. It was created by Charles IV as Nové Město's cattle market (Dobytčí trh), though now it actually signals the southern limit of the city's commercial district.

The Gothic **Novoměstská radnice**, at the northern end of the square, was once a town hall to rival that of Staré Město. After the amalgamation of Prague's separate towns in 1784, however, it was used solely as a criminal court and prison. It was here that Prague's **first defenestration** took place on July 30, 1419, when the radical Hussite preacher Jan Želivský and his penniless religious followers stormed the building, mobbed the Catholic councillors and burghers and threw several of them out of the town hall windows onto the pikes of the Hussite mob below. Václav IV, on hearing the news, suffered a stroke and died just two weeks later. So began the long and bloody Hussite Wars.

*For details of Prague's second defenestration, see p.67*

Following the defeat of Protestantism two centuries later, the Jesuits were allowed to demolish 23 houses on the east side of the square to make way for their college (now one of the city's main hospitals) and the accompanying church of **sv Ignác** (St Ignatius). The latter is modelled, like so many Jesuit churches, on the Gesù in Rome, but it's worth looking in if only for the wedding-cake stucco on the ceiling.

At the southern end of the square is the so-called **Faustův dům** (Faust House), a late Baroque building with a long and diabolical history of alchemy. An occult priest from Opava owned the house in the fourteenth century, and, two hundred years later, the English alchemist and international con-man Edward Kelley was summoned here by the eccentric Emperor Rudolf II to turn base metal into gold. The building is also the traditional setting for the Czech version of the Faust legend, with the arrival one rainy night of a penniless and homeless student, Jan Šťastný (meaning *Faustus* or lucky). Finding money in the house, he decided to keep it – only to discover that it was put there by the Devil, who then claimed his soul in return. Seemingly unperturbed by the historical fate of the site, a new pharmacy has set up shop on the ground floor.

## Towards the river: Resslova

West off Karlovo náměstí, Resslova is a noisy extension of Ječná, heading towards the Vltava. A short way down is the eighteenth-century church of **sv Cyril and Metoděj**, the main base of the

> **The Assassination of Reinhard Heydrich**
>
> The assassination of Reinhard Heydrich in 1942 was the only attempt the Allies ever made on the life of a leading Nazi. It's an incident which the Allies have always billed as a great success in the otherwise rather dismal seven-year history of the Czech resistance. But, as with all acts of brave resistance during the war, there was a price to be paid. Given that the reprisals meted out on the Czech population were entirely predictable, it remains a controversial, if not suicidal, decision to have made.
>
> The target, Reinhard Tristan Eugen Heydrich, was a talented and upwardly mobile anti-Semite (despite rumours that he was partly Jewish himself), a great organiser and a skilful concert violinist. He was a late recruit to the Nazi Party, signing up in 1931, after having been dismissed from the German Navy for dishonourable conduct towards a woman. However, he swiftly rose through the Party ranks to become, in the autumn of 1941, *Reichsprotektor* of the puppet state of *Böhmen und Mähren* – effectively, the most powerful man in the Czech Lands. Although his rule began with brutality, it soon settled into the tried and tested policy which Heydrich liked to call *Peitsche und Zucker* (literally, "whip and sugar").
>
> On the morning of May 27, 1942, as Heydrich was being driven by his personal bodyguard in his open-top Mercedes from his manor house north of Prague to his office in Hradčany, three Czechoslovak agents (parachuted in from England) were taking up positions in the northeastern suburb of Libeň. As the car pulled into Kirchmayer Boulevard (now V Holešovičkách), one of them, a Slovak called Gabčík, pulled out a gun and tried to shoot. The gun stuck but Heydrich's bodyguard, rather than driving out of the situation, slowed down and attempted to shoot back. At this point, another agent, Kubiš, threw a grenade at the car. The blast injured Heydrich and stopped the car, but failed to harm his bodyguard, who immediately jumped out and began chasing Gabčík down the street, shooting. Gabčík pulled out a second gun, shot the bodyguard dead and hopped on board an approaching tram.
>
> Back at the Mercedes, Kubiš had been badly injured himself and, with blood pouring down his face, jumped on his bicycle and rode into town. Heydrich, seemingly only slightly wounded, flagged down a delivery van and hitched a lift to hospital. However, he died eight days later from shrapnel wounds and was given full Nazi honours at his Prague funeral; the cortège passed down Wenceslas Square, in front of a crowd of thousands – the Nazis made attendance compulsory. Revenge was quick to follow. The day after Heydrich's funeral, the village of Lidice (see p.187) was burnt to the ground.
>
> The plan to assassinate Heydrich had been formulated in the early months of 1942 by the Czechoslovak government-in-exile in London, without consultation with the Czech Communist leadership in Moscow, and despite fierce opposition from the resistance within Czechoslovakia. Since it was clear that the reprisals would be horrific, the only logical explanation for the plan is that this was precisely the aim of the government-in-exile's operation – to forge a solid wedge of resentment between the Germans and Czechs. In this respect, if in no other, the operation was ultimately successful.

Orthodox church in the Czech republic since the 1930s, but originally constructed for the Roman Catholics by Bayer and Dientzenhofer. Amid all the traffic, it's extremely difficult to imagine the scene here on June 18, 1942, when seven of the Czechoslovak secret agents involved in the most dramatic assassination of World War II (see box above) were besieged in the church by over 300 members of the SS and Gestapo. For most of the night the Nazis fought a pitched battle, trying explosives, flooding and any other method they could think of to drive the men out of their stronghold in the crypt. Eventually, all seven agents committed suicide rather than give themselves up.

There's a plaque at street level on the south wall commemorating those who died; in the crypt itself, which is rarely open, a small exhibition with photos details the incident. On the opposite side of the street is the church of sv Václav na Zderaze (St Wenceslas at Zderaz), whose origins predate Nové Město itself. Nowadays it's used by the modern Hussites, among whose adherents was the Art-Nouveau sculptor, František Bílek, who designed the church's pews and crucifix.

## Along the embankments

Magnificent turn-of-the-century mansions line the Vltava's right bank, almost without interruption, for some two kilometres from the Charles Bridge south to the rocky outcrop of Vyšehrad. It's a long walk, even just along the length of **Masarykovo and Rašínovo nábřeží**, though there's no need to do the whole lot in one go: you can hop on a tram (#3, #7 or #17) at various points, drop down from the embankments to the waterfront itself, or escape to one of the two islands connected to them, **Střelecký and Slovanský ostrov**.

### Hlahol and the Mánes Gallery

Most of the buildings along the waterfront are private apartments, and therefore inaccessible. One exception is the Art-Nouveau concert hall, Hlahol, at Masarykovo nábřeží 16, designed by the architect of the main railway station, Josef Fanta, with a pediment mural by Mucha and statues by Šaloun – check with the *PIS* when the next concert is. Another break comes with the striking white functionalist mass of the **Mánes Gallery** (Tues–Sun 10am–6pm), halfway down Masarykovo nábřeží. Designed in open-plan style by Otakar Novotný in 1930, it spans the narrow channel between Slovanský ostrov (see below) and the waterfront, close to the onion-domed Šítek water tower. The gallery is named after Josef Mánes, a traditional nineteenth-century landscape painter and Czech nationalist, and puts on some of the more unusual exhibitions in Prague; there are two cafés, and an upstairs restaurant, suspended above the channel.

### Two islands

Slovanský ostrov (commonly known as Žofín), accessible via Mánes, came about as a result of the natural silting of the river in the eighteenth century. By the late nineteenth century it had become one of the city's foremost pleasure gardens, where, as the composer Berlioz remarked, "bad musicians shamelessly make abominable music in the open air and immodest young males and females indulge in brazen dancing, while idlers and wasters . . . lounge about smoking foul tobacco and drinking beer". On a good day, things seem pretty much unchanged from those heady times. Concerts, balls, and other social gatherings take place here, and there are rowing boats for hire from May to October.

Closer to the other bank, and accessible via most Legií (Legion's Bridge) up by the National Theatre, Střelecký ostrov, or Shooters' Island, is where the army held their shooting practice, on and off, from the fifteenth until the nineteenth century. Later, it became a favourite spot for a Sunday promenade and it's still popular, especially in summer. The first *Sokol* festival took place here in 1882 (see p.85); the first May Day demonstrations in 1890, and, one hundred years on, having been used and abused by the Communists for propaganda purposes, the traditional low-key *Májales* celebrations have returned.

## Palackého náměstí
At **Palackého náměstí**, the buildings along the embankment retreat for a moment to reveal an Art-Nouveau sculpture to rival Šaloun's monument in Staroměstské náměstí (see p.97): the **Monument to František Palacký**, the great nineteenth-century Czech historian, politician and nationalist, by Stanislav Sucharda. Like the Hus Monument, which was unveiled three years later, this mammoth project – fifteen years in the making – had missed its moment by the time it was finally completed in 1912, and found universal disfavour. The critics have mellowed over

*For details of fish
restaurants near
the embankment,
see Chapter 11*

---

**Havel on the waterfront**

Since the beginning of the Charter 77 movement, **Václav Havel**, his wife Olga and his brother Ivan have lived in the top-floor flat of Rašínovo nábřeží 78\*. So permanent was the surveillance on Havel (apart from his four and a half years in prison) that the secret police set up a small prefab hut (since removed) on the other side of the road from which they could monitor his movements in relative comfort.

In 1990, Havel rejected the draughty, pompous rooms of the Hrad (the traditional place of residence for the president), preferring to stay put here. Even though he spends less time here now, his house has become something of a shrine. After forty years of Stalinist heroics, it's a fittingly modest object of pilgrimage – a typical four-storey mansion, no doubt beautiful when it was first designed (and owned) by his grandfather, a respected Art-Nouveau architect, but now shabby and run-down. There's no armed guard, no name on the bell, no plaque, yet despite the lack of anything to see, there are usually one or two people talking *sotto voce* and pointing up to the top floor, not to mention the lines of goodwill graffiti scrawled on the wall.

---

\*The embankment was previously named after Engels; Alois Rašín was the interwar Minister of Finance, who was assassinated by a non-Party communist in the 1920s.

the years, and nowadays it's appreciated for what it is – an energetic and inspirational piece of work. Ethereal bronze bodies, representing the world of the imagination, shoot out at all angles, contrasting sharply with the plain stone mass of the plinth, and below, the giant seated figure of Palacký himself, representing the real world.

## Vyšehradská and Ke Karlovu

Behind Palackého náměstí, off Vyšehradská, the twisted concrete spires of the **Emmaus monastery** (Emauzy) are an unusual modern addition to the Prague skyline. The monastery was one of the few important historical buildings to be damaged in the last war, in this case by a stray American bomb. Charles IV founded the monastery for Croatian Benedictines, who used the Old Slavonic liturgy (hence its Czech name, na Slovanech, or "at the Slavs"), but after the Battle of Bílá hora, it was handed over to the more mainstream Spanish Benedictines. The cloisters contain some extremely valuable Gothic frescoes, but since the return of the monks from their forty-year exile, it's become increasingly difficult to gain access to them.

Behind Emmaus is one of Kilian Ignaz Dientzenhofer's little gems, the church of **sv Jan Nepomucký na skalce** (St John of Nepomuk on the rock), perched high above Vyšehradská, with a facade that displays the plasticity of the Bavarian's Baroque style in all its glory. Heading south, the road descends to a junction, where you'll find the entrance to the city's **botanical gardens** (Botanická zahrada; daily 10am–4/5/6pm), laid out in 1897 on a series of terraces up the other side of the hill; though far from spectacular, they're one of the few patches of green in this part of town.

On the far side of the gardens, Apolinářská runs along the south wall and past a grim red-brick maternity hospital before joining up with Ke Karlovu. Head left up here and the first street off to the right is Na bojišti, which is usually packed with tour coaches. The reason for this is the **U kalicha** pub, on the right, which was immortalised in the opening passages of the consistently popular comic novel *The Good Soldier Švejk*, by Jaroslav Hašek. In the story, on the eve of the Great War, Švejk (*Schweik* to the Germans) walks into *U kalicha*, where a plain-clothes officer of the Austrian constabulary is sitting drinking and, after a brief conversation, finds himself arrested in connection with the assassination of Archduke Ferdinand. Whatever the pub may have been like in Hašek's day (and even then, it wasn't his local), it's now unashamedly oriented towards reaping in the Deutschmarks, and about the only authentic thing you'll find inside is the beer.

*There's another memorial to Dvořák in his birthplace in Nelahozeves, see p.165*

Further down Ke Karlovu, set back from the road behind wrought-iron gates, is the russet country house **Vila Amerika** (Tues–Sun 10am–5pm), one of the most successful secular works of Kilian Ignaz Dientzenhofer. Finished in 1720, it now houses a museum devoted to **Antonín Dvořák**, easily the most famous of all Czech composers, who for many years had to play second fiddle to Smetana in the orchestra at the National Theatre, where Smetana was the conductor. When in his forties, Dvořák received an honorary degree from Cambridge before leaving for the "New World", and his gown is one of the very few items of memorabilia to have found its way into the museum, along with the programme of a concert given at London's Guildhall in 1891. But there's compensation for what the display cabinets may lack in the tasteful period rooms, the composer's music wafting in and out, and the tiny garden dotted with Baroque sculptures.

## The Police Museum and Na Karlově church

There's a metro station (I. P. Pavlova) not far from Vila Amerika, but if you've got a few hundred more metres left in you, continue south down Ke Karlovu. At the end of the street, the former Augustinian monastery of Karlov is now the **Police Museum** (Muzeum Policie; Tues–Sun 10am–5pm; closed July & Aug), formerly the Museum of the Security Forces – and, in the heyday of "normalisation" in the 1970s, one of the most fascinating museums in the city. Works by Trotsky, photos of Bob Dylan, plays by Havel and contraband goods were all displayed in the grand room of dissidence; closed-circuit TV watched over your every move; and the first thing you saw on entry were 200 pistols confiscated from western secret agents pointing at you from the wall. But the most famous exhibit was undoubtedly a stuffed German shepherd dog called Brek, who saw twelve years' service on border patrols, intercepted sixty "law-breakers", was twice shot in action and eventually retired to an old dogs' home.

With the barbed wire and border patrols all but disappeared, and the police at the nadir of their popularity, the new exhibition concentrates on road and traffic offences, and the force's latest challenges: forgery, drugs and murder. It's not what it used to be, but it's still mildly amusing, with several participatory displays, including a *Scalextric* race track, road-crossing practice, and a quiz on the Highway Code (in Czech).

Attached to the museum is **Na Karlově** church, founded by Charles IV (of course), designed in imitation of Charlemagne's tomb in Aachen, and quite unlike any other church in Prague. If it's open, you should take a look at the dark interior, which was remodelled in the sixteenth century by Bonifaz Wohlmut. The stellar vault has no central supporting pillars – a remarkable feat of engineering for its time, and one which gave rise to numerous legends about the architect being in league with the devil.

From outside the church, there's a great view south across the Botič valley, to the twin delights of the skyscraper *Hotel Forum* and the low-lying **Palác kultury** (Palace of Culture), originally used for party congresses and now the country's biggest concert venue; to the right of the Palác kultury is Vyšehrad (covered in Chapter 7). The nearest metro (Vyšehrad) is across Nuselské most; alternatively, you can walk down to the the bottom of the valley and catch a tram (#7, #18 or #24).

# Vyšehrad and
# the eastern suburbs

By the end of his reign in 1378, Charles IV had laid out his city on such a grand scale that it wasn't until the industrial revolution hit Bohemia in the mid-nineteenth century that the first suburbs began to sprout up around the boundaries of the medieval town. A few were rigidly planned, with public parks and grid street plans; most grew with less grace, trailing their tenements across the hills, and swallowing up existing villages on the way. The majority still retain an individual identity, which makes them worth checking out on even a short visit to the city.

Vyšehrad, which was actually one of the earliest points of settlement in Prague, is something of an exception to all this, and is much the most enticing of the outlying areas. Its cemetery contains the remains of Bohemia's artistic elite; the ramparts afford superb views over the river; and below its fortress, there are several examples of Czech Cubist architecture. The rest of this chapter is given over to Vinohrady and Žižkov, the suburbs proper, each of which contains one or two specific sights to guide your wandering.

## Vyšehrad

At the southern tip of Nové Město, around 3km south of the city centre, the rocky red-brick fortress of VYŠEHRAD (literally "High Castle") has more myths attached to it per square inch than any other place in Bohemia. According to Czech legend, this is the place where the Slav tribes first settled in Prague, where the "wise and tireless chieftain" Krok built a castle, and whence his youngest daughter Libuše went on to found *Praha* itself. Alas, the archaeological evidence doesn't bear this claim out, but it's clear that Vratislav II (1061–92), the first Bohemian ruler to bear the title "king", built a royal palace here, to get away from his younger brother who was lording it in the Hrad. Within half a century the royals had moved back to

Hradčany, into a new palace, and from then on Vyšehrad began to lose
its political significance.

Charles IV had a system of walls built to link Vyšehrad to the newly founded Nové Město, and decreed that the *králová cesta* begin from here; these fortifications were destroyed by the Hussites in 1420, but the hill was settled again over the next two hundred years. In the mid-seventeenth century, the Habsburgs turfed everyone out and rebuilt the place as a fortified barracks, only to tear it down in 1866 to create a public park. The Czech *národní obrození* movement became interested in Vyšehrad when only the red-brick fortifications were left as a reminder of its former strategic importance, rediscovering its history and its legends, and gradually transforming it into a symbol of Czech nationhood.

For all its national historical significance, Vyšehrad today offers a pretty unremarkable set of buildings, and it's worth visiting mainly as an afternoon escape from the human congestion of the city, or in the evening to watch the sun set behind the Hrad.

## The fortress

There are several approaches to the **fortress** (see map on p.144), depending on where you arrive in Vyšehrad. From the metro station, Vyšehrad, walk west past the modern Palác kultury, and enter through the Leopoldová brána (**a**); if you've come by tram #3, #7 or #21, which pass along the waterfront, you can either wind your way up Vratislavova and enter through the Cihelná brána (**b**), or take one of the two steep stairways leading up through the trees to a small side entrance in the west wall.

The last approach brings you out right in front of the blackened sandstone church of **sv Petr and Pavel** (**c**), rebuilt in the 1880s in an unexciting neo-Gothic style on the site of an eleventh-century basilica. The twin openwork spires are the fortress's most familiar landmark; the church itself has been closed since archaeologists began to search for the remains of the eleventh-century royal palace here some years ago.

### The Vyšehrad Cemetery

One of the first initiatives of the *národní obrození* movement was to establish the **Vyšehrad Cemetery** (Vyšehradský hřbitov; daily May–Sept 8am–7pm; March, April & Oct 8am–6pm; Nov–Feb 9am–4pm), which spreads out to the north and east of the church. It's a measure of the part that artists and intellectuals played in the foundation of the nation, and the regard in which they are still held, that the most prestigious graveyard in the city is given over to them: no soldiers, no politicians, not even the Communists managed to muscle their way in here. Sheltered from the wind by its high walls, lined on two sides by arcades, it's a small cemetery, filled with well-kept graves, many of them designed by the country's leading sculptors.

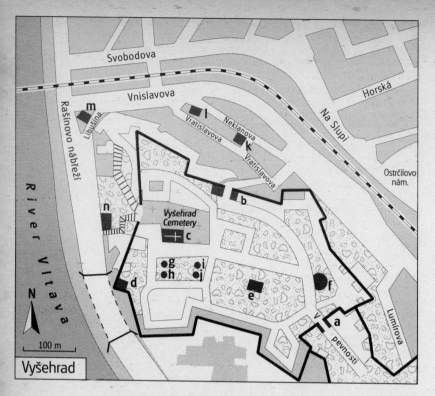

**Vyšehrad**

To the uninitiated only a handful of figures are well-known, but for the Czechs the place is alive with great names (there's a useful plan of the most notable graves at the entrance nearest the church). Dvořák's grave, under the arches, is one of the more showy ones, with a mosaic inscription, studded with gold stones, glistening behind wrought-iron railings. Smetana, who died twenty years earlier, is buried in comparatively modest surroundings near the Slavín monument (see below). The Spring Music Festival begins with a procession from his grave to the Obecní dům, on the anniversary of his death.

Other graves that attract (mostly Czech) pilgrims are those of the nineteenth-century writer Božena Němcová, by the east end of the church; and Karel Čapek – his grave faces the arcades – who coined one of the two Czech words to have entered the English language – "robot". Several graves of lesser-known individuals stand out artistically, too: in particular, Bílek's towering statue of *Sorrow* on the grave of V. B. Třebizský, which aroused a storm of protest when it was first unveiled; Bohumil Kafka's headstone for Dr J. Kaizl, with a woman's face peeping out from the grave; and Karel Hladík's modern *Cathedral* sculpture, which sits above his own grave.

*There's an A–Z of leading Czechs, past and present, on p.269*

The focus of the cemetery, though, is the **Slavín monument**, a big bulky stele, covered in commemorative plaques and topped by a sarcophagus and a statue representing Genius. It's the communal resting place of over fifty Czech artists, including the painter Alfons Mucha, the sculptors Josef Václav Myslbek and Ladislav Šaloun, the architect Josef Gočár, and the opera singer Ema Destinová.

The grave of the Romantic poet **Karel Hynek Mácha** was the assembly point for the demonstration on November 17, 1989, which triggered the Velvet Revolution. This was organised to commemorate the fiftieth anniversary of the funeral of **Jan Opletal**, a student at the university who was killed during the student protests against the Nazi occupation. His funeral took place on November 17, 1939, and provoked more violent disturbances: the Nazis responded by executing various student leaders, packing thousands off to the camps and shutting down all Czech higher education institutes. In 1989, a 50,000-strong crowd gathered at the cemetery, and attempted to march to Wenceslas Square, only to be stopped short in Národní, where the infamous *masakr* took place (see box, p.127).

*Mácha's remains were brought here from a cemetery in Litoměřice in 1938, when the Nazis took over the Sudetenland, see p.172*

### The rest of the fortress

The rest of the deserted fortress makes for a pleasant afternoon stroll; you can walk almost the entire length of the ramparts, which give some superb views out across the city. The small museum of historical drawings in one of the bastions (d) and the exhibition in the new deanery (e) are both pretty dull, though you might want to head for the latter to buy some postcards. The rotunda of sv Martin (f) – one of a number of Romanesque rotundas scattered across Prague – is the sole survivor of the medieval fortress, originally built by Vratislav II in the eleventh century but heavily restored by the nineteenth-century nationalists.

Time is better spent lounging on the patch of grass to the south of the church, where you'll come across the gargantuan statues by Myslbek that used to grace the city's Palackého most. Four couples are dotted across the green, all taken from Prague legends: *Přemysl and Libuše* (g), the husband and wife team who founded Prague and started Bohemia's first royal dynasty, the Přemyslids; *Lumír and Píseň* (h), the legendary Czech singer and his muse, Song; *Záboj and Slavoj* (i), two mythical Czech warriors; and *Ctirad and Šárka* (j), for whose story, see p.159.

## Czech Cubism in Vyšehrad

Even if you harbour only a passing interest in modern architecture, it's worth seeking out the cluster of **Cubist villas** below the fortress in Vyšehrad. Whereas Czech Art Nouveau was heavily influenced by the Viennese Secession, it was Paris rather than the imperial capital that provided the stimulus for the short-lived but extremely productive Czech Cubist movement. In 1911, the *Skupina výtvarných umělců* or *SVU* (Group of Fine Artists) was founded in Prague, and quickly became the movement's organising force. **Pavel Janák** was the *SVU*'s chief theorist, **Josef Gočár** its most illustrious exponent, but **Josef Chochol** was the most successful practitioner of the style in Prague.

Cubism is associated mostly with painting, and the unique contribution of its Czech offshoot was to apply the theory to furniture (most of which is now in the vaults of the UPM, see p.116) and **architecture**. In Vyšehrad alone, Chochol completed three buildings, close to one another below the fortress, using prismatic shapes and angular lines to produce the sharp geometric contrasts of light and dark shadows characteristic of Cubist painting. Outside Czechoslovakia, only the preparatory drawings by the French architect Duchamp-Villon for his *Maison Cubiste* (never undertaken), can be considered remotely similar.

The *SVU*'s plans were cut short by World War I, after which Janák and Gočár attempted to establish a specifically Czechoslovak style of architecture incorporating prewar Cubism. The style was dubbed **Rondo-Cubism** since the prismatic moulding had been replaced by semicircles, but only a few projects got off the ground before Czech architects turned to the functionalist ideals of the international modernist movement.

### The buildings

The most impressive example of Czech Cubist architecture, brilliantly exploiting its angular location, is the apartment block **nájemný obytný dům (k)**, at Neklanova 30, which dates from 1913. Further along Neklanova at no. 2, Antonín Belada built the street facade **uliční průčelí (l)**, and around the corner is the most ambitious project of the lot – Chochol's **Kovařovicova vila (m)**, which backs onto Libušina. The front, on Rašínovo nábřeží, is presently concealed behind some overenthusiastic shrubs, but it's still possible to appreciate the clever, slightly askew layout of the garden, designed right down to its zigzag garden railings. Further along the embankment is Chochol's largest commission, the **rodinný trojdům (n)**, a large building complex with room enough for three families.

---

**Cubist and Rondo-Cubist buildings in Prague**

Prague's unique Cubist and Rondo-Cubist buildings, most of which are covered in the text, are scattered right across the city. For those taken with the style, we've provided a checklist below.

# Vinohrady

PRAGUE

Southeast of Nové Město is the well-to-do nineteenth-century suburb of
**VINOHRADY**, home over the years to many of the country's most
notable personages. Although these days it has a run-down air about it,
it's still a desirable part of town to live in, boasting two spacious parks
– the **Riegrovy sady**, to the north, and the **Havlíčkovy sady**, to the
south – and a fabulous array of turn-of-the-century mansions. In terms
of conventional sightseeing, Vinohrady is definitely a low priority, but
there are a few places here (and in neighbouring Žižkov) worth visiting, most of them quick and easy to reach by metro.

    If Vinohrady has a centre, it's **náměstí Míru** (metro náměstí Míru),
a leafy square centred on the neo-Gothic church of sv Ludmila. From
here, block after block of decaying tenements, each covered in its own
individual garment of sculptural decoration, form a grid-plan of grand
bourgeois avenues stretching eastwards to the city's great cemeteries
(see below).

### Plečník's church

Vinohrady's other main square, **náměstí Jiřího z Poděbrad** (metro
Jiřího z Poděbrad), halfway between náměstí Míru and the cemeteries,
contains Prague's most celebrated modern church, **Nejsvětější Srdce
Páně** (Most Sacred Heart of Our Lord), built in 1928 by Josip Plečník,
the Slovene architect responsible for much of the remodelling of the
Hrad (see box on p.59). It's a marvellously eclectic and individualistic
work, employing a sophisticated potpourri of architectural styles: a
classical pediment, a Gothic rose window, and a great slab of a tower
with a giant transparent face, as well as the bricks and mortar of
contemporary constructivism. Plečník also had a sharp eye for detail;
look out for the little gold crosses inset into the brickwork like stars,
inside and out, and the celestial orbs of light suspended above the
heads of the congregation.

# Žižkov

PRAGUE

Unlike Vinohrady, **ŽIŽKOV** is a traditionally working-class area – and
was a Communist Party stronghold even before the war, earning it the
nickname "Red Žižkov". Nowadays it's home to a large proportion of
Prague's Romany community and other less privileged sections of
Czech society. The main reason for venturing into Žižkov is to visit its
two landmarks – ancient (Vítkov hill) and modern (the television tower)
– and the city's main cemeteries, on the borders of Žižkov and
Vinohrady.

### The Žižkov television tower

At over 100m, the Žižkov television tower (Televizní vysílač) is the
tallest (and the most unpopular) building in Prague. Close up, though,

it's difficult not to be impressed by this truly intimidating piece of futuristic architecture, its smooth grey exterior giving no hint of humanity. In the course of its construction, the Communists saw fit to demolish part of a nearby Jewish cemetery, that had served the community between 1787 and 1891; a small section survives to the northwest of the tower.

Begun in the 1970s in a desperate bid to keep out West German television, the tower has only become fully operational within the last few years, and now boasts a café four metres below ground, a restaurant on the fifth floor, and a **viewing platform** (výhlídka; daily 9am–10pm) on the eighth floor. For a not inconsiderable 50kčs, you can take the lift up there, though given the tower's position in a thoroughly uninspiring part of town, the view is not among the city's best. To get to the tower, take the metro to Jiřího z Poděbrad and walk northeast a couple of blocks.

## The cemeteries

Approaching from the west, the first and the largest of Prague's vast cemeteries – each of which is bigger than the entire Jewish quarter – is the **Olšany cemetery** (Olšanské hřbitovy; metro Flora), originally created for the victims of the great plague epidemic of 1680. The perimeter walls are lined with glass cabinets, stacked like shoe-boxes, containing funereal urns and mementoes, while the graves themselves are a mixed bag of artistic achievements, reflecting the funereal fashions of the day as much as the character of the deceased. The cemetery is divided into districts and crisscrossed with cobbled streets; at each gate there's a map, and an aged janitor ready to point you in the right direction at the mention of a name.

*There's a shrine to Palach and other martyrs of the Communist era on Wenceslas Square, see p.124*

Probably the most famous person buried here is **Jan Palach**, the philosophy student who set fire to himself in protest against the 1968 Soviet invasion. Over 750,000 people attended his funeral in January 1969, and in an attempt to put a stop to the annual vigils at his graveside, the secret police removed his body in 1973 and reburied him in

---

### Jaroslav Seifert of Žižkov

Czechoslovakia's Nobel prize-winning poet, **Jaroslav Seifert** (1901–1986) was born and bred in the Žižkov district. He was one of the founding members of the Czechoslovak Communist Party, and in 1920 helped found *Devětsil*, the most daring and provocative avant-garde movement of the interwar republic. Always accused of harbouring bourgeois sentiments, Seifert and eight other Communist writers were expelled from the Party when Gottwald and the Stalinists hijacked the Party at the Fifth Congress in 1929. After the 1948 coup, he became *persona non grata*, though he rose to prominence briefly during the 1956 Writers' Union congress, when he attempted to lead a rebellion against the Stalinists. Later on, he became involved in Charter 77, and in 1984, amidst much controversy, he became the one and only Czech to win the Nobel Prize for Literature.

---

his home town, 60km outside Prague. His place was taken by an unknown woman, Marie Jedličková, who for the next seventeen years had her grave covered in flowers instead. Finally, in 1990, Palach's body was returned to Olšany; you'll find it to the east of the main entrance on Vinohradská.

To the east of Olšany cemetery, and usually totally deserted, is the **war cemetery** (Vojenský hřbitov); the entrance is 200m up Jana Želivského, on the right (metro Želivského). Its centrepiece is the monument to the 436 Soviet soldiers who lost their lives on May 9, 1945 in the liberation of Prague, surrounded by a small, tufty meadow dotted with simple white crosses. Nearby, the graves of Czechs who died fighting for the Habsburgs on the Italian front in World War I are laid out in a semicircle.

### The New Jewish Cemetery
Immediately south of the war cemetery is the **New Jewish Cemetery** (Nový židovský hřbitov; April–Aug 8am–5pm; Sept–March 8am–4pm; closed Fri & Sat), founded in the 1890s, when the one by the Žižkov television tower was full (see p.148). It's a melancholy spot, particularly so in the east of the cemetery, where large empty allotments wait in vain to be filled by the generation who perished in the Holocaust. In fact, the community is now so small that it's unlikely the graveyard will ever be full. Most people come here to visit **Franz Kafka**'s grave, 400m east along the south wall and signposted from the entrance. He is buried, along with his mother and father (both of whom outlived him), beneath a plain headstone; the plaque below commemorates his three sisters who died in the camps.

*For more on Kafka's associations with Prague, see p.114*

## Žižkov hill
**Žižkov hill** (also known as Vítkov) is the thin green wedge of land that separates Žižkov from Karlín, another industrial district to the north. From its westernmost point, which juts out almost to the edge of Nové Město, can be had what's probably the definitive panoramic view over the city centre. It was here, on July 14, 1420, that the Hussites enjoyed their first and finest victory at the **Battle of Vítkov**, under the inspired leadership of the one-eyed general, Jan Žižka (hence the name of the district). Ludicrously outnumbered by something like ten to one but fanatically motivated, Žižka and his Táborite troops thoroughly trounced Emperor Sigismund and his papal forces.

The giant granite **Žižkov monument** was built between the wars as a memorial to the new nation, though its pompous brutality was just as well suited to its postwar use as a Communist mausoleum: presidents Gottwald, Zápotocký and Svoboda were all buried here, along with the Unknown Soldier and various Party hacks. Žižkov was an ideal resting place, lying as it does in the heart of "Red Žižkov", from where the Communists drew so much of their working-class support; in 1990, however, the bodies were reinterred elsewhere to protect them from desecration.

## Žižkov

*The pre-1914 military museum is covered on p.71*

To get to the monument, take the metro to Florenc, walk under the railway lines, and then up the steep lane U památníku. On the right as you climb the hill is the post-1914 section of the **Military Museum** (Vojenské muzeum; Tues–Sun April–Oct 8.30am–5pm; Nov–March 9.30am–4.30pm), guarded by a handful of unmanned tanks, howitzers and armoured vehicles. Before 1989, this place was a glorification of the Warsaw Pact, pure and simple; its recent overhaul has produced a much more evenly balanced account of both world wars, particularly in its treatment of the previously controversial subjects of the Czechoslovak Legion, the Heydrich assassination (see p.135) and the Prague Uprising.

# Chapter 8

# The northern and western suburbs

T he northern and western suburbs, on the left bank of the
Vltava, cover a much larger area than those to the east of the
river. They are also far more varied: some, like Holešovice and
parts of Smíchov, date from the time of the industrial revolution,
whereas the much posher areas of Dejvice and Střešovice were laid out
and built between the wars. The left bank also boast plenty of green-

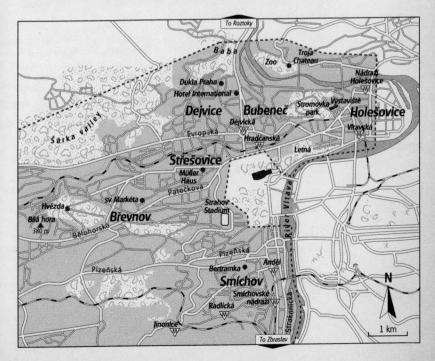

ery, including the city's largest public park, Stromovka. All this goes to make up a fascinating patchwork of communities, which few tourists bother to see. It's worth the effort, though, if only to remind yourself that Prague doesn't begin and end at the Charles Bridge.

There are several specific sights in each suburb that can lend structure to your meanderings. A few, like the Mozart Museum in Smíchov and the Technical Museum in Holešovice, are included in most people's tours of the city. Others – like the functionalist villa quarters in Dejvice and Střešovice – are more specialised; and some are simply unknown to most visitors, like the Renaissance chateau of Hvězda, and the Museum of Czech sculpture in the monastery at Zbraslav.

PRAGUE

# Holešovice and Bubeneč

The districts of HOLEŠOVICE and BUBENEČ, tucked into a huge U-bend in the Vltava, have little in the way of magnificent architecture, but they make up for it with two huge splodges of green: to the south Letná, where Prague's greatest gatherings occur, and to the north the Stromovka park, bordering the Výstaviště funfair and international trade fair; within easy reach, across the river, is Prague's only genuine chateau, Troja.

## A small piece of Hradčany

For convenience, we've included in this chapter the small patch of Hradčany that lies to the northeast of the castle. The easiest way to this part of town is to take the metro to Hradčanská and head up Tychonova, a street flanked on one side by a military barracks and training ground, on the other by a series of semi-detached houses. These include Josef Gočár's rodinný dvojdům at nos. 4–6, built in a restrained Cubist style similar to that employed on the Dům U černé Matky boží in Staré Město (see p.101).

At the top of Tychonova, the leafy avenue of Marianské hradby slopes down to the left, past the Belvedere, to the Chotkovy sady beyond: Prague's first public park, founded in 1833 by the ecologically minded city governor, Count Chotek. The atmosphere here is a lot more relaxed than in the nearby Royal Gardens, and you can happily stretch out on the grass and soak up the sun, or head for the south wall, which enjoys an unrivalled view of the bridges and islands of the Vltava. At the centre of the park there's a bizarre grotto-like memorial to the nineteenth-century Romantic poet Julius Zeyer, an elaborate monument from which life-sized characters from Zeyer's works, carved in white marble, emerge from the blackened rocks amid much drapery.

*The Belvedere and the Royal Gardens are both covered in Chapter 2, see p.62*

### The Bílkova vila

Across the road from the park, hidden behind its overgrown garden at Mieckiewiczova 1, the Bílkova vila (mid-May to Sept Tues–Sun 9am–5pm) honours one of Czechoslovakia's most unusual sculptors,

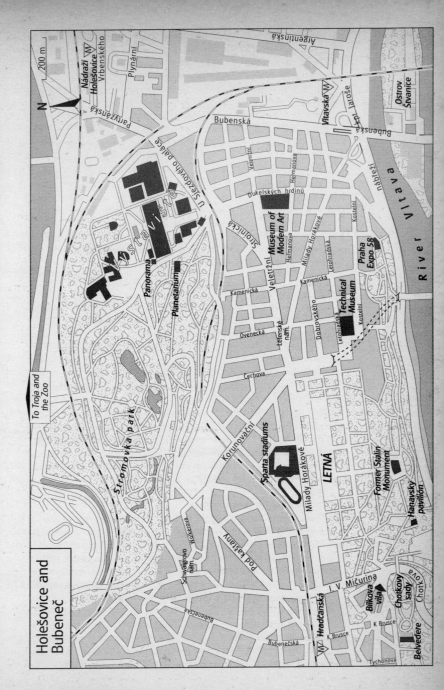

Holešovice and Bubeneč

N 200 m

Nádraží Holešovice Vrbenského

Plynární

Partyzánská

To Troja and the Zoo

U Sjezdového paláce

Výstaviště

Panorama

Planetarium

Stromovka park

Schwaigrovo nám.

Pod kaštany

Wolkerova

Bubenská

Kamenická

Schwaigrovo nám.

Korunovační

Bubenečská

Bubenečská

Hradčanská

I. V. Mičuring

Bílkova vila

K Brusce

Brusce

Tychonova

Argentinská

Vltavská

Bubenská

kpt. Jaroše

Ostrov Štvanice

River Vltava

nábřeží

Veletržní Museum of Modern Art

Dukelských hrdinů

Veletržní

Heřmanova

Milady Horákové

Letohradská

Praha Expo 58

Kostelní

Technical Museum

Kamenická

Dobrovského

Kamenická

Ovenecká

tetenské nám.

Čechova

Sparta stadiums

Milady Horákové

LETNÁ

Former Stalin Monument

Hanavský pavilón

Chotkovy sady

Chotkova

Belvedere

Šrobárova

František Bílek. Born in 1872 in a part of South Bohemia steeped in the
Hussite tradition, Bílek lived a monkish life, spending years in spiritual
contemplation, reading the works of Hus and other Czech reformers.
The villa was built in 1911 to Bílek's own design, intended as both a
"cathedral of art" and the family home. Even so, at first sight, it's a
strangely mute red-brick building, out of keeping with the extravagant
Symbolist style of Bílek's sculptures: from the outside, only the front
porch, supported by giant sheaves of corn, and the sculptured figures in
the garden – the fleeing Comenius and followers – give a clue as to what
lies within.

Inside, the brickwork gives way to bare stone walls lined with
Bílek's religious sculptures – giving the impression you've walked into a
chapel rather than an artist's studio. In addition to his sculptural and
relief work in wood and stone, often wildly expressive, there are also
ceramics, graphics and a few mementoes of Bílek's life. His work is
little known outside his native country, but his contemporary admirers
included Franz Kafka, Julius Zeyer, and Otakar Březina, whose poems
and novels provided the inspiration for much of Bílek's art.

## Letná

Cross over the bridge at the eastern end of the Chotkovy sady, and
you'll find yourself on the flat green expanse of the **Letná plain**, traditional assembly point for invading and besieging armies. It was laid out
as a public park in the mid-nineteenth century, but its main post-1948
function was as the site of the May Day parades. For these, thousands
of citizens were dragooned into marching past the south side of the
city's main football ground, the Sparta stadium, where the old
Communist cronies would take the salute from a giant red podium.

On November 26, 1989, the park was the scene of a more genuine
expression of popular sentiment, when over 750,000 people gathered
here to join in the call for a general strike against the Communist
regime. Unprecedented scenes followed in April 1990, when a million
Catholics came to hear Pope John Paul II speak on his first visit to an
eastern European country other than his native Poland.

### The former Stalin monument

Letná's – indeed Prague's – most famous monument is one which no
longer exists. The **Stalin monument**, the largest in the world, was
once visible from almost every part of the city: a thirty-metre-high
granite sculpture portraying a procession of people being led to
Communism by the Pied Piper figure of Stalin, popularly dubbed "the
bread queue". Designed by Otakar Švec, who committed suicide before
it was unveiled, it took 600 workers 500 days to erect the 14,000-ton
monster, which was revealed to the cheering masses on May 1, 1955.
This was the first and last popular celebration to take place at the
monument. Within a year, Krushchev had denounced his predecessor
and, after pressure from Moscow, the monument was blown to smith-
ereens by a series of explosions spread over a fortnight in 1962.

All that remains above ground is the statue's vast concrete platform, on the southern edge of the Letná plain, now a favourite spot for skateboarders and another good viewpoint, with the central stretch of the Vltava glistening in the afternoon sun. Built into the hillside below is Prague's one and only nuclear bunker, intended to preserve the Party elite, post-armageddon. For years, it was actually used to store the city's slowly rotting potato mountain; more recently it has been sporadically squatted and used as a nightclub venue.

If you're in need of some refreshment, head for the café at the nearby **Hanavský pavilón**, originally built for the 1891 Prague Exhibition in a flamboyant style which anticipated the arrival of Art Nouveau a few years later.

Holešovice and Bubeneč

## East of Letná: the Museum of Technology and the Museum of Modern and Contemporary Art

At present Holešovice boasts just one fully functioning museum, the **Museum of Technology** (Tues–Sun 10am–5pm) on Kostelní, which contains Vojta Náprstek's technological collection, plus a host of old planes, trains and automobiles, and an impressive gallery of motorbikes. The showpiece is the hangar-like main hall, packed with machines from Czechoslovakia's industrial heyday between the wars, when the country's Škoda cars and Tatra limos were really something to brag about. Upstairs, there are displays tracing the development of early photography, and a collection of some of Kepler and Tycho de Brahe's astrological instruments. Below ground, a mock-up of a coal mine offers guided tours every other hour, kicking off at 11am.

*The Náprstek Museum, containing his American, Australian and African collections, is covered on p.106*

The **Museum of Modern and Contemporary Czech Art** is at present no more than a plan, despite constant rumours that it is to open imminently. The 1928 Trade Fair building being restored for the purpose – ten minutes' walk northeast of the Museum of Technology, at the corner of Dukelských hrdinů and Veletržní (tram #5, #12, #17 or #19) – is a magnificent seven-storey glass curtain-wall design that's in many ways Prague's ultimate functionalist masterpiece. It certainly blew Le Corbusier's mind, as he himself admitted in 1930: "When I first saw the Trade Fair building in Prague I felt totally depressed, I realised that the large and convergent structures I had been dreaming of really existed somewhere, while at the time I had just built a few small villas".

*Exhibitions of twentieth-century Czech art are currently staged by the Jízdárna, see p.62*

## Výstaviště and Stromovka park

Five minutes' walk north up Dukelských hrdinů takes you right to the front gates of the **Výstaviště**, a motley assortment of buildings, originally created for the 1891 Prague Exhibition, that have served as the city's main trade fair arena and funfair ever since. The Communist Party held its rubber-stamp congresses here from 1948 until the late 1970s, and more recently several brand new permanent structures were built for the 1991 Prague Exhibition. The canopy over the main

entrance, off U Sjezdového paláce, is one of these – a modern echo of
the flamboyant glass and iron **Průmyslový palác** at the centre of the
complex.

The park is at its busiest on summer weekends, when hordes of
Prague families descend on the place to down hot dogs, drink beer and
listen to traditional brass band music. Apart from the annual fairs and
lavish special exhibitions, there are a few permanent attractions, such
as the city's **planetarium** (Mon–Thurs 8am–noon & 1–6pm, Fri 8am–
noon, Sat & Sun 10am–6pm; hours can vary); the **Maroldova
panoráma** (daily 9am–5pm), a giant diorama of the 1434 Battle of
Lipany (see *Contexts* for the significance of this battle); and the
**Dětský svět**, a funfair and playground for kids. Another permanent
fixture that will hopefully be restored in the not too distant future is
the panoramic cinema screen, near the diorama.

To the west is the *královská obora* or royal enclosure, more
commonly known as **Stromovka park**, Prague's largest and leafiest
public park. Originally the fourteenth-century hunting grounds for the
noble occupants of the Hrad, it gained various rare trees, and a lake,
fed by a canal from the Vltava, thanks to one of Rudolf II's ambitious
horticultural schemes. From here, you can wander northwards to Troja
and the city's zoo (see below), following a path that leads under the
railway, over the canal, and on to the Císařský ostrov (Emperor's
Island) – and from there to the right bank of the Vltava.

# Troja

Though still well within the municipal boundaries, the suburb of
TROJA, across the river to the north of Holešovice and Bubeneč, has a
distinctly provincial air. Its most celebrated sight is the **chateau** of the
same name, perfectly situated against a hilly backdrop of vines. Troja's
other attraction is the city's slightly dilapidated, but still enormously
popular **zoo**.

### The chateau

The **Troja Chateau** (Trojský zámek; April–Sept Tues–Sun 9am–5pm;
bus #112 from metro Nádraží Holešovice) was designed by Jean-
Baptiste Mathey for the powerful Šternberk family towards the end of
the seventeenth century. Despite a recent renovation and rusty red
repaint, its plain early Baroque facade is no match for the action-
packed, blackened figures of giants and titans who battle it out on the
chateau's monumental balustrades. To visit the **interior**, you'll have to
join one of the guided tours. The star exhibits are the gushing frescoes
depicting the victories of the Habsburg Emperor Leopold I (1657–
1705) over the Turks, which cover every inch of the walls and ceilings
of the grand hall. Alternatively, you can simply take a wander through
the chateau's pristine French-style formal **gardens** (open all year), the
first of their kind in Bohemia.

### The zoo

On the other side of U trojského zámku, which runs along the west wall of the chateau, is the city's capacious zoo (zoologická zahrada; daily April 7am–5pm; May 7am–6pm; June–Sept 7am–7pm; Oct–March 7am–4pm), founded in 1931 on the site of one of Troja's numerous hillside vineyards. Despite its rather weary appearance, all the usual animals are on show here, and kids, at least, have few problems enjoying themselves. Thankfully, a programme of modernisation is currently underway, though only the new lion and tiger building, to the south, has so far been completed. In the summer, you can take a "ski-lift" (lanová dráha) from the duck pond to the top of the hill, where the prize exhibits – a rare breed of miniature horse known as Przewalski – hang out.

# Dejvice, Střešovice and beyond

Spread across the hills to the northwest of the city centre are the leafy, garden suburbs of **Dejvice** and **Střešovice**, peppered with onceswanky villas, built between the wars for the upwardly mobile Prague bourgeoisie and commanding magnificent views across the north of the city. Both districts are short on conventional sights, but interesting to explore all the same. Some distance further west, the **Šárka valley** is just about as far as you can get from an urban environment without leaving the city. To the south of Šárka are the battlefield of **Bílá hora**, and the **Hvězda** park, which contains a pretty star-shaped chateau that's well worth the effort to see.

## Dejvice

**DEJVICE** was planned and built in the early 1920s for the First Republic's burgeoning community of civil servants and government and military officials. Its unappealing main square, **Vitězné náměstí** (metro Dejvická), is practically unavoidable if you're planning to explore any of the western suburbs, since it's a major public transport interchange. There's nothing much of note in this central part of Dejvice, though you can't help but notice the **Hotel International** at the end of Jugoslávských partyzanů, a gift from Stalin that is disturbingly similar to the universally loathed Palace of Culture in Warsaw.

### Baba

Dejvice's most intriguing villas are located to the north in **Baba** (bus #131 from metro Hradčanská), a model neighbourhood of 33 functionalist houses, each individually commissioned and built under the guidance of one-time Cubist, Pavel Janák. A group of leading architects affiliated to the Czech Workers' Alliance, inspired by a similar project in Stuttgart, initiated what was, at the time, a radical housing project to provide simple, single-family villas. The idea was to use space and open-plan techniques rather than expensive materials to create a luxurious living space.

Despite the plans of the builders, the houses were mostly bought up by Prague's artistic and intellectual community. Nevertheless, they have stood the test of time better than most utopian architecture, not least because of the fantastic site – facing south and overlooking the city. Some of them remain exactly as they were when first built, others have been thoughtlessly altered, but as none of them is open to the public you'll have to be content with surreptitious peeping from the street.

## Střešovice

STŘEŠOVICE has no central square and is dominated rather by its wealthy villa quarter, Ořechovka. The most famous of the villas is the **Müller Haus** at Na hradním vodojemem 14 (tram #1, #2 or #18), designed by the Brno-born architect, Adolf Loos. Completed in 1930 (after planning permission had been refused ten times), it was one of Loos' few commissions, a typically uncompromising white box, wiped smooth with concrete rendering. Now grey with pollution, it's not exactly a wonder to behold, and since you can't get inside, there's no way to appreciate the careful choice of rich materials and minimal furnishings that were Loos' hallmark. There are plans to turn the house into a museum to Loos – regarded by many as one of the founders of modern architecture – but for the moment, surrounded by hundreds of similarly boxy houses, you may well wonder what all the fuss is about.

## The Šárka valley

If you've had your fill of postcards and crowds, take tram #20 or #26 to the last stop and walk north down into the Šárka valley, a peaceful limestone gorge that twists eastwards back towards Dejvice. The first section (Divoká Šárka) is particularly dramatic, with grey-white crags rising up on both sides – it was here that Šárka plunged to her death (see below). Gradually the valley opens up, with a grassy meadow to picnic on, and a swimming pool nearby, both fairly popular on summer weekends. There are various points further east from which you can pick up a city bus back into town, depending on how far you want to walk. The full walk to where the Šárka stream flows into the Vltava is about 6 or 7km all told, though none of it is particularly tough going.

## Bílá hora, Hvězda and Břevnov

A couple of kilometres southwest of Dejvice, trams #8 and #22 terminate close to the once entirely barren limestone summit of **Bílá hora** (White Mountain). It was here, on November 8, 1620, that the first battle of the Thirty Years' War took place, sealing the fate of the Czech nation for the following three hundred years. In little more than an hour, the Protestant forces under Count Thurn and the "Winter King" Frederick of Palatinate were roundly beaten by the Catholic troops of the Habsburg Emperor Maximilian. As a more or less direct consequence, the Czechs lost their aristocracy, their religion, their scholars and, most importantly, the remnants of their sovereignty.

### Šárka and Ctirad

The Šárka valley takes its name from the Amazonian Šárka, who, according to Czech legend, committed suicide here sometime back in the last millennium. The story begins with the death of Libuše, the founder and first ruler of Prague. The women closest to her, who had enjoyed enormous freedom and privilege in her court, refused to submit to the new patriarchy of her husband, Přemysl. Under the leadership of a woman called Vlasta, they left Vyšehrad and set up their own proto-feminist, separatist colony on the opposite bank of the river.

They scored numerous military victories over the men of Vyšehrad, but never managed to finish off the men's leader, a young warrior called Ctirad. In the end they decided to ensnare him and tied one of their own warriors naked to a tree, sure in the knowledge that Ctirad would take her to be a maiden in distress and come to her aid. Šárka offered to act as the decoy, and everything went according to plan. However, in her brief meeting with Ctirad, Šárka fell madly in love with him and, overcome with grief at what she had done, threw herself off the aforementioned cliff. And just in case you thought the legend had a feminist ending, it doesn't. Roused by the cruel murder of Ctirad, Přemysl and the lads have a final set-to with Vlasta and co, and butcher the lot of them.

To get to the hill from the tram stop, walk west, take the first road on the right, Nad višňovkou, and then turn right when you see the monument. There's nothing much to see now, apart from the small monument (*mohyla*), and a pilgrims' church, just off Nad višňovkou. This was erected by the Catholics to commemorate the victory, which they ascribed to the timely intercession of the Virgin Mary – hence its name, **Panna Marie Vítězná** (St Mary the Victorious).

A short distance to the northeast of Bílá hora is the hunting park of **Hvězda** (obora Hvězda), scene of a last-ditch counterattack launched by the Moravian Brethren during the battle. Nowadays it's one of Prague's most beautiful and peaceful parks, with soft, green avenues of trees radiating from a bizarre star-shaped building (Hvězda means "Star") that was designed by the Archduke Ferdinand of Tyrol for his wife in 1555. Fully restored in the 1950s, it houses a **museum** (Tues–Sat 9am–4pm, Sun 10am–5pm) devoted to the reactionary writer Alois Jirásek (1851–1930), who popularised old Czech legends during the *národní obrození*, and the artist Mikuláš Aleš (1852–1913), whose drawings were likewise inspired by Czech history. There's also a small exhibition on the Battle of Bílá hora (see above) on the top floor. It's the building itself, though – decorated with delicate stucco work and frescoes – that's the greatest attraction; it makes a perfect setting for the chamber music concerts occasionally staged here.

Despite the park's proximity to Bílá hora, the only entrances are on the north side, near the #1, #2 and #18 tram terminal on Heyrovského náměstí. Rather than heading straight back into town, if you've time to spare, the idyllic Baroque monastery of sv **Markéta** in

### Jan Patočka

The main road which runs past the Břevnov monastery is named after Jan Patočka (1907–77), one of the first three spokespersons of the human rights group, Charter 77. Patočka was educated before the war at the Charles University and the Sorbonne, where he studied under Edmund Husserl, later becoming professor of philosophy in Prague. As a humanist philosopher, he was barred from a position at the university, but continued to write, translate and edit numerous works. On March 1, 1977, he was interrogated for eleven hours by the secret police, and suffered a heart attack; he died ten days later in Strahov hospital.

When Patočka was buried in Břevnov cemetery, on March 16, it was not without considerable interference from the security forces. Flower shops across the city were instructed not to accept orders for wreaths or flowers for the ceremony; access roads to Břevnov were closed, and several people were arrested trying to reach the cemetery. In the end, over 1000 managed to attend, all of them filmed by the police.

Břevnov is just five minutes' walk east of the park, down Zeyerova alej. Founded as a Benedictine abbey by Saint Adalbert, tenth-century bishop of Prague, it was worked over in the eighteenth century by both Christoph and Kilian Ignaz Dientzenhofer, and bears their characteristic interconnecting ovals, inside and out. The monks have recently returned, which may paradoxically make it easier to gain access to the church. To get back into town, take tram #8 or #22 from just below the monastery.

# The south: from Smíchov to Zbraslav

SMÍCHOV is for the most part an old nineteenth-century working-class suburb, home to the city's largest brewery, and a large community of Romanies, its skyline peppered with satanic mills and chimneys dutifully belching out smoke. To the west, as it gains height, the run-down tenements give way to another of Prague's sought-after villa quarters. To the north, it borders with Malá Strana, and in fact takes in a considerable part of the woods of Petřín, south of the Hunger Wall (see p.87).

This part of Petřín, which you can gain access to from náměstí Sovětských tankistů (tram #6, #9 or #12), belonged to the Kinský family, whose Empire villa until recently housed an old collection of folk costumes and art, part of the original 1891 exhibition; its future is currently uncertain. Just north of the villa, hidden in the trees, is a wooden church that was brought here, log by log, from an Orthodox village in Ruthenia (now part of Ukraine) in 1929. Churches like this are still common in eastern Slovakia, and this is a particularly ornate example from the eighteenth century, with multiple domes like piles of giant acorns.

## Bertramka

As long ago as 1838, the Dušeks' **Bertramka Villa** (April–Sept Tues–Fri 2–5pm, Sat & Sun 10am–noon & 2–5pm; Oct–March Tues–Fri 1–4pm, Sat & Sun 10am–noon & 1–4pm; metro Anděl), halfway up Mozartova, was turned into a shrine to Mozart, who stayed here on several occasions towards the end of his life. Very little survives of the house he knew, since a fire on New Year's Day 1871, not that this has deterred generations of Mozart lovers from flocking here. These days, what the museum lacks in memorabilia, it makes up for in Rococo ambience and the odd Mozart recital. To get to Bertramka, take the metro to Anděl, walk a couple of blocks west up Plzeňská, then left up Mozartova.

*The south:
Smíchov to
Zbraslav*

*For more on
Mozart's links
with Prague, see
box on p.81*

---

**The Pink Tank**

Smíchov's most recent claim to fame was the episode of the **pink tank**. Until very recently, Tank 23 sat proudly on its plinth in náměstí Sovětských tankistů (Soviet tank drivers' square), one of a number of obsolete tanks generously donated by the Soviets after World War II to serve as monuments to the 1945 liberation. Tank 23 was supposedly the first tank to arrive to liberate Prague, on May 9, hotfoot from Berlin; the circumstances of its arrival, however, are shrouded in controversy.

Apparently, the first offer of assistance to the Prague Uprising, which began on May 5, came from units of the anti-Communist Russian Liberation Army (KONR), under the renegade general, Andrei Vlasov. Vlasov was a high-ranking Red Army officer, who was instrumental in pushing the Germans back from the gates of Moscow, but switched sides after being captured by the Nazis in 1942. Under orders from Moscow, the resistance in Prague refused the KONR's overtures. Vlasov himself was keen to fight on against the Red Army, while his men wanted nothing more than to surrender to the Americans – in fact, the KONR were eventually forced to fight alongside the SS until the very end. After the war, the Americans handed Vlasov over to the Russians who tried him *in camera* as a traitor, and executed him.

The unsolicited reappearance of Soviet tanks on the streets of Prague in 1968 left most Czechs feeling somewhat ambivalent towards the old monument. And in the summer of 1991, situationist artist David Černý painted the tank bubble-gum pink, and placed a large phallic finger on top of it, while another mischievous Czech daubed "Vlasov" on the podium. Since the country was at the time engaged in delicate negotiations to end the Soviet military presence in Czechoslovakia, the new regime, despite its mostly dissident leanings, roundly condemned the act as unlawful. Havel, in his characteristically even-handed way, made it clear that he didn't like tanks anywhere, whether on the battlefield or as monuments.

In the end, the tank was hastily repainted khaki green and Černý was arrested under the familiar "crimes against the state" clause of the penal code, which had been used by the Communists with gay abandon on several members of the present government. In protest at the arrest of Černý, twelve members of the federal parliament turned up the following day in their overalls and, taking advantage of their legal immunity, repainted the tank pink. Finally, the government gave in, released Černý and removed the tank from public view. There's now no trace of tank, podium or plaque, though the square's name is still holding out against the odds.

## Zbraslav

One of the best art museums in Prague is in the little-visited village of
ZBRASLAV, 10km south of the city, though now within the municipal
boundaries (bus #241, #243, #255, ČSAD, or local train from metro
Smíchovské nádraží). Přemyslid King Otakar II built a hunting lodge
here, which was later turned into a Cistercian monastery and now
houses the National Gallery's collection of modern Czech sculpture
(Tues–Sun 10am–6pm). The sculptures are imaginatively strewn about
the chambers, courtyards and gardens of the Baroque buildings. The
ground floor is filled with the work of Josef Václav Myslbek (1848–
1929), who laid the groundwork for the remarkable outpouring of
Czech sculpture in the first half of this century. There are also some
outstanding works by the likes of Ladislav Šaloun, who was responsible for the Hus Monument, unveiled in 1912, Stanislav Sucharda, who
sculpted the Palacký Monument, completed three years later, and Otto
Gutfreund, whose Cubist creations predate those of Picasso and co –
not to mention *The Motorcyclist* by Otakar Švec, the only extant work
by the man responsible for the Stalin Monument.

# Chapter 9

# Out from the City

ew capital cities can boast such extensive unspoilt tracts of
woodland so near at hand as Prague. Once you leave the
half-built high-rise estates of the outer suburbs behind, the
traditional provincial feel of Bohemia (Čechy) immediately makes

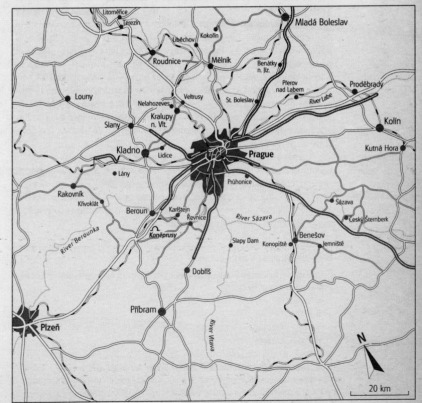

itself felt. Its towns and villages still huddle below the grand residences of their former lords, their street layout little changed since medieval times.

To the north, several such chateaux grace the banks of the Vltava, including the wine-producing town of **Mělník**, on the Labe (Elbe) plain. Beyond Mělník lie the wooded gorges of the **Kokořínsko** region, too far for a day trip, but perfect for a weekend in the country. Further away, but better served by public transport, are **Terezín**, the wartime Jewish ghetto, and the neighbouring town of **Litoměřice**. One of the most obvious day-trip destinations is to the east of Prague: **Kutná Hora**, a medieval silver mining town with one of the most beautiful Gothic churches in the country, and a macabre gallery of bones in the suburb of Sedlec.

Further south, there's a couple of chateaux worth visiting along the **Sázava** valley; while nearby, two more chateaux, **Průhonice** and **Konopiště**, are set in exceptionally beautiful and expansive grounds – with a car, you could take in all four in a day. Southwest of Prague, a similar mix of woods and rolling hills surrounds the popular castle of **Karlštejn**, a gem of Gothic architecture, dramatically situated above the River Berounka. There are numerous possibilities for walking in the region around Karlštejn, and further upstream, in the forests of **Křivoklátsko**. West of Prague, near Kladno, there are two places of pilgrimage: **Lány** is the resting place of the founder of modern Czechoslovakia, and summer residence of the president; and **Lidice**, razed to the ground by the SS, is another town which recalls the horror of Nazi occupation. Finally, beer lovers might consider a trip to the *Pilsner Urquell* brewery in **Plzeň**, centre of the country's beer industry, home of the Škoda engineering works and an interesting medieval town in its own right.

*For details on public transport systems, and addresses of car hire firms, see p.16*

**Transport** throughout Bohemia is fairly straightforward, thanks to a comprehensive network of railway lines and regional bus services, though connections can be less than smooth, and journeys slow. If you're planning to try and see more than one or two places outside Prague, however, or one of the more difficult destinations to reach, it might be worth considering hiring a car.

---

**Accommodation Prices**

Each place to stay in this chapter has a price symbol corresponding to one of five **price categories:**

① Under 750kčs

② 750–1250 kčs

③ 1250–2000 kčs

④ 2000–3000kčs

⑤ 3000kčs and upwards

All prices are for the cheapest **double room** available, which usually means without private bath or shower in the less expensive places. For a **single room**, expect to pay around two-thirds the price of a double.

---

# North along the Vltava

One of the quickest and most rewarding trips out of the capital is to follow the Vltava as it twists northwards across the plain towards the River Labe at Mělník. This is the beginning of the so-called **záhrada Čech** (Garden of Bohemia), a flat and fertile region whose cherry blossoms are always the first to herald the Bohemian spring, and whose roads in summer are lined with stalls overflowing with fruit and vegetables. But the real reason to venture into this flat landscape is to visit the chateaux that lie along the banks of the river, all easily reached from Prague by public transport.

## Around Kralupy

The Nobel prize-winning poet Jaroslav Seifert didn't beat about the bush when he wrote that KRALUPY NAD VLTAVOU "is not a beautiful town and never was". It paid an unusually heavy price in the last war, bombarded from the air, and postwar industrial development has left it with "smokestacks . . . like phantom trees, without branches, without leaves, without blossoms, without bees". Now, Kralupy's oil refineries and chemical plants have spread across both sides of the river, but it's still worth making the 45-minute train journey from Prague, as just a few kilometres to the north, on either side of the Vltava, are two fine chateaux: Nelahozeves on the left bank, and Veltrusy on the right – again both accessible by train.

### Nelahozeves

Shortly after pulling out of Kralupy, the train passes through a short tunnel and comes to rest at Nelahozeves zastávka, the first of two stations in the village of NELAHOZEVES. Above the railway sits the village's plain, barracks-like chateau (April–Oct Tues–Sun 9am–5pm), recently given a new lease of life by a sgraffito face-lift. The chateau was built by a group of fairly undistinguished Italian builders for one of the lackeys of the Habsburg Emperor Ferdinand I and now, stripped of its furniture, it serves as an art repository for European paintings from the collections of three great aristocratic families: the Pernštejns, the Rožmberks and the Lobkovics. The best stuff, sadly, is either in Prague galleries or on permanent loan elsewhere, leaving little to gloat over here, but there are some good portraits spanning the centuries, and you can get something to eat in the chateau restaurant.

The country's most famous composer, **Antonín Dvořák** (1841–1904), was born and bred under the shadow of the chateau, at the house (no. 12) next door to the post office. Dvořák was originally apprenticed to a butcher, but on the recommendation of his schoolmaster, was sent to the Prague Organ School instead. Throughout a successful career, he continued to draw inspiration from his homeland. If there's someone around at the house (officially open Tues–Thurs, Sat & Sun 9am–noon & 2–5pm), you can have a quick look at the great man's rocking chair, and various other personal effects.

*There's another museum dedicated to Dvořák in Prague, see p.138*

**Veltrusy**

The industrial suburbs of Kralupy stop just short of the gardens of the chateau of **Veltrusy** (Tues–Sun March, April & Sept 9am–noon & 1–4pm; May–Aug 8am–noon & 1–5pm), over the bridge from the second of the stations in Nelahozeves (one stop on from Nelahozeves zastávka). The classic Baroque symmetry of Veltrusy makes for an altogether more satisfying experience than the chateau at Nelahozeves, its green shutters and henna-dyed wings pivoting round a bulbous, green-domed building that recalls earlier country houses in France or Italy. It was built in the early eighteenth century as a plaything for the upwardly mobile Counts of Chotek, its 290 acres of surrounding woodland perfect for a little light hunting.

If you fancy staying, there's a very good **campsite** (April to mid-Nov) just outside the chateau grounds – a great spot for watching the barges on the Vltava, but no place for a dip given the pollutants that pour into the river further upstream. On the road to the campsite and chateau, several houses offer cheap **private rooms**.

# Mělník

Occupying a commanding site at the confluence of the Vltava and Labe rivers, MĚLNÍK, 33km north of Prague, lies at the heart of Bohemia's tiny wine-growing region. The town's history goes back to the ninth century, when it was handed over to the Přemyslids as part of Ludmilla's dowry when she married Prince Bořivoj. And it was here, too, that she introduced her heathen grandson Václav (later to become Saint Wenceslas) to the joys of Christianity. Viticulture became the town's economic mainstay only after Charles IV, aching for a little of the French wine of his youth, introduced grapes from Burgundy (where he was also king).

### The old town

Mělník's greatest monument is its Renaissance **chateau** (Tues–Sun March, April & Sept 9am–4pm; May–Aug 8am–noon & 1–5pm), perched high above the flat plains and visible for miles around. The present building, covered in the familiar sgraffito patterning, houses the local museum, and more of the apparently unending collection of old masters that belonged to its last aristocratic owners, the Lobkovic family – displayed in magnificently proportioned rooms, which also provide great views out over the plain.

Below the chateau, vines cling to the south-facing terraces, as the land plunges into the river below. From beneath the great tower of Mělník's onion-domed church of **sv Petr and Pavel**, next door to the chateau, there's an even better view of the rivers' confluence, and the subsidiary canal, once so congested with vessels that traffic lights had to be introduced to avoid accidents. The rest of the old town is pleasant enough for some casual strolling, though pretty small – not much more than an arcaded main square and an old medieval gateway.

**Practicalities**

Beyond Nelahozeves, the main line from Prague veers northwest, away
from Mělník, which means that there's no direct train service here from
Prague. There is, however, a regular bus service, which takes around an
hour; to reach the older part of town from the **bus station**, simply head
up Krombholcova in the direction of the big church tower. If your next
destination is Liběchov or Litoměřice, you have the choice of either the
bus or the train; the **train station** is still further from the old town, a
couple of blocks northeast of the bus station, down Jiřího z Poděbrad.

If you're hoping to stay, there are **private rooms** available on
Legionářů, to the north of the old town, and on Palackého náměstí, off
the main square; plus the modern hotel, *Ludmila* (☎0206/25 78; ②),
1.5km down the road to Prague. As for **food and drink**, the chateau
restaurant is as good (and cheap) a place as any to sample some of the
local wine (and enjoy the view): the red *Ludmila* is the most famous
of Mělník's wines, but if you prefer white, try a bottle of *Tramín* to
accompany the fresh trout (thankfully not pulled out of the Vltava or
Labe below). If the tour groups are monopolising the chateau restaurant, you'll have to be content with the basic food and *Krušovice* beer
served at the *Zlatý beránek* on the main square in the old town, or *U
sv Václava* at Svatováclavská 22, a new *vinárna* beside the main
entrance to the chateau. The *Zámecka pivnice*, opposite, was temporarily closed at the time of writing.

## Liběchov

Seven kilometres north and ten minutes by train from Mělník – just out
of sight of the giant coal-fired power station that provides most of
Prague's electricity – is the rhubarb-and-custard coloured **chateau**
(Tues–Sun 9am–noon & 1–3.30pm) at LIBĚCHOV (Liboch). Even without the sickly colour scheme, it's a bizarre place: formal and two-
dimensional when viewed from the French gardens at the front, but
bulging like an amphitheatre around the back by the entrance. Inside
is another surprise, a **museum of Asian and Oriental cultures** featuring endless Buddhas, Mongolian printing equipment, Balinese monster
gear and Javanese puppets – all of which make for a fascinating half-
hour tour. The main dining hall, now full of Asian musical instruments,
is curious, too, smothered in its original barley-sugar decor with little
sculpted jesters crouching mischievously in the corners of the ceiling.

*The museum is an
offshoot of the
Náprstek Museum
in Prague, see
p.106*

For all the chateau's excesses, the **village** itself is little more than a
*hostinec* and a bend in the road, but straggling up the valley are the
remains of what was once an attractive spa resort for ailing Praguers.
Many of the old *Gasthäuser* are still standing, including the *Pension
Stüdl* where Kafka spent the winter of 1918. It was here that he met
and became engaged to Julie Wohryzek, daughter of a Jewish shoe-
maker from Prague – a match vigorously opposed by his father. Kafka
was prompted to write his vitriolic *Letter to His Father*, which he
passed on to his mother, who wisely made sure it never got any further.

---

**The Levý heads: A Walk from Liběchov**

For a brief and not too strenuous walk from Liběchov, take the blue-marked
path opposite the chateau, which follows the Liběchovka stream and then
heads east towards some thickly wooded hills. The first hill contains some
unremarkable sandstone caves, but the second is covered in sandstone rocks,
two of which have been sculpted into giant grimacing faces, one with a goat-
ish beard, the other baring its teeth. Known as the Čertovy hlavy (Devil's
heads), these are the work of the nineteenth-century sculptor Václav Levý,
who was the cook for a while at Liběchov chateau, until his boss, Count Veith,
encouraged him to take up sculpture and became one of his leading patrons.

---

The only working pension nowadays is the private *Hotel Aveco*, Pod
kostelíčkem 20 (☎0206/971 156; ②), off the road to Dubá. On the
other side of the River Liběchovka, there's a **campsite** (mid-April to
Sept), a possible base for hikes into the Kokořínsko region.

## Kokořínsko

Northeast of Mělník, you leave the low plains of the Labe for a plateau
region known as **Kokořínsko**, a hidden pocket of wooded hills which
takes its name from the Gothic castle rising through the tree tops at its
centre. The sandstone plateau has weathered over the millennia to
form sunken valleys and bizarre rocky outcrops, which means there's a
lot of scope for some gentle hiking here. With picturesque valleys such
as the Kokořínský důl, do: ed with well-preserved, half-timbered
villages and riddled with marked paths, it comes as a surprise that the
whole area isn't buzzing all summer.

At the centre of the region is the village of **KOKOŘÍN**, whose
dramatic setting and spectacular fourteenth-century **castle** (April &
Oct Sat & Sun 9am–4pm; May–Aug Tues–Sun 8am–5pm; Sept Tues–
Sun 9am–5pm) greatly inspired the Czech nineteenth-century
Romantics. The castle is a perfect hideaway, ideal for the robbers who
used it as a base after it fell into disrepair in the sixteenth century. Not
until the end of the nineteenth century did it get a new lease of life,
from a jumped-up local landowner, Václav Špaček, who bought himself
a title and refurbished the place as a family memorial. There's precious
little inside and no incentive to endure the half-hour tour, as you can
explore the ramparts and climb the tallest tower on your own.

Unless you've got your own transport, Kokořínsko is not really
feasible as a day trip from Prague. In summer, there's one direct **bus** a
week from the Praha-Holešovice bus station (leaving at around
7.45am); otherwise, take the regular buses to Mělník and change
there. Alternatively, you could catch the local train from Mělník to
MŠENO, from where it's a three-kilometre walk west to Kokořín on the
green-marked path. Finding **accommodation** shouldn't be too much of
a problem; there's the *Hotel Dolina* in Kokořín (☎0206/26; ②), a
cluster of campsites at KOKOŘÍNSKÝ DŮL, a couple of kilometres down
the valley, and private rooms in KANINA, 2km further east.

# Terezín

The road from Prague to Berlin passes right through the fortress town of TEREZÍN (Theresienstadt), just over 60km northwest of the capital. Purpose-built in the 1780s by the Habsburgs to defend the northern border against Prussia, it was capable of accommodating 14,500 soldiers and hundreds of prisoners. In 1941, the whole town was turned into a **Jewish ghetto**, and used as a transit camp for Jews whose final destination was Auschwitz.

Although the **Main Fortress** (Hlavní pevnost) has never been put to the test in battle, Terezín remains a garrison town. Today, it's an eerie, soulless place, built to a dour eighteenth-century grid plan, its bare streets still ringing with the sounds of soldiers and military police. As you enter, the red-brick fortifications are still an awesome sight, though the huge moat has been put out of action by local gardening enthusiasts.

## A brief history of the ghetto

In October 1941, Reinhard Heydrich and the Nazi high command decided to turn the whole of Terezín into a Jewish ghetto. It was an obvious choice: fully fortified, close to the main Prague–Dresden railway line, and with an SS prison already established in the Lesser Fortress nearby. The original inhabitants of the town – less than 3500 people – were moved out, and transports began arriving at Terezín from many parts of central Europe. Within a year, nearly 60,000 Jews were interned here in appallingly overcrowded conditions; the monthly death rate rose to 4000. In October 1942, the first transport left for Auschwitz. By the end of the war, 140,000 Jews had been deported to Terezín; fewer than 17,500 remained when the ghetto was finally liberated on May 8, 1945.

One of the perverse ironies of Terezín is that it was used by the Nazis as a cover for the real purpose of the *Endlösung* or "final solution", devised at the Wannsee conference in January 1942 (at which Heydrich was present). The ghetto was made to appear self-governing, with its own council, its own bank printing ghetto money, its own shops selling goods confiscated from the internees on arrival, and even a café on the main square. For a while, a special "Terezín family camp" was even set up in Auschwitz, to continue the deception. The deportees were kept in mixed barracks, allowed to wear civilian clothes and – the main purpose of the whole thing – send letters back to their loved ones in Terezín telling them they were OK. After six months "quarantine", they were sent to the gas chambers.

Despite the fact that Terezín was being used by the Nazis as cynical propaganda, the ghetto population turned their unprecedented freedom to their own advantage. Since the entire population of the Protectorate (and Jews from many other parts of Europe) passed through Terezín, the ghetto had an enormous number of outstanding

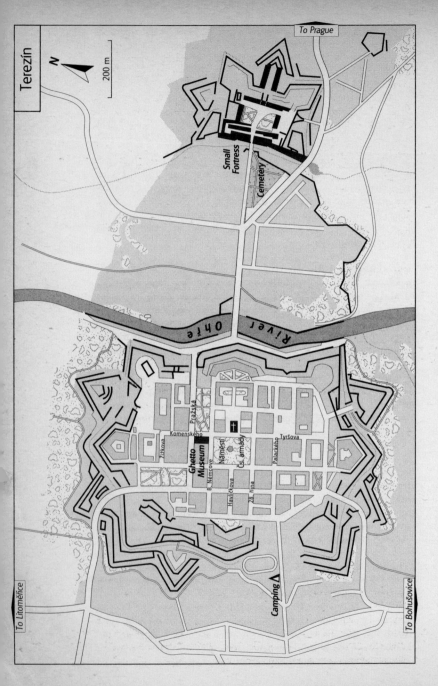

Terezín

N

200 m

To Prague

Small Fortress

Cemetery

River Ohře

To Litoměřice

Žižkova

Pražská

Komenského

Ghetto Museum

B. Němcové

Havlíčkova

Náměstí

Čs. armády

28. října

Palackého

Tyršova

Camping

To Bohušovice

Jewish artists, musicians, scholars and writers. Thus, in addition to the officially sponsored activities, countless clandestine cultural events were organised in the cellars and attics of the barracks: teachers gave lessons to children, puppet theatre productions were held, and literary evenings were put on.

Towards the end of 1943, the so-called *Verschönerung* or "beautification" of the ghetto was implemented, in preparation for the arrival of the International Red Cross inspectors. Streets were given names instead of numbers, and the whole place was decked out as if it were a spa town. When the International Red Cross asked to inspect one of the Nazi camps, they were brought here and treated to a week of Jewish cultural events. A circus tent was set up in the main square; a children's pavilion erected in the park; numerous performances of a children's opera, *Brundibár* (Bumble Bee), staged; and a jazz band, called the *Ghetto Swingers*, performed. The Red Cross visited Terezín twice, once in June 1943, and again in April 1945; both times the delegates filed positive reports.

## The Ghetto Museum

The unnerving feel of the place apart, there's just one thing to see here, the **Ghetto Museum** (Muzeum Ghetta; daily 9am–6pm), which was finally opened in 1991, on the fiftieth anniversary of the arrival of the first transports in Terezín. After the war, the Communists had followed the consistent Soviet line by deliberately ignoring the Jewish perspective on Terezín. Instead, the emphasis in the museum set up in the Lesser Fortress (see below) was on the war as an anti-fascist struggle, in which good (Communism and the Soviet Union) had triumphed over evil (Fascism and Nazi Germany). It wasn't until the Prague Spring of 1968 that the idea of a museum dedicated specifically to the history of the Jewish ghetto first emerged. In the 1970s, however, the intended building was turned into a Museum of the Ministry of the Interior instead.

Now that it's open, this extremely informative and well laid-out exhibition at last attempts to do some justice to the extraordinary and tragic events which took place here between 1941 and 1945, including background displays on the measures which led up to the *Endlösung*. There's also a fascinating video (with English subtitles) showing clips of the Nazi propaganda film shot in Terezín – *Hitler gives the Jews a Town* – intercut with harrowing interviews with survivors.

## The Lesser Fortress

On the other side of the River Ohře, east down Pražská, lies the **Lesser Fortress** (Malá pevnost; daily 9am–5pm), built as a military prison in the 1780s, at the same time as the main fortress. The young Bosnian, Gavrilo Princip, who succeeded in shooting Archduke Ferdinand in 1914, was interned and died here during World War I. In 1940 it was turned into an SS prison by Heydrich and, after the war, it became the official memorial and museum of Terezín.

There are guides available (usually survivors from Terezín), or else you can simply buy the brief broadsheet guide to the prison in English, and walk around yourself. The infamous Nazi refrain *Arbeit Macht Frei* (Work Brings Freedom) is daubed across the entrance on the left, which leads to the exemplary washrooms, still as they were when built for the Red Cross tour of inspection. The rest of the camp has been left empty but intact, and graphically evokes the cramped conditions under which the prisoners were kept half-starved and badly clothed, subject to indiscriminate cruelty and execution. The main **exhibition** is housed in the smart eighteenth-century mansion set in the prison gardens, which was home to the camp *Kommandant*, his family and fellow SS officers. A short documentary, intelligible in any language, is regularly shown in the cinema that was set up in 1942 to entertain the prison officers.

### Practicalities

Terezín is about a one-and-a-half-hour **bus** ride from Prague's Florenc terminal, and therefore easy to visit on a day trip. The nearest train station to Terezín is at BOHUŠOVICE, 2km south of the fortress. There's a smart new **restaurant**, *Teresian*, on the main square, which serves simple but good Czech food. It's difficult to imagine a less appealing place to stay, but stay you may at the **campsite** (May to mid-Sept) just west of town; the *Parkhotel* is currently closed, but there's a hotel and rooms in Litoměřice, just 3km away (see below).

# Litoměřice

If the idea of lingering in Terezín is unappealing, it might be worth walking or catching the bus 3km north to LITOMĚŘICE (Leitmeritz), at the confluence of the Ohře and the Labe rivers. The town has been an ecclesiastical centre since the Přemyslid Spytihněv II founded a collegiate chapter here in 1057. From the eleventh century onwards, German craftsmen flooded into Litoměřice, thanks to its strategic trading position on the Labe, and it soon became the third or fourth city of Bohemia. Having survived the Hussite Wars by the skin of its teeth, it was devastated in the Thirty Years' War. But its most recent upheaval came in 1945, when virtually the entire population (which was predominantly German) was forcibly expelled from the country.

The main reason people come here now is to pay their respects at Terezín, just south of the town (see above); however Litoměřice is of more than passing interest, since virtually the entire town is a museum to **Octavio Broggio**. Broggio was born here in 1668 and, along with his father Giulio, redesigned the town's many churches following the arrival of the Jesuits and the establishment of a Catholic bishopric here in the mid-seventeenth century. The reason for this zealous re-Catholicisation was Litoměřice's rather too eager conversion to the heretical beliefs of the Hussites and its disastrous allegiance to the Protestants in the Thirty Years' War.

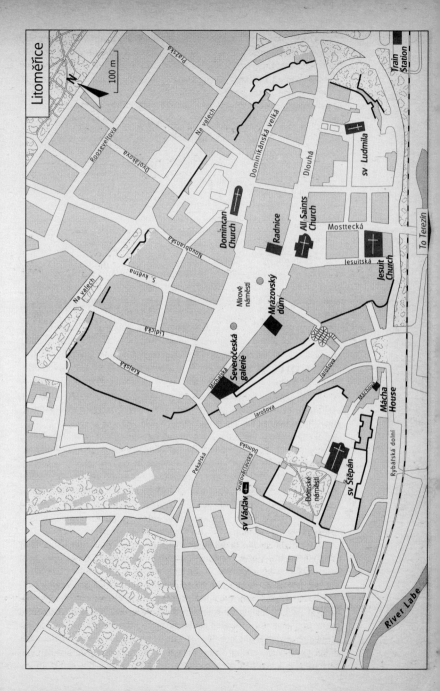

Litoměřice

N

100 m

Blažská

Na valech

Roosveltova

Dvořákova

Dominikánská velká

Dlouhá

sv Ludmila

Train Station

Dominican Church

Novobranská

Radnice

All Saints Church

Mosttecká

To Terezín

Jesuitská

Jesuit Church

S. května

Mírové náměstí

Mrázovský dům

Lidická

Severočeská galerie

Na valech

Michalská

Kraiská

Jarošova

Jarošova

Máchov

Mácha House

Rybářská dolní

Pekarská

Svatověchrska

Domská

Dómské náměstí

sv Václav

sv Štěpán

River Labe

Since 1989, the town has begun to pick up the pieces after forty years of neglect. Restoration work is continuing apace, and the re-establishment here of Bohemia's one and only Catholic seminary has brought some pride back to the town.

## The Town

Stepping out of the train station, you'll notice the last remaining bastion of the old town walls across the road; behind it lies the histori-cal quarter, entered via the wide boulevard of Dlouhá. There's no better place to get an understanding of the town's rich religious heri-tage than at the hybrid church of **All Saints** at the top of the street. It started life as a Romanesque church and now boasts the only Gothic spire left on the skyline, a beautiful wedge-shaped affair reminiscent of Prague's right bank. Broggio designed the present Baroque facade, though the oppressively low ceiling and dusty furnishings inside are disappointing, with the notable exception of the fifteenth-century panel painting by the Master of Litoměřice.

*The Master of Litoměřice was also responsible for much of the decoration in the Chapel of sv Václav in the St Vitus Cathedral, see p.63*

The town's vast cobbled marketplace, **Mírové náměstí**, once one of the most important in Bohemia, now boasts only a couple of build-ings from before the Thirty Years' War. The best known is the **Mrázovský dům**, on the south side of the square at no. 15, whose owner, a devout Hussite, had a huge wooden *kalich* (chalice) – the symbol of all Hussites – plonked on the roof in 1537. The other build-ing that stands out is the arcaded fourteenth-century **radnice**, at the eastern end of the square, rebuilt in Renaissance style and covered in sgraffito decoration. It's now the town **museum** (Tues–Sun 10am–noon & 1–5pm), worth a quick spin round, if only for the coffered sixteenth-century ceiling of the council hall; there's still precious little mention in the exhibition of the 1945 expulsions.

West of the square, the **Severočeská galerie** (Tues–Sun 9am–noon & 2–5pm) occupies a wonderfully rambling sixteenth-century building on Michalská, its inner courtyard draped in ivy and echoing to the trickle of a modern fountain. Exhibitions doing the Bohemian circuit stop off here, supplementing the already handsome permanent collec-tion of Czech works and the sculpture terrace around the back.

### Cathedral hill

On a promontory 500m southwest of the town centre, the **Cathedral hill**, where the bishop and his entourage once held residence, was originally entirely separate from the town, with its own fortifications. On its northern slope, the small, pasty chapel of **sv Václav** (St Wenceslas) is in many ways the younger Broggio's finest work, grand despite its cramped proportions and location. But the real reason to come out here is to wonder at the former cathedral of **sv Štěpán** (St Stephen), which looks out onto the quiet grassy enclosure of Dómské náměstí. Redesigned by Giulio Broggio (among others) in the second half of the seventeenth century, sv Štěpán marked the start of the extensive rebuilding of Litoměřice. The cathedral's interior is full of light touches missing from the later churches, set against the dark wood and gloomy altar paintings from the school of the Saxon master Lucas Cranach. Outside, the freestanding campanile adds a peculiarly Tuscan touch.

A path along the north side of sv Štěpán leads down the cobbled lane of Máchova, where the Czech poet **Karel Hynek Mácha** died in 1836. The corner house at no. 3 – built after Mácha's untimely death – contains a small exhibition (Tues–Sun 10am–5pm) on the life of the poet who, in the true style of the Romantics, died of consumption at the age of 26. His most famous poem, *Máj* (May), was hijacked by the Communists as their May Day anthem. He used to be buried in the local cemetery, but when the Nazis drew up the Sudetenland borders Litoměřice lay inside the Greater German Reich, so the Czechs dug him up and reinterred him in the Vyšehrad cemetery in Prague (see p.141). Once you've reached the bottom of the cathedral hill, the stairway of the Máchovy schody will take you back up into town.

## Practicalities

From the **train station**, which is also where **buses** terminate, *ČEDOK* is only a short walk up Dlouhá. They can help you find you a **room**, though the only hotel at present is the high-rise *Sechezy* (☎0416/24 51; ②), at Vrchlického 10 in the housing estate northeast of town. There's a **campsite** with bungalows (and an open-air cinema) open June to September in the woods between the railway line and the river. The *Hotel Rak* on the main square (no longer in fact a hotel) serves good Czech food and beer from Louny in its ground-floor vaults, and also has a new nightclub in the backrooms. Alternatively, there are several new snack bars and bistros on Novobranská.

# Northeast of Prague

The scenery **northeast of Prague** is as flat as it is around Mělník, a rich blanket of fields spreading over the plain as far as the eye can see. Two places you might consider heading for are **Mladá Boleslav**, where Škoda cars are produced, and **Přerov nad Labem**, an open-air museum of the kind of folk architecture that was common in Bohemia less than a century ago. With transport of your own, you could quite easily visit both in a day.

## Přerov nad Labem

The **skansen** (folk village) at PŘEROV NAD LABEM was the first of its kind when it was founded in 1895. Later, in the 1950s and 1960s, skansens became quite a fad, as collectivisation and urbanisation wiped out traditional rural communities, along with their distinctive folk culture and wooden architecture. During the summer Přerov's skansen is busy with tour groups from Prague, wandering through the various half-timbered and stone buildings, some brought here plank by plank from nearby villages, some from Přerov itself. Particularly evocative is the reconstructed eighteenth-century village school, with a portrait of the Austrian Emperor taking pride of place amid the Catholic icons and a delicate paper theatre that was used in drama lessons.

To get to the village, take one of the slow buses from Prague to Poděbrady and get off at the crossroads just after the turn-off to Mochov – the village is 1km north.

## Mladá Boleslav

*The true home of the Škoda empire is its heavy engineering plant at Plzeň, see p.188*

Trains from Praha-Vysočany take an hour and a half to reach MLADÁ BOLESLAV (Jungbunzlau), where Laurin & Klement set up a bicycle factory in the mid-nineteenth century. They went on to produce the country's first car in 1905, and eventually merged with the Škoda industrial empire. The factory has produced all Škoda cars since that time, and currently churns out the latest model, the *Favorit*.

The main reason for coming here is to visit the **Škoda Museum** (Mon–Fri 7am–6pm, Sat 9am–1pm), which exhibits over 25 old Škodas and Laurin & Klements in its showroom. The exhibition starts off, as the factory itself did, with an L & K bicycle and a couple of

---

**Škoda: the cars and jokes**

For Czechs, the Škoda industrial empire is a great Czech achievement and a source of national pride. It's doubly ironic, then, that the word *Škoda* means "shame" or "pity" in Czech – a marketing own-goal were it not the name of the founding father of the Czech car industry, **Emil Škoda**. The latest Škoda model, assembled at the Mladá Boleslav plant, has been very favourably received, even in the west (whence a large proportion of its components derive), and is in great demand from the new Czech bourgeoisie. In 1989, there was a three-year waiting list, despite a retail price of over 90,000 Czech crowns (over twice the average yearly salary). In one of the most controversial deals in the current privatisation programme, Volkswagen will soon have a majority stake in the firm.

Škoda cars have, however, long been the laughing stock of western European car buffs. A few sample groaners:

Customer to garage mechanic: "Have you got a petrol cap for a Škoda?"
Garage mechanic to customer: "It's a fair swap".

Q: What do you call a Škoda convertible?
A: A skip.

Q: What's the difference between a Jehovah's Witness and a Škoda?
A: You can close the door on a Jehovah's Witness.

Q: How do you double the value of your Škoda?
A: Fill up the petrol tank.

Q: Why do Škodas have heated rear windows?
A: To keep your hands warm as you're pushing it along.

---

motorbikes. There are also several vintage vehicles and a 1917 fire engine, but the vast majority of the cars date from the 1920s and 1930s – big, mostly black, gangster-style motors. The museum is on třída Václava Klementa, northeast of the town centre, and not at all well signposted. Diagonally opposite the museum, and handy for orientation, is a park with a palatial neo-Baroque *Gymnasium* at the far end. There's a wonderfully provincial Art-Nouveau theatre close by, brightly painted in white, gold and blue.

The **old town** lies to the east of the River Jizera, in a tight bend of one of its tributaries, the Klenice. It has little going for it besides its fading Renaissance **radnice**, and the **castle** tucked into the southernmost part of town, now the local museum and exhibition space. However, if you're looking for somewhere to **eat**, the *Jihočeská hostinec*, beside the castle entrance, has a big fish restaurant, *Rýbářská*, with an amazing menu that includes pike, eel and plaice. The *Hotel Věnec*, also on the main square (☎0326/24 93; ①), currently offers some ridiculously cheap **rooms**.

# Kutná Hora

For two hundred and fifty years or so, **KUTNÁ HORA** (Kuttenberg) was one of the most important towns in Bohemia, second only to Prague. At the end of the fourteenth century its population was equal to that of London, its shantytown suburbs straggled across what are now green fields, and its ambitious building projects set out to rival those of the capital itself. Today, Kutná Hora is a small provincial town with a population of just over 20,000, but the monuments dotted around it, and the remarkable monastery and ossuary in the suburb of **Sedlec**, make it one of the most enjoyable of all possible day trips from Prague.

### A brief history

Kutná Hora's road to prosperity began in the late thirteenth century with the discovery of **silver deposits** in the surrounding area. German miners were invited to settle and work the seams, and around 1300 Václav II founded the royal mint here and sent for Italian craftsmen to run it. Much of the town's wealth was used to fund the beautification of Prague, but it also allowed for the construction of one of the most magnificent churches in central Europe and a number of other prestigious Gothic monuments in Kutná Hora itself.

At the time of the Hussite Wars, the town was mostly German, and therefore staunchly Catholic; local miners used to throw captured Hussites into the deep mine shafts and leave them to die of starvation. Word got out, and the town was besieged and eventually taken by Žižka's fanatical Táborites in 1421, only to be recaptured by Sigismund and his papal forces shortly afterwards, and again by Žižka, the following year.

While the silver stocks remained high the town was able to recover its former prosperity, but at the end of the sixteenth century the mines dried up and Kutná Hora's wealth and importance came to an abrupt end – when the Swedes marched on the town during the Thirty Years' War, they had to be bought off with beer rather than silver. The town has never fully recovered, shrivelling to less than a third of its former size, its fate emphatically sealed by a devastating fire in 1770.

## The Town

The small, unassuming houses that line the town's medieval lanes give little idea of Kutná Hora's former glories. The same can be said of the main square, **Palackého náměstí**, now thoroughly provincial in character.

A narrow alleyway on the south side of the square leads to the leafy Havlíčkovo náměstí, off which is the **Vlašský dvůr** (Italian Court), originally conceived as a palace by Václav II, and for three centuries the town's bottomless purse. It was here that Florentine minters produced the Prague Groschen (*pražské groše*), a silver coin widely used throughout central Europe until the nineteenth century. The building itself has been mucked about with over the years, most recently – and most brutally – by nineteenth-century restorers, who left only the chestnut trees, a fourteenth-century oriel window (capped by an unlikely looking wooden onion dome) and the statue of a miner unmolested. The original workshops of the minters have been bricked in, but the outlines of their little doors and windows are still visible in the courtyard. The short **guided tour** (daily every half-hour 10am– 6pm) of the old chapel, treasury and royal palace gives you a fair idea of the building's former importance.

Outside the court is a statue of the country's founder and first president, T. G. Masaryk, twice removed – once by the Nazis and once by the Communists – but now returned to its pride of place. Before you leave, take a quick turn in the court gardens, which climb down in steps to the Vrchlice valley below. This is undoubtedly Kutná Hora's best profile, with a splendid view over to the church of sv Barbora (see opposite).

Behind the Vlašský dvůr is **sv Jakub** (St James), the town's oldest church, begun a generation or so after the discovery of the silver deposits. Its grand scale is a clear indication of the town's quite considerable wealth by the time of the fourteenth century, though in terms of artistry it pales in comparison with Kutná Hora's other ecclesiastical buildings. The leaning tower is a reminder of the precarious position of the town, the church's foundations prone to subsidence from the disused mines below. If you want to see some of these, head for the **Hrádek**, an old fort which was used as a second mint and now serves as the **Silver Mining Museum** (Muzeum a středověké důlní dílo; April–Oct Tues–Sun 8am–noon & 1–5pm). Here you can pick up a white coat, miner's helmet and torch, and visit some of the medieval mines that were discovered beneath the fort in the 1960s.

To Bus Station
(100 m)

Kutná Hora

100 m

N

To Sedlec & Main
Train Station (2 km)

Na valech

Na valech

Jiřího z Poděbrad

Former
Ursuline
Convent

Vocelova

Sedlecká

Na Náměti

Leská

Na valech

Kollárova

Vladislavova

Panna Marie
na Náměti

Kamenný
dům

Šultysova

Plague
Column

Palackého
nám.

Tylova

Post Office

Husova

Kašna

Havlíčkovo
nám.

Husova

Barborská

sv Jakub

Vlašský dvůr

Smíškova

Hrádek

Former Jesuit
College

Barborská

Na valech

River Vrchlice

sv Barbora
Church

## The church of sv Barbora

Kutná Hora's church of **sv Barbora** (summer Tues–Sun 8am–noon &
1–5pm; winter 9am–noon & 1–4pm) is arguably the most beautiful
church in central Europe. Not to be outdone by the great monastery at
Sedlec (see overleaf) or the St Vitus Cathedral in Prague, the miners of
Kutná Hora began financing the construction of a great Gothic cathedral of their own, dedicated to Saint Barbara, the patron saint of
miners and gunners. The foundations were probably laid by Parler in
the 1380s, but work was interrupted by the Hussite wars, and the
church remains unfinished, despite a flurry of building activity at the
beginning of the sixteenth century by, among others, Benedikt Reith.

The approach road to the church, Barborská, is lined with a
parade of gesticulating Baroque saints and cherubs that rival the sculptures on the Charles Bridge; on the right-hand side is the palatial
former **Jesuit College**. The church itself bristles with pinnacles, finials
and flying buttresses which support its most striking feature, a roof of
three tent-like towers, culminating in unequal needle-sharp spires.
Inside, cold light streams through the plain glass windows, illuminat-

ing a playful vaulted nave whose ribs form branches and petals stamped with coats of arms belonging to Václav II and the local miners' guilds. The wide spread of the five-aisled nave is remarkably uncluttered: a Gothic pulpit – half wood, half stone – creeps tastefully up a central pillar, and black and gold Renaissance confessionals hide discreetly in the north aisle. On the south wall is the Minters' Chapel, decorated with fifteenth-century wall frescoes showing the Florentines at work, while in the ambulatory chapels some fascinating paintings – unique for their period – depict local miners at work.

### The rest of the town

There are a few minor sights worth seeking out in the rest of the town. On Rejskovo náměstí, the squat, many-sided **Kašna** (fountain) by Matouš Rejsek strikes an odd pose – anything less like a fountain would be hard to imagine. At the bottom of the sloping Šultyskovo náměstí is a particularly fine **Morový sloup** (Plague Column), giving thanks for the end of the plague of 1713; while just around the corner from the top of the square is one of the few Gothic buildings to survive the 1770 fire, the **Kamenný dům**, built around 1480 and covered in an ornate sculptural icing. This used to contain an unexceptional local museum, which has now been moved a couple of blocks down Poděbradova, to Kilian Ignaz Dientzenhofer's unfinished **Ursuline convent**. Only three sides of the convent's ambitious pentagonal plan were completed, its neo-Baroque church added in the late nineteenth century while sv Barbora was being restored.

## Sedlec

Buses #1 and #4 run 3km northeast to SEDLEC, once a separate village but now a suburb of Kutná Hora. Adjoining Sedlec's defunct eighteenth-century Cistercian monastery (now the largest tobacco factory in Europe) is the fourteenth-century church of **Panna Marie** (St Mary), imaginatively redesigned in the eighteenth century by Giovanni Santini, who specialised in melding Gothic with Baroque. Here, given a plain French Gothic church gutted during the Hussite wars, Santini set to work on the vaulting, adding his characteristic sweeping stucco rib patterns, relieved only by the occasional Baroque splash of colour above the chancel steps. For all its attractions, however, the church seems to be permanently covered in scaffolding, and closed except for the occasional service.

Cross the main road, following the signs, and you come to the monks' graveyard, where an ancient Gothic chapel leans heavily over the entrance to the macabre subterranean **kostnice** or ossuary (Tues–Sun summer 8am–noon & 1–5pm; winter 9am–noon & 1–4pm), full to overflowing with human bones. When holy earth from Golgotha was scattered over the graveyard in the twelfth century, all of Bohemia's nobility wanted to be buried here and the bones mounted up until there were over 40,000 complete sets. In 1870, worried about the ever-growing piles, the authorities commissioned František Rint to do something creative with them. He rose to the challenge and moulded out of bones four giant bells, one in each corner of the crypt, designed wall-to-ceiling skeletal decorations, including the Schwarzenberg coat of arms, and, as the centrepiece, put together a chandelier made out of every bone in the human body. Rint's signature (in bones) is at the bottom of the steps.

## Practicalities

The simplest way to get to Kutná Hora is to take a bus from the Praha-Florenc or Praha-Želivského terminals (1hr 30min). Fast trains from Prague's Masarykovo nádraží take around an hour (there's only one in the morning); slow ones take two hours; trains from Praha hlavní nádraží involve a change at Kolín. The main railway station (Kutná Hora hlavní nádraží) is a long way out of town, near Sedlec; bus #2 or #4 will take you into town, or there's an occasional shuttle train service to Kutná Hora město, near the centre of town.

The town has a highly efficient system of orientation signs, and at almost every street corner a pictorial list of the chief places of interest keeps you on the right track. Having said that, the train station signposted is not the main one; and signs even point the way to the *turistická ubytovna* (tourist hostel), which was under reconstruction at the time of writing. The *pokladna* (ticket office) in the Vlašský dvůr also serves as a tourist information point, and can arrange reasonably priced private rooms. Otherwise, the only hotels are the modern *Mědínek*, on Palackého náměstí (☎0327/2741 or 2743; ②), and a small, very cheap private hotel at Barborská 24 (☎ 0327 2113; ①).

As for eating and drinking, Kutná Hora was in desperate need of a good restaurant at the time of writing. If *U Anděla*, the cheap *pivnice* near the Kamenný dům, closes, as looks increasingly likely, you'll be left with only the *Mědínek* for nourishment, until somewhere new appears. If it's just a hot drink you want, the *kavárna v zahradě*, at the bottom of Palackého náměstí, has tables outside and stays open until 10pm.

# Průhonice and the Sázava valley

A short train ride southeast of Prague is enough to transport you from the urban sprawl of the capital into one of the prettiest regions of central Bohemia, starting with the park at Průhonice. Until the motorway to Brno and Bratislava ripped through the area in the 1970s, the roads and railways linking the three big cities took the longer, flatter option, further north along the Labe valley. As a result, commerce and tourism passed the Sázava Valley by, and, with the notable exception of Konopiště, it remains undeveloped, unspoilt and out of the way.

# Průhonice

Barely outside the city limits, and just off the country's one and only motorway, PRŮHONICE throngs with Czech weekenders during the summer season. For the great majority, it's the 625-acre **park** (April–Oct) they come to see and not the **chateau**, a motley parade of neo-Renaissance buildings, most of them closed to the public anyway. The park is a botanical and horticultural research centre, so the array of flora is unusually good here. Though few do, it's worth paying a passing visit to the chateau's **art gallery**, which features a permanent collection of twentieth-century Czech paintings and sculpture, including a hefty series of canvases by the Czech Cubists.

There's a regular *ČSAD* **bus** service to Průhonice from the Praha-Chodov bus terminal, or else you could conceivably walk the 4km cross-country from metro Háje. Being so near Prague, it's a popular place to **stay the night**: the choice is between the flash new *Pension Charlie* on Hlavní (☎75 06 83; ②) and the tatty old hotel, *Tulipán*, on the road to the motorway (☎75 95 30; ①). For something to **eat**, look no further than *U zámku*, the local *hostinec* by the chateau entrance.

# Sázava and Český Šternberk

Rising majestically above the slow-moving waters of the river Sázava, the **Sázava monastery** (April & Sept Sat & Sun 9am–4pm; May–Aug Tues–Sun 8am–noon & 1–5pm) was founded by the eleventh-century Prince Oldřich, on the instigation of a passing hermit called **Prokop** (St Procopius), whom he met by chance in the forest. The Slavonic liturgy was used at the monastery and, for a while, Sázava became an important centre for the dissemination of Slavonic texts. Later, a large Gothic church was planned, and this now bares its red sandstone nave to the world, incomplete but intact. The chancel was converted into a Baroque church and, later still, the Tieg family bought the place and started to build themselves a modest chateau. Of this architectural hotchpotch, only the surviving Gothic frescoes – in the popular "Beautiful Style", but of a sophistication unmatched in Bohemian art at the time – are truly memorable. The village itself thrived on the glass trade, and the rest of the monastery's overlong guided tour concentrates on the local glassware.

Without your own transport, it'll take a good hour and a half by bus or train to cover the 55km from Prague to Sázava. Of the two, the **train** ride (change at ČERČANY) is the more visually absorbing, at least by the time you join the branch line that meanders down the Sázava valley. There's a **campsite** (June to mid-Sept) by the river, and a hotel, *Na Růžku*, on the road to Benešov (☎0328/91550; ①), should you need a place to stay.

## Český Šternberk

Several bends in the Sázava river later, the great mass of the **castle** at ČESKÝ ŠTERNBERK (April & Oct Sat & Sun 9am–4pm; May–Aug Tues–

Sun 8am–5pm; Sept Tues–Sun 9am–5pm) is strung out along a knife's edge above the river – a breathtaking sight. Unfortunately, that's all it is, since apart from its fiercely defensive position, little remains of the original Gothic castle. Add to that the dull guided tour, the castle's popularity with coach parties, and the full two-hour journey by train or bus from Prague (again, change trains at Čerčany), and you may decide to skip it altogether.

## Konopiště

Other than for its proximity to Prague, the popularity of **Konopiště** (April, Sept & Oct Tues–Sun 9am–noon & 1–4pm; May–Aug Tues–Sun 8am–noon & 1–5pm) remains a complete mystery. From the beginning of the season to the last day of October, coach parties from all over the world home in on this unexceptional Gothic castle, stuffed with dead animals and dull weaponry. The only interesting thing about the place is its historical associations: King Václav IV was imprisoned for a while by his own nobles in the castle's distinctive round tower, and Archduke Franz Ferdinand lived here until his assassination in Sarajevo in 1914. The archduke's prime interest seems to have been the elimination of any living creature foolish enough to venture into the castle grounds: between 1880 and 1906, he killed no fewer than 171,537 birds and animals, the details of which are recorded in his *Schuss Liste* displayed inside.

There's a choice of two equally tedious **guided tours**: the shorter forty-minute tour of the *Zámecké sbírky* takes you past the stuffed bears, deer teeth and assorted lethal weapons; the tour of the *Zámecké salony* is less gruesome but ten minutes longer. There are occasionally tours in English, French and German, too, so ask at the box office before you sign up. Alternatively, simply head off into the 225-acre **park**, which boasts several lakes, a rose garden and a deer park.

As Konopiště is only 45km from Prague you shouldn't have to stay the night, though there is a **campsite** (May–Sept) and **motel** not far from the castle car park. The castle is a fifteen-minute walk or short bus ride west from the railway station at BENEŠOV.

### Jemniště

Castle enthusiasts are better advised to visit the simple Baroque **chateau** (April, Sept & Oct Tues–Sun 9am–noon & 1–4pm; May–Aug Tues–Sun 8am–noon & 1–5pm) hidden in the woods above the nearby village of JEMNIŠTĚ. To get there, you'll need to change trains at Benešov, getting off at POSTUPICE, twenty-five minutes down the line, and then walking fifteen minutes from there. It's worth the effort because the chateau is rarely visited (it should come as no surprise if you're the only taker for the brief guided tour), yet contains an impressive collection of seventeenth-century pictorial maps and plans and a small selection of Empire furniture.

# Along the Berounka river

The green belt area to the **west of Prague** has its fair share of rolling hills, but spend more time here and you'll find it's easily the most varied of the regions around the city, and consequently one of the most popular escapes for urban Czechs. The **River Berounka** carves itself an enticingly craggy valley up to Charles IV's magnificent country castle at **Karlštejn**, the busiest destination of all, and continues further upstream to the castle of **Křivoklát**.

## Around Karlštejn

Trains for KARLŠTEJN leave Praha-Smíchov station roughly every hour, and take about forty minutes to cover the 28km from Prague. Over the river from the station is a small T-shaped village (now part of Karlštejn village but originally the separate hamlet of Budňany), strung out along one of the tributaries of the Berounka – pretty, but not enough to warrant a coach park the size of a football pitch. It's the **castle** (Tues–Sun March, April & Oct–Dec 9am–noon & 1–4pm; May–Sept 8am–noon & 1–6pm), occupying a defiantly unassailable position above the village, which draws in the mass of tourists. Designed in the fourteenth century by Matthias of Arras for Emperor Charles IV, as a giant safe-box for the imperial crown jewels and his large personal collection of precious relics, it quickly became Charles' favourite retreat from the vast city he himself had masterminded. Women were strictly forbidden to enter the castle, and the story of his third wife Anna's successful break-in (in drag) became one of the most popular Czech comedies of the nineteenth century.

The castle was ruthlessly restored in the nineteenth century and now looks much better from a distance. Inside, the centuries of neglect and the restoration work have taken their toll. Guided tours last around half an hour, and begin from the main inner courtyard. Most of the rooms visited contain only the barest of furnishings, the empty spaces taken up by uninspiring displays on the history of the castle. However, the top two chambers make the whole trip worthwhile – though unfortunately, only the emperor's residential **Mariánská věž** is open to the public at the moment. It was here that Charles shut himself off from the rest of the world, with any urgent business passed to him through a hole in the wall of the tiny ornate chapel of sv **Kateřina**.

*A small selection of Master Theodoric's panels are exhibited in Prague's Convent of sv Jiří, see p.68*

A wooden bridge leads on to the highest point of the castle, the **Velká věž**, where the castle's finest treasure, the **Holy Rood Chapel** (Kaple svatého kříže), has been closed now for over ten years. Traditionally, only the Emperor, the archbishop and the electoral princes could enter this guilded treasure house, whose six-metre-thick walls contain 2200 semiprecious stones and 128 painted panels, the work of Master Theodoric, Bohemia's greatest fourteenth-century painter. The imperial crown jewels, once secured here behind nineteen separate locks, were removed to Hungary after an abortive attack by

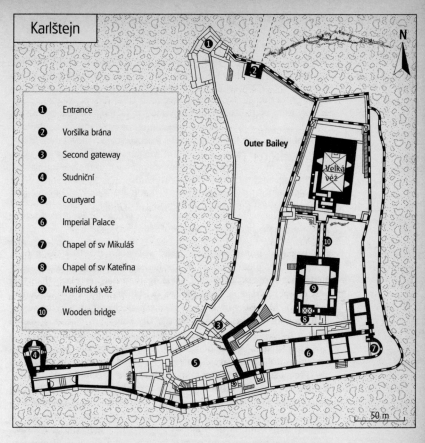

Karlštejn

- ❶ Entrance
- ❷ Voršilka brána
- ❸ Second gateway
- ❹ Studniční
- ❺ Courtyard
- ❻ Imperial Palace
- ❼ Chapel of sv Mikuláš
- ❽ Chapel of sv Kateřina
- ❾ Mariánská věž
- ❿ Wooden bridge

Outer Bailey

Velká věž

50 m

N

the Hussites, while the Bohemian jewels are now stashed away in the cathedral in Prague.

### Walks around Karlštejn and the Český kras

There are some great possible hikes in the countryside around Karlštejn. From ŘEVNICE, two stops on the train before Karlštejn – the unlikely village in which Martina Navrátilová spent her tennis-playing childhood – several marked paths cover the stiff climb through the forests of the Hpebeny ridge. Armed with a *Praha okolí* map, these are easy enough to follow; you can pick up a bus back to Prague from MNÍŠEK on the other side of the hills.

From SRBSKO (one stop on from Karlštejn), a red-marked path winds its way through the woods to Sv Jan pod Skálou, whose dramatically situated monastery was until recently a secret police training camp. This is also the place where the country's remaining aristocrats were imprisoned following the 1948 coup. Again, you can catch a bus back to Prague easily enough from VRÁŽ, a kilometre or so to the north.

Another option from Srbsko is to take the yellow-marked path west into the Český kras (Bohemian Karst). The geology of this region has fascinated scientists since the early nineteenth century, but the one set of caves open to the public, the Koněpruské jeskyně (daily April–Oct), 3km west of Srbsko, lay undiscovered until 1950. Nowadays they're not so easy to miss, thanks to the Hollywood-style giant white lettering on the hillside above. Much more fascinating than the dripstone decorations, however, was the simultaneous discovery of an illegal mint in the upper level of the caves. A full set of weights, miners' lamps and even the remains of food were found here, dating back to the second half of the fifteenth century. To reach the caves other than by foot, you'll need to catch one of the infrequent buses from the soap-producing town of BEROUN (50min by train from Praha hlavní nádraží).

## Křivoklátsko

The beautiful mixed woodland that makes up the UNESCO nature reserve of Křivoklátsko, further up the Berounka, is just out of reach of the day-trippers, making it an altogether sleepier place than the area around Karlštejn. The agonised twists (křivky) of the Berounka cast up the highest crags of the region, which cluster around the castle of Křivoklát (Tues–Sun April, Sept & Oct 9am–4pm; May–Aug 8am–noon & 1–5pm) – somehow elevated above everything around it.

With such a perfect location in the heart of the best hunting ground in Bohemia, Křivoklát naturally enjoyed the royal patronage of the Přemyslids, whose hunting parties were legendary. From the outside it's a scruffy but impressive stronghold, dominated by the round tower where the English alchemist Edward Kelley found himself incarcerated after falling out with Rudolf II and, in an attempt to escape, jumped out of the window. The one-hour guided tour takes in most of the castle's good points, including the Great Hall and the chapel, both of which date back to the thirteenth century and have an austere beauty quite at odds with the castle's reputation as a venue for bacchanalian goings-on.

### Practicalities

Apart from a direct Saturday morning service, all journeys by train from Prague to Křivoklát require a change at Beroun. Buses from the Praha-Dejvice terminal run frequently only at weekends, and take around an hour and a half. Křivoklát castle is the region's only real sight, though you could happily spend days exploring the surrounding countryside on the network of well-marked footpaths. However, unless you're staying at one of the two campsites (June–Sept), a short walk up the river near ROZTOKY, you'll have to hole up in RAKOVNÍK (30min beyond Křivoklát on the train), a deeply provincial town with just one posh hotel and a good local beer to recommend it.

# Around Kladno

As you approach KLADNO, just under 30km west of Prague, it's difficult to miss the low blue barracks of the *Poldí* steelworks on the edge
of town, which used to provide employment for almost the entire town
but are currently running at a third of normal capacity. It was here in
1921 that the Communist Party was founded, and Kladno's miners and
steelworkers were rewarded with some of the best wages in the country after the 1948 coup. Nowadays, it typifies the problems and contra-
dictions of the post-Communist situation: what will happen to a town
of over 70,000 people whose livelihood depends on an industry that's
both economically and ecologically unsound?

The only reason to come here is to catch one of the **buses** that
leave around midday for **Lány** (see below), though you can avoid
Kladno altogether by taking the slow train to Chomutov from Prague's
Masarykovo nádraží and getting out 3km northeast of Lány at
STOCHOV. If you're heading for **Lidice**, take the bus to Kladno from
Praha-Dejvice, and get off at the turn-off to the village.

## Lidice

The small mining village of LIDICE, 18km northwest of Prague, hit
world headlines on June 10,´1942, at the moment when it ceased to
exist. On the flimsiest pretext, it was chosen as scapegoat for the assassination of the Nazi leader Reinhard Heydrich. All 184 men from the
village were rounded up and shot by the SS, the 198 women were sent
to Ravensbrück concentration camp, and the 98 children either went
with their mothers, or, if they were Aryan enough, were packed off to
"good" German homes, while the village itself was burnt to the ground.

*For a detailed
account of
Heydrich's
assassination, see
p.135*

Knowing all this as you approach Lidice makes the modern village
seem almost perversely unexceptional. At the end of the straight tree-
lined main street, 10 června 1942, there's a dour concrete memorial
with a small but horrific **museum** (daily April–Sept 8am–4pm; Oct–
March 8am–5pm) that continually shows a short film about Lidice,
including footage shot by the SS themselves as the village was burning.
The spot where the old village used to lie is just south of the memorial,
now merely smooth green pasture punctuated with a few simple
symbolic reminders: the foundations of the old school, a wooden cross
and a common grave.

After the massacre, the "Lidice shall live" campaign was launched
and villages all over the world began to change their name to Lidice.
The first was Stern Park Gardens, Illinois, soon followed by villages in
Mexico and other Latin American countries. From Coventry to
Montevideo, towns twinned themselves with Lidice, so that rather than
"wiping a Czech village off the face of the earth" as Hitler had hoped,
the Nazis created a symbol of anti-fascist resistance.

There's no place, nor reason, to stay and most people come here as
a day trip from Prague on one of the regular buses from Praha-Dejvice.

# Lány

On summer weekends, Škoda-loads of Czech families, pensioners and assorted pilgrims make their way to LÁNY, a plain, grey village by the edge of the Křivoklát forest, 12km beyond Kladno. They congregate in the pristine cemetery to pay their respects to one of Czechoslovakia's most important historical figures, Tomáš Garrigue Masaryk, the country's founding father and president from 1918 to 1935.

The Masaryk plot is separated from the rest of the cemetery (*hřbitov*) by a little wooden fence and flanked by two bushy trees. Tomáš is buried alongside his American wife, Charlotte Garrigue Masaryková, who died some fifteen years earlier, and their son Jan, who became Foreign Minister in the post-1945 government, only to die in mysterious circumstances shortly after the Communist coup. After laying their wreaths, the crowds generally wander over to the presidential summer chateau, with its blue-liveried guards, on the other side of the village. Its rooms are strictly out of bounds, but the large English gardens, orangerie and deer park, which were landscaped by Josip Plečnik, are open to the public at weekends and on public holidays.

*For details of the controversy surrounding Jan Masaryk's death, see p.74*

---

### TGM

**Tomáš Garrigue Masaryk** – known affectionately as TGM – was born in 1850 in Hodonín, a town in a part of Moravia where Slovaks and Czechs lived harmoniously together. His father was an illiterate Slovak peasant who worked for the local bigwig, his mother a German, while Tomáš himself trained as a blacksmith. From such humble beginnings, he rose to become professor of philosophy at the Charles University, a Social Democrat MP in the Viennese Reichskrat, and finally the country's first, and longest-serving, president. A liberal humanist through and through, Masaryk created what was, at the time, probably the most progressive democracy in central Europe, featuring universal suffrage, an enviable social security system and a strong social democratic thrust. At the time of his death in 1937, Czechoslovakia was one of the few democracies left in Central Europe, "a lighthouse high on a cliff with the waves crashing on it on all sides", as Masaryk's less fortunate successor, Edvard Beneš, put it. The whole country went into mourning – a year later the Nazis marched into Sudetenland.

After the 1948 coup, the Communists began to dismantle the myth of Masaryk, whose name was synonymous with the "bourgeois" First Republic. All mention of him was removed from textbooks, street names were changed and his statue was taken down from almost every town and village in the country. However, during liberalisation in 1968, his bespectacled face and goatee beard popped up again in shop windows, and his image returned again in 1989 to haunt the beleagured Communists.

---

# Plzeň

PLZEŇ is the largest city in Bohemia after Prague, with a population of 175,000. Parts of the city defy description, such is their state of disrepair, and the skyline is a symphony of smoke and steam, the results of which can be seen in the colour of the city's tap water. Yet despite its overwhelmingly industrial character, there are compensations – a large number of students, eclectic architecture and an unending supply of (probably) the best beer in the world – all of which make Plzeň a justifiably popular stopoff on the main railway line between Prague and the west.

Plzeň

## Some history

Plzeň (or Pilsen as it is still called in the west) was built on beer and bombs. In 1850 it was a small town of 14,000, of whom the vast majority were German; then in 1859 an ironworks was founded and quickly snapped up by the Czech capitalist Emil Škoda, under whose control it drew an ever-increasing number of Czechs from the countryside. Within thirty years, the overall population had trebled while the number of Germans had decreased. Although initially simply an engineering plant, it was transformed into a huge armaments factory (second only to Krupps in Germany) by the Austrian government during World War I. Inevitably, it attracted the attention of Allied bombers during World War II. Nowadays, apart from producing the country's rolling stock, it also has the dubious privilege of having manufactured all the dodgy Soviet-designed nuclear reactors for the Warsaw Pact. However, since cancelled orders are now mounting up, and the wisdom of nuclear power being openly questioned in eastern Europe for the first time, the factory may soon have to switch tack again.

*Škoda cars are currently put together in Mladá Boleslav, see p.176*

## Arrival, orientation and accommodation

Fast trains from Prague take between one and a half and two hours to reach Plzeň, making it just about possible to visit on a day trip. The town's railway stations are works of art in themselves: of the two, your likeliest point of arrival is Plzeň hlavní nádraží (main station), east of the city centre, rather than the Jižní předměstí (south station), 750m southwest of the centre. The bus terminal, for all national and international arrivals, is on the west side of town. From the bus or the main train station, the city centre is just a short walk away or a few stops on tram #1 or #2.

Finding a vacancy in one of Plzeň's hotels presents few problems, though rooms don't come cheap. At the lower end of the market are the faded splendour and Hollywood stairways of the *Slovan*, Smetanovy sady 1 (☎019/335 51; ②), and moving up a bit there's the *Continental*, Zbrojnická 8 (☎019/330 60; ③), or the ugly *Central*, náměstí Republiky 33 (☎019/326 85; ③).

Private rooms are available from *ČEDOK*, Prešovská 10 (Mon–Fri 8am–noon & 2–6pm, Sat 8am–noon), for slightly less per person than the *Slovan*. In July and August, student hostels offer cheap dorm accommodation – go to *CKM* on Dominikanská to find out the latest addresses. Bus #20 will drop you at the *Bílá hora* campsite, in the northern suburb of the same name, where Plzeňites go to swim on summer days.

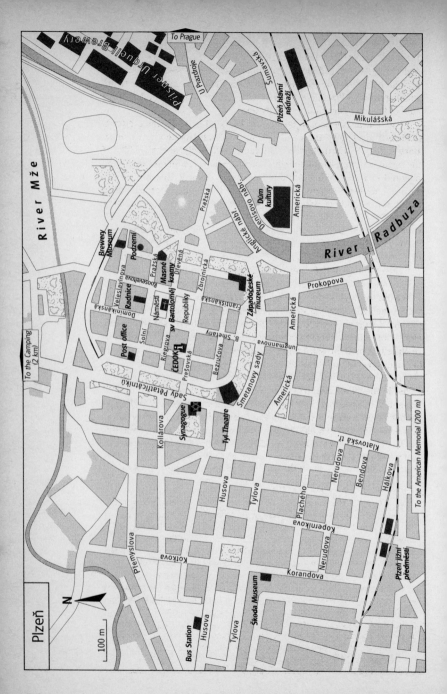

Plzeň

N

100 m

To Prague

Pilsner Urquell Brewery

U Prazdroje

Šumavská

Plzeň hlavní nádraží

Mikulášská

River Mže

Prašská

Anglické nábř.

Denisovo nábř.

Dům kultury

Americká

River Radbuza

Brewery Museum

Podzemí

Pražská

Masné krámy

Dřevená

Roosveltova

Velešlavínova

Radnice

Dominikánská

Prokopova

Zbrojnická

Náměstí

sv Bartoloměj

Republiky

Františkánská

Západočeské muzeum

Americká

Solní

Riegrova

Post office

ČEDOK

Dlouhá

Přešovská

B. Smetany

Bezručova

Smetanovy sady

Tungmannova

To the Camping (2 km)

Sady Pětatřicátníků

Kollárova

Synagogue

Tyl Theatre

Smetanovy sady

Americká

Husova

Tylova

Plachého

Nerudova

Bendova

Hálkova

Klatovská tř.

To the American Memorial (200 m)

Přemyslova

Kotkova

Koperníkova

Nerudova

Korandova

Plzeň jižní předměstí

Bus Station

Husova

Tylova

Husova

Škoda Museum

Stepping out of the main station onto Americká, you're confronted with a variety of bad-taste Communist buildings, some still in the process of completion. Close by, the River Radbuza, one of four rivers running through Plzeň, doesn't bear close inspection, but the historical core of the city, beyond it, certainly does.

Laid out in chessboard fashion by Václav II in 1295, the old town is still dominated by the exalted heights of the Gothic church of sv Bartoloměj (St Bartholomew), stranded awkwardly in the middle of the main square, its bile-green spire reaching up more than one hundred metres, making it the tallest in the country. The rest of the square – náměstí Republiky – presents a full range of architectural styles: some buildings, like the squat, grey *Hotel Central*, as recent as the 1960s, others, like the Italianate Stará radnice (Old Town Hall), smothered in sgraffito earlier this century, dating from the sixteenth century. Rudolf II based himself next door, at no. 41, for the best part of a year, in an effort to avoid the ravages of the 1599 Prague plague.

The vast majority of Plzeň's buildings, however, hail from the city's heyday during the industrial expansion around the turn of the century. In the old town, this produced some wonderful variations on historical themes and Art-Nouveau motifs, particularly to the north and west of the main square. West of Sady Pětatřicátníků, there are still more blocks of late nineteenth-century residential apartments, boasting vestiges of ornate mosaics and sculpturing, now barely visible beneath the black layer of pollution eating away at their fanciful facades.

On Sady Pětatřicátníků itself stands the largest surviving synagogue in the whole country, its neo-Romanesque facade caked in dirt. The smaller prayer hall inside was in use until very recently, and there are plans now to turn it into a museum on Plzeň's Jewish history along with a concert and exhibition hall. Diagonally opposite is the flamboyant Tyl Theatre, named after Josef Kajétan Tyl, the composer of the Czech half of the national anthem, who died in Plzeň in 1856.

---

### The American Liberation of Plzeň

On May 6, 1945, General Patton's US Third Army liberated Plzeň. Less than 100km of virtually open road lay between the Americans and Prague, by then into the second day of its costly uprising against the Nazis. However, the agreement between the Allies at Yalta was that Prague should be liberated by the Soviets, who were, at the time, still 200km from Prague, en route from Berlin. Patton offered to march on Prague, and, in fact, on May 7, three US armoured cars reached the outskirts of the city, but the order was to stay put.

Following the 1948 coup, the Communists took down all the monuments, and deleted all references in history books to the American liberation of Plzeň. They even went so far as to say that the Americans had deliberately hung back from Prague, allowing thousands to die in the uprising. Finally, in May 1990, the city was able once again to celebrate the liberation, and with large numbers of US army veterans present, a new memorial was erected on Chodské náměstí, just off Klatovská třída.

Plzeň

## Beer and the brewery

Whatever its other attractions, the real reason most people come to Plzeň is to sample its famous beer, *Plzeňský Prazdroj* or **Pilsner Urquell** (its more familiar Germanised export name). Beer has been brewed in the town since its foundation in 1295, but it wasn't until 1842 that the famous *Bürgerliches Brauhaus* was built by the German banker Bleichröder, after a near-riot by the townsfolk over the declining quality of their beer. The new brew was a bottom-fermented beer which quickly became popular across central Europe, spawning thousands of paler imitations under the generic name of *Pilsner* or *Pils* – hence the brewers' addition of the suffix *Prazdroj* or *Urquell* (meaning "original"), to show just who thought of it first. The reason for the superiority of Plzeň's beer is said to be the combination of the soft local water and world-renowned Žatec hops.

Joining a guided tour of the brewery is now relatively easy, except that no one seems to be quite sure of the exact times. Either turn up at the brewery gates at 12.30pm any day except Wednesday, as the brewery suggests, or ask at *ČEDOK*, who tend to tell a different story. Alternatively, if the technological details of brewing don't grab you, try the historical angle at the Brewery Museum instead (see below), and/ or go for a glass of the real thing at the *Restaurace Prazdroj* at U Prazdroje 1, next to the brewery's triumphal arch. This was built in 1892 to commemorate its fiftieth birthday – and has appeared on every authentic bottle of *Pilsner Urquell* ever since. Plzeň's annual beer festival, incidentally, is held in October.

## Plzeň's museums

Plzeň has a fair few museums, the biggest being the copper-topped **Západočeské muzeum** (due to reopen towards the end of 1992). A neo-Baroque extravaganza, it was built in the nineteenth century to help educate the peasants who were flocking to the city; only a few of its mammoth selection of exhibits deserve close attention, notably the art section, which boasts some of the best examples of twentieth-century Czech painting outside Prague. A little to the north, beneath the elongated vaults of the Gothic **Masné krámy** (Butchers' Stalls), the gallery puts on temporary art exhibitions (Tues–Fri 10am–6pm, Sat 10am–1pm, Sun 9am–5pm) and hosts concerts on Sunday mornings.

At the end of the beautiful, narrow, *fin-de-siècle* Veleslavínova is the most popular of Plzeň's museums, the **Brewery Museum** (pivovarské muzeum; Tues 1–4.30pm, Wed–Sun 9am–4.30pm), housed in what was originally a Gothic malthouse and later a pub. A more than sufficient consolation for those who fail to get into the brewery itself, its friendly anglophile custodian can furnish you with an information sheet in English, and get the old *Würlitzer* organ going while you check out the exhibits: the smallest beer barrel in the world (a mere one-centimetre cube), case after case of kitsch Baroque beer mugs, and much else besides.

Unfortunately, unless you're an automotive engineer you won't get much from the **Škoda Museum**, by the factory on Korandova (Mon–Fri 7am–3.30pm), which has displays on the insides of train engines and suchlike. For an exhibition of old Škoda cars, you'll have to go Mladá Boleslav (see p.176).

## Eating, drinking and entertainment

All the hotels in town have **restaurants** attached to them, but for something more basic – and authentically Czech – you might as well combine your eating with your drinking. Apart from the aforementioned *Restaurace Prazdroj* (see above), you can get *Pilsner Urquell* (and cheap grub) at the *Pivnice na parkánu* (Mon–Fri 10.30am–11pm, Sat 10.30am–midnight), next door to the Brewery Museum, and at *U kanóna*, Rooseveltova 18 (daily 10am–9pm). *Gambrinus*, Plzeň's other beer, is best drunk at *U Žumbery* on Bezručova (currently under restoration). As for cafés, try *U Bedřicha* on B. Smetany (10am–10pm).

Plzeň's wonderful Beaux-Arts **Tyl Theatre** is the city's main venue for opera and ballet. Most other concerts and cultural events take place at the *Dům kultury* on Americká, but in summer the **Festival of Folk Songs** (July) is just one of the events held at the *Přírodní divadlo*, Plzeň's open-air theatre, set in the botanical gardens of Lochotínský park, near the university medical faculty (tram #3 or #4 from outside the Tyl Theatre). Czechoslovakia's longest-running puppet duo, Spejbl and Hurvínek, originated at Plzeň's **puppet theatre**, *Divadlo dětí Alfa* at Americká 17 (entrance is on Jungmannova), which still puts on daily performances plus the occasional film.

# Prague: Listings

# Chapter 10

# Finding a Place to Stay

Prague's hotel problem is notorious. Not only are there still just 10,000 beds in the city – many of them currently unavailable due to reconstruction work – but they are extremely expensive for what you get. As a result, most tourists now stay in private accommodation, easy enough to arrange either from the UK, or on arrival in Prague. There are several **accommodation agencies** to choose from at the airport, the main train station, and elsewhere in Prague (see box below for addresses). If you're determined to stay in a hotel, you'll need to book well in advance, especially during the high season (Easter to October, and the two weeks around Christmas and New Year). ČEDOK in London (see *Basics* for address) can do this for you, but their choice of hotels is limited, and prices start at around £40 for a double. ČEDOK in Prague has a wider selection, but still doesn't handle the bottom end of the market. As yet, the only method of ensuring a cheap hotel room is to contact the hotel yourself by letter, phone or fax – a time-consuming and often frustrating business.

## Private accommodation

The (almost) endless supply of **private rooms** in Prague means it's not really necessary to book in advance – although it can be worth doing to save time, and for some peace of mind, especially if you're arriving in July or August (see "Getting There" in *Basics* for lists of relevant travel agencies). If you arrive without a room reservation, the easiest thing to do is head for one of the **booking offices** at the airport or main train station. If the queues are horrendous, as

they can be in peak season, then try one of the other agencies in town (see box below). Alternatively, if you hang around at the station, airport or outside one of the agencies, you're almost certain to be approached by a tout. Most offers are genuine, but make sure you ask for a receipt before you pass over any money. In any case, you should check exactly how far out of the centre you're going to be (and preferably see the room) before committing yourself.

### Accommodation agencies in Prague

**Agentura B & B**
28 října 9, Nové Město (☎ 26 82 20; daily 8/9am–6/7pm).
Private rooms from 350kčs per person.

**AVE Ltd**
Offices at the airport and the main train station (☎ 236 56 60; daily summer 6am–11pm; winter 6am–4pm).
Private rooms from 350kčs.

**ČEDOK**
Panská 5, Nové Město (☎ 212 71 11; April–Nov Mon–Fri 9am–10pm, Sat 8.30am–6pm, Sun 8.30am–4.30pm; Dec–March Mon–Fri 9am–8pm, Sat & Sun 8.30am–2pm).
For the top end of the hotel market only.

**Hello Ltd**
Senovážné náměstí 3, Nové Město (☎ 224 283; daily 9am–10pm).
Hostels for 250kčs per person; private rooms from 350kčs; private apartments from 600kčs per person.    *contd.*

## Finding a Place to Stay

**IFB**
Václavské náměstí 38, Nové Město (☎26
03 33; Mon–Fri 9am–1pm & 2–6pm, Sat
9am–4pm).
Private rooms from 500kčs per person,
plus some hotels.

**Pragotur**
U Obecního domu 2, Staré Město (☎232
22 05; April–Oct Mon–Fri 8am–10pm,
Sat 8am–8pm, Sun 8am–3pm; March,
Nov & Dec Mon–Fri 8am–8pm, Sat 8am–
6pm, Sun 8am–3pm; Jan Mon–Fri 8am–
6pm; Feb Mon–Fri 8am–8pm, Sat 8am–
6pm). Deals with the lower end of the
hotel market and will also book private
rooms from 350kčs per person.

**Toptour**
Rybná 3, Staré Město (☎232 10 77;
Mon–Fri 9am–8pm, Sat & Sun 10am–
7pm). Private rooms from 500kčs per
person, and self-contained apartments
from 1000kBs a night.

## Hotels

**Hotels** in Prague are expensive, and, with a
few notable exceptions, nondescript.
Nevertheless, since demand still far
exceeds supply, in summer they are
booked up solid months in advance. So,
unless you're here off season, there's really
no point in trekking around any of the
hotels listed below on the off chance they
will have vacancies. Besides, Prague's
cheaper hotels are scattered throughout the
city, with virtually none in the older quarters
of Hradčany, Malá Strana and Staré Město.
The best policy is to contact the hotel
before you leave for Prague and attempt to
make a reservation.

### Around náměstí Republiky

The hotels within spitting distance of
náměstí Republiky tend to be fairly extor-
tionate, with a much cheaper, run-down
cluster just a couple of blocks east, near
the Wilsonova flyover – where the Těšnov
train station used to be.

**Axa**, Na poříčí 40, Nové Město; ☎232 72
34; metro Florenc. Just five minutes' walk
from náměstí Republiky, and a particular
favourite with young German tour groups.
②.

**Centrum**, Na poříčí 31, Nové Město; ☎231
00 09. Directly opposite the *Axa*, and at
present undergoing a much-needed period
of refurbishment. ② but currently under
reconstruction.

**Hybernia**, Hybernská 24, Nové Město; ☎22
04 31. At the time of writing, as gloomy as
ever, but no doubt soon to fall under the
onslaught of the developers. ②.

**Merkur**, Těšnov 9, Nové Město; ☎231 68
40. Few mod cons here as yet, and so, for
the moment, one of the few cheap central
hotels in Prague. ②.

---

### Accommodation Prices

The hotel lists below are divided according to area; within each section the lists are
arranged alphabetically within price range. After each entry you'll find a symbol which
corresponds to one of five **price categories**:

① Under 750kčs

② 750–1250 kčs

③ 1250–2000 kčs

④ 2000–3000kčs

⑤ 3000kčs and upwards

All prices are for the cheapest **double room** available, which usually means without
private bath or shower in the less expensive places. For a **single room**, expect to pay
around two-thirds the price of a double.

Note that a large number of the hotels listed below are currently closed, undergoing
extensive modernisation – and others will no doubt follow in the near future. This is
bound to result in higher prices when they reopen; the prices quoted below should, therefore, be taken only as a guideline.

---

**Central**, Rybná 8, Staré Město; ☎232 43 51. One of the very few hotels in Staré Město – no work of art, but true to its name and surprisingly cheap. ③.

**Opera**, Těšnov 13, Nové Město; ☎231 56 09. Moderately priced nineteenth-century hotel and remarkably pleasant considering it's right by the flyover. ③.

**Atlantic**, Na poříčí 9, Nové Město; ☎231 85 12. Modern, and therefore a cut above its neighbours in terms of both facilities and price. ④.

**Botel Albatros**, nábřeží Ludvíka Svobody, Nové Město; ☎231 36 34. Double cabins for rent on a moored boat at the end of Revoluční. Not quite as romantic or cheap as you might expect, but the best of the city's three floating "botels". ④.

**Meteor**, Hybernská 6, Nové Město; ☎22 42 02. Recently completely refurbished, and now nothing like as cheap as its immediate neighbours. ④.

**Paříž**, U Obecního domu 1, Staré Město ☎232 20 51. A mostly quite modern interior to this turn-of-the-century hotel, superbly located off náměstí Republiky and therefore over £100 a double. ⑤.

**Ungelt**, Štupartská 1, Staré Město; ☎232 04 71. Unbelievably well positioned, exclusive little hotel in the backstreets of the old town, but over £100 a double since its recent modernisation. ⑤.

### Around Wenceslas Square

There's no question that these hotels are right in the centre of things, though it's worth bearing in mind that Wenceslas Square (Václavské náměstí) doubles as Prague's red-light district and nightclub zone by night.

**Juliš**, Václavské náměstí 22; ☎235 28 85. Tired-looking 1930s functionalist hotel, halfway down Wenceslas Square, which was known as the *Tatran* under the Communists and has only recently reverted to its original name. ③.

**Evropa**, Václavské náměstí 25; ☎236 52 74. Without doubt, the most beautiful hotel in Prague, sumptuously decorated in Art-Nouveau style (except for the rooms them-

selves). Surprisingly, it's not the most expensive, but it's incredibly difficult to get a room here, since *ČEDOK* don't deal with them and they claim not to take bookings more than fourteen days in advance – and yet they're always full. ④.

**Alcron**, Štěpánská 40; ☎235 92 16. Top-notch 1930s hotel, just off Wenceslas Square. A favourite haunt of western journalists during the 1968 Prague Spring. ⑤ but currently under reconstruction.

**Palace**, Panská 12; ☎26 83 41. Originally built in the 1900s but tastelessly modernised recently and now over £150 a double. ⑤.

### Southern Nové Město

Only a metro stop or two from the centre of things, though in parts blighted by heavy traffic flow.

**Moráň**, Václavská 5; ☎29 42 51; metro Karlovo náměstí. A very basic place just off Karlovo náměstí, with few facilities – and therefore a prime candidate for reconstruction. ②.

**Hlavkova**, Jenštýnská 1; ☎29 21 39; metro Karlovo náměstí. Spartan but clean hotel one block south of Resslova. Large breakfast included in price of room. ③.

**Koruna**, Opatovická 16; ☎29 39 33. Hidden in the backstreets three blocks south of Národní. ③.

**Kriváň**, náměstí I. P. Pavlova 5; ☎29 33 41; metro I. P. Pavlova. Not the greatest part of town to be in, but very close to Wenceslas Square – expect the price to rise. ③ but currently under reconstruction.

### The southern suburbs

There really are very few advantages to staying in characterless suburbs like Nusle or Krč, though they are, for the most part, well served by the city's fast transport system.

**Nusle**, Závišova 30, Nusle; tram #7, #18 or #24 from metro Karlovo náměstí. Spartan, modern hotel down in the Botič valley. Bookable only through the *CAS* accommodation agency at the main train station. ②.

## Finding a Place to Stay

# Finding a Place to Stay

**Michle**, Nuselská 124, Michle; ☎42 71 17. Not that easy to get to: take tram #11 from behind the National Museum, at the top of Wenceslas Square. ③.

**Botel Racek**, Podolské nábřeží, Podolí; ☎42 57 93; tram #3, #17 or #21. Suffering the worst views of all Prague's "botels", this is definitely a last resort. ④.

**Forum**, Kongresová 1, Nusle; ☎41 02 38; metro Vyšehrad. Highly impressive views from this £100-a-double skyscraper which boasts Prague's one and only bowling alley. ⑤.

**Panorama**, Milevská 7, Krč; ☎41 61 11; metro Pankrác. Ugly skyscraper hotel just off the motorway to Brno; marginally cheaper, and with slightly fewer facilities than the *Forum*. ⑤.

## Vinohrady, Žižkov and beyond

Vinohrady and Žižkov, both good-looking run-down nineteenth-century neighbourhoods, contain some of Prague's cheapest hotels, all within easy access of the fast metro system. Unfortunately, the vast majority are currently under reconstruction, and may well reopen with much higher prices.

**Juventus**, Blanická 10, Vinohrady; ☎25 51 51; metro náměstí Míru. One of the few cheap Vinohrady haunts still functioning at the time of going to press. ①.

**Libeň**, Rudé armády 37, Libeň; ☎82 82 27; metro Palmovka. Not your usual tourist locale, but very convenient for Prague's Hare Krishna restaurant (see p.210). ①.

**Národní dům**, Bořivojova 53, Žižkov; ☎27 53 65; tram #5, #9 or #26 from metro Hlavní nádraží. Turn-of-the-century hotel, once Prague's cheapest. ① but currently under reconstruction.

**Ostaš**, Orebitská 8, Žižkov; ☎27 28 60; tram #5, #9 or #26 from metro Hlavní nádraží. Another former bargain hotel. ① but currently under reconstruction.

**Tichý**, Seifertova 65, Žižkov; ☎27 30 79; tram #9, #10, #13 or #26. *Tichý* means silent, but don't believe it – this hotel is right on the main road. ① but currently under reconstruction.

**Ametyst**, Jana Masaryka 11, Vinohrady; ☎25 92 56; metro náměstí Míru and/or tram #6 or #11. Neo-Rennaissance pile with a wonderful view overlooking the Botič valley. ② but currently under reconstruction.

**Beránek**, Bělehradská 110, Vinohrady; ☎25 45 44. Previously an extremely cheap hotel, where Maxim Gorky once stayed. It remains to be seen what it will have turned into when it reopens. ② but currently under reconstruction.

**Luník**, Londýnská 50, Vinohrady; ☎25 27 01; metro I. P. Pavlova. A short hop away from Wenceslas Square. ② but currently under reconstruction.

**Zotavovna**, Sokolovská, Karlín; metro Invalidovna. Within minutes of the centre of town by metro; must be booked through *Pragotur*. ③.

## Holešovice, Bubeneč, Dejvice and beyond.

These hotels are spread over a wide area ranging from the tenements of Holešovice to the leafy garden suburbs of Bubeneč, Dejvice and beyond.

**Moravan**, U Uranie 22, Holešovice; ☎80 29 05; metro Nádraží Holešovice. Not a jolly part of town, but within easy reach of the Stromovka park. ①.

**Savoy**, Keplerova 6, Hradčany; ☎53 74 57. Its position – at the western end of Hradčany – is magnificent, but it's unlikely to hold its previously unbeatable prices. ③ but currently under reconstruction.

**International**, Podbaba, Dejvice; ☎331 91 11; tram #20 or #25. Classic, pompous 1950s Stalinist hotel with plenty of dour social realist friezes and large helpings of marble. ④.

**Splendid**, Ovenecká 33, Bubeneč; ☎37 33 51; tram #1, #8, #25 or #26; stop Letenské *náměstí*. Situated in a pleasant part of town, right by the Stromovka park. ④ but currently under reconstruction.

**Parkhotel**, Veletržní 20, Holešovice; ☎380 71 11; tram #5, #12 or #17. Fairly professionally run hotel from the 1960s, just a short distance from the Výstaviště fairground. ⑤.

## Smíchov

Smíchov is one of the poorer, traditionally industrial parts of Prague, but it's just a step away from Malá Strana and Petřín Hill.

**Balkán**, Svornosti 28; ☎54 07 77; metro Anděl. One of the cheapest functioning hotels in Prague; recently privatised but still reassuringly run-down. ①.

**Praga**, Plzeňská 29; ☎54 87 41; metro Anděl. Previously extremely cheap and basic. ① but currently under reconstruction.

**U Blaženký**, U Blaženký 1; ☎53 82 66; metro Anděl. Nice hilltop location, just up from the Mozart Museum, and with a good cheap restaurant. ③.

**Botel Admirál**, Hořejší nábřeží; ☎54 74 45; metro Anděl. The largest of Prague's floating "botels", perversely positioned the wrong side of the river for a really good view of the Hrad. ④.

## Youth Hostels

Prague has very few **hostels**, official (*IYHF*) or otherwise. Those that do exist generally cost about two-thirds the price of a private room – around 250kčs a night – though one or two are very cheap. All hostels are heavily oversubscribed in summer, so ring ahead where possible to save a fruitless journey; none of them require a membership card. To find out the latest on the Prague hostel scene, go to the *CKM* **youth agency** at Žitná 10, Nové Město (☎29 29 84; 7am–7pm; closed Sun). In July and August, *CKM* also let out rooms in student hostels.

**Dukla Karlín**, Malého 1, Karlín; ☎22 20 09; metro Florenc. Situated in the insalubrious locale of the Praha-Florenc bus station. Reception opens at 6pm and you'll be turfed out at 8am the next morning – a definite last resort.

**Hotel Praha**, Žitná 42, Nové Město; metro Karlovo náměstí. Billed as "the cheapest hotel in Prague", this place charged just 50kčs for a camp bed on a gym floor in the summer of 1991. Open July & Aug only; reception 6–11am & 5–11pm.

**Juniorhotel "B & B"**, Jankovcova 163, Holešovice; metro Nádraží Holešovice. A private youth hostel in a sort of scout hut

by the river Vltava – sounds scenic but isn't. Dorm beds 250kčs.

**Juniorhotel Praha**, Žitná 12, Nové Město; ☎29 99 41; metro Karlovo náměstí. This is supposedly the official *IYHF* hostel – members get a reduced rate – and it's invariably full. There are plans to open a new *IYHF* hostel in the near future; ask at the *CKM* office, across the street, for the latest.

**Strahov**, Spartakiádní 5, Strahov; tram #8 or #22, stop Pohořelec, then a short walk. Permanent student hostel which may well be able to squeeze you in.

**Ubytovna Raketa**, Havličkova 2, Nové Město. A cheap dorm-style hostel near náměstí Republiky.

**Na Vlachovce**, Rudé armády 217, Kobylisy; tram #5, #17 or #25; open May–Sept. Cheap, two-sleeper giant beer barrels – heaven or hell depending on your tastes.

**Finding a Place to Stay**

## Campsites

Prague abounds in **campsites** and most are relatively easy to get to by public transport. Facilities, on the whole, are rudimentary and badly maintained, but the prices reflect this. Note that most Prague campsites close down from the end of October to the end of March.

**Troja**, Trojská 157, Troja; ☎84 28 33; bus #112 roughly hourly, or tram #5, #17 or #25 then a short walk, from metro Nádraží Holešovice; open mid-April to Sept. Good location, 3km north of the centre, on the road to the Troja chateau. As well as this official site, a whole series of others have sprung up on Trojská, ranging from people's back gardens to two fully equipped sites.

**Aritma Džbán**, Nad lávkou 3, Vokovice; ☎36 85 51; tram #20 or #26 from metro Dejvická; open all year. 4km west of the centre, near the Šárka valley. Tents only.

**Kotva Braník**, U ledáren 55, Braník; ☎46 13 97; tram #3 or #17 along the right bank of the Vltava; open April–Oct. 6km south of the city.

**Caravancamp Motol**, Plzeňská, Motol; ☎52 47 14; tram #4, #7 or #9 from metro Anděl; open April–Sept. 5km west of the city centre.

# Chapter 11

# Eating and Drinking

Every restaurant, *pivnice* and *vinárna* in Prague has either closed down or been privatised in the last year or so, so it's not surprising that **eating and drinking** is a bit unpredictable at the moment, with enormous variations in price and quality. A few authentic ethnic eateries have started up, though traditional Czech food still predominates. New western-style outfits are also beginning to appear, charging prices that westerners find very reasonable but few Czechs can afford. Meanwhile, the number of cheap Czech *pivnice* has considerably reduced, particularly downtown.

The biggest mistake most first-time visitors make is to confine their eating and drinking to the obvious sightseeing areas, where prices are generally much higher, quality often a low priority, and, in summer, spare tables a real find. It's worth venturing, instead, into the southern section of Nové Město, which hides a number of good-value restaurants; or to suburbs like Vinohrady, Nusle or Bubeneč, just ten minutes' travel from the centre.

In the **high season**, Prague can be unbearably crowded, and its restaurants rarely manage to cope. There are, however, a number of ways around the problem: reserve a table in advance; eat your main meal at lunchtime (as most Praguers do), when the rest of the city's tourists are busy sightseeing; or try somewhere a bit further from the centre of town. If you're intent on **drinking** plenty of Bohemia's world-class beers, bear in mind that, with precious few exceptions, Prague's *pivnice* close around 10 or 11pm.

## "Breakfast", snacks and fast food

Unless a continental breakfast is included in the price of your accommodation, you're going to find it hard to know exactly what to eat for breakfast and where to eat it. The Czechs get up so early, they rarely bother with more than a gulp of grainy black coffee, and perhaps a slice of bread and salami. A few of the newer bakeries offer croissants, sundry pastries and coffee all under the same roof, but most don't. The state subsidised stand-up buffets (*bufet*), favoured by many Czech workers, are slowly disappearing. Instead, sandwiches (*sendvič*) are starting to catch on, and there are various new fast-food places to try out (not all of them *McDonald's*). If you get up much past 10am, you might as well join Prague's working population for lunch.

### Hradčany and Malá Strana

**Golden Bun**, Mostecká 3. Burgers, kebabs and falafel. Open daily until 8.30pm.

**Saté**, Pohořelec 4. Convenient fast-food place with a vaguely Indonesian bent, but small portions and zero atmosphere. Open daily 10am–8pm.

**U labutí** (The Swan), Hradčanské náměstí 11. A cheap snack bar, not the posh *vinárna* (in the same building), with outside tables in summer. Open Mon–Sat 10am–6pm.

### Staré Město and Josefov

**Bonal**, Staroměstské náměstí 4. Flash Czech-German joint venture selling sandwiches, pastries and some of the best coffee in Prague. Stand-up only. Open daily 9am–9pm.

**Country Life**, Melantrichova 15. Cramped, popular stand-up buffet within a health food shop, which serves vegan snacks – though you'll have to buy a lot to fill yourself up. Open Mon–Fri until 7pm; Sun until 1pm.

**Frank's Bistro**, Na můstku (right by the bottom end of Wenceslas Square). A convenient but uninspiring stomach filler, run by an LA expat, serving pizza, pasta and other snacks. Open daily 7am–10pm.

**Lahůdky u čapů**, Staroměstské náměstí 24. Stand-up Czech *bufet* in what the Czechs call a deli. Open Mon–Sat until 7pm.

**U Bindrů**, Staroměstské náměstí 26 (opposite the astronomical clock). A larger, more westernised buffet than the above. Open daily until 9pm in summer, 7pm in winter.

**US Burger**, Masná 2. Uncompromising name, though the roast chicken is actually a better bet than the so-called burgers. Open daily 10am–10pm.

### Nové Město

**Arbat**, Na příkopě 29. Before *McDonald's*, this bland but extremely popular hamburger outlet was the only fast-food joint in town – it remains to be seen how it handles the competition. Open daily 7.30am–11pm.

**McDonald's**, Vodičková 15. Opened in March 1992 on the site of an old school dining hall, its main virtue is that it also sells draught *Pilsner Urquell*. Open daily 8am–11pm.

**Palace**, Panská 12 (on corner with Jindřišská). Situated in the basement of the most expensive hotel in Prague, this is no place to linger (there are no tables, only counters), but a good spot to binge on fresh produce and the self-service salad bar. Open daily 6–11am & noon–midnight.

**Pekárna Dahlen**, Senovážné náměstí 3. Cheap, smoky and tacky, this new "bakery" serves hot and cold Czech snacks.

**Poříčská pekárna**, Na poříčí 30. One of the new-style Viennese bakeries, selling coffee and pastries. Open Mon–Fri 7am–7pm, Sat until 1pm.

**Rybárna**, Václavské náměstí 43. Stand-up buffet with fish in batter and fishy salads on offer. Open daily until 8pm.

**Snack Bar India**, Štěpánská 63. Tandoori dishes, curries and other mildly hot snacks. Vegetarians be warned: the rice contains meat. Open 11am–11pm; closed Sat.

## Cafés and bars

Prague can no longer boast a café society to rival the best in Europe, as it could at the beginning of this century, though a few of the classic haunts survive. Nevertheless, many Praguers still spend a large part of the day smoking and drinking in the city's cafés, particularly in the summer, when the tables spill out onto the streets and squares. At all the places picked out below, the emphasis is more on drinking than eating, and in many the only food on offer will be cakes.

### Hradčany and Malá Strana

**Café de Colombia**, Mostecká 3. French radio, Colombian coffee, but very few tables under its Gothic vaults. Open daily noon–midnight.

**Kajetánka**, Hradčanské náměstí (below the wall which overlooks the city). Fantastic view which the prices are starting to reflect. Open Tues–Sat 11am–10pm, Sun & Mon 11am–8pm.

**Malostranská kavárna**, Malostranské náměstí 28. A time-honoured café founded in 1874 in a late eighteenth-century palace. Despite the changes, it's still a good place to meet for coffee and cakes either inside or on the summer terrace, provided you can get a table. Open daily 7am–11pm.

**Rubín**, Malostranské náměstí 9. Arty cellar café with the occasional live music or theatre show. Open 3pm–1am.

**U tří houslíček** (The Three Violins), Nerudova 12. Just one of a number of small wine bars that line the climb up to the castle. Open Tues–Sat 3.30–11.30pm.

### Staré Město and Josefov

**A Scéna** (also known as Lávka), Novotného lávka (below the Smetana Museum). Tiny, trendy and lively riverside café, with tables

**Eating and Drinking**

## Eating and Drinking

outside in summer. Superb view of the castle; occasional theatre and music gigs inside. Open daily noon–2am.

**Bílý jelínek**, U radnice. Small designer coffee-and-cake place, which is currently being redesigned; situated just off Staroměstské náměstí.

**Blatnička**, Michalská. Perfect for a stand-up wine hit, but if you want to sit down you'll have to cross the street to *Blatnice* (see below). Open 10am–10pm.

**Paříž**, U obecního domu 1. The prices are sky-high for Prague, but there's a certain faded elegance about this hotel *kavárna*. Open daily until 1am.

**U zelené lipy** (The Green Lime Tree), Melantrichova 12. Convenient, smoky caffeine halt en route from Staroměstské náměstí to Wenceslas Square. Open daily 10am–11pm.

**Výčep selského vina**, Stupartská. A tiny but popular wine bar in a side street off Staroměstské náměstí, the clientele frequently spilling out on to the street.

### Nové Město

**Becher Club**, Masarykovo nábřeží 38. Intimate bar behind the national theatre, perfect for a pre- or post-theatrical *becherovka*. Open daily until midnight.

**Beránkova-Osvěžovna**, Masarykovo nábřeží (two doors down from the *Becher Club*). The first of two much plainer cafés behind the national theatre. Go for the hot chocolate. Open daily until 11.30pm.

**Café Bunkr**, Lodecká 2. Posey (but cheap) café attached to the club of the same name. Open daily until 5am.

**Café Four**, Soukenická 2. Another posey stopoff, decked out in black marble, just off Revoluční en route to the *Bunkr*. Open until 11pm.

**ČKD dům**, Na příkopě 1. Sadly the top-floor terrace (with its amazing view of Wenceslas Square) is closed for the moment, but the ground floor is still functioning. Strictly coffee only. Open daily 10am–11.30pm.

**Hotel Evropa**, Václavské náměstí 25. *The* place to be seen on Wenceslas Square. If you want to appreciate the sumptuous Art-Nouveau decor, take breakfast inside. Open daily 10am–11.30pm.

**Juliš**, Václavské náměstí 22. Functionalist café on the second floor, severely battered over the years. Open daily 7am–midnight; naff live band in the evening.

**Mánes**, Masarykovo nábřeží 250. Pristine white functionalist café, one floor above the gallery, with a view onto the island. The entrance is around the side from the gallery.

**Obecní dům**, náměstí Republiky. The *kavárna*, with its famous fountain, is in the more restrained south hall of this huge Art-Nouveau complex. Ask for the cake trolley. Open daily 7am–11pm.

**Paris-Praha**, Jindřišská 7. Small, chic café selling *Gauloise* singles; next door to the French delicatessen of the same name. Open Mon–Fri 8.30am–7pm, Sat 8.30am–1pm.

**Slavia**, Národní 1. Incredibly smoky atmosphere, lousy music, excruciatingly slow service, and unbelievably bad coffee. Yet this place remains an enduring and endearing Prague institution (see p.129). Open 8am–midnight.

## Restaurants, pubs and wine bars

For a full meal, you can go to a *restaurace*, a *pivnice* or a *vinárna*. A *pivnice* is primarily a beer hall for serious (predominantly male) drinkers, but most also serve food, and some even have separate (generally more mixed) dining areas (*jídelna*). *Restaurace* span the range from glorified *pivnice* to extremely posh affairs, run by tuxedoed waiters with Viennese airs and graces. A *vinárna* is traditionally a more intimate affair, perhaps with a little live music, a long wine list, and late opening hours. Having said all that, the differences between all three can be very vague indeed.

Most places serve traditional Czech food – beef or pork and dumplings or potatoes – though there are a number of new restaurants offering **international cuisines** – mainly Chinese and Italian – which make a change from the calorific local fare.

The listings are divided into geographical areas, and into price categories, too – cheap, medium and expensive. As a rough guide, you'll be able to get a three-course meal with drinks for:

**Cheap** under 150kčs a head

**Medium** 150–300kčs a head

**Expensive** 300kčs and upwards

While 300kčs for a meal is hardly expensive to a westerner, it still is for most Czechs – you're unlikely to share your table with any locals. Bear in mind, too, that the full repercussions of privatisation have yet to take effect, and that many of the places listed below may close down or double their prices overnight.

The Czechs eat their main meal of the day at lunchtime (when you'll be offered the widest choice of dishes), and most kitchens stop taking orders around 10pm. At all but the cheapest *pivnice*, it's recommended that you **reserve a table** in advance, especially in the high season: either ring the number provided, or call in earlier in the day.

### Hradčany and Malá Strana

Hradčany and Malá Strana are two of the nicest parts of the city in which to spend the evening. However, they also contain some of Prague's most exclusive (and expensive) restaurants and *vinárna*, so make sure you check the prices before committing yourself.

#### CHEAP

**Baráčnická rychta**, Na tržiště 22 (down a narrow passageway off Nerudova). A real survivor – a small backstreet *pivnice* squeezed in between the embassies, with a cheap and filling restaurant attached. Open daily 11am–11pm.

**Jadran**, Mostecká 21 (through the archway and across the courtyard). One of the few really cheap *vinárna* left in Malá Strana, though, unfortunately, it closes early – and may yet close for good. Open daily 11am–10pm.

**Český rybářský svaz** (Czech Fishermen's Club), U Sovových mlýnů; ☎53 02 23. Worth the trouble to get to – it's hidden away in the park on Kampa island. The manager has an appropriately sailor-like beard, and the fish is fresh from the Sázava river. Open Mon–Sat 1–9pm.

**U černého vola** (The Black Bear), Loretánské náměstí 1. Does a brisk business providing the popular light beer *Velkopopovický kozel* in huge quantities to thirsty local workers. Open 9.30am–9pm.

**U kocoura** (The Cat), Nerudova 2. The last surviving pub on Nerudova, which was bought by the Beer Party in January 1992 to prevent it, too, from disappearing. Serves some of the best *Pilsner Urquell* in town; the food doesn't stretch much beyond sausages. Open daily until 11pm.

#### MEDIUM

**Nebozízek** (Little Auger), Petřínské sady 411; ☎53 79 05; funicular from Újezd to first stop. You used to go here for the view, not the food; now you can enjoy both. Adventurous Czech cuisine and incredibly attentive service. Open daily 11am–6pm & 7–11pm.

**U čerta** (The Devil's), Nerudova 4; ☎53 09 75. Good steaks, some veggie dishes, and not the ripoff you'd expect, given its prime location on the *králová cesta* up to the castle, but expect it to be fairly full. Open daily noon–3pm & 6–11pm.

**U Lorety**, Loretánské náměstí 8; ☎53 13 95. Bang next door to the Loreto chapel, and facing the monster Černín Palace, this is a great place to eat outside in summer. Familiar Czech menu, but served with more than the usual flair. Open daily noon–11pm.

**U svatého Tomáše** (St Thomas's), Letenská 12. A brewery was set up here by the Augustinians as long ago as 1358, making this easily the oldest *pivnice* in Prague, though the Communists closed down the brewery in 1953. Nowadays it's just a pub serving traditional grub and dark *Braník* beer, rather too conveniently situated on the tourist trail, as reflected by the surly service. Open daily 11am–11pm.

## Eating and Drinking

*For a glossary of Czech terms for food and drink,*
*see p.32*

## Eating and Drinking

**U tří pštrosů** (The Three Ostriches), Dražického náměstí 12; ☎53 61 51. A Rennaisance house right by the Charles Bridge – exclusive and overrated. Reservations are a must, though you may have more luck at lunchtimes. Open daily 11am–3pm & 6–11pm.

### EXPENSIVE

**Lobkovická vinárna**, Vlašská 17; ☎53 01 85. Fresh asparagus and mushrooms washed down with Mělník wine. A popular and relatively expensive restaurant. Open daily noon–3pm & 6.30pm–midnight.

**U malířů** (The Artist's), Maltézské náměstí 11; ☎53 18 83. A converted sixteenth-century house that used to belong to an artist called Jiří Šic (pronounced "Shits"). Now one of the best (and most expensive – upwards of 2000kčs a head) restaurants in Prague, run by a French catering company who use fresh produce flown in daily from Paris. Open Mon–Sat 11.30am–3.30pm & 7pm–2am.

**U Mecenáše**, Malostranské náměstí 10; ☎53 38 81. Well-known medieval *vinárna* where Václav IV used to drink (a lot). The menu features the usual hearty steaks, plus Bulgarian moussaka – all top-quality stuff and, with some restraint, currently around 500–750kčs a head. Open 5pm–1am; closed Sat.

**U zlaté hrušy** (The Golden Pear), Nový Svět 3 ☎53 11 33. Romantic, exclusive, intimate – and about 1000kčs a head. Open daily 6.30pm–12.30am.

### Staré Město and Josefov

Staré Město has probably the highest concentration of eating places in Prague.

---

### Vegetarian places

At the moment, these are the only exclusively vegetarian eateries in Prague:

---

Prices, even in the *pivnice*, tend to be higher than elsewhere, so if you're on a meagre budget, it's best to stay away from the more obvious tourist spots like Karlova, Staroměstské náměstí and Celetná.

### CHEAP

**Blatnice**, Michalská. Snack bar, *vinárna*, wine sales, and a popular restaurant in the cellar. Open Mon–Sat noon–midnight.

**Krušovická pivnice**, Široká 20. Once one of the best *pivnice* in Prague; nowadays spoilt by the pretentious decor and its proximity to Josefov. Nevertheless, it still serves *Krušovice* beer, one of Bohemia's finest lagers. Cold food only. Open daily 10am–10pm.

**Pivnice ve skořepce**, Skořepka 1; ☎22 80 81. Unfriendly staff, but if you manage to get a table they serve huge helpings of pork, chicken and duck, and litre mugs of *Gambrinus*. Open Mon–Fri 11am–10pm, Sat 11am–8pm.

**Pizzeria Mikuláš**, Benediktská 16; ☎231 57 27. Stuck in a backstreet off Revoluční, which no doubt contributes to the fact that this is one of the best pizza places in Prague; try the *krabí* (crab). Open Mon–Sat 11.30am–10pm.

**U dvou koček** (The Two Cats), Uhelný trh. Rowdy *Pilsner Urquell* pub, best known nowadays as a hangout for pimps and prostitutes. Open Mon–Sat 10am–11pm.

**U Golema**, Maislova 8; ☎23 18 00. Small, swish and intimate serving some tasty Jewish specialities. Reasonably priced, too. Open Mon–Fri 10am–10pm.

**U Medvídků** (The Little Bears), Na Perštýně 7. Another Prague institution going back to the thirteenth century. Nowadays, the food is not great, and the beer, *Budvar* (the original Budweiser), not always what it should be, but it's central, unpretentious and roomy. Open Mon–Sat 11am–11pm.

**U supa** (The Vulture), Celetná 22. Lively fourteenth-century pub serving cheap Czech meals and very strong, dark *Braník* beer, either inside or on the cobbles of its cool, vaulted courtyard. Open Mon–Sat 11am–9pm.

**U sv Salvátora**, Staroměstské náměstí. Fairly quiet, pleasant *vinárna*, despite its location, serving food and reasonably priced wine until late. Open 11am–1am.

**U Vejvodů**, Jilská 4. Classic medieval *pivnice* in the warren of streets south of Karlova. The usual filling Czech dishes on offer, washed down with *Smíchov* beer. Open Mon–Fri until 10pm, but closed for reconstruction at the time of writing.

MEDIUM

**Berjozka**, Rytířská 31; ☎22 38 22. The best Russian restaurant in town. Open Mon–Sat 11am–11pm.

**Košer jídelna**, Maislova 18. Indifferent self-service kosher restaurant in the Jewish town hall, frequented mostly by Prague's dwindling Jewish community. Open 11.30am–1pm.

**U králova dvora** (The King's Court), Královorska. Refreshingly untacky, roomy café-restaurant behind the Obecní dům, where you've a good chance of getting a table. Standard Czech dishes on offer. Open daily 10am–11pm.

**U Rudolfa**, Maislova 5; ☎232 26 71. A small *vinárna* in the Jewish Quarter serving tasty meat dishes, grilled in front of you by the chef. If there are no free tables, you can eat at the bar. Open daily 10am–10pm.

EXPENSIVE

**Bellevue**, Smetanovo nábřeží 18; ☎235 95 99. The view of the Charles Bridge and Prague Castle is outstanding, and the food's not bad either. Anywhere that serves fresh vegetables and crispy French fries is a cut above most Prague outfits. Open daily 11am–11pm.

**Reykjavik**, Karlova 20 (no reservations accepted). The owners really are Icelandic, though the cuisine – around 350kčs a head – is pretty international. The soups and starters are definitely worth going for, but the best feature is the wonderful variety of fresh(ish) fish, flown in from you know where. Open daily 11am–11pm.

**U Sixtů**, Celetná 2; ☎236 79 80. Beautiful setting underneath Gothic vaults, and an unusually varied menu, featuring fresh

salmon, rabbit, veal and venison. Spoiled only by slow service, disappointing desserts and prices that approach 750kčs per person. There's a café on the ground floor. Open daily noon–1am.

**U zátiší** (Still Life), Liliova 1; ☎26 51 07. Exquisitely prepared international cuisine with fresh vegetables and regular non-meat dishes, all served in *nouvelle cuisine* sized portions by professional waiters. Set menus 350–500kčs. Open noon–3pm & 6–11pm.

## Nové Město

Nové Město covers quite a large area, and you'll need to use public transport to get to some of the recommendations listed below. As a general rule, the prices along the "golden cross" of Národní, Na příkopě and Wenceslas Square will be higher than elsewhere.

CHEAP

**Adria palác**, Národní 40. Large dining hall on the first floor of the Rondo-Cubist Adria Palace, with a summer terrace overlooking Národní. Ripe for privatisation.

**Arco**, Hybernská 16. Don't expect period furnishings (yet) from the café which gave its name to the *Arconaut Circle* (Kafka, Kisch, Brod et al). Open until 11pm.

**Branický sklípek**, Vodičkova 26. One of the few places where you can down the lethal *Braník 14°* brew. Open daily until 11pm.

**Hlavní nádraží**, Wilsonova. Sleazy restaurant on the first floor of the main train station, decorated with huge Art-Nouveau murals – architectural curiosity value only.

**Na rybárně** (The Fishmonger's), Gorazdova 17. Wonderful fish restaurant in a cosy cellar, tucked away in the backstreets behind Havel's riverside flat. Good *Pilsner Urquell* on tap. Open Mon–Fri 4pm–1am.

**Obecní dům**, náměstí Republiky. The service may be slow and the food nothing special, but the palatial Art-Nouveau decor is infinitely more satisfying than any Czech meal. Open daily until 11pm.

**Orlík**, Masarykovo nábřeží 10. A popular late-night *vinárna*, with den-like alcoves and *MTV*. Czech and Chinese food available until 1am. Open daily 5pm–2am.

## Eating and Drinking

## Eating and Drinking

**Rybárna/Baltic gril**, Václavské náměstí 43. Cheap if you stick to the carp and trout; less so, if you go for the salmon or prawns. Open 10am–11pm; closed Sat.

**U bubeníčků**, Myslíkova 8. Great place to down a few beers and eat some simple Czech cuisine, after visiting the Mánes gallery. Open daily until 11pm.

**U Fausta**, Karlovo náměstí 4; ☎29 01 12. Quiet, fairly sleazy *vinárna*, well off the tourist track. Food served all day. Open Mon–Fri noon–2am.

**U Fleků**, Křemencova 11. Famous medieval *pivnice* where the unique dark 13° beer, *Flek*, has been exclusively brewed and consumed since 1499. Despite seats for over five hundred, you may still have to fight for a bench. The food is perfectly OK, but it's best to go during the day. Open daily 9am–11pm.

**U Pešků**, Sokolská 50; metro I. P. Pavlova. Large and lively beer hall on one of Prague's most unhealthy streets, plus a smaller, more sedate *jídelna* serving some interesting Czech dishes – look out for the goose (*hus*). Open daily until 11pm.

**U Pinkasů**, Jungmannovo náměstí 15. Famed as the first *pivnice* in Prague to serve *Pilsner Urquell* (which it still does). Despite its proximity to Wenceslas Square, it still manages to keep a few Czech regulars. Open daily until 11pm.

**U šupů**, Spálená 41; ☎29 93 10. A *vinárna* which specialises in "Chinese" cuisine and fresh mushrooms; there's a takeaway booth in the same building dispensing *krokety se žampiony*. Open daily until 11pm.

**U zlatého tygra** (The Golden Tiger), Husova 17. Beery *pivnice* frequented by Prague's literary crowd, including the pub's permanent resident, writer and bohemian, Bohumil Hrabal.

**U zpěváčků** (The Choir Boy), Na struze 7. Walking from the national theatre, the first bit you come to is the *vinárna*, which stays open late and is famous for the spaghetti dish that makes up its entire menu. Around the corner, the *pivnice* is a completely different scene (and closes much earlier): a loud, smoky workers/musicians' pub with an ironic line in Marxist-Leninist tracts, and the local *Staropramen* on tap. *Vinárna* open Mon–Sat 5pm–2am, Sun 5pm–midnight; *Pivnice* open daily 11am–10pm.

### MEDIUM

**Crazy Daisy**, Vodičkova 9; ☎235 00 21 Rather misleading American name and trendy bistro-bar decor for what is really just a better-than-average Czech restaurant. Fish and veggie dishes available, not to mention blueberry pie. Open daily 10am–11pm.

**Mayur**, Štěpánská 61; ☎236 99 22. A worthy approximation of an Indian restaurant, offering a range of spicy meat dishes that make a welcome change from standard Bohemian fare. Open noon–4pm & 6–11pm; closed Sat.

**Peking**, Legerova 64; ☎29 35 31; metro I. P. Pavlova. Passable Chinese food, and triple-glazing to keep out the noise of the traffic. Open Mon–Sat until 11pm.

**Pod křídlem**, Národní 10 (corner with Voršilská). Usual Czech fare in unusual surroundings at unusually high prices. Sometimes features chicken, venison and the odd veggie dish on its menu, but its main virtue is its late closing. Open daily 11am–2am.

**Viola**, Národní 7; ☎26 67 32. Small, nominally Italian restaurant with a wide range of steaks and pasta dishes, topped with indifferent sauces. Also puts on cabaret and live bands. Open daily noon–midnight.

**Vltava**, Rašínovo nábřeží; ☎29 49 64. A tasty and little-known fish restaurant right by the water's edge, below the main road. Open daily 11am–10pm.

### Vyšehrad and the southern suburbs
#### CHEAP

**Pizzeria West**, náměstí bratří Synků 511, Nusle; ☎43 45 02; tram #6 or #11 from metro I. P. Pavlova. One of Prague's better pizzerias, run by some very friendly Macedonian Slavs. Try the *Scandinavská* topped with caviar and sardines. Open daily 10.30am–10.30pm.

## Around Midnight

After about 11pm, your choices are limited if you want a full sit-down meal. At any of the late-opening restaurants listed below you should be able to get something to eat at least half an hour before the closing times given.

**Bistro Evropské**
Evropská 300,
Veleslavín.
Until 3am.                          p.210

**CG-čínský restaurace**
Janáčkovo nábřeží 1,
Smíchov.
Until midnight.                     p.211

**Lobkovická vinárna**
Vlašská 17,
Malá Strana.
Until midnight.                     p.206

**Na rybárně**
Gorazdova 17,
Nové Město.
Until 1am.                          p.207

**Na slamníku**
Schwaigrova 7,
Bubeneč.
Until midnight.                     p.210

**Orlík**
Masarykovo nábřeží 10,
Nové Město.
Until 2am.                          p.207

**Pizzeria Babetka**
Jana Želivského 10,
Žižkov.
Until 2am.                          p.210

**Pod křídlem**
Národní 10,
Nové Město.
Until 2am.                          p.208

**Rebecca**
Olšanské náměstí 8,

Žižkov.
Until 7am.                          p.210

**Royal**
Slezská 134,
Vinohrady.
Until midnight.                     p.210

**U Fausta**
Karlovo náměstí 4,
Nové Město.
Until 2am.                          p.208

**U malířů**
Maltézské náměstí 11,
Malá Strana.
Until 2am.                          p.206

**U Mecenáše**
Malostranské náměstí 10,
Malá Strana.
Until 1am.                          p.206

**U Sixtů**
Celetná 2,
Staré Město.
Until 1am.                          p.207

**U zlaté hrušy**
Nový Svět 3,
Hradčany.
Until 12.30am.                      p.206

**U zpěváčků**
Na struze 7,
Nové Město.
Until midnight.                     p.208

**Viola**
Národní 7,
Nové Město.
Until midnight.                     p.208

**U soudků**, Branická, Braník; tram #3 or #17, stop Modřanská. An ordinary Czech *pivnice*, not worth a special trip, but perfect for a pre-Braník theatre forage. Open daily until 10pm.

**Vyšehradského nádraží**, Svobodová 4; tram #3, #7, #17, #18, #21 or #24. Vyšehrad is short of watering holes; this one is close by the Cubist villas down in the Botič valley. Open Mon–Fri 9am–6pm.

### MEDIUM

**Dlouhá zeď** (The Great Wall), sidliště Pankrác, Michle; metro Pankrác, then one stop southwest on bus #188. Huge Chinese-run restaurant, in the middle of a housing estate, which serves seriously delicious Chinese food. The menu is long, but the portions are small, so you need to order plenty of dishes. Open Tues–Sun 11am–3pm & 5.30–11pm.

## Eating and Drinking

**Orient**, Bělehradská 14, Nusle; ☎43 09 13; tram #6 or #11 from metro I. P. Pavlova. A real treat down in the seemingly unpromising Botič valley. Good-value, authentic Chinese food, with a great selection of desserts, too. Open daily 11am–3pm & 5–11pm.

**Vinárna na Vyšehradě**, by the cemetery in Vyšehrad; tram #3, #7, #17 or #21. Tasteless decor and the usual unhurried service, but convenient if you're here to watch the sunset. Open Tues–Sat noon–midnight, Sun noon–10pm.

### Vinohrady, Žižkov and beyond
CHEAP

**Pizzeria Babetka**, Jana Želivského 10, Žižkov; tram #15 or #19 from metro Želivského. Unlikely location for one of the city's better pizzerias. Big portions, and a vegetarian option, but still a noticeable lack of fresh produce. Open daily until 2am.

**Rebecca**, Olšanské náměstí 8, Žižkov; tram #5, #9 or #26 from metro Hlavní nádraží. Tiny non-stop bistro serving meat and pasta dishes, plus sundry other snacks. Open daily 9am–8pm & 9pm–12am.

**Toscana**, Vinohradská, Vinohrady (one block west from metro Flora). Popular new pizza place featuring a *Quattro Formaggi* topped with real Gorgonzola. Open noon–10pm; closed Fri & Sat.

**U koleje** (The College), Slavíkova 24, Vinohrady; metro Jiřího z Poděbrad. Pubs have been closing down in droves since privatisation, but this one has survived and thrived since. Cigarette smoke, beer, meat and dumplings all guaranteed. Open daily 11am–10pm.

**ÚKDŽ**, náměstí Míru 9; metro náměstí Míru. An old nineteenth-century *Národní dům* (now owned by the Railway Workers' Union) far from the tourist centre of town, with a good restaurant, and ballroom dancing on the first floor. Convenient for the Vinohrady theatre.

**U Góvindy**, Na hrázi 5, Libeň; metro Palmovka. Newly opened Hare Krishna (*Haré Kršna* in Czech) restaurant serving organic veggie slop. Operates a pay-what-you-can system. Open Mon–Fri 11am–5pm.

**Zdar**, Vinohradská 164, Vinohrady (halfway between metros Flora and Želivského). Situated opposite the big Olšany cemetery, this place specialises in serious game dishes. Open daily 11am–10pm.

MEDIUM

**Royal**, Slezská 134, Vinohrady; ☎73 91 94; metro náměstí Míru. Vaguely Greek restaurant (olives, feta cheese and retsina all available) with upwardly mobile aspirations. Open Tues–Sat 6pm–midnight.

EXPENSIVE

**China-restaurant**, Francouzská 2; ☎25 26 43; metro náměstí Míru. Stunningly unimaginative name for what is one of Prague's best ethnic restaurants. Good Chinese food, prepared and served by an all-Chinese staff. Open daily 11am–11pm.

**Principe**, Anglická 23, Vinohrady; ☎25 96 14; metro náměstí Míru. A new Italian restaurant with the airs, graces and prices of the real thing. The food is pretty special for Prague, too, but it's not difficult to blow 750kčs or more per person here. Open noon–2.30pm & 6–11.30pm.

### Holešovice, Bubeneč and Dejvice
CHEAP

**Bistro Evropské**, Evropská 300, Veleslavín; tram #20 or #26, penultimate stop. If you are staying on this side of town, this is the place to go for late-night munchies. Standard Czech menu, with the occasional veggie dish thrown in. Open Mon–Sat 5pm–3am, Sun 5–10pm.

**Na slamníku** (The Straw Bed), Schwaigrova 7, Bubeneč; bus #131 from metro Hradčanská. The perfect place to end up after a stroll in Stromovka: a *pivnice* serving good Czech grub and wonderful *Krušovice* beer. Open daily 4pm–midnight.

**U písecké brány**, Na valech (corner with K Brusce), Hradčany; metro Hradčanská. Good out-of-the-way *pivnice* near Bílek's Villa, serving Prague's own *Staropramen* beer; tables outside in the summer.

MEDIUM

**Praha EXPO 58**, Letenské sady, Bubeneč; ☎37 45 46. Restaurant and café on the seventh floor of this period piece, built, as the name suggests, for the 1958 World Expo in Montréal. A great view over the Vltava. Closed for reconstruction at the time of writing.

### EXPENSIVE

**U zlatého rožně** (The Golden Spit), Československé armády 22, Bubeneč; metro Dejvická; ☎312 10 32. Deep in the heart of ambassador-land, this exclusive new restaurant serves a startling variety of international dishes from catfish to Chinese cuisine. Open daily until midnight.

## Smíchov and Barrandov

### CHEAP

**Mateo**, Arbesovo náměstí 15, Smíchov; tram #6, #9 or #12. A real find in Prague – a whole variety of fresh salads, plus pasta and other meaty and non-meaty Italian-style dishes. Open Mon–Fri 9am–9pm.

**Terasy na Barrandově**, Barrandovská 171, Hlubočepy; bus #105, or #120 from metro Smíchovské nádraží. Cliff-top functionalist café, with its own lighthouse; the height of fashion in the 1930s, currently closed for reconstruction.

**U Blaženky**, U Blaženky 1, Smíchov; metro Anděl. Convenient hotel restaurant if you're up at Bertramka for a Mozart concert.

**U soudků** (The Judge's), náměstí Sovětských tankistů (corner with Holečkova); tram #6, #9 or #12. Cosy, unpretentious Czech *vinárna*, with a few eastern dishes to liven up an otherwise quite predictable menu. Open daily until 11pm.

### MEDIUM

**CG-čínský restaurace**, Janáčkovo nábřeží 1, Smíchov; ☎54 91 64; tram #4, #7, #14 or #16. Genuine Chinese cuisine, hence the high prices, popularity and obligatory reservations. Open daily 11.30am–midnight.

**Eating and Drinking**

# Chapter 12

# Clubs and live venues

Although there's infinitely more choice than there was prior to 1989, Prague still has nothing like the number of **clubs** you'd expect from a European capital. The dance craze has yet to hit Prague in any significant way; pure dance clubs are the exception away from the tacky meat markets around Wenceslas Square. The **live music** scene is a bit more promising, and many nightclubs double as live music venues, although Czech reggae or skinhead punk may not suit everyone's tastes.

One good thing about going clubbing in Prague is that, compared to the west, it's phenomenally cheap. Admission to live gigs or nightclubs is rarely more than 50kčs, and drinks are only slightly more expensive than usual. And, if you can handle it, a few places stay open until 5 or 6am.

To find out the latest on the city's up-and-coming events, scour the fly posters around town, or check the listings sections in *Prognosis, Prague Post*, or the Czech listings weekly *Program*, or monthly *Přehled*.

## Rock, pop and dance music

*See Basics p.39 for a brief rundown of the local talent*

Major western bands only rarely include Prague in their European tours, as tickets here have to be sold at a fraction of their price in the west. However, there are gigs by Czech bands almost every night in the city's clubs and discos – a selection of the better ones is listed below.

**Barbara**, Jungmannovo náměstí 14, Nové Město. Regular Euro-disco joint that's recently become something of a gay nightspot. Open Mon–Sat until 4am.

**Bar Club**, Hybernská 10, Nové Město. Incredibly uninspiring name for one of the city's best nightspots. A very mixed crowd, including many of Prague's African students, goes down to the basement ballroom for the club's nightly *Reggae Sound System* – loud, proud and very early 1980s. Open until 5am; closed Wed & Sun.

**Borát**, Újezd 18, Malá Strana; tram #6, #9 or #22 from metro Národní třída. A dark and dingy post-punk den which sprawls across three floors of a knackered old building close to the funicular railway. Open daily until 6am.

**Bunkr**, Lodecká 2, Nové Město; ☎231 45 35. Currently flavour of the month, *Bunkr* is, as you might guess, a converted wartime bunker, painted black, and fitted with the longest bar (and slowest service) in Prague. Open until 5am; live music from 9pm.

**Classic Club**, Pařížská 4, Staré Město. Mainstream dance music, plus an hour or so of 1960s classics for the older crowd that frequents the place. Open until 2am.

**Futurum**, Zborovská 7, Smíchov; tram #4, #14 or #16 from metro Karlovo náměstí. Soft metal disco. Open until 5am.

**Junior Klub Na Chmelnici**, Koněvova 219, Žižkov; ☎82 85 98. The main venue for domestic indie bands. Doubles as an alternative theatre venue, too.

**Klub Delta**, Vlastina 887, Liboc; ☎301 92 22; tram #20 or #26 to last stop. Pretty mainstream stuff way out in Prague 6; positively local if you're camping at Džbán. Open Thurs–Sat until 2am.

**Klub Na Petynce**, Radimova 2, Břevnov; ☎35 28 18; bus #108, #174 or #235 from metro Hradčanská. Standard indie venue, so expect bands like *Gregory Peccary* and the *Yo Yo Band*. Gigs (and the odd seminar) start around 7.30pm – check it's not a seminar.

**Lucerna**, Vodičkova 36, Nové Město; ☎235 26 48. Grand old turn-of-the-century ballroom with dripping balconies. now the favoured venue for largish Czech gigs and the trendier imported acts (Siouxsie played here early 1992).

**Mamma Klub**, Elišky Krásnohorské 7, Staré Město. Popular with local students and tourists, with some serious dancing going down for once.

**New D Club**, Vinohradská 38, Vinohrady; short walk from metro Muzeum. Bizarre hybrid club which operates a genre rota: Mon – Folk; Tues – Country; Wed – Reggae; Thurs – Rock; Fri – Dance music; Sat – Reggae; Sun – Jazz. Open until 2am.

**Rock Café**, Národní 22, Nové Město. Tries hard to evoke the underground, but is considered passé in the fickle world of Prague clubbing since it made its name in the early days of post-Communist euphoria.

Open daily until 3am; live music from 10.30pm.

**Strahov 007**, Strahov stadium, Spartakiádní; tram #8 or #22. Student club with regular thrashy gigs by the local talent; wear black. Open Thurs & Fri until 11pm or later.

## Jazz

Despite a long indigenous tradition, Prague these days has just a handful of good jazz clubs, and audiences remain predominantly foreign. With little money to attract foreign acts, however, the artists are almost exclusively Czech, and do the entire round of venues each month. The one exception to all this is the annual **international jazz festival** in October, which attracts big names from abroad, such as Winston Marselis, B. B. King and Jan Garburek.

**Agharta Jazz Centrum**, Krakovská 5, Nové Město; ☎22 45 58. New jazz club in a side street off the top end of Wenceslas Square. Open daily 8pm–midnight.

**Jazz Art Club**, Vinohradská 40, Vinohrady; ☎25 76 54; short walk from metro Muzeum. Conveniently enough, next door to the New D Club. Open Tues–Sun until 2am.

Clubs and live venues

---

---

**Clubs and live venues**

**Malostranská beseda**, Malostranské náměstí 21, Malá Strana; ☎ 53 90 24. Venue with a varied booking policy but often features jazz acts. Music from 8pm.

**Press Jazz Club**, Pařížská 9, Staré Město; ☎ 53 18 35. Large former conference hall, with poor acoustics, but you're pretty well guaranteed a seat, and the acts are as good (or bad) as anywhere else. Open until 2am.

**Reduta**, Národní 20, Nové Město; ☎ 20 38 25. Prague's best-known jazz club – advisable to book a table in advance. Open Mon–Sat until 2am.

# Chapter 13

# The Arts

Alongside the city's numerous pubs, restaurants and clubs, there's a rich **cultural life** in Prague. Classical music is strongly represented with a busy schedule of concerts throughout the year, often atmospherically set in one of the city's countless palaces, churches or – in summer – gardens. Czech **theatre** and **film** are in a state of turmoil at the moment as the industry tries to come to terms with the loss of state subsidy and diminished audiences – not to mention freedom of expression. Even if you don't speak Czech, there are performances worth catching – Prague has a strong tradition of **mime** and "black theatre", and many cinemas show films in their original language. **Rock, pop** and **jazz** gigs have been covered in the previous section.

## TICKETS

The major venues all have their own box offices, and in addition to these there are now several **ticket agencies** throughout the city. The most comprehensive, **Sluna**, has outlets in the Alfa arcade on Wenceslas Square and Černá růže arcade on Panská; the **PIS** on Na příkopě, also sells tickets for most events. Ticket **prices**, with a few notable exceptions, are still extremely cheap for westerners. And don't despair if everything is officially sold out (*výprodano*), as standby tickets are often available at the venue's box office on the night.

Lastly, you should bear in mind that some (though by no means all) theatres and concert halls are **closed in July and August**.

## LISTINGS AND INFORMATION

The English-language **listings** in *Prognosis* and *Prague Post* are selective, but do at least pick out the events which may be of interest to the non-Czech speaker. Also in English are the free handout *The Month In Prague* and the monthly *Přehled*, both available from any *PIS* office. For a truly comprehensive rundown of the week's events, buy a copy of *Program*, which is in Czech but easy enough to decipher. Any additional **information** you might need can usually be obtained from one of the *PIS* offices around town.

## Classical music, opera and ballet

**Classical concerts** take place throughout the year in Prague, but by far the biggest annual event is the *Pražské jaro* (Prague Spring), the country's most prestigious **international music festival**. It traditionally begins on May 12, the anniversary of Smetana's death, with a performance of *Má vlast*, and finishes on June 2 with a rendition of Beethoven's Ninth Symphony.

The main venues are listed below, but keep an eye out for concerts in the city's churches and palaces, gardens and courtyards (listed separately below). Classical concerts tend to be booked out by a combination of tour groups and season-ticket holders, but it's generally fairly easy to get hold of standby tickets an hour or so before the performance. The cost of tickets can vary enormously: most are extremely inexpensive, but prices for some events,

**The Arts**

such as opera at the Stavovské divadlo, are beginning to approach western levels.

### Permanent concert halls

**Stavovské divadlo** (formerly the Tylovo divadlo), Ovocný trh, Staré Město; ☎22 86 58. Prague's oldest opera house, looking superb after its recent renovation, puts on a mixture of opera, ballet and straight theatre (with simultaneous headphone translation available).

**Smetanovo divadlo**, Wilsonova, Nové Město; ☎26 97 46; metro Muzeum. A sumptuous nineteenth-century opera house, built by the city's German community, and now the number-two venue for opera and ballet.

**Smetanova síň**, Obecní dům, náměstí Republiky, Nové Město; ☎232 98 38. Fantastically ornate Art-Nouveau concert hall which kicks off the Prague Spring festival, and is also home to the Czech Philharmonic Orchestra (ČF).

**Hlahol**, Masarykovo nábřeží, Nové Město. There's no regular programme at Hlahol, home to the Hlahol Choir, but if you get the chance to catch something here, take it. The hall is decorated by, among others, the Art-Nouveau artist Alfons Mucha.

**Palác kultury**, 5 května 65, Nusle; ☎416 11 11; metro Vyšehrad. Prague's largest indoor venue, putting on anything from classical music to the odd pop concert. In addition to the main Congresový sal, there are several smaller concert halls, a cinema, nightclub, restaurant and café here.

### Other concert venues

The following is a selection of churches, palaces and gardens that regularly hold concerts. Unless a telephone number is given, tickets can only be bought in advance from a ticket agency.

**Anežský klášter** (Convent of sv Anežka), U milosrdiných 17, Staré Město. Gothic chapel in a restored convent. See p.102.

**Basilica sv Jiřího**, náměstí U sv Jiří, Hradčany. Atmospheric Romanesque church in Prague Castle. See p.68.

**Bertramka**, Mozartova 169, Smíchov; metro Anděl. See p.161.

**Dům U kamenného zvonu**, Staroměstské náměstí 13, Staré Město; ☎231 02 72. See p.100.

**Emauzy**, Vyšehradská 49, Nové Město; ☎29 38 50. See p.138.

**Hvězda**, obora Hvězda, Liboc; ☎36 79 38; tram #1, #2 or #18. See p.159.

**Kostel U Kilmentská**, Klimentská 1, Nové Město. See p.96.

**Lobkovický palác** (Lobkovic Palace), Jiřská 3, Hradčany. At the eastern edge of the Castle. See p.70.

**Martinický palác**, Hradčanské náměstí 8, Hradčany. See p.71.

**Míčovna**, Prague Castle, Hradčany. Renaissance real-tennis court in the Royal Gardens. See p.62.

**Národní kulturní památka Vyšehrad**, Nové proboštství (New Deanery), Vyšehrad. See p.145.

**Ryířský sál**, Valdštejn Palace, Valdštejnské náměstí 4, Malá Strana.

**Španělský sál** (Spanish Hall), Prague Castle, Hradčany.

**sv Jakub**, Štupartská, Staré Město. Great organ recitals. See p.102.

**sv Mikuláš**, Staroměstské náměstí, Staré Město. See p.99.

**Valdštejnská zahrada**, Letenská, Malá Strana. Open-air concerts at the *sala terrena*. See p.84.

## Theatre

**Theatre** has always had a special place in Czech culture, one which the events of 1989 only strengthened. Not only did the country end up with a playwright as president, but it was the capital's theatres that served as information centres during those first few crucial weeks.

Predictably enough, the economic situation is making things very difficult for Prague's theatres; audiences nowadays are often small and/or overwhelmingly made up of visitors. Most plays in Prague are performed in Czech, but mime, puppetry and "black theatre" are still strongly represented, and are thriving on the international audiences.

## Mainstream theatres

**Činoherní klub**, Ve Smečkách 26, Nové Město; ☎235 23 70; metro Muzeum. Regularly puts on good repertoire stuff from ancient to modern.

**Divadlo DISK**, Karlova 8, Staré Město; ☎26 53 77. During term time, this is the main venue for the city's drama students' productions, while in summer it's given over to "black theatre".

**Divadlo na Vinohradech**, náměstí Míru 7, Vinohrady; ☎25 70 41; metro náměstí Míru. An ornate nineteenth-century theatre that puts on anything from the classics to comedy, and even the occasional concert.

**Divadlo za branou II**, Národní 40, Nové Město; ☎26 00 33. Theatre showing the multimedia extravaganza that went down so well at the Montréal EXPO 58. It's been going ever since and is a bit too obviously tourist-oriented for some.

**Labyrint**, Štefánikova 57, Smíchov; ☎54 50 27. Formerly the *Realistické divadlo*, which was at the centre of the 1989 events, this is now one of Prague's main arty fringe theatres.

**Národní divadlo**, Národní 2, Nové Město; ☎20 53 64. Prague's grandest nineteenth-century theatre puts on a wide variety of plays, opera and ballet. Worth visiting for the decor alone.

**Nová scéna**, Národní 40, Nové Město; ☎20 62 60. This is Prague's most modern and versatile stage. Mostly straight theatre, with the occasional opera or ballet, and now the main stage for the multimedia *Laterna magika*.

**Semafor**, Alfa arcade, Václavské náměstí, Nové Město; ☎26 14 49. Another multimedia venture founded in the 1960s, now catering mostly to Prague's foreign visitors.

**Studio Ypsilon**, Spálená 16, Nové Město; ☎29 22 55. One of the city's leading – slightly alternative – repertoire theatres.

## Black theatre, mime and puppetry

**Branické divadlo pantomimy** (Braník Pantomime Theatre), Branická 63, Braník; ☎46 05 07; tram #3 or #17, stop Modřanská. Puts on an adventurous mixture of mime and pantomime featuring Czech and foreign troupes. Hosts an international festival of mime every June.

**Divadlo minor**, Senovážné náměstí 28, Nové Město; ☎22 51 41. Children's puppet shows most days; adult shows on Wed evenings.

**Divadlo na zábradlí**, Anenské náměstí 5, Staré Město; ☎236 04 49. Havel's old haunt back in the 1960s, now home base for the Ladislav Fialka troupe, founded by the great-grandfather of Czech mime who died in 1991. Shows straight theatre as well as mime.

**Divadlo Spejbla a Hurvínka**, Římská 45, Vinohrady; ☎25 16 66. Features the indomitable puppet duo, Spejbl and Hurvínek, created by Josef Skupa earlier this century and still going strong at one of the few puppets-only theatre in the country.

**Národní divadlo marionet** (National Marionette Theatre), Žatecká 1, Staré Město; ☎232 34 29. Kids' matinees and adult evening shows using traditional all-string marionettes. Also listed under *Divadélko říše loutek*.

**Studio Gag**, Národní 25, Nové Město; ☎26 54 36. Mime artist Boris Hybner's legendary slapstick studio theatre.

**Studio Rampa**, Branická 41, Braník; ☎46 05 07; tram #3 or #17. Studio theatre attached to the main Braník Pantomime Theatre up the road (see above).

## Film

More than half the **films** shown in Prague cinemas are American productions, usually around nine months' old and dubbed into Czech. *Prague Post* and *Prognosis* publish a list of films to be shown in their original language; in Czech publications *české titulky* (meaning Czech subtitles) are the words to look for. Most of the city's central main screens are either on or just off Wenceslas Square. The **cinemas** listed below are all that's left of Prague's once vast array of film clubs and art house cinemas. Keep a look out, too, for films shown at the various national cultural institutions around town (see p.44 for addresses).

**The Arts**

**The Arts**

**Alfa**, Václavské náměstí 28, Nové Město. A sadly underused 70mm screen that is, without doubt, the best place to see new releases.

**Dlabačov**, Bělohorská 24, Střešovice; ☎311 53 28; tram #8 or #22. At around 5 and 8pm daily, you can see classics of the likes of *Butch Cassidy and the Sundance Kid*.

**Miš Maš**, Veletržní 61, Holešovice; tram #1, #8, #25 or #26. Newly opened art house cinema screening recently released art films.

**Pražský filmový klub**, Sokolovská, Karlín; ☎231 57 05; metro Florenc. This place shows some seriously offbeat and unusual material from the archives. You need to become a member (for a nominal fee).

## The Visual Arts: galleries and exhibition space.

Prague has dozens of private art galleries and exhibition halls, in addition to the temporary displays on show in its museums and major galleries. For a full rundown of the latest offerings, consult the "galerie a výstavy" section of *Přehled*. Listed below are some of the best-known galleries, where you can be fairly sure of finding something interesting at most times of the year.

**Belvedér**, Mariánské hradby 1, Hradčany. Open Tues–Sun 10am–6pm. See p.62.

**Dům U kamenného zvonu**, Staroměstské náměstí 13, Staré Město. Open Tues–Sun 10am–6pm. See p.100.

**Galerie bratří Čapků**, Jugoslávská 20, Vinohrady. Open Tues–Sun 10am–1pm & 2–6pm.

**Galerie Hollar**, Smetanovo nábřeží 6, Nové Město. Open Tues–Sun 10am–1pm & 2–6pm.

**Jízdárna**, U prašného mostu, Hradčany. Open Tues–Sun 10am–6pm. See p.62.

**Mánes**, Masarykovo nábřeží 250, Nové Město; ☎29 55 77. Open Tues–Sun 10am–6pm. See p.136.

**Středoevropská galerie**, Husova 19, Staré Město; ☎236 07 00. Open daily 10am–6pm.

**U Hybernů**, náměstí Republiky, Nové Město. Open daily 9am–6pm. See p.130.

**ÚLUV**, Národní 36, Nové Město. Open Tues–Sun 10am–6pm.

**UPM**, 17 listopadu 2, Staré Město; ☎232 00 51. Open Tues–Sun 10am–6pm. See p.116.

# Chapter 14

# Kids' Activities

If you've tried the patience of your offspring with too many Baroque churches and art galleries, any of the suggestions below should head off a rebellion. Most have been covered in the text, so you can get more information by turning to the relevant page. In the summer, the streets are positively alive with buskers and street performers, while for **sporting** suggestions, see the next section.

**Castles** Many of the castles outside Prague are at least as much fun for children as adults – try especially Křivoklát (see p.186) and Kokořín (see p.168).

**Český kras** A karst region, 32km southwest of Prague, with caves of stalactites and stalagmites in weird and wonderful formations. See p.185.

**Cinema** The *American Hospitality Centre* on Malé náměstí shows children's films on Saturday mornings.

**Museums** Some which might be of particular interest to children include the Technical Museum (see p.155); National Museum (see p.125); Police Museum (see p.139); and the Military museums (see p.71 and 150).

**Petřín Hill** Take the funicular railway to the top for a spectacular view of Prague, followed by a visit to the observatory, the Bludiště (Mirror Maze) and a climb up the miniature Eiffel Tower. See p.86.

**Přerov nad Labem**, 32km east of Prague. Open-air museum of wooden folk architecture and farms, plus a schoolroom from the last century with a miniature paper theatre. See p.175.

**Puppet theatre** See "The Arts" section for details of where to find puppet theatre for children in Prague.

**Trams** Any tram will do, but, for preference, the regular #22 goes round some great hairpins.

**Výstaviště** Large turn-of-the-century funfair with various rides and activities in the summer, and a planetarium and adventure playground, *Dětský svět*, open all year.

**Zoo** All the usual beasts and birds, plus a children's train, swings and slides. See p.157.

# Chapter 15

# Sports

Prague is almost entirely surrounded by hills, woods and rivers, which means it's easy to do a day's **hiking** while based in the city. Sports facilities are more of a problem, with only a few easily accessible for tourists. If you want to check **forthcoming sports events**, get hold of *Program* or ask at a *PIS* office.

## Soccer and ice hockey

Prague's – and Czechoslovakia's – top **soccer** team, **Sparta Praha**, play at the Sparta stadium by the Letná plain (five-minute walk from metro Hradčanská); every other international match is played there too. The other local teams are the army team, **Dukla Praha**, whose stadium is in Dejvice, just below the Baba housing development (tram #20 or #25 from metro Dejvická); **Slavia Praha**, who play in Vršovice, just off U Slavie (tram #4, #7, #22 or #24); and **Bohemians**, whose ground is nearer to town, off Vršovická (tram #6, #7 or #24).

**Tickets** for all matches are extremely cheap, and can be bought at the ground on match day (even Sparta have only sold out twice in the last twenty-odd years). The season runs from September to December and March to June, and matches are usually held on a Sunday afternoon.

### Ice hockey

**Ice hockey** is the country's second most popular sport (the national side came third in the 1992 Winter Olympics), and, as for football, **Sparta Praha** are one of the country's most successful teams. Their *zimní*

*stadión* (winter stadium) is next door to the Výstaviště exhibition grounds in Holešovice (tram #5, #12 or #17).

**Tickets** can be bought from the stadium on the day, and again cost very little. Matches are fast, physical, and can take anything up to three hours; they take place on Tuesday, Friday and sometimes Sunday afternoon.

## Swimming

The waters of the Vltava, Beroun and Labe are all pretty polluted – the Sázava is marginally better – so for a clean swim your best bet are the city's swimming pools.

**YMCA/Fitcentrum**, Na poříčí 12, Nové Město. 25m pool – the oldest in Prague. Open Mon–Sat irregular hours – check with the *PIS*.

**Plavecký stadión**, Podolská 74, Podolí; tram #3 or #17, stop Kublov. 50m indoor pool, plus a 33m outdoor one which is open all year and heated to at least 26°C. Open Mon–Fri irregular hours, Sat 10am–8pm & Sun 8am–8pm.

## Ice skating

Given the nation's penchant for ice hockey, it's not surprising that **ice skating** (*bruslení*) is Prague's most popular winter activity. There's no shortage of rinks (*zimní stadión*) in the city, although public opening hours are limited. Most rinks don't rent out skates, but you can buy or rent them cheaply from shops like the one at the corner of Milady Horákové and Kamenická in Holešovice.

**Nikolajka**, U Nikolajky 28, Smíchov; five-minute walk up the hill from metro Anděl. Open Fri 1.30–4.30pm, Sun 1–4pm.

**HC Praha**, Na dlouhém lánu, Dejvice; tram #2, #20 or #26, stop Bořislavka. Open Thurs, Sat & Sun 3–5pm, Fri 5–7pm.

**Štvanice**, ostrov Štvanice, Holešovice; five-minute walk on to the island from metro Florenc. Open Thurs, Fri & Sun 8.30–11.30am, Sat 1–4pm.

## Bowling, billiards and boating

Prague's one and only **bowling alley** – *Beer and Bowling* – is in the *Hotel Forum*, but with just four lanes it's not exactly well equipped. Open daily 2.30pm–12.30am; metro Vyšehrad; phone ☎419 01 51 to make a reservation.

**Billiards** is better catered for with ten tables to choose from in the hall at the Strahov stadium. Open daily 11am–11pm; bus #132 or #217 from metro Anděl.

**Boats** can be hired during the summer from Slovanský ostrov (also known as Žofín), the island off Masarykovo nábřeží. From May to mid-September boat **trips** leave from below the Palackého most –

north to Roztoky (1hr 20min) or south to Štěchovice (3hr) and the Slapy dam (4hr).

## Sports centres and saunas

**YMCA/Fitcentrum**, Na poříčí 12, Nové Město. Sauna, massage and 25m pool. Opening hours are extremely irregular, so check with *PIS*.

**Fitcentrum Dlabačov**, Bělohorská 24, Střešovice; ☎ 311 53 28; tram #8 or #22. Sauna, table tennis and a 25m pool. Open 1–9pm.

**Fitcentrum Natur**, nábř kapt. Jaroše 3, Holešovice; metro Vltavská. Gym and sauna. Complex open Mon–Sat 9am–midnight. Sauna open 2–8pm; women only Mon, Wed & Thurs; men only Tues & Fri.

## Horse racing

Prague's main racecourse is at **Velká Chuchle**, 5km or so south of the city centre; bus #129, #172, #241, #243, #244, #255 or *osobní* train from Smíchovské nádraží. Steeplechase and hurdles May–Oct Sun afternoons; trots all year round on Thurs. There's a smaller trot course on **Císařský ostrov**, north of the Stromovka park, May–Oct only.

Sports

# Chapter 16

# Shopping

Consumer goods always had a low priority under the centralised state-run economy of the Communist system, and the country is only now beginning to develop a consumer culture that visitors from the west would recognise.

Many of the cheap Czech goods of the past are disappearing from the shops as factories across the country close. Numerous multinationals like *Benetton* have already taken their place, with prices the same as in the west. The few bargains that still exist are in goods like glass, ceramics, cutlery, CDs, cassettes, LPs and books, and of course smoked meats, salamis and alcohol – particularly vodka – all of which the Czechs continue to produce at a fraction of western prices.

Shop **opening hours** are typically Monday–Friday 9am–noon/1pm and 2–5/6pm, Saturday 8/9am–noon/1pm, although various department stores and food shops open earlier or run right through lunch; more unusual hours are given below.

## Department Stores

**Bílá labuť**, Na poříčí 23, Nové Město. Built in the 1930s, when its functionalist design turned more than a few heads. Nowadays it's in need of serious renovation.

**Kotva**, náměstí Republiky 8, Nové Město. One of two modern department stores in the city centre; spread over five floors, with a food section in the basement.

**Máj**, Národní 26, Nové Město. Prague's other big modern department store. Four floors, selling everything from food to hi-fis.

## Markets and food stores

Prague is chronically short of good **markets** of all types, despite the introduction of free enterprise. For health food-starved visitors, a few outlets now stock some basic ingredients, as listed below.

### Markets

**Bubenské nábřeží**, Holešovice; metro Vltava. Prague's seediest sprawling market, housed in the city's disused abbatoir. Everything from German coffee to Swedish porn. Daily Mon–Sat.

**Havelská**, Staré Město. Food, flowers and sundry goods are sold here Mon–Sat.

**Sparta football stadium**, Milady Horákové, Holešovice; five minutes' walk from metro Hradčanská. Anything goes at this giant car-boot sale. Sat & Sun mornings only.

**V kotcích**, Staré Město. Cheap but naff Czech clothes in the street that runs parallel to Havelská. Open Mon–Sat.

### Food and health food stores

**Bio-Market**, Mostecká 3, Malá Strana. Just your average Czech *potraviny* except for its long hours, and a couple of shelves devoted to basic health foods. Open Mon–Sat 7am–10pm, Sun 10am–6pm.

**Country Life**, Melantrichova 15, Staré Město. Everything from dried bananas to seaweed.

**Frionor**, Vodičkova 34, Nové Město. Frozen Norwegian fish and TV dinners galore.

**Fruits de France**, Jindřišská 9, Nové Město. Unusually good selection of fruit and vegetables from strawberries to fresh herbs.

**Sýp**, Šénova 2232, Chodov; metro Chodov. Newly privatised supermarket selling mostly food, but including everything from artichoke hearts to pineapple. Open Mon–Fri 8am–8pm, Sat 8am–6pm.

## Books, maps and graphics

There is still no bookshop in Prague that stocks a really good selection of English-language books, but the following places do at least have more than most.

**Bohemian Ventures**, nám. Jana Palacha, Staré Město. Located on ground floor of Philosophy Faculty, specialises in English-language books (including cheap Penguins).

**Cizojazyčná literatura**, Na příkopě 27, Nové Město. Stocks a large contingent of Kafka and Agatha Christie, plus postcards, posters, maps and guides.

**ČKD dům**, Na příkopě, Nové Město. Good on glossy coffee-table books, guides and maps. Open daily until 6pm.

**Karel Křenek**, Celetná 32, Staré Město. Secondhand and antiquarian dealer, with only a handful of English books, but lots of maps, graphics and art books.

**Senovážné náměstí 6**, Nové Město. Small, idiosyncratic collection of Penguin dictionaries, Agatha Christie and other murder pulp.

## Music

At the moment, CDs sell for about a quarter to a third of western prices; some cassettes and LPs are even cheaper. The choice, however, tends to be quite limited, particularly in western pop music. Classical buffs will fare much better, not just with the Czech composers, but cheap copies of Mozart, Vivaldi and other classics.

**Bonton**, Malostranské náměstí 31, Malá Strana. Pop, rock and jazz CDs.

**Dedika**, Celetná 32, Staré Město. Very good on Czech classical and traditional folk.

**Supraphon**, ČKD dům, Na příkopě, Nové Město. Mostly classical.

## Souvenirs

**Cristallino**, Celetná 12, Staré Město. Simple, classic and modern styles of Bohemian glassware.

**Dřevené hračký**, Jilská 7, Staré Město. Wonderfully simple wooden toys for kids.

**Jan Huněk**, Pohořelec 2, Hradčany. Antiques, especially clocks and glassware.

**Loutkami**, Nerudova 47, Malá Strana. Quite the widest selection of puppets, old and new, for sale anywhere in Prague: hand, glove and rod puppets, plus marionettes.

**Panorama**, Staroměstské náměstí 15, Staré Město. Folk dolls, crockery, and a wide choice of Mucha cards and posters.

**Sazka Sportka**, Londýnská, Vinohrady. *Sparta Praha* soccer souvenirs.

**Starožitnosti**, Národní 36, Nové Město. Antiques, from 1930s glassware to Baroque kitsch.

Shopping

# The Contexts

# A History of Prague

The famous pronouncement (attributed to Bismarck) that "he who holds Bohemia holds mid-Europe" gives a clear indication of the pivotal role the region has played in European history. As the capital of Bohemia, Prague has been fought over and occupied by German, Austrian, French and even Swedish armies. Consequently, it is virtually impossible to write a history of the city without frequent reference to the wider events of European history. One of the constant themes

that runs throughout Prague's history, however, has been the conflicts between the city's Germans and Czechs, Protestants and Catholics. The history of Prague as the capital of Czechoslovakia is less than a hundred years old, beginning with the foundation of the country in 1918. Since then, the country's numerous tragedies, mostly focused on Prague, have been exposed to the world at regular intervals – 1938, 1948, 1968 and, most recently (and most happily), 1989.

## Beginnings

According to Roman records, the area now covered by Bohemia was inhabited as early as 500 BC by a Celtic tribe – the **Boii**, who gave their name to the region. Very little is known about the Boii except that around 100 BC they were driven from their territory by a Germanic tribe, the **Marcomanni**, who occupied Bohemia. The Marcomanni were a semi-nomadic people and later proved awkward opponents for the Roman Empire, which wisely chose to use the River Danube as its natural eastern border.

The disintegration of the Roman Empire in the fifth century AD corresponded with a series of raids into central Europe by eastern tribes: firstly the **Huns**, who displaced the Marcomanni, and later the **Avars**, who replaced the Huns around the sixth century, settling a vast area including the Hungarian plains and parts of what is now Czechoslovakia. Around the same time, the **Slav tribes** entered Europe from somewhere east of the Carpathian mountains. To begin with, at least, they appear to have been subjugated by the Avars. The first successful Slav rebellion against the Avars seems to have taken place in the seventh century, under the Frankish leadership of **Samo**, though the kingdom he created, which was centred on Bohemia, died with him around 658 AD.

# The Great Moravian Empire

The next written record of the Slavs in the region isn't until the eighth century, when East Frankish (Germanic) chroniclers report a people known as the **Moravians** as having established themselves around the River Morava, a tributary of the Danube. It was an alliance of Moravians and Franks (under Charlemagne) which finally expelled the Avars from central Europe in 796 AD. This cleared the way for the establishment of the **Great Moravian Empire**, which at its peak included Slovakia, Bohemia and parts of Hungary and Poland. Its significance in terms of modern Czechoslovakia is that it was the first and last time (until the establishment of the modern republic, for which it served as a useful precedent) that the Czechs and Slovaks were united under one ruler.

The first attested ruler of the empire, **Mojmír**, found himself at the political and religious crossroads of Europe under pressure from two sides: from the west, where the Franks and Bavarians (both Germanic tribes) were jostling for position with the papacy; and from the east, where the Patriarch of Byzantium was keen to extend his influence across eastern Europe. Mojmír's successor, **Rastislav** (850–870), plumped for Byzantium, and invited the missionaries Cyril and Methodius to introduce Christianity, using the Slav liturgy and Eastern rites. Rastislav, however, was ousted by his nephew, **Svätopluk** (871–894), who captured and blinded his uncle, allying himself with the Germans instead. With the death of Methodius in 885, the Great Moravian Empire fell decisively under the influence of the Catholic Church.

Svätopluk died shortly before the **Magyar invasion** of 896, an event which heralded the end of the Great Moravian Empire and a significant break in Czecho-Slovak history. The Slavs to the west of the River Morava (the Czechs) swore allegiance to the Frankish Emperor, Arnulf; while those to the east (the Slovaks) found themselves under the yoke of the Magyars. This separation, which continued for the next millennium, is one of the major factors behind the distinct social, cultural and political differences between Czechs and Slovaks.

# The Přemyslid Dynasty: legends and history

The Czechs have a **legend** for every occasion and the founding of Bohemia and Prague are no exception. The mythical mound of Říp, the most prominent of the pimply hills in the Labe (Elbe) plain, north of Prague, is where Čech, the leader of a band of wandering Slavs, is alleged to have founded his new kingdom, Čechy (Bohemia). His brother Lech, meanwhile, headed further north to found Poland.

Some time in the seventh or eighth century AD, **Krok** (aka Pace), a descendant of Čech, moved his people south from the plains to the rocky knoll that is now Vyšehrad (literally "High Castle"). Krok was succeeded by his youngest daughter, **Libuše**, the country's first and last female ruler, who, handily enough, was endowed with the gift of prophecy. Falling into a trance one day, she pronounced that the tribe should build a city "whose glory will touch the stars", at the point in the forest where they found an old man constructing the threshold of his house. He was duly discovered on the Hradčany hill, overlooking the Vltava, and the city was named *Praha*, meaning threshold.

Subsequently, Libuše was compelled to take a husband, and again she fell into a trance, this time pronouncing that they should follow her horse to a ploughman, whose descendants would rule over them. Sure enough, a man called Přemysl (which means ploughman) was discovered, and became the mythical founder of the Přemyslid dynasty which ruled Bohemia until the fourteenth century.

So much for the legend. Historically, Hradčany, and not Vyšehrad, was where the first Slav settlers established themselves. The Vltava was relatively shallow at this point, and it probably seemed a safer bet than the plains of the Labe. The earliest recorded Přemyslid was Prince Bořivoj, the first Christian ruler of Prague, baptised in the ninth century by the Slav apostles Cyril and Methodius (see opposite). Other than being the first to build a castle on Hradčany, nothing very certain is known about Bořivoj, nor about any of the other early Přemyslid rulers, although there are numerous legends, most famously that of Prince Václav (Saint Wenceslas), who was martyred by his pagan brother Boleslav the Cruel in 929 (see p.64).

## Bohemia under the Přemyslids

Cut off from Byzantium by the Hungarian kingdom, Bohemia lived under the shadow of the Holy Roman Empire from the start. In 950, Emperor Otto I led an expedition against Bohemia, making the kingdom officially subject to the empire and its king one of the seven electors of the emperor. In 973, under Boleslav the Pious (967–999), a bishopric was founded in Prague, subordinate to the archbishopric of Mainz. Thus, by the end of the first millennium, German influence was already beginning to make itself felt in Bohemian history.

The thirteenth century was the high point of Přemyslid rule over Bohemia. With Emperor Frederick II preoccupied with Mediterranean affairs and dynastic problems, and the Hungarians and Poles busy trying to repulse the Mongol invasions from 1220 onwards, the Přemyslids were able to assert their independence. In 1212, Otakar I (1198–1230) managed to extract a "Golden Bull" (formal edict) from the emperor, securing the royal title for himself and his descendants (who thereafter became kings of Bohemia). Prague prospered too, benefiting from its position on the central European trade routes. Merchants from all over Europe settled there, and in 1234 the first of Prague's historic five towns, Staré Město, was founded to accommodate them.

As a rule, the Přemyslids welcomed German colonisation, none more so than Otakar II (1253–78), the most distinguished of the Přemyslid kings, who systematically encouraged German craftsmen to settle in the kingdom. The switch to a monetary economy and the discovery of copper and silver deposits heralded a big shift in population from the countryside to the towns. German immigrants founded whole towns in the interior of the country, where German civic rights were guaranteed them, for example Kutná Hora, Mělník and, in 1257, Malá Strana in Prague. At the same time, the territories of the Bohemian crown were expanded to include not only Bohemia and Moravia but also Silesia and Lusatia to the north (now divided between Germany and Poland).

The beginning of the fourteenth century saw a series of dynastic disputes – messy even by medieval standards – beginning with the death of Václav II from consumption and excess in 1305. The following year, the murder of his son, the heirless, teenage Václav III, marked the **end of the Přemyslid dynasty** (he had four sisters, but female succession was not recognised in Bohemia). The nobles' first choice of successor, the Habsburg Albert I, was murdered by his own nephew, and when Albert's son, Rudolf I, died of dysentery not long afterwards, Bohemia was once more left without any heirs.

## The Luxembourg dynasty

The crisis was finally solved when the Czech nobles offered the throne to **John of Luxembourg** (1310–46), who was married to Václav III's youngest sister. German by birth, but educated in France, King John spent most of his reign participating in foreign wars, with Bohemia footing the bill, and John himself paying for it first with his sight, and finally with his life, on the field at Crécy in 1346. His son, **Charles IV** (1346–78), was wounded in the same battle, but thankfully for the Czechs lived to tell the tale.

It was Charles who ushered in Prague's **golden age**. Although born and bred in France, Charles was a Bohemian at heart (his mother was Czech and his real name was Václav): he was also extremely intelligent, speaking five languages fluently and even writing an autobiography. In 1344, he had wrangled an archbishopric for Prague, independent of Mainz, and two years later he became not only king of Bohemia, but also, by election, Holy Roman Emperor. In the thirty years of his reign, Charles transformed Prague into the new capital of the empire, and one of the most important cities in fourteenth-century Europe. He established institutions and buildings that still survive today – the university, St Vitus Cathedral, the Charles Bridge, a host of monasteries and churches – and founded an entire new town, **Nové Město**, to accommodate the influx of students and clergy. Artists and architects from all over the continent were summoned to work in his new capital, while Charles himself cobbled together a vast collection of art and relics. As emperor, Charles was also entitled to issue the all-important Golden Bull edicts, which helped to strengthen Bohemia's position. He promoted Czech as the official language alongside Latin and German and, perhaps most importantly of all, presided over a period of peace in central Europe while western Europe was tearing itself apart in the Hundred Years' War.

Charles' son, **Václav IV**, who assumed the throne in 1378, was no match for such an inheritance. Stories that he roasted an incompetent cook alive in his own spit, shot a monk whilst hunting, and tried his own hand at lopping off people's heads with an axe, are almost certainly myths. Nevertheless, he was a legendary drinker, prone to violent outbursts, and so unpopular with the powers that be that he was imprisoned twice – once by his own nobles, and once by his brother, Sigismund. His reign was also characterised by religious divisions within the Czech Lands and in Europe as a whole, beginning with the **Great Schism** (1378–1417), when rival popes held court in Rome and Avignon. This was a severe blow to Rome's centralising power, which might otherwise have successfully combated the assault on the Church that was already under way in the Czech Lands towards the end of the fourteenth century.

# The Czech Reformation

Right from the start, Prague was at the centre of the Czech reform movement. The increased influence of the Church, and the independence from Mainz established under Charles, led to a sharp increase in debauchery, petty theft and alcoholism among the clergy – a fertile climate for militant reformers like Jan Milič of Kroměříž, whose fiery sermons drew crowds of people to hear him at Prague's Týn Church. In Václav's reign, the attack was led by the peasant-born preacher **Jan Hus**, who gave sermons at Prague's Bethlehem Chapel in 1402, and the following year became the first Czech to hold the influential position of Rector of Prague University.

Hus's main inspiration was the English reformist theologian John Wycliffe, whose heretical works found their way to Bohemia via Václav's sister, Anne, who married King Richard II. Worse still, as far as Church traditionalists were concerned, Hus began to preach in the language of the masses (ie Czech) against the wealth, corruption and hierarchical tendencies within the Church at the time. A devout, mild-mannered man himself, as Rector he became embroiled in a dispute between the conservative German archbishop and clergy and the Wycliffian Czechs at the university. Václav backed Hus, for political and personal reasons – Hus was the confessor to his wife, Queen Sophie – and in 1409 issued the **Kutná Hora Decree**, which rigged the voting within the university in the Czechs' favour. The Germans, who made up the majority of the students, immediately left the university in protest.

The scene was set for an international showdown – and a civil war. Widening his attacks on the Church, Hus began to preach against the sale of religious indulgences to fund the inter-papal wars, thus incurring the enmity of Václav, who received a percentage of the sales. In 1412 Hus and his followers were expelled from the university and excommunicated, and spent the next two years as itinerant preachers spreading their reformist gospel throughout Bohemia. In 1414 Hus was summoned to the **Council of Constance** to answer charges of heresy. Despite a guarantee of safe conduct from Emperor Sigismund, Hus was condemned to death and, having refused to renounce his beliefs, was burned at the stake on July 6, 1415.

Hus's martyrdom sparked off **widespread riots** in Prague, initially uniting virtually all Czechs – clergy and laity, peasant and noble (including many of Hus's former opponents) – against the decision of the council, and, by inference, against the Catholic Church and its conservative, mostly German, clergy. The Hussites immediately set about reforming church practices, most famously by administering communion *sub utraque specie* ("in both kinds", ie bread and wine) to the laity, as opposed to the Roman Catholic practice of reserving the wine for the clergy.

## The Hussite Wars: 1419–1434

In 1419, Václav inadvertently provoked further large-scale rioting by endorsing the re-admission of anti-Hussite priests to their parishes. In the ensuing violence, several Catholic councillors were thrown to their death from the windows of Prague's Novoměstská radnice, in Prague's **first defenestration** (see p.134). Václav himself was so enraged (not to say terrified) by the mob that he suffered a stroke and died, "roaring like a lion", according to a contemporary chronicler. The pope, meanwhile, declared an international crusade against the Czech heretics, under the leadership of Emperor Sigismund, Václav's brother and, since Václav had failed to produce an heir, next in line for the Bohemian throne.

Already, though, cracks were appearing in the Hussite camp. The more radical reformers, who became known as the **Táborites**, broadened their attacks on the Church hierarchy to include all figures of authority and privilege. Their message found a ready audience among the oppressed classes in Prague and the Bohemian countryside, who went around eagerly destroying church property and massacring Catholics. Such actions were deeply disturbing to the Czech nobility and their supporters who backed the more moderate Hussites – known as the **Utraquists** (from the Latin *sub utraque specie*) – who confined their criticisms to religious matters.

For the moment, however, the common Catholic enemy prevented a serious split developing amongst the Hussites, and under the inspirational military leadership of the Táborite **Jan Žižka**, the Hussites' (mostly peasant) army enjoyed some miraculous early victories over the numerically superior "crusaders", most notably at the Battle of Vítkov in Prague in 1420. The Bohemian Diet quickly drew up the **Four Articles of Prague**, a compromise between the two Hussite camps, outlining the basic tenets about which all Hussites could agree, including communion "in both kinds". The Táborites, meanwhile, continued to burn, loot and pillage ecclesiastical institutions from Prague to the far reaches of the kingdom. At the **Council of Basel** in 1433 Rome reached a compromise with the Utraquists over the Four Articles, in return for ceasing hostilities. The peasant-based Táborites rightly saw the deal as a victory for the Bohemian nobility and the status quo, and vowed to continue the fight. However, the Utraquists, now in cahoots with the Catholic forces, easily defeated the remaining Táborites at the **Battle of Lipany**, outside Kolín, in 1434. The Táborites were forced to withdraw to the fortress town from which they took their name, Tábor. Poor old Sigismund, who had spent the best part of his life fighting the Hussites, died only three years later.

By the end of the Hussite Wars, the situation for the majority of the population – landless serfs, and as such virtual slaves to the local feudal lords – had changed very little. The most significant development in terms of **social structure** was in the balance of power between the Czechs and Germans of Bohemia. Temporarily, at least, the seemingly inexorable German immigration had been checked. The merchant class was still predominantly German and the peasantry mostly Czech, but now, for the first time, there were additional religious differences between the two communities which only increased the mutual distrust.

## Compromise and Counter-Reformation

Despite the agreement of the Council of Basel, the pope refused to acknowledge the Utraquist church in Bohemia. The Utraquists nevertheless consolidated their position, electing the gifted **George of Poděbrady** as first Regent and then King of Bohemia (1458–71). The first and last Hussite king, George (Jiří to the Czechs) is remembered primarily for his commitment to promoting religious tolerance and for his far-sighted efforts in trying to establish some sort of "Peace Confederation" in Europe.

On George's death, the Bohemian Estates handed the crown over to the Polish Jagiellonian dynasty, who ruled in absentia, effectively relinquishing the reins of power to the Czech nobility. In 1526, the last of the Jagiellonians, King Louis, was decisively defeated by the Turks at the Battle of Mohács, and died shortly afterwards, leaving no heir to the throne. The Roman Catholic Habsburg, Ferdinand I, was elected king of Bohemia – and what was left of Hungary – in order to fill the power vacuum, marking the **beginning of Habsburg rule** over what is now Czechoslovakia. Ferdinand adroitly secured automatic hereditary succession over the Bohemian throne for his dynasty, in return for which he accepted the agreement laid down at the Council of Basel back in 1433.

In 1546, the Utraquist Bohemian nobility provocatively joined the powerful Protestant Schmalkaldic League in their (ultimately successful) war against the Holy Roman Emperor, Charles V. When armed conflict broke out in Bohemia, however, victory fell to Ferdinand, who took the opportunity to extend the influence of Catholicism in the Czech Lands, executing several leading Protestant nobles, persecuting the reformist Unity of Czech Brethren, who had figured prominently in the rebellion, and inviting Jesuit missionaries to establish churches and seminaries in the Czech Lands.

Like Václav IV, **Emperor Rudolf II** (1576–1611), Ferdinand's eventual successor, was moody and wayward, and by the end of his reign Bohemia was once more rushing headlong into a major international confrontation. But Rudolf also shared characteristics with Václav's father, Charles, in his genuine love of the arts, and in his love of Prague, which he re-established as the royal seat of power, in preference to Vienna, which was then under threat from the Turks. He endowed Prague's galleries with the best Mannerist art in Europe, and, most famously, invited the respected astrologists Tycho de Brahe and Johannes Kepler, and the infamous English alchemists John Dee and Edward Kelley, to Prague.

Czechs tend to regard Rudolfine Prague as a second golden age, but as far as the Catholic Church was concerned, Rudolf's religious tolerance and indecision were a disaster. In the early 1600s, Rudolf's melancholy began to veer dangerously close to insanity, a condition he had inherited from his Spanish grandmother, Joanna the Mad. And in 1611, the heirless Rudolf was forced to abdicate by his brother **Matthias**, to save the Habsburg house from ruin. Ardently Catholic, but equally heirless, Matthias proposed his cousin **Ferdinand II** as his successor in 1617. This was the last straw for Bohemia's mostly Protestant nobility, and the following year conflict erupted again.

### The Thirty Years' War: 1618–1648
On May 23, 1618, two Catholic governors appointed by Ferdinand (and their secretary) were thrown out of the windows of Prague Castle – the country's **second defenestration** (see p.67) – an event that's now taken as the official beginning of the complex religious and dynastic conflicts collectively known as the **Thirty Years' War**. Following the defenestration, the Bohemian Diet expelled the Jesuits and elected the youthful Protestant "Winter King", Frederick of the Palatinate, to the throne. In the first decisive set-to of the war, on November 8, 1620, the Czech Protestants were utterly defeated at the

Battle of **Bílá hora** (Battle of the White Mountain) by the imperial Catholic forces under Count Tilly. In the aftermath, twenty-seven Protestant nobles were executed on Prague's Staroměstské náměstí, and the heads of ten of them displayed on the Charles Bridge.

It wasn't until the Protestant Saxons occupied Prague in 1632 that the heads were finally taken down and given a proper burial. The Catholics eventually drove the Saxons out, but for the last ten years of the war, Bohemia became the main battleground between the new champions of the Protestant cause – the Swedes – and the imperial Catholic forces. In 1648, the final battle of the war was fought in Prague, when the Swedes seized Malá Strana, but failed to take Staré Město, thanks to the stubborn resistance of Prague's Jewish, and newly Catholicised student populations on the Charles Bridge.

## The Dark Ages and the Enlightenment

The Thirty Years' War ended with the **Peace of Westphalia**, which, for the Czechs, was as disastrous as the war itself. An estimated five-sixths of the Czech nobility went into exile, their properties handed over to loyal Catholic families from Austria, Spain and Italy. Bohemia had been devastated, towns and cities laid waste, and the total population reduced by almost two-thirds. On top of all that, Bohemia was now decisively within the Catholic sphere of influence, and the full force of the **Counter-Reformation** was brought to bear on its people. All forms of Protestantism were outlawed, the education system was handed over to the Jesuits and, in 1651 alone, over two hundred "witches" were burned at the stake in Bohemia.

The next two centuries of Habsburg rule are known to the Czechs as the **dark ages**. The focus of the empire shifted back to Vienna, Austria's absolutist grip over the Czech Lands catapulted the remaining nobility into intensive Germanisation, while fresh waves of German immigrants reduced Czech to a despised dialect spoken only by peasants, artisans and servants. The situation was so bad that Prague and most other urban centres became practically all-German cities. By the end of the eighteenth century, the Czech language was on the verge of dying out, with government, scholarship and literature carried out exclusively in German. For the newly ensconced Germanised aristocracy, and for the Catholic Church, of course, the good times rolled and Prague was endowed with numerous Baroque palaces, churches, monasteries and monuments.

After a century of iron-fisted Habsburg rule, dispute arose over the accession of Charles VI's daughter, **Maria Theresa** (1740–80), to the Habsburg throne. In the course of the ensuing war, Prague was briefly occupied by the Bavarian and French armies, though ultimately the Empress retained hold of Bohemia. Later, during the Seven Years' War, Prague was once more captured, this time by the Prussians, in 1757; though it was Silesia, not Bohemia, that was the price of this defeat.

Maria Theresa's reign also marked the beginning of the **Enlightenment** in the Habsburg Empire. Despite her own personal attachment to the Jesuits, the empress acknowledged the need for reform, and followed the lead of Spain, Portugal and France in expelling the order from the empire in 1773. But it was her son, **Joseph II** (1780–90), who, in the ten short years of his reign, brought about the most radical changes to the social structure of the Habsburg lands. His 1781 Edict of Tolerance allowed a large degree of freedom of worship for the first time in over 150 years, and went a long way towards lifting the restrictions on Jews within the empire. The following year, he ordered the dissolution of the monasteries, and embarked upon the abolition of serfdom.

Despite all his reforms, Joseph was not universally popular. Catholics – some ninety percent of the Bohemian population – viewed him with disdain, and even forced him to back down when he decreed that Protestants, Jews, unbaptised children and suicides should be buried in consecrated Catholic cemeteries. His centralisation and bureaucratisation of the empire placed power in the hands of the Austrian civil service, and thus helped entrench the Germanisation of Bohemia. He also offended the Czechs by breaking with tradition and not bothering to hold an official coronation ceremony in Prague.

## The Czech *národní obrození*

The Habsburgs' enlightened rule inadvertently provided the basis for the economic prosperity and social changes of the **Industrial Revolution**, which in turn fuelled the Czech national revival of the nineteenth century. The textile, glass, coal and iron industries began to grow, drawing ever more Czechs from the countryside and swamping the hitherto mostly Germanised towns and cities, including Prague. A Czech working class, and even an embryonic Czech bourgeoisie emerged, and, thanks to Maria Theresa's reforms, new educational and economic opportunities were given to the Czech lower classes.

For the first half of the century, the Czech national revival or **národní obrození** was confined to the new Czech intelligentsia, led by philologists like Josef Dobrovský and Josef Jungmann at the Charles University or *Karolinum* in Prague. Language disputes (in schools, universities and public offices) remained at the forefront of Czech nationalism throughout the nineteenth century, only later developing into demands for political autonomy from Vienna. The leading figure of the time was the historian **František Palacký**, a Protestant from Moravia who wrote the first history of the Czech nation, rehabilitating Hus and the Czech reformists in the process. He was in many ways typical of the early Czech nationalists – pan-Slavist, virulently anti-German, but not yet entirely anti-Habsburg.

### 1848 and all that

The fall of the French monarchy in February 1848 prompted a crisis in the German states and in the Habsburg Empire. The new Bohemian bourgeoisie, both Czech and German, began to make political demands – freedom of the press, of assembly, of religious creeds. In Prague, liberal opinion became polarised between the Czech- and German-speakers. Palacký and his followers were against the dissolution of the empire and argued instead for a kind of multinational federation. Since the empire contained a majority of non-Germans, Prague's own Germans were utterly opposed to Palacký's scheme, campaigning for unification with Germany to secure their interests. So when Palacký was invited to the Pan-German National Assembly in Frankfurt in May, he refused to go. Instead, he convened a **Pan-Slav Congress** the following month, which met on Prague's Slovanský ostrov, an island in the Vltava. Meanwhile, the radicals and students (on both sides) took to the streets of Prague, barricades went up, and the local Austrian commander, Prince Windischgrätz (whose famous dictum was "Man begins with Baron") declared martial law. On June 16, Windischgrätz bombarded Prague; the following morning the city capitulated – the counter-revolution in Bohemia had begun. The upheavals of 1848 left the absolutist Habsburg Empire shaken but fundamentally unchanged and served to highlight the sharp differences between German and Czech aspirations in Bohemia.

## Dualism

The Habsburg recovery was, however, short-lived. In 1859, and again in 1866, the new emperor, Franz Joseph II, suffered humiliating defeats at the hands of the Italians and Prussians respectively. In order to buy some more time, the compromise or *Ausgleich* of 1867 was drawn up, establishing the so-called **Dual Monarchy** of Austria-Hungary – two independent states united by one ruler.

For the Czechs, the *Ausgleich* came as a bitter disappointment. While the Magyars became the Austrians' equals, the Czechs remained second-class citizens. The Czechs' failure in bending the emperor's ear was no doubt partly due to the absence of a Czech aristocracy that could bring its social weight to bear at the Viennese court. Nevertheless, the *Ausgleich* did mark an end to the absolutism of the immediate post-1848 period, and, compared to the Hungarians, the Austrians were positively enlightened in the wide range of civil liberties they granted, culminating in universal male suffrage in 1907.

The industrial revolution continued apace in Bohemia, bringing an ever-increasing number of Czechs into the newly founded suburbs of Prague, such as Smíchov and Žižkov. Thanks to the unfair voting system, however, the German minority managed to hold onto power in the Prague city council until the 1880s. By the turn of the century, Germans made up just five percent of the city's population – fewer than the Czechs in Vienna – and of those more than half were Jewish. Nevertheless, German influence in the city remained considerable, far greater than their numbers alone warranted; this was due in part to economic means, and in part to overall rule from Vienna.

Under Dualism, the Czech **národní obrození** flourished. Towards the end of the century, Prague was endowed with a number of symbolically significant Czech monuments, like the National Theatre (built by private subscription), the National Museum and the Rudolfinum. Inevitably, the movement also began to splinter, with the liberals and conservatives, known as the **Old Czechs**, advocating working within the existing legislature to achieve their aims, and the more radical **Young Czechs** favouring a policy of non-cooperation. The most famous political figure to emerge from the ranks of the Young Czechs was the Prague university professor **Tomáš Garrigue Masaryk**, who founded his own Realist Party in 1900 and began to put forward the (then rather quirky) concept of closer cooperation between the Czechs and Slovaks.

The Old Czechs, backed by the new Czech industrialists, achieved a number of minor legislative successes, but by the 1890s, the Young Czechs had gained the upper hand and conflict between the Czech and German communities became a daily ritual in the boulevards of the capital – a favourite spot for confrontations being the promenade of Na příkopě. Language was also a volatile issue, often fought out on the shop and street signs of Prague. In 1897 the **Badeni Decrees**, which put Czech on an equal footing with German in all dealings with the state, drove the country to the point of civil war, before being withdrawn by the cautious Austrians.

## World War I

At the outbreak of **World War I**, the Czechs and Slovaks showed little enthusiasm for fighting alongside their old enemies, the Austrians and Hungarians, against their Slav brothers, the Russians and Serbs. As the war progressed, large numbers defected to form the **Czechoslovak Legion**, which fought on the Eastern Front against the Austrians. Masaryk travelled to the USA to curry favour for a new Czechoslovak state, while his two deputies, the Czech Edvard Beneš and the Slovak Milan Štefánik, did the same in Britain and France.

Meanwhile, the Legion, which by now numbered some 100,000 men, became embroiled in the Russian revolutions of 1917, and, when the Bolsheviks made peace with Germany, found itself cut off from the homeland. The uneasy cooperation between the Reds and the Legion broke down when Trotsky demanded that they hand over their weapons before heading off on their legendary **anabasis**, or march back home, via Vladivostok. The soldiers refused and became further involved in the Civil War, for a while controlling large parts of Siberia and, most importantly, the Trans-Siberian Railway, before arriving back to a tumultuous reception in their new joint republic.

In the summer of 1918, the Slovaks finally threw in their lot with the Czechs, and the Allies recognised Masaryk's provisional Czechoslovak government. On October 28, 1918, as the Habsburg Empire began to collapse, the new **Czechoslovak Republic** was declared in Prague. In response, the German-speaking border regions (later to become the Sudetenland) declared their own *Deutsch-Böhmen* (German-Bohemian) government, loyal to the Austrians. Nothing came of the latter, and by the end of the year Czechoslovak troops had gained control of the Sudetenland with relatively little resistance.

Last to opt in favour of the new republic was **Ruthenia** (officially known as Sub-Carpatho Ruthenia), a rural backwater of the old Hungarian Kingdom which became officially part of Czechoslovakia by the Treaty of St Germain in September 1919. Its incorporation was largely due to the campaigning efforts of Ruthenian emigrés in the USA. For the new republic the province was a strategic bonus, but otherwise a huge drain on resources.

## The First Republic

The new nation of Czechoslovakia began postwar life in an enviable economic position – **tenth in the world industrial league table** – having inherited seventy to eighty percent of Austria-Hungary's industry intact. Prague regained its position at the centre of the country's political and cultural life, and in the interwar period was embellished with a rich mantle of Bauhaus-style buildings. Less enviable was the diverse make-up of the country's population –

a melange of minorities which would in the end prove its downfall. Along with the 6 million Czechs and 2 million Slovaks who initially backed the republic, there were over 3 million Germans and 600,000 Hungarians, not to mention sundry other Ruthenians (Rusyns), Jews and Poles.

That Czechoslovakia's democracy survived as long as it did is down to the powerful political presence and skill of **Masaryk**, the country's president from 1918 to 1935, who shared executive power with the cabinet. It was his vision of social democracy that was stamped on the nation's new constitution, one of the most liberal of the time (if a little too bureaucratic and centralised), aimed at ameliorating any ethnic and class tensions within the republic by means of universal suffrage, land reform and, more specifically, the Language Law, which ensured bilinguality to any area where the minority exceeded twenty percent.

The elections of 1920 reflected the mood of the time, ushering in the left-liberal alliance of the **Pětka** (The Five), a coalition of five parties led by the Agrarian, Antonín Švehla, whose slogan "We have agreed that we will agree" became the keystone of the republic's consensus politics between the wars. Gradually all the other parties (except the Fascists and Communists) – among them Hlinka's Slovak People's Party and most of the Sudeten German parties – began to participate in (or at least not disrupt) parliamentary proceedings. On the eve of the Wall Street Crash, the republic was enjoying an economic boom, a cultural renaissance and a temporary *modus vivendi* among its minorities.

### The Thirties

The 1929 Wall Street Crash plunged the whole country into crisis. Economic hardship was quickly followed by **political instability**. In Slovakia, Hlinka's People's Party fed off the anti-Czech resentment that was fuelled by Prague's manic centralisation, consistently polling around thirty percent, despite its increasingly nationalist/separatist position. In Ruthenia, the elections of 1935 gave only 37 percent of the vote to parties supporting the republic, the rest going to the Communists, pro-Magyars and other autonomist groups.

But without doubt the most intractable of the minority problems was that of the Sudeten Germans, who occupied the heavily industrialised border regions of Bohemia and Moravia. Nationalist sentiment had always run high in the Sudetenland, whose German-speakers resented having been included in the new republic, but it was only after the Crash that the extremist parties began to make significant electoral gains. Encouraged by the rise of Nazism in Germany, and aided by rocketing Sudeten German unemployment, the proto-Nazi **Sudeten German Party** (SdP), led by a gym teacher by the name of Konrad Henlein, was able to win over sixty percent of the German-speaking vote in the 1935 elections.

Although constantly denying any wish to secede from the republic, after 1935 Henlein and the SdP were increasingly funded and directed from Nazi Germany. To make matters worse, the Czechs suffered a severe blow to their morale with the death of Masaryk late in 1937, leaving the country in the less capable hands of his Socialist deputy, Edvard Beneš. With the Nazi annexation of Austria (the *Anschluss*) on March 11, 1938, Hitler was free to focus his attention on the Sudetenland, calling Henlein to Berlin on March 28 and instructing him to call for outright autonomy.

### The Munich Crisis

On April 24, 1938, the SdP launched its final propaganda offensive in the **Karlsbad Decrees**, demanding (without defining) "complete autonomy". As this would clearly have meant surrendering the entire Czechoslovak border defences, not to mention causing economic havoc, Beneš refused to bow to the SdP's demands. Armed conflict was only narrowly avoided and, by the beginning of September, Beneš was forced to acquiesce to some sort of autonomy. On Hitler's orders, Henlein refused Beneš's offer and called openly for the secession of the Sudetenland to the German Reich.

On September 15, as Henlein fled to Germany, the British prime minister, Neville Chamberlain, flew to Berchtesgaden on his own ill-conceived initiative to "appease" the Führer. A week later, Chamberlain flew again to Germany, this time to Bad Godesburg, vowing to the British public that the country would not go to war (in his famous words) "because of a quarrel in a far-away country between people of whom we know nothing". Nevertheless, the French issued draft papers, the British Navy was mobilised, and the whole of Europe fully expected war. Then, in the early hours of September 30, in one of the most treacherous and self-interested acts of modern European diplomacy, prime ministers Chamberlain (for Britain) and Deladier (for France) signed the **Munich Diktat** with Mussolini and Hitler, agreeing – without consulting the Czechoslovak government – to all of Hitler's demands. The British and French public were genuinely relieved, and Chamberlain flew back to cheering home crowds, waving his famous piece of paper that guaranteed "peace in our time".

## The Second Republic

Betrayed by his only Western allies and fearing bloodshed, Beneš capitulated, against the wishes of most Czechs. Had Beneš not given in, however, it's doubtful anything would have come of Czech armed resistance, surrounded as they were by vastly superior hostile powers. Beneš resigned on October 5 and left the country. On October 15, **German troops occupied Sudetenland**, to the dismay of the forty percent of Sudeten Germans who hadn't voted for Henlein (not to mention the half a million Czechs and Jews who lived there). The Poles took the opportunity to seize a sizeable chunk of North Moravia, while in the short-lived "rump" **Second Republic** (officially known as Czecho-Slovakia), the one-eyed war veteran Emil Hácha became president, Slovakia and Ruthenia electing their own autonomous governments.

The Second Republic was not long in existence before it too collapsed. On March 15, 1939, Hitler informed Hácha of the imminent Nazi occupation of what was left of the Czech Lands, and persuaded him to demobilise the army, again against the wishes of many Czechs. The Germans encountered no resistance (nor any response from the Second Republic's supposed guarantors, Britain and France) and swiftly set up the Nazi **Protectorate of Bohemia and Moravia**. The Hungarians effortlessly crushed Ruthenia's brief independence, while the Slovak People's Party, backed by the Nazis, declared **Slovak independence**, under the leadership of the Catholic priest Jozef Tiso.

# World War II

In the first few months of the occupation, left-wing activists were arrested, and Jews were placed under the infamous Nuremberg Laws, but Nazi rule in the Protectorate was not as harsh as it would later become – the economy even enjoyed something of a mini-boom. But in late October and November 1939, Czech students in Prague began a series of demonstrations against the Nazis, who responded by closing down all institutions of higher education. In 1941 a leading SS officer, **Reinhard Heydrich**, was put in charge of the Protectorate. Arrests and deportations followed, reaching fever pitch after Heydrich was assassinated by the Czech resistance in June 1942 (see p.135). The "final solution" was meted out on the country's remaining Jews, who were transported first to the ghetto in Terezín, and then on to the extermination camps. The rest of the population were frightened into submission – very few acts of active resistance being undertaken in the Czech Lands until the Prague Uprising of May 1945 (see below).

By the end of 1944, Czechoslovak and Russian troops had begun to liberate the country, starting with Ruthenia, which Stalin decided to take as war booty despite having guaranteed to maintain Czechoslovakia's pre-Munich borders. On April 4, 1945, under Beneš's leadership, the provisional **Národní fronta** government – a coalition of Social Democrats, Socialists and Communists – was set up in Košice. On April 18, the US Third Army, under General Patton, crossed the border in the west, meeting very little German resistance. The people of Prague finally rose up against the Nazis on May 5, many hoping to prompt an American offensive from Plzeň, which the Third Army were on the point of taking. In the end, the Americans made the politically disastrous (but militarily wise) decision not to cross the demarcation line that had been agreed between the Allies at Yalta. Two crack German armoured divisions, not to mention some extremely fanatical SS troops, remained in position near the capital. Some 1600 barricades were erected, and around 30,000 Praguers held out against the numerically superior German troops, backed up by tanks and artillery, until they finally capitulated on May 8. The Russians entered the city the following day.

## The Third Republic

Violent reprisals against suspected collaborators and the German-speaking population in general began as soon as the country was liberated. All Germans were immediately given the same food rations as the Jews had been given during the war. Starvation, summary executions and worse resulted in the deaths of thousands of ethnic Germans. With considerable popular backing and the tacit approval of the Red Army, Beneš began to organise the **forced expulsion of the German-speaking population**, referred to euphemistically by the Czechs as the *odsun* (transfer). Only those Germans who could prove their anti-Fascist credentials were permitted to stay – the Czech community was not called on to prove the same – and by the summer of 1947, nearly 2.5 million Germans had been expelled or had fled in fear. On this occasion, Sudeten German objections were brushed aside by the Allies, who had given Beneš the go-ahead for the *odsun* at the postwar Potsdam Conference. Attempts by

Beneš to expel the Hungarian-speaking minority in similar fashion, however, proved unsuccessful.

On October 28, 1945, in accordance with the leftist programme thrashed out at Košice, sixty percent of the country's industry was nationalised. Confiscated Sudeten German property was handed out by the largely Communist-controlled police force, and in a spirit of optimism and/or opportunism, people began to join the Communist Party (KSČ) in droves, membership more than doubling in less than a year. In the **May 1946 elections**, the Party reaped the rewards of their enthusiastic support for the *odsun*, of Stalin's vocal opposition to Munich, and of the recent Soviet liberation, emerging as the strongest single party in the Czech Lands with up to forty percent of the vote (the largest ever for a European Communist Party in a multi-party election). In Slovakia, however, they failed to push the Democrats into second place, with just thirty percent. President Beneš appointed the KSČ leader, **Klement Gottwald**, prime minister of another Národní fronta coalition, with several strategically important cabinet portfolios going to Party members, including the ministries of the Interior, Finance, Labour and Social Affairs, Agriculture, and Information.

Gottwald assured everyone of the KSČ's commitment to parliamentary democracy, and initially at least even agreed to participate in the Americans' Marshall Plan (the only Eastern Bloc country to do so). Stalin immediately summoned Gottwald to Moscow, and on his return the KSČ denounced the Plan. By the end of 1947, the Communists were beginning to lose support, as the harvest failed, the economy faltered and malpractices within the Communist-controlled Ministry of the Interior were uncovered. In response, the KSČ began to up the ante, constantly warning the nation of imminent "counter-revolutionary plots", and arguing for greater nationalisation and land reform as a safeguard.

Then in February 1948 – officially known as **"Victorious February"** – the latest in a series of scandals hit the Ministry of the Interior, prompting the twelve non-Communist cabinet ministers to resign en masse in the hope of forcing a physically weak President Beneš to dismiss Gottwald. No attempt was made, however, to rally popular support against the Communists. Beneš received over 5000 resolutions supporting the Communists and just 150 opposing them. Stalin sent word to Gottwald to take advantage of the crisis and ask for military assistance – Soviet troops began massing on the Hungarian border. It was the one time in his life when Gottwald disobeyed Stalin; instead, by exploiting the divisions within the Social Democrats he was able to maintain his majority in parliament. The KSČ took to the streets (and the airwaves), arming "workers' militia" units to defend the country against counter-revolution, calling a general strike and finally, on February 25, organising the country's biggest ever demonstration in Prague. The same day Gottwald went to an indecisive (and increasingly ill) Beneš with his new cabinet, all Party members or "fellow travellers". Beneš accepted Gottwald's nominees and the most popular Communist coup in Eastern Europe was complete, without bloodshed and without the direct intervention of the Soviets. In the aftermath of the coup, an estimated two million Czechs and Slovaks fled abroad.

# The People's Republic

Following Victorious February, the Party began to consolidate its position, a relatively easy task given its immense popular support and control of the army, police force, workers' militia and trade unions. A **new constitution** confirming the "leading role" of the Communist Party and the "dictatorship of the proletariat" was passed by parliament on May 9, 1948. President Beneš refused to sign it, resigned in favour of Gottwald, and died (of natural causes) shortly afterwards. Those political parties that were not banned or forcibly merged with the KSČ were prescribed fixed-percentage representation within the so-called "multi-party" Národní fronta.

With the Cold War in full swing, the **Stalinisation** of Czechoslovak society was quick to follow. In the Party's first Five Year Plan, ninety percent of industry was nationalised, heavy industry (and in particular the country's defence industry) was given a massive boost and compulsory collectivisation forced through. Party membership reached an all-time high of 2.5 million, and "class-conscious" Party cadres were given positions of power, while "class enemies" (and their children) were discriminated against. It wasn't long, too, before the Czechoslovak mining "gulags" began to fill up with the regime's political opponents – "kulaks", priests and "bourgeois oppositionists" – numbering over 100,000 at their peak.

Having incarcerated most of its non-Party opponents, the KSČ, with a little prompting from Stalin, embarked upon a ruthless period of internal bloodletting. As the economy nose-dived, calls for intensified "class struggle", rumours of impending "counter-revolution" and reports of economic sabotage by fifth columnists filled the press. An atmosphere of fear and confusion was created to justify **large-scale arrests of Party members** with an "international" background – those with a wartime connection with the West, Spanish Civil War veterans, Jews and Slovak nationalists.

In the early 1950s, the Party organised a series of Stalinist **show-trials** in Prague, the most spectacular of which was the trial of Rudolf Slánský, who had been second only to Gottwald in the KSČ before his arrest. He and thirteen other leading Party members (eleven of them Jewish, including Slánský) were sentenced to death as "Trotskyist-Titoist-Zionists". Soon afterwards, Vladimír Clementis, the former KSČ foreign minister, was executed along with other leading Slovak comrades (Gustáv Husák, the post-1968 president, was given life imprisonment).

### After Stalin

Gottwald died in mysterious circumstances in March 1953, nine days after attending Stalin's funeral in Moscow (some say he drank himself to death). The whole nation heaved a sigh of relief, but the regime seemed as unrepentant as ever. The arrests and show-trials continued. Then, on May 30, the new Communist leadership announced a drastic currency devaluation, effectively reducing wages by ten percent, while raising prices. The result was a wave of isolated **workers' demonstrations** and rioting in Plzeň and Prague. Czechoslovak army units called in to suppress the demonstrations proved unreliable, and it was left to the heavily armed workers' militia and police to disperse the crowds and make the predictable arrests and summary executions.

So complete were the Party purges of the early 1950s, so sycophantic (and scared) the surviving leadership, that Khrushchev's 1956 thaw was virtually ignored by the KSČ. An attempted rebellion in the Writers' Union Congress was rebuffed and an enquiry into the show-trials made several minor security officials scapegoats for the "malpractices". The genuine mass base of the KSČ remained blindly loyal to the Party for the most part; Prague basked under the largest statue of Stalin in the world; and in 1957, the dull, unreconstructed neo-Stalinist **Antonín Novotný** – later proved to have been a spy for the Gestapo during the war – became First Secretary and President.

## Reformism and Invasion

The first rumblings of protest against Czechoslovakia's hardline leadership appeared in the official press in 1963. At first, the criticisms were confined to the country's worsening economic stagnation, but soon developed into more generalised protests against the KSČ leadership. Novotný responded by order-ing the belated release and rehabilitation of victims of the 1950s purges, permitting a slight cultural thaw and easing travel restrictions to the West. In effect, he was simply buying time. The half-hearted economy reforms announced in the 1965 **New Economic Model** failed to halt the recession, and the minor political reforms instigated by the KSČ only increased the pressure for greater reforms within the Party.

In 1967, Novotný attempted a pre-emptive strike against his opponents. Several leading writers were imprisoned, Slovak Party leaders were branded as "bourgeois nationalists" and the economists were called on to produce results or else forego their reform programme. Instead of eliminating the opposition, though, Novotný unwittingly united them. Despite Novotný's plea to the Soviets, Brezhnev refused to back a leader whom he saw as "Khrushchev's man in Prague", and on January 5, 1968, the young Slovak leader **Alexander Dubček** replaced Novotný as First Secretary. On March 22, the war hero Ludvík Svoboda dislodged Novotný from the presidency.

### 1968: The Prague Spring

By inclination, Dubček was a moderate, cautious reformer – the perfect compromise candidate – but he was continually swept along by the sheer force of the reform movement. The virtual **abolition of censorship** was probably the single most significant step Dubček took. It transformed what had been until then an internal Party debate into a popular mass movement. Civil society, for years muffled by the paranoia and strictures of Stalinism, suddenly sprang into life in the dynamic optimism of the first few months of 1968, the so-called "Prague Spring". In April, the KSČ published their Action Programme, propos-ing what became popularly known as "socialism with a human face" – federali-sation, freedom of assembly and expression, and democratisation of parliament.

Throughout the spring and summer, the reform movement gathered momentum. The Social Democrat Party (forcibly merged with the KSČ after 1948) re-formed, anti-Soviet polemics appeared in the press and, most famously of all, the writer and lifelong Party member Ludvík Vaculík published his personal manifesto entitled "**Two Thousand Words**", calling for radical de-Stalinisation within the Party. Dubček and the moderates denounced the manifesto and reaffirmed the country's support for the Warsaw Pact military alliance. Meanwhile, the Soviets and their hardline allies – Gomulka in Poland and Ulbricht in the GDR – viewed the Czechoslovak developments on their doorstep very gravely, and began to call for the suppression of "counter-revolutionary elements" and the reimposition of censorship.

As the summer wore on, it became clear that the Soviets were planning military intervention. Warsaw Pact manoeuvres were held in Czechoslovakia in late June, a Warsaw Pact conference (without Czechoslovak participation) was convened in mid-July and, at the beginning of August, the Soviets and the KSČ leadership met for **emergency bilateral talks** at Čierná nad Tisou on the Czechoslovak–Soviet border. Brezhnev's hardline deputy, Alexei Kosygin, made his less than subtle threat that "your border is our border", but did agree to withdraw Soviet troops (stationed in the country since the June manoeuvres) and gave the go-ahead to the KSČ's special Party Congress scheduled for September 9.

In the early hours of August 21, fearing a defeat for the hardliners at the forthcoming KSČ Congress, and claiming to have been invited to provide "fraternal assistance", the Soviets gave the order for the **invasion of Czechoslovakia** to be carried out by all the Warsaw Pact forces (only Romania refused to take part). Dubček and the KSČ reformists immediately condemned the invasion before being arrested and flown to Moscow for "negotiations". President Svoboda refused to condone the formation of a new government under the hardliner Alois Indra, and the people took to the streets in protest, employing every form of non-violent resistance in the book. Individual acts of martyrdom, like the self-immolation of **Jan Palach** on Prague's Wenceslas Square, hit the headlines, but casualties were light compared to the Hungarian uprising of 1956 – the cost in terms of the following twenty years was much greater.

## Normalisation

In April 1969, there were anti-Soviet riots during the celebrations of the country's double ice hockey victory over the Soviets. On this pretext, another Slovak, **Gustáv Husák**, replaced the broken Dubček as First Secretary, and instigated his infamous policy of **"normalisation"**. Over 150,000 fled the country before the borders closed, around 500,000 were expelled from the Party, and an estimated one million people lost their jobs or were demoted. Inexorably, the KSČ reasserted its absolute control over the state and society. The only part of the reform package to survive the invasion was **federalisation**, which gave the Slovaks greater freedom from Prague (on paper at least), though even this was severely watered down in 1971. Dubček, like countless others, was forced to give up his job, working for the next twenty years as a minor official in the Slovak forestry commission.

An unwritten social contract was struck between rulers and ruled during the 1970s, whereby the country was guaranteed a tolerable standard of living (second only to that of the GDR in Eastern Europe) in return for its passive collaboration. Husák's security apparatus quashed all forms of dissent during the early 1970s, and it wasn't until the middle of the decade that an organised opposition was strong enough to show its face. In 1976, the punk rock band *The Plastic People of the Universe* was arrested and charged with the familiar "crimes against the state" clause of the penal code. The dissidents who rallied to their defence – a motley assortment of people ranging from former KSČ members to right-wing intellectuals – agreed to form **Charter 77** (*Charta 77* in Czech), with the purpose of monitoring human rights abuses in the country. One of the organisation's prime movers and initial spokespersons was the absurdist Czech playwright **Václav Havel**. Havel, along with many others, endured relentless persecution (including long prison sentences) over the next decade in pursuit of Charter 77's ideals. The initial gathering of 243 signatories had increased to over 1000 by 1980, and caused panic in the moral vacuum of the Party apparatus, but consistently failed to stir a fearful and cynical populace into action.

### The Eighties

In the late 1970s and early 1980s, the inefficiencies of the economy prevented the government from fulfilling its side of the social contract, as living standards began to fall. Cynicism, alcoholism, absenteeism and outright dissent became widespread, especially among the younger (post-1968) generation. The **Jazz Section** of the Musicians' Union, who disseminated "subversive" western pop music (like pirate copies of "Live Aid"), highlighted the ludicrously harsh nature of the regime when they were arrested and imprisoned in the mid-1980s. Pop concerts, religious pilgrimages and, of course, the anniversary of the Soviet invasion all caused regular confrontations between the security forces and certain sections of the population. Yet still a mass movement like Poland's Solidarity failed to emerge.

With the advent of **Mikhail Gorbachev**, the KSČ was put in an extremely awkward position, as it tried desperately to separate *perestroika* from comparisons with the reforms of the Prague Spring. Husák and his cronies had prided themselves on being second only to Honecker's GDR as the most stable and orthodox of the Soviet satellites – now the font of orthodoxy, the Soviet Union, was turning against them. In 1987, **Miloš Jakeš** – the hardliner who oversaw Husák's normalisation purges – took over smoothly from Husák as General (First) Secretary and introduced *přestavba* (restructuring), Czechoslovakia's lukewarm version of *perestroika*.

## The Velvet Revolution

Everything appeared to be going swimmingly for the KSČ as it entered 1989. Under the surface, however, things were becoming more and more strained. As the country's economic performance worsened, divisions were developing within the KSČ leadership. The protest movement was gathering momentum: even the Catholic Church had begun to voice dissatisfaction, compiling a staggering 500,000 signatures calling for greater freedom of worship. But the 21st anniversary of the Soviet invasion produced a demonstration of only 10,000, which was swiftly and violently dispersed by the regime.

During the summer, however, more serious cracks began to appear in Czechoslovakia's staunch hardline ally, the GDR. The trickle of East Germans fleeing to the West turned into a mass exodus, forcing Honecker to resign and, by the end of October, prompting nightly mass demonstrations on the streets of Leipzig and Dresden. The opening of the Berlin Wall on November 9 left Czechoslovakia, Romania and Albania alone on the Eastern European stage still clinging to the old truths.

All eyes were now turned upon Czechoslovakia. Reformists within the KSČ began plotting an internal coup to overthrow Jakeš, in anticipation of a Soviet denunciation of the 1968 invasion. In the end, events overtook whatever plans they may have had. On Friday, **November 17**, a 50,000-strong peaceful demonstration organised by the official Communist youth organisation was viciously attacked by the riot police. Over 100 arrests, 500 injuries and one death were reported (the fatality was later retracted) in what became popularly known as the *masakr* (massacre). Prague's students immediately began an occupation strike, joined soon after by the city's actors, who together called for an end to the Communist Party's "leading role" and a general strike to be held for two hours on November 27.

## Civic Forum and the VPN

On Sunday, November 19, on Václav Havel's initiative, the established opposition groups like Charter 77 met and agreed to form Občanské fórum or **Civic Forum**. Their demands were simple: the resignation of the present hardline leadership, including Husák and Jakeš; an enquiry into the police actions of November 17; an amnesty for all political prisoners; and support for the general strike. In Bratislava, a parallel organisation, Veřejnosť proti nasiliu or **People Against Violence** (VPN), was set up to coordinate protest in Slovakia.

On the Monday evening, the first of the really big **nationwide demonstrations** took place – the biggest since the 1968 invasion – with more than 200,000 people pouring into Prague's Wenceslas Square. This time the police held back and rumours of troop deployments proved false. Every night for a week people poured into the main squares in towns and cities across the country, repeating the calls for democracy, freedom and the end to the Party's monopoly of power. As the week dragged on, the Communist media tentatively began to report events, and the KSČ leadership started to splinter under the strain, with the prime minister, **Ladislav Adamec**, alone in sticking his neck out and holding talks with the opposition.

## The end of one-party rule

On Friday evening, Dubček, the ousted 1968 leader, appeared before a crowd of 300,000 in Wenceslas Square, and in a matter of hours the entire Jakeš leadership had resigned. The weekend brought the largest demonstrations the country had ever seen – over 750,000 people in Prague alone. At the invitation of Civic Forum, Adamec addressed the crowd, only to be booed off the platform. On Monday, November 27, eighty percent of the country's workforce joined the two-hour **general strike**, including many of the Party's previously stalwart allies, such as the miners and engineers. The following day, the Party agreed to an end to one-party rule and the formation of a new "coalition government".

A temporary halt to the nightly demonstrations was called and the country waited expectantly for the "broad coalition" cabinet promised by Prime Minister Adamec. On December 3, another Communist-dominated line-up was announced by the Party and immediately denounced by Civic Forum and the VPN, who called for a fresh wave of demonstrations and another general strike for December 11. Adamec promptly resigned and was replaced by the Slovak Marián Čalfa. On December 10, one day before the second threatened general strike, Čalfa announced his provisional **"Government of National Understanding"**, with Communists in the minority for the first time since 1948 and multi-party elections planned for June 1990. Having sworn in the new government, President Husák, architect of the post-1968 "normalisation", finally threw in the towel.

By the time the new Čalfa government was announced, the students and actors had been on strike continuously for over three weeks. The pace of change had surprised everyone involved, but there was still one outstanding issue: the election of a new president. Posters shot up all round the capital urging **"HAVEL NA HRAD"** (Havel to the Castle – the seat of the presidency). The students were determined to see his election through, continuing their occupation strike until Havel was officially elected president by a unanimous vote of the Federal Assembly, and sworn in at the Hrad on December 29.

## Into the 1990s

Czechoslovakia started the new decade full of optimism for what the future would bring. On the surface, the country had a lot more going for it than its immediate neighbours (with the possible exception of the GDR). The Communist Party had been swept from power without bloodshed, and, unlike the rest of Eastern Europe, Czechoslovakia had a strong interwar democratic tradition with which to identify – Masaryk's First Republic. Despite Communist economic mismanagement, the country still had a relatively high standard of living, a skilled workforce and a manageable foreign debt.

In reality, however, the situation was somewhat different. Not only was the country economically in a worse state than most people had imagined, it was also environmentally devastated, and its people were suffering from what Havel described as "post-prison psychosis" – an inability to think or act for themselves. The country had to go through the painful transition "from being a big fish in a small pond to being a sickly adolescent trout in a hatchery". As a result, it came increasingly to rely on its new-found saviour, the humble playwright-president, Václav Havel.

In most people's eyes, "Saint Václav" could do no wrong, though he himself was not out to woo his electorate. His call for the rapid withdrawal of Soviet troops was popular enough, but his apology for the postwar expulsion of Sudeten Germans was deeply resented, as was his generous amnesty which eased the country's overcrowded prisons. The amnesty was blamed by many for the huge **rise in crime** in 1990. Every vice in the book – from racism to homicide – raised its ugly head in the first year of freedom. In addition, there was still a lot of talk about the possibility of "counter-revolution", given the thousands of unemployed StB (secret police) at large. Inevitably, accusations of previous StB involvement rocked each political party in turn in the run-up to the elections.

Despite all the inevitable hiccups and the increasingly vocal Slovak nationalists, Civic Forum/VPN remained high in the opinion polls. The **June 1990 elections** produced a record-breaking 99 percent turnout. With around sixty percent of the vote, Civic Forum/VPN were clear victors (the Communists got just thirteen percent) and Havel immediately set about forming a broad "Coalition of National Sacrifice", including everyone from Christian Democrats to former Communists.

### The economy

The main concern of the new government remains how to transform an outdated command-system economy into a **market economy** that can compete with its EC neighbours. The argument over the speed and model of economic reform eventually caused Civic Forum to split into two main camps: the centre-left Občánské hnutí or **Civic Movement** (OH), led by the foreign minister and former dissident Jiří Dienstbier, who favoured a more gradualist approach; and Občánská democratická strana or the right-wing **Civic Democratic Party** (ODS), headed by the finance minister **Václav Klaus**, whose pronouncement that the country should "walk the tightrope to Thatcherism" sent shivers up the spines of those familiar with the UK in the 1980s. Havel has sensibly tried to remain aloof from arguments over the economy, though there can be no doubt that, given a free choice, he would ally himself more with OH than ODS.

Klaus is currently putting the country through the most radical privatisation programme in the former eastern bloc. In the first stage, small businesses were auctioned off, many going for well over the 500,000kčs which any one person could have saved under the last regime. The second stage, still ongoing at the time of going to press, is the unique **coupon privatisation**. Every citizen was offered the right to buy 2000kčs worth of privatisation coupons, which would then be converted into shares in whatever business they saw fit. Potentially a quite radical democratising move, this has been watered down by the involvement of various less than scrupulous investment agencies, to which many people have pledged their coupons, and who then make the final decision as to where the money is invested. After a slow start, a staggering nine million people have now taken up the offer. However, given that an estimated forty percent of the businesses being floated are likely to go under in the first year, it only remains to be seen whether this programme of privatisation will go any way to solving the country's economic malaise.

Thanks to severe devaluation, the Czechoslovak crown now seems to be holding its own against the major western currencies, and inflation is stabilising, though industrial production has dropped by more than 25 percent and unemployment in some parts of the country is now a major concern. The only place where vacancies exceed the unemployment figures is Prague. Nevertheless, life for someone on the national average wage is becoming more and more difficult, and society is in danger of developing into the classic Third World model of a small number of haves, set against a large number of have-nots.

## Princes, kings, emperors and presidents

### The Přemyslid dynasty
Princes
Bořivoj I d. 895
Spytihněv I 895–905
Vratislav I 905–921
Václav I 921–929
Boleslav I 929–972
Boleslav II 972–999
Boleslav III 999–1002
Vladivoj 1002–1003
Jaromir 1003–1012
Ulrich 1012–1034
Břetislav I 1034–1055
Spytihněv II 1055–1061
Vratislav II (king from 1086) 1061–1092
Břetislav II 1092–1110
Bořivoj II 1110–1120
Vladislav I 1120–1125
Soběslav I 1125–1140
Vladislav II (as king, I) 1140–1173
Soběslav II 1173–1189
Otho 1189–1191
Václav II 1191–1192
Otakar I (king from 1212) 1192–1230

Kings
Václav I 1230–1253
Otakar II 1253–1278
Václav II 1278–1305
Václav III 1305–1306

### Habsburgs
Rudolf I 1306–1307
Henry of Carinthia 1307–1310

### The Luxembourg dynasty
John 1310–1346
Charles I (as emperor, IV) 1346–1378

Václav IV 1378–1419
Sigismund 1436–1437

### Habsburgs
Albert 1437–1439
Ladislav the Posthumous 1439–1457

### Czech Hussite
George of Poděbrady 1458–1471

### The Jagiellonian dynasty
Vladislav II 1471–1516
Louis I 1516–1526

### The Habsburg dynasty
Ferdinand I 1526–1564
Maximilian 1564–1576
Rudolf II 1576–1612
Matthias 1612–1619
Ferdinand II 1619–1637
Ferdinand III 1637–1657
Leopold I 1657–1705
Joseph I 1705–1711
Charles II (as emperor, VI) 1711–1740
Maria Theresa 1740–1780
Joseph II 1780–1790
Leopold II 1790–1792
Franz 1792–1835
Ferdinand IV (I) 1835–1848
Franz Joseph 1848–1916
Charles III 1916–1918

### Presidents
Tomáš Garrigue Masaryk 1918–1935
Edvard Beneš 1935–1938 & 1945–1948
Klement Gottwald 1948–1953
Antonín Zápatocký 1953–1957
Antonín Novotný 1957–1968
Ludvík Svoboda 1968–1975
Gustáv Husák 1975–1989
Václav Havel 1989–

# Czech Cinema

The Czechs are undoubtedly proud of their cinema. The cities may be polluted, the economy might be bankrupt, but everybody knows that, certainly in the 1960s, Czechoslovakia produced some of the finest films – and some of the finest film-makers – in the world.

Pessimists maintain that the weight of that "golden age" is a factor dragging down Czech cinema today. A generation of film-makers have returned from exile or emerged from obscurity to produce films that are no longer exciting or innovative. Not only do they dominate the film-making institutions, but as idol figures they dominate the thinking of younger film-makers, whose contemporary works are pale imitations of forgotten classics. More charitably, the "New Wave" of the 1960s can be seen as a high point in a long and distinguished cinematic tradition, which – although it may now be in the form of television or co-productions – shows every sign of continuing.

## Interwar cinema: Avant-garde to erotic

From the early days, the Czech contribution to European cinema has not been just great films and outstanding directors. Even in the 1920s, foreign companies were coming to use the facilities at the Barrandov **studios** in Prague – built by Vaclav Havel's ubiquitous architect grandfather – or the Baťa documentary studios in Zlín; and Czech film technicians, like the cameramen Jan Roth and Otto Heller, were much in demand abroad.

With around thirty films produced annually, the Czech **avant-garde** were excited by the possibilities of cinema. In pioneering articles, the leading theoretician of the *Devĕtsil* group, Karel Teige, saw not only the possibility of an art for the masses, but what he called "pure cinematography", an opportunity to escape from (bourgeois) objective realism. The Czech public was perhaps less discerning. The most famous prewar film, *Extase* (1933), was notorious not for the Devĕtsil motifs of circles, trains and picture poem montages from the director **Gustav Machatý**, but for the (briefly naked) appearance of a young Slovak actress, later to become famous as Hedy Lamarr. Machatý never recovered from his initial success; his career was dogged by proposals to make a pornographic sequel.

There were initially strong ties with early **German cinema**. Paul Wagner's expressionist classic *The Golem* (1920) was based on the Prague legend. Karl

Junghans made *Such is Life* (1929) with a Czech cast, and Přemysl Pražský's silent classic *Battalion* (1927) showed the extent of German influence. However, the coming of sound and the rise of fascism propelled most Czech film-makers in different directions.

Czech theatre contributed an important influence with **E.F. Burian** switching from directing for the stage to the screen and Voskovec and Werich bringing their successful blend of comedy and politics from the Liberated Theatre in Prague (now the ABC Theatre just off Wenceslas Square) to films like *Your Money or Your Life* (1932) and *The World is Ours* (1937). Their domestic popularity was enormous, comparable only with Chaplin, and Werich in particular remained a powerful figure in Czech culture long after the war. He continued writing and making films and records into the 1970s, ceasing only when the authorities threatened to prevent him receiving vital surgery.

## Nazi occupation and nationalisation

The **Nazi takeover** did not spell the end of Czech film production. Although many film-makers took their talents into exile – notably the director Karel Lamač, and actors Hugo Haas and Jiří Voskovec – others managed to continue working, albeit on more lyrical and less controversial themes. Frič, Vávra and Burian, who were all to be major figures in Czech cinema, continued working during the occupation.

One reason they were able to do so was that the Germans envisaged a major role for the film industry in Czechoslovakia. The Barrandov studios were greatly expanded and produced over a hundred features for the Reich. In 1945, Czechoslovakia found itself with the largest undamaged film complex in Europe and the surviving community of film-makers had already decided how best to manage it. As President Beneš put it, "If there is anything in our country ripe for nationalisation, it is film!"

Public support for the arts was not unknown in Czechoslovakia (theatre had been subsidised since the 1880s) but cinema had acquired a new prominence. In October 1945 the **Prague film academy (FAMU)** was founded and film students started to gather in the *Café Slavia*. A surge of film-making began, under the direction of Vítězslav Nezval, once *Devětsil* poet, now Minister of Information. With other studios badly damaged, Barrandov again became an international production centre, whilst Vávra, Frič and Weiss (fresh back from his spell at the British Crown Film Unit) demonstrated the strength of domestic talent.

Meanwhile, freed from commercial pressures and advertising fashions by nationalisation, Czech **animation** began to bloom. **Jiří Trnka**, the master of puppet animation, produced *The Czech Year* in 1947, while Hermína Týrlová and Karel Zeman were experimenting with combining filters, live action and cut-out cartoons at the Baťa studios at Zlín.

## Under the Communists

When the Communists took power, they inherited a centralised film industry and quickly began implementing the new orthodoxy of **social realism** that had been laid down in Moscow by Zhadnov two years earlier. Vávra, Frič, Trnka –

even Burian – were all curbed by the new bureaucracy. Bright talents like the student directors Vojtěch Jásny and Karel Kachyňa were kept away from feature films.

The authorities were not consistent, however. While for most of the 1950s Czech cinema produced an unappetising diet of girls in love with tractors, war epics and uninspiring biographies, some unusual gems emerged. **Alfred Radok** (founder of the *Laterna magika* theatre company) made *The Longest Journey* (1950), a striking portrait of the Terezín ghetto, and **Martin Frič** made a two-part intellectual comedy about the limits of absolute power, based on the golem myth and starring Jan Werich: *The Emperor's Baker* and *The Baker's Emperor* (1951). Zeman managed his surreal *The Invention of Destruction* in 1957 and Trnka produced *The Cybernetic Grandma* in 1962 – demonstrating that animation is perhaps harder to control politically than normal film.

After the ideological savaging of the Stalinist era, when feature film production dropped as low as eight films a year, a slightly more relaxed attitude prompted a series of questioning and often elegant films from directors like Ladislav Helge (*The Great Solitude*, 1959 – on the difficulty of being a rural party official), and Zdeněk Brnych (whose *Local Romance*, 1957, produced the term "dingy realism").

## The Czech New Wave

Although there was a sudden freeze with a conference on Czechoslovak cinema in 1959 at Banska Bystrica – which ended the promising careers of Krska and Svitaček – production reached 35 films a year in the early 1960s and a trend away from predictable conformity became apparent. The great partnerships of Czech cinema between directors **Jan Kadar** and **Elmar Klos**, and between scriptwriter **Jan Procházka** and director **Karel Kachyňa** got under way. Vojtěch Jásny and Štefan Uher both found their way past the censor and inspired a new and bolder generation.

Assisting these film-makers were various young students from FAMU. They were not only directors, but cameramen like Jan Kučera and Miroslav Ondriček, and Miroslav Hájek the editor. As economic sluggishness produced turmoil within the Communist Party, these students were to find a new contemporary voice and lead the Czech New Wave.

Their teachers showed the way. Jásny's *Cassandra Cat* (1963) starred Werich in a fairy tale about a cat who saw people in their true colours; Kadar and Klos's *The Shop on Main Street* (1964) described the fascist puppet state of wartime Slovakia; and Kachyňa's *Long Live the Republic* looked at the liberation from the Nazis with a new objectivity (1964).

The student directors took the contemporary feel and the flexibility modern cameras allowed to produce stunning low-budget films. **Věra Chytilová** completed her *Something Different* (a woman's point of view) in 1963. **Miloš Forman** was filming his first feature, *Black Peter*, out on the streets in the same year. **Jan Němec** took Arnošt Lustig's autobiographical story of boys fleeing from the Nazis and turned it into a terrifying vision of youth in a hostile world with *Diamonds of the Night* (1964). **Pavel Juraček** brought Kafka back to Prague with *Josef Kilian* (1964), a nightmare tale of a man trying to find the shop he had borrowed a cat from. A number of young directors were brought together in producing the various *Pearls at the Bottom* (1965), each based on short stories by the surrealist writer Bohumil Hrabal.

The New Wave was characterised by energetic and innovative camera work, a brazen questioning of assumptions and a darkly humorous accuracy in observing contemporary mores. As the political uncertainty in the Party deepened, the films became more daring: in *Daisies* (1966) Chytilová had two girls having a food fight at an official banquet; in *The Fireman's Ball* (1967) Forman hilariously satirised bureaucratic incompetence; and in *The Report on the Party and the Guests* (1966), Němec depicted a chilling party where the guests couldn't leave. Trnka contributed the blatantly allegorical *The Hand* (1966), and in the same year Jiří Menzl won an Oscar for his delightfully irreverent look at wartime resistance – *Closely Observed Trains*, again based on a Hrabal story.

By the time the tanks rolled in, a number of even stronger films were already in production. Jaromír Jireš' version of Milan Kundera's mournful novel about the 1950s, *The Joke*, came out – briefly – in 1969, as did Evald Schorm's bitterly funny *End of the Priest* (with a script by Josef Škvorecký). Menzl's *Larks on the String* (1969) had the same lead (Vlastimil Brodský) in a Hrabal tale of love and politics amongst the labour gangs at a Kladno steel works. Most terrifying, in *The Ear* (1970), Kachyňa and Procházka produced an image of an entire society under surveillance.

All these films were **banned**, along with Vojtěch Jásny's lyrically melancholy *All My Good Countrymen* (1969), arguably the finest film of the period, and, not surprisingly *The Uninvited Guest*, which starred a youthful Landovsky (currently an MP) as a mysterious visitor who arrives one night and refuses to leave.

## Post-1968: normalisation and exile

The era of normalisation blighted the burgeoning Czech film industry. While Chytilová and Menzl, in particular, produced some interesting work in the 1970s, and Ondriček became one of the world's most valued cameramen, little of note emerged from Czechoslovakia in the drab decades after 1969. Dozens of film-makers fled, including Kadar and Němec, while many of those who stayed found themselves excluded from regular film-making and isolated from international film trends.

The most successful **director in exile** has undoubtedly been **Miloš Forman**. His most famous films, *Amadeus* (which was filmed in Prague) and *One Flew Over The Cuckoo's Nest*, had a particular relevance to Czechoslovakia, where artists still suffered the vagaries of official patronage, and mental hospitals were one of numerous institutions used to curb individual will. They only secured public release in full after the revolution of 1989. Several other major foreign films were made in Czechoslovakia, including *Slaughterhouse 5* and *Yentl* (a picture of Barbra Streisand still hangs proudly in Prague's kosher restaurant).

One outstanding Czech film-maker who just about continued to function was **Jan Švankmajer**, although he had to move to Bratislava for a while to evade official restrictions. He was not associated with the New Wave, partly because he had not been at FAMU, and partly because he saw himself as primarily a surrealist rather than solely a film-maker. He used an enforced break from film-making to conduct a series of "touch experiments", exploring the nature of objects. When he returned to animation, he produced a series of stunning films including *Dimensions of a Dialogue*, *Down to the Cellar* and the feature-length *Alice*. In recent years he has been acknowledged in the west as one of the giants of contemporary animation, and he continues to work with his dedicated team in his studio in Nový Svět.

## The Velvet Revolution and after

The revolution, in which FAMU students played a prominent part, raised enormous expectations of Czech cinema. These were further encouraged when Czech audiences for the first time had an opportunity to view some of the finest films that had been buried in the archives. However, the **post-revolutionary films** of Němec (*In the Heat of Royal Love*, 1990) and Menzl (*Threepenny Opera*, 1991 – using Havel's script) and Chytilová's depiction of Mozart in Prague have all been disappointing.

Jan Svěrak secured an Oscar nomination in 1992 with his *Elementary School*, but few of the younger film-makers have made a significant impression. *Tank Division* (Wit Olmer, 1990) was the first privately financed Czech film since the 1940s. It recouped its budget, but its script (based on a Škvorecký story) is typical of the post-revolutionary films in being a reminiscent, mildly funny tale, full of cheap anti-Communist gibes laced with a tedious sexism.

Meanwhile, foreign crews have been flocking to use Czech **facilities** and **locations**. Whether Czechs are able to have more than a menial influence on the big co-productions, or earn enough to fund significant domestic production is far from certain. As in much of eastern Europe, Czechs are resigned to making fewer films, but hope to make better ones. The years of isolation and decay have taken their toll, however, not only in equipment and technology but also in terms of creative thinking. The slogan that Švankmajer painted during the revolution – "More Imagination Please" – has so far fallen on deaf ears within the film community.

With all the *Star Wars* films to catch up on, Czech cinemas are largely full of western imports – but occasionally something local will slip through. For the foreign visitor, Prague cinemas are certainly worth a look in. Not only does the strong visual style of the Czech classics lessen the language barrier, but cheap ticket prices and truly sumptuous interiors make Prague an ideal place to view the latest releases (as long as they're subtitled rather than dubbed). *Lucerna*, *Flora*, *Pasáž* and *Illusion* are still picture palaces; *Dlabachov* and *Sokolovo* are the best places to hunt for art house classics.

David Charap

# Women in Prague

Bronwyn Brady lived in Prague for six months in 1991, teaching English in the nearby mining town of Kladno. The article below is a personal account, based on the experiences of the women she met and worked with.

Czech society remains profoundly patriarchal, and in discussions with my women friends and students, it was seldom that any of them would criticise their men. Men's work is still seen as inherently more valuable than women's work, and housework and child-care are definitely not men's work. Coming from South Africa, I was more than aware that feminism was not universally well-regarded but I was intrigued to find in Prague an attitude that has since been expressed by Jiřina Vrabková, in an unpublished paper for the Women's Conference on Security and Cooperation in Europe (March 1992). She pointed out that:

> "Feminism" and "emancipation" are very bad words here. There is the widespread opinion that our women are emancipated enough thanks to the previous regime . . . Feminism here means something bad, either another "ism" which means one ideology replaced by another, or a vision of the militant, frustrated, unsuccessful, usually ugly women who are hostile towards men.

(Young women's priorities and visions for the year 2000).

## The economy

As in most places, the two things from which women suffer most in Czechoslovakia are the economy and the environment. Under socialism it was a crime not to have a job. Women were expected to contribute fully to the economy, unless they were having children, in which case they were allowed three years' maternity leave to be at home with their infant children. A state grant went with this leave, but not enough to make the mother independent of the father of the child. The social and professional isolation of the situation could often be unbearable, and Sylvie, my doctor friend, counts herself as having been extremely lucky to have been able to return to work only a few months after her son was born. Women were expected on the one hand to be devoted socialist individuals working for the common good, and on the other devoted socialist mothers and housewives.

Now, post revolution, it is essential for women to **work**: it takes two basic salaries to keep a household running – and even then only just. Maternity benefits remain inadequate. Economic pressure has effectively replaced legislation as the medium of women's oppression. To the majority of women it seems there has been little benefit from a change in government. It is small wonder that the concerns of women in Czechoslovakia differ from those in the west. Marie, for instance, is tired of bearing the full burden of **child-care**, home management, a job and the attendant exhaustion; she wants to be able to choose to stay at home and raise her children herself, instead of submitting them to the dubious care of a kindergarten. Other women are not interested in pursuing their careers as they are certain that, despite legislation to prevent it, they will never be paid the same as a man in the same job.

The growing level of **prostitution** in Prague is a symptom of this economic pressure. Women who speak several languages and provide escort services for the increasing numbers of international businessmen can earn as much as three times a monthly salary in one night. And of course, it's tax free. Those working the streets earn less, but it nevertheless serves to supplement the family income: "My husband doesn't like it, but he agrees, knowing that I could never earn such a high salary".

## The Environment

My first cue into environmental issues came from my flatmate, Anna, and her friend Iva. Twenty-three and twenty-four years old, they think it is now probably too late to contemplate having **children**. Both have lived in or around Prague all their lives, and feel that they have now absorbed too many teratogens to make the risk (of congenital malformations) worthwhile. Women accept that their children will suffer from allergies, and need to be kept indoors during winter when thermal inversion covers the city in smog; and that they will need to be sent out of the city periodically to spend time in the mountains, breathing clean air. Air pollution is top of the environment ministry's list for attention.

The first major piece of environmental legislation debated in Prague after the revolution dealt with the disposal of waste. During the debate, the environment minister, Vavroušek, discussed the possibility of introducing additional legislation to commit mothers to testing their breast-milk before they began to feed their babies. **PCBs** (polychlorinated biphenyls) have entered the food chain: they are present in meat and dairy products, and so in human beings. In the event, this did not enter the legislation, but it served to shock the population into a new awareness of the extent of environmental pollution.

### Women's initiatives

The situation is, inevitably, much more complex than I have represented, which perhaps increases the sense of the weight of the burden that women bear. But it makes it even more exciting to see women's initiatives underway to change things.

The name that always springs to mind when organisation is discussed is that of the **Prague Mothers**, whose name rather belies them. These are women who have organised around the environment, and they are extremely vocal in challenging local government and industry on their environmental performance. My friend Vladimír, who works for local government in environmental planning, is often on the receiving end of their phone calls. He flinches at the mention of their name, in a way that suggests that they are doing their job well. A national women's organisation does exist – Český svaz ženy, the Czech Union of Women – but it is a carry-over from pre-revolution days, and irremediably tarred with the "communist" brush. There is substantial doubt as to whether it will ever become the grassroots organisation its current leaders would like it to be.

In *Academia*, the social work department at the Charles University has recently established a women's studies course. And there are women deputies in parliament – although none for whom women's issues would take first place. On the whole, they work as part of the system, playing the power games of politicians and allowing issues perceived as "women's" to be pushed to the back burner.

In Jiřina Vrabková's conclusion to her paper, she states that she is "very pessimistic about Czech women's positive awareness of their emancipation and the possibility of getting rid of anachronisms in the near future". I am more hopeful than that. I don't know that things will turn out entirely as we envisage, but I do know that it took Prague to teach me the value of the interstices in society which women can appropriate for themselves. And the power of people to survive despite everything.

# Books

The recent upsurge of interest in all things eastern European has had a number of positive repercussions. In addition to the eye-witness accounts of the "Velvet Revolution", several new histories of the country have appeared in print and there's a much wider choice of Czech fiction than ever before, including several previously untranslated women writers. If you encounter any difficulties, the best source of specialist books on all things Czech is *Collets International Bookshop*, 129 Charing Cross Road, London W1 (☎071/734 0782).

Where two publishers are given, the first is the UK publisher, the second the US.

## History, Politics and Society

Janusz Bugajski *Czechoslovakia – Charter 77's Decade of Dissent* (Praeger). Informative, comprehensive but rather dry account of Charter 77's background and campaigns, as well as information on a host of other dissident activities in the 1980s.

Mark Frankland *The Patriots' Revolution* (Sinclair Stevenson/I. R. Dee). Falls somewhere between Garton Ash's eye-witness account and Glenny's more lengthy analysis, but fails to be convincing either way.

Timothy Garton Ash *We The People: The Revolutions of 89* (Granta, Penguin). A personal, anecdotal, eye-witness account of the Velvet Revolution (and the events in Poland, Berlin and Budapest), and for that reason by far the most compelling of all the post-1989 books.

Misha Glenny *The Rebirth of History: Eastern Europe in the Age of Democracy* (Penguin). Eight chapters in all, one of which deals with Czechoslovakia, focusing on the events of 1990 and the problems of the future rather than the Velvet Revolution itself. Correspondent for *The Guardian* and *BBC*, Glenny knows his stuff, but don't expect any jokes.

Karel Kaplan *Report on the Murder of the General Secretary* (I. B. Tauris/ Ohio State University Press). Detailed study of the most famous of the anti-Semitic Stalinist show trials, that of Rudolf Slánský, number two in the KSČ until his arrest.

Jaroslav Krejčí *Czechoslovakia at the Crossroads of European History* (I. B. Tauris). Fairly breezy, lacklustre account of Czechoslovakia's history by a 1968 Czech emigré. Despite its recent publication, it contains only the briefest summary of the events of November 1989.

Hans Renner *A History of Czechoslovakia since 1945* (Routledge, o/p). General history by one of the 1968 emigré generation, finishing with the accession of Jakeš to General Secretary in December 1987.

David Selbourne *Death of a Dark Hero – Eastern Europe 1987–90* (Cape). A collection of articles by a leading journalist on eastern Europe. Several deal with Prague, mostly personal accounts of meetings with the country's leading dissidents, before and after the revolution.

**R. W. Seton-Watson** *The History of the Czechs and Slovaks* (Hutchinson, o/p/ Transatlantic, o/p). Seton-Watson's highly informed and balanced account, written during World War II, is hard to beat. The Seton-Watsons were lifelong Slavophiles but managed to maintain a scholarly distance in their writing, rare amongst emigré historians.

**Ivan Svítek** *The Unbearable Burden of History*. No prizes for guessing what inspired the title of this recent history, which starts with the crisis of 1938, and ends with the revolution of 1989.

**Elizabeth Wiskemann** *Czechs and Germans* (Oxford, o/p/AMS Press). Researched and written in the build-up towards Munich, this is the most fascinating and fair treatment of the Sudeten problem. Meticulous in her detail, vast in her scope, Wiskemann nevertheless manages to suffuse the weighty text with enough anecdotes to keep you gripped. Unique.

**Sharon L. Wolchik** *Czechoslovakia in Transition: Politics, Economics and Society* (Pinter). Dry, but detailed and well-researched sociological study of the country, published in 1991.

**Zbyněk Zeman** *Prague Spring; A Report on Czechoslovakia 1968* (Penguin, o/p). Short, straightforward, and in many ways the easiest of the books on 1968, including useful background stuff on the country's postwar history.

## Essay, memoirs and biography

**Stephen Brook** *The Double Eagle: Vienna, Budapest and Prague* (Picador). Taking their shared Habsburg tradition as a starting point, Brook's readable, personal foray gives an illuminating picture of dissident life in Prague in the late 1980s before the neo-Stalinist bubble finally burst.

**Margarete Buber-Neumann** *Milena* (Collins Harvill/Schocken). A moving biography of Milena Jesenská, one of interwar Prague's most beguiling characters, who befriended the author while they were both interned in Ravensbrück concentration camp.

**Neil Butterworth** *Dvořák* (Omnibus/ Paganiniana Publications). An extremely accessible illustrated biography of the country's best known composer.

**Jana Cerná** *Kafka's Milena* (Souvenir Press). Another biography of Milena Jesenská, this time written by her daughter, a surrealist poet, whose own works were banned under the Communists.

*Dubček Speaks* (I. B. Tauris). Verbatim account of Dubček's interview in early 1989 with Andras Sugar, one of Hungary's leading political writers, in which Dubček spoke for the first time in public about the events of the 1968 Prague Spring.

**Timothy Garton Ash** *Uses of Adversity* (Granta, Penguin). A collection of Garton Ash's journalistic pieces on Eastern Europe, written mostly in the 1980s, including several informative pieces on Czechoslovakia.

**Patrick Leigh Fermor** *A Time of Gifts* (Penguin/Viking Penguin). The first volume of Leigh Fermor's trilogy based on his epic walk along the Rhine and Danube rivers in 1933–34. In the last quarter of the book he reaches Czechoslovakia, indulging in a quick jaunt to Prague before crossing the border into Hungary. Written forty years later in dense, luscious and highly crafted prose, it's an evocative and poignant insight into the culture of *Mitteleuropa* between the wars.

*Granta 30: New Europe!* (Penguin). Published at the beginning of 1990, this state-of-the-continent anthology includes Graham Swift's *Looking for Jiří Wolf*, as well as a series of brief reactions to events by a dozen or so European intellectuals.

**Patricia Hampl** *A Romantic Education* (Houghton Mifflin). An account of the author searching for her Czech roots in pre-1989 Prague.

**Václav Havel** *Living in Truth* (Faber & Faber); *Letters to Olga* (Faber/Owl Books); *Disturbing the Peace* (Faber/ Knopf), *Open Letters: Selected Prose* (Faber/Vintage); *Summer Meditations* (Faber & Faber). The first essay in *Living in Truth* is "Power of the Powerless", Havel's lucid, damning indictment of the inactivity of the Czechoslovak masses in the face of "normalisation". *Letters to Olga* is a collection of Havel's letters written under great duress (and heavy censorship) from prison in the early 1980s to his wife, Olga – by turns philosophising, nagging, effusing, whingeing. *Disturbing the Peace* is probably Havel's most accessible work yet: a series of autobiographical questions and answers in which he talks interestingly about his childhood, the events of 1968 when he was in Liberec, and the path to Charter 77 and beyond (though not including his reactions to being thrust into the role of president). Summer Meditations is Havel's most recent collection of essays.

**Václav Havel et al** *Power of the Powerless* (Hutchinson/M. E. Sharp). A collection of essays by leading Chartists, kicking off with Havel's seminal title-piece. Other contributors range from the dissident Marxist Petr Uhl to devout Catholics like Václav Benda.

*High Hopes – Young Voices of Eastern Europe* (Virago). A series of short personal accounts by young people across the former eastern bloc, expressing their often mixed feelings about the events of 1989.

**Miroslav Holub** *The Dimension of the Present Moment* (Faber & Faber). A series of very short musings/essays by this unusual and clever scientist-poet.

**Heda Margolius Kovaly** *Prague Farewell* (Gollancz/Penguin). An autobiography that starts in the concentration camps of World War II, ending with the author's flight from Czechoslovakia in 1968. Married to one of the Party

hacks executed in the 1952 Slánský trial, she tells her story simply, and without bitterness. The best account there is on the fear and paranoia whipped up during the Stalinist terror.

**Nikolaus Martin** *Prague Winter* (Peter Halban). Brought up in Prague in the 1930s, Martin ended up in Terezín, Czechoslovakia's most notorious ghetto and concentration camp, because of his mother's Jewish background. This autobiography follows his life up to and including the 1948 Communist coup, after which he escaped to Canada.

*New Left Review* (Number 179). Contains a rare interview with leading Charter 77 spokesperson and dissident Marxist Petr Uhl, conducted during the heady first few months after the Velvet Revolution.

*Jan Patočka – Philosophy and Selected Writings* (Chicago UP). A collection of essays by one of the first of Charter 77's spokespeople, on subjects ranging from Charter 77 itself to Husserl and phenomenology.

**Jan Šejna** *We Will Bury You* (Sidgwick & Jackson, o/p). The memoirs of Czechoslovkia's highest ranking military defector, who fled to the West in February 1968. The memoir part is the most interesting, the sections uncovering the Commies' secret plan to take over the world little short of hysterical.

**William Shawcross** *Dubček and Czechoslovakia 1918–1990* (Hogarth Press/Simon & Schuster). Biography of the most famous figure of the 1968 Prague Spring, updated to include Dubček's role in the 1989 Velvet Revolution.

**Michael Simmons** *The Reluctant President* (Methuen). The definitive (and so far the only) biography of Václav Havel, by the long-time *Guardian* reporter.

**Phyllis Myrtle Clarke Sisperova** *Not Far From Wenceslas Square* (The Book Guild). Autobiography of an English woman who married a Czech airman in World War II, and afterwards settled in Prague, only to be arrested during the 1950s "terror". She was released and finally returned to England in 1955 amid a blaze of publicity in the West.

**Josef Škvorecký** *Talkin' Moscow Blues* (Faber/Ecco Press). Without doubt the most user-friendly of Škvorecký's works, containing a collection of essays on his wartime childhood, Czech Jazz, literature and contemporary politics, all told in his inimitable, irreverent and infuriating way.

*The Spirit of Thomas G. Masaryk 1850–1937* (Macmillan/St Martins). An anthology of writings on philosophy, religion, Czech history and politics by the country's founder and first president, affectionately known as TGM.

**Ludvík Vaculík** *A Cup of Coffee with My Interrogator* (Readers International). A Party member until 1968, and signatory of Charter 77, Vaculík revived the *feuilleton*, a short political critique – a journalistic literary genre once much loved in central Europe. This collection dates from 1968 onwards. His first novel, *The Axe* (Andre Deutsch, o/p/Northwestern University Press), is *the* definitive account of the forced collectivisation of the 1950s.

**Zbyněk Zeman** *The Masaryks – The Making of Czechoslovakia* (I. B. Tauris). Written in the 1970s while Zeman was in exile, this is a very readable, none too sentimental biography of the country's founder Tomáš Garrigue Masaryk, and his son Jan Masaryk, the postwar Foreign Minister who died in mysterious circumstances shortly after the 1948 Communist coup.

## Czech fiction

**Karel Čapek** *Towards a Radical Centre* (Catbird Press); *The War with the Newts* (Picador/Northwestern University Press); *Nine Fairy Tales* (Northwestern UP). Čapek was the literary and journalistic spokesperson for Masaryk's First Republic, but he's better known in the West for his plays, some of which feature in this anthology.

**Ladislav Fuks** *The Cremator* (Marion Boyars); *Mr Theodore Mundstock* (Four Walls Eight Windows). The first novel is a story about a man who works in a crematorium in occupied Prague, and is about to throw in his lot with the Nazis when he discovers that his wife is half-Jewish. The second is set in Prague 1942, as the city's Jews wait to be transported to Terezín.

**Jaroslav Hašek** *The Good Soldier Švejk* (Penguin/Viking Penguin); *The Bachura Scandal* (Angel Books). The former is a rambling, picaresque tale of Czechoslovakia's most famous fictional fifth columnist, *Švejk*, who wreaks havoc in the Austro-Hungarian army during World War I, by Bohemia's most bohemian writer. The latter is a collection of zany short stories on life in prewar Prague.

**Václav Havel** *The Memorandum* (Methuen, o/p/Grove Weidenfeld); *Three Vaněk Plays*; *Temptation*; *Redevelopment* (all Faber & Faber/ Grove Weidenfeld). Havel's plays are not renowned for being easy to read (or watch). *The Memorandum* is one of his earliest works, a classic absurdist drama that, in many ways, sets the tone for much of his later work, of which the *Three Vaněk Plays*, featuring Ferdinand Vaněk, Havel's *alter ego*, are perhaps the most successful.

**Bohumil Hrabal** *Closely Observed Trains* (Abacus/Viking Penguin); *The Death of Mr Baltisberger* (Abacus); *I Served the King of England* (Picador/ Vintage); *Too Loud a Solitude* (Abacus/ Harcourt Brace Jovanovich). A thoroughly mischievous writer, Hrabal's slim but superb *Closely Observed Trains* is one of the postwar classics, set in the last days of the war and relentlessly unheroic; it was made into an equally brilliant film by Jiří Menzl. *I Served the King of England* follows the antihero Dítě through the crucial decade after 1938. *Too Loud a Solitude*, about a waste-paper disposer under the Communists, is also being made into a film, again by Menzl.

**Alois Jirásek** *Old Czech Legends* (Forest Books). A major figure in the nineteenth-century Czech *národní obrození*, Jirásek popularised Bohemia's legendary past. This collection includes all the classic texts, including the story of the founding of the city by the prophetess Libuše.

**Franz Kafka** *The Collected Novels of Franz Kafka*; *Letters to Felice*; *Diaries* (all Minerva/Schocken). A German-Jewish Praguer, Kafka has drawn the darker side of central Europe – its claustrophobia, paranoia and unfathomable bureaucracy – better than anyone else, both in a rural setting, as in *The Castle*, and in an urban one, in one of the great novels of the twentieth century, *The Trial*.

**Eva Kantůrková** *My Companions in the Bleak House* (Quartet/Viking Penguin). Kantůrková spent a year in Prague's Ruzyně prison, and *Companions* is a well-observed novel based around the characters within the prison's women's wing, the measure of their kindness, violence and despair mirroring the outside world.

**Ivan Klíma** *A Summer Affair* (Penguin); *My Merry Mornings* (Readers International); *First Loves* (Penguin/Norton); *Love and Garbage* (Penguin/Knopf); *Judge on Trial* (Chatto), *My Golden Trades* (Granta). A survivor of Terezín, Klíma is another writer in the Kundera mould as far as sexual politics goes, but his stories are a lot lighter. His latest novel, *Judge on Trial*, is one of his best, concerning the moral dilemmas of a Communist judge.

**Milan Kundera** *Laughable Loves* (Faber); *The Farewell Party* (Penguin/Viking Penguin); *The Joke*; *The Book of Laughter and Forgetting*; *Life is Elsewhere* (all Faber/Viking Penguin); *The Unbearable Lightness of Being*; *The Art of the Novel*; *Immortality* (all Faber/HarperCollins). Milan Kundera is Czechoslovakia's most popular writer – at least with non-Czechs. Certainly, if you can stand his sexual politics, his books are very obviously "political",

particularly *The Book of Laughter and Forgetting*, which led the Communists to revoke Kundera's citizenship. *The Joke*, written while he was still living in Czechoslovakia, and in many ways his best work, is set in the very unfunny era of the Stalinist purges. Its clear, humorous style is far removed from the carefully poised posturing of his most famous work, *The Unbearable Lightness of Being*, set in and after 1968, and successfully turned into a film some twenty years later.

**Arnošt Lustig** *Diamonds of the Night*; *Darkness Casts No Shadow*; *Night and Hope* (all Quartet/Northwestern University Press); *A Prayer for Kateřina Horovitová* (Quartet/Overlook Press); *Indecent Dreams* (Northwestern University Press). A Prague Jew exiled since 1968, Lustig spent World War II in Terezín, Buchenwald and Auschwitz, and his novels and short stories are consistently set in the Terezín camp.

**Gustav Meyrink** *The Golem* (Dedalus/Ariadne); *The Angel of the West Window* (Dedalus/Dover). Meyrink was another of Prague's weird and wonderful characters who started out as a bank manager, but soon came involved in cabalism, alchemy and drug experimentation. His *Golem*, based on Rabbi Löw's monster, is one of the classic versions of the tale, set in Jewish quarter. *The Angel at the West Window* is a historical novel about John Dee, the English alchemist who was invited to Prague in the late sixteenth century by Rudolf II.

**Ladislav Mňačko** *The Taste of Power* (Weidenfeld & Nicolson, o/p/Praeger, o/p). Now exiled in Israel, Mňačko is one of the few Slovak writers to have been widely published abroad, most frequently this novel about the corruption of ideals that followed the Communist takeover.

**Libuše Moníková** *The Facade* (Chatto/Knopf). Humorous novel about the adventures of a group of anarchic artists who cause havoc in Communist Bohemia and Siberia.

*New Writing in Czechoslovakia* (Penguin, o/p). First published in 1969, this is one of the easiest collections of Czech and Slovak writing to get hold of secondhand.

**Leo Perutz** *By Night Under the Stone Bridge* (Harvill/Arcade Publishing). A Jewish-German Praguer who emigrated to Israel and wrote a series of historical novels. This one is set in Rudolfine Prague, and, among other things, tells the story of the emperor's love affair with the wife of Mordecai Maisl.

**Josef Škvorecký** *The Cowards* (Penguin/Ecco Press); *The Swell Season* (Picador/Ecco Press); *The Bass Saxophone* (Picador/Pocket Books); *Miss Silver's Past* (Picador, o/p/Ecco Press); *Dvořák in Love* (Hogarth, o/p/Norton); *The Engineer of Human Souls* (Picador); *The Miracle Game* (Faber & Faber/Norton). A relentless anti-Communist, Škvorecký is typically Bohemian in his bawdy sense of humour and irreverence for all high moralising. *The Cowards* (which briefly saw the light of day in 1958) is the tale of a group of irresponsible young men in the last days of the war, an antidote to the lofty prose from official authors at the time. *The Bass Saxophone* is based around Škvorecký's other great love, jazz, while *Dvořák in Love* and *The Engineer of Human Souls* are both set in and around the Czech emigré communities of the "New World", where Škvorecký has lived since 1968.

**Josef Škvorecký** *The Mournful Demeanor of Lieutenant Boruvka*; *Sins for Father Knox*; *The Return of Lieutenant Boruvka* (all Faber & Faber/Norton). Less well known (and understandably so) are Škvorecký's detective stories featuring a podgy, depressive Czech cop, which he wrote in the 1960s at a time when his more serious work was banned. The later book, *The Return of Lieutenant Boruvka*, is set in Škvorecký's new home, Canada.

**Zdena Tomin** *Stalin's Shoe* (Dent, o/p/Dodd Mead, o/p); *The Coast of Bohemia* (Picador). Although Czech-born, Tomin writes in English (the language of her exile since 1980), with a style and fluency all her own. *Stalin's Shoe* is the compelling and complex story of a girl coming to terms with her Stalinist childhood, while *The Coast of Bohemia* is based on Tomin's experiences of the late 1970s dissident movement, when she was an active member of Charter 77.

**Ludvík Vaculík** *The Guinea Pigs* (Northwestern UP). Vaculík was expelled from the Party in the midst of the Prague Spring in 1968; this novel, set in Prague, catalogues the slow dehumanisation of Czech society in the aftermath of the Sovet invasion.

**Jiří Weil** *Life With a Star*; *Mendelssohn is on the Roof* (Flamingo/Viking Penguin). A novel written just after the war and based on Weil's experiences as a Czech Jew in Prague as the Nazis occupied Czechoslovakia.

# Poetry

**Jaroslav Čejka, Michal Černík and Karel Sýs** *The New Czech Poetry* (Bloodaxe). Slim, but interesting volume by three Czech poets; all in their late forties, all very different. Čejka is of the Holub school, and comes across simply and strongly; Černík is similarly direct; Sýs the least convincing.

*Child of Europe – A New Anthology of East European Poetry* (Penguin). This collection contains many hitherto untranslated Czech poets, including Ivo Šmoldas, Ewald Murrer and Jana Štroblová.

**Sylva Fischerová** *The Tremor of Racehorses: Selected Poems* (Bloodaxe). Poet and novelist, Fischerová is one of the new generation of Czech writers, though in many ways she is continuing in the Holub tradition. By turns powerful, obtuse and personal, as was necessary to escape censorship during the late 1980s.

**Miroslav Holub** *The Fly* (Bloodaxe); *Poems Before & After* (Bloodaxe); *Vanishing Lung Syndrome* (Faber/Oberlin College Press). Holub is both a scientist and scholar, and his poetry reflects this unique fusion of master poet and chief immunologist. Regularly banned in his own country, he is the Czech poet *par excellence* – classically trained, erudite, liberal and westward-leaning. *Vanishing Lung Syndrome* is his latest volume; the other two are collections.

**Vladimír Janovic** *The House of the Tragic Poet* (Bloodaxe). A bizarre epic poem set in the last days of Pompeii in 79 AD, and centred around six young men who are rehearsing a satyr play.

**Rainer Maria Rilke** *Selected Poems* (Penguin/HarperCollins). Rilke's upbringing was unexceptional, except for the fact that his mother brought him up as a girl until the age of six. In his adult life, he became one of Prague's leading Jewish-German authors of the interwar period.

**Jaroslav Seifert** *The Selected Poetry of Jaroslav Seifert* (Andre Deutsch, o/p/ Collier Macmillan). Czechoslovakia's one and only Nobel prize-winning author, Seifert was a founder-member of the Communist Party and the avant-garde arts movement *Devětsil*, later falling from grace and signing the Charter in his old age. His longevity means that his work covers some of the most turbulent times in Czechoslovak history, but his irrepressible lasciviousness has been known to irritate.

## Literature by Foreign Writers

**Bruce Chatwin** *Utz* (Picador/Viking Penguin). Chatwin is one of the "exotic" school of travel writers, hence this slim, intriguing and mostly true-to-life account of an avid crockery collector from Prague's Jewish quarter.

**Martha Gellhorn** *A Stricken Field* (Virago, o/p/Viking Penguin). The story of an American journalist who arrives in Prague just as the Nazis march into Sudetenland. Based on the author's own experiences, this is a fascinating, if sentimental, insight into the panic and confusion in "rump" Czecho-Slovakia

after the Munich Diktat. First published in 1940.

**Ellis Peters** *The Piper on the Mountain* (Headline). Ellis Peters, whose real name is Edith Pargeter, is the author of the popular crime series *The Chronicles of Brother Cadfael*. A woman with strong Czech connections, Peters has chosen Prague and the Slovak Tatra mountains as the setting for this modern-day detective story.

**Zina Rohan** *The Book of Wishes and Complaints* (Flamingo). Rohan is a British-born writer of German-Jewish and Russian-Yugoslav origin, who married a Czech. The story revolves around a young country girl, Hana, who moves to Prague and embarks upon a voyage of self-discovery against the backdrop of the 1968 Prague Spring.

## Art, Photography and Film

*Czech Modernism 1900–1945* (Bullfinch Press). Wide-ranging and superbly illustrated, this American publication records the journey of the Czech modern movement through Cubism and Surrealism to Modernism and the avant-garde. The accompanying essays by leading art and film critics cover fine art, architecture, film, photography and theatre.

*Devětsil – Czech Avant-Garde Art, Architecture and Design of the 1920s and 30s* (Museum of Modern Art, Oxford). Published to accompany the 1990 Devětsil exhibition at Oxford, this is the definitive account of interwar Czechoslovakia's most famous left-wing art movement, which attracted artists from every discipline.

*Disorientations – Eastern Europe in Transition* (Thames & Hudson). A self-explanatory book of photographs accompanied by text by Pavel Kohout

**Peter Hames** *The Czechoslovak New Wave* (Californian UP). An intelligent and detailed history of the golden age of Czechoslovak cinema during the 1960s, but a bit mean on the stills.

**Josef Koudelka** (Photo Poche, o/p). Without doubt the most original Czech photographer and purveyor of fine Prague Spring photos. This pocket-size monograph is occasionally available in secondhand art bookshops.

**Miroslav Lamač** *Osma a skupina 1907–1917* (Odeon, o/p/Szwede Slavic).

Czech text, but with a good selection of colour reproductions (mostly of paintings) of the Cubist phase in Czech art.

*Josef Sudek – A Photographer's Life* (John Murray/Aperture). Hauntingly beautiful set of sepia photographs by the old man of Czech photography, who died in the 1970s.

# Language

The official language of the Czech federal republic is Czech (český), a highly complex western Slav tongue. If you know some German, brush up on that, since, among the older generation in particular, German is still the most widely spoken second language, and as a western visitor you'll be expected to know at least some. Russian, once the compulsory second language, has been practically wiped off the school curriculum, and the number of English-speakers has been steadily increasing. That said, any attempt to speak Czech will be heartily appreciated, if a little difficult to understand for a people unaccustomed to hearing foreigners stumble through their language.

## Pronunciation

English-speakers often find Czech impossibly difficult to pronounce. In fact, it's not half as daunting as it might first appear from the traffic jams of consonants which crop up on the page. Apart from a few special letters, each letter and syllable is pronounced as it's written – the trick is always to stress the first syllable of a word, no matter what its length; otherwise you'll render it unintelligible.

### Short and long vowels

Czech has both short and long vowels (the latter being denoted by a variety of accents). The trick here is to lengthen the vowel without affecting the principal stress of the word, which is invariably on the first syllable.

a like the u in cup
á as in father
e as in pet
é as in fair
ě like the ye in yes
i or y as in pit
í or ý as in seat
o as in not
ó as in door
u like the oo in book
ů or ú like the oo in fool

### Vowel combinations and dipthongs

There are very few dipthongs in Czech, so any combinations of vowels not mentioned below should be pronounced as two separate syllables.

au like the ou in foul
ou like the oe in foe

### Consonants and accents

There are no silent consonants, but it's worth remembering that r and l can form a syllable if standing between two other consonants or at the end of a word, as in Brno (Br–no) or Vltava (Vl–ta–va). The consonants listed below are those which differ substantially from the English. Accents look daunting, but the only one which causes a lot of problems is ř, probably the most difficult letter to say in the entire language – even Czech toddlers have to be taught how to say it.

c like the **ts** in boats
č like the **ch** in chicken
ch like the **ch** in the Scottish loch
ď like the **d** in duped
g always as in **goat**, never as in general
h always as in **have**, but more energetic
j like the **y** in yoke
kd pronounced as **gd**
ľ like the **lli** in colliery

mě pronounced as **mnye**
ň like the **n** in nuance
p softer than the English **p**
r as in **rip**, but often rolled
ř like the sound of **r** and **ž** combined
š like the **sh** in shop
ť like the **t** in tutor
ž like the **s** in pleasure; at the end of a word like the **sh** in shop

---

### A Czech language guide

There are very few **teach-yourself Czech** courses available and each has drawbacks. *Colloquial Czech* by James Naughton is a bit fast and furious for most people; *Teach Yourself Czech* is a bit dry for some. The best portable **dictionary for Czech** is the *kapesní slovník*, most easily purchased in Czechoslovakia. Colletts produce a useful phrasebook called *Travellers' Czech*.

| **Basic words and phrases** | | **Left** | *nalevo* |
| --- | --- | --- | --- |
| Yes | *ano* | Right | *napravo* |
| No | *ne* | Straight on | *ovně* |
| Excuse me/don't mention it | *prosím/Není zač* | Where is . . .? | *kde je . . .?* |
| Sorry | *pardon* | How do I get to Prague? | *jak se dostanu do* |
| Thank you | *děkuju* | | *Prahy ?* |
| Bon appetit | *dobrou chuť* | How do I get to the | *jak se dostanu k* |
| Bon voyage | *šťastnou cestu* | university? | *univerzitě?* |
| Hello/goodbye (informal) | *ahoj* | By bus | *autobusem* |
| Goodbye (formal) | *na shledanou* | By train | *vlakem* |
| Good day | *dobrý den* | By car | *autem* |
| Good morning | *dobré ráno* | By foot | *pěšky* |
| Good evening | *dobrý večer* | By taxi | *taxíkem* |
| Good night (when leaving) | *dobrou noc* | Ticket | *jízdenka lístek* |
| How are you? | *jak se máte?* | Return ticket | *zpátečá jízdenka* |
| Today | *dnes* | Railway station | *nádraží* |
| Yesterday | *včera* | Bus station | *autobusové nádraží* |
| Tomorrow | *zítra* | Bus stop | *autobusová zastávka* |
| The day after tomorrow | *pozítra* | When's the next train | *kdy jde další vlak* |
| Now | *hnet* | to Prague? | *do Prahy?* |
| Later | *později* | Is it going to Prague? | *jde to do Prahy?* |
| Leave me alone | *pusť mě* | Do I have to change? | *musím přestupovat?* |
| Go away | *jdi pryč* | Do I need a | *musím mit* |
| Help! | *pomoc!* | reservation? | *místenku?* |
| This one | *tento* | | |
| A little | *trócha* | | |
| Large/small | *velký/malý* | **Questions and answers** | |
| More/less | *více/méně* | Do you speak English? | *mluvíte anglicky?* |
| Good/bad | *dobrý/špatný* | I don't speak German | *nemluvím německy* |
| Hot/cold | *horký/studený* | I don't understand | *nerozumím* |
| With/without | *s/bez* | I understand | *rozumím* |
| | | Speak slowly | *mluvte pomalu* |
| | | How do you say that | *jak se tohle řekne* |
| **Getting around** | | in Czech? | *česky?* |
| Over here | *tady* | Could you write it | *mužete mi to* |
| Over there | *tam* | down for me? | *napsat?* |

| | | | |
|---|---|---|---|
| What | *co* | Departure | *odjezd* |
| Where | *kde* | Police | *policie* |
| When | *kdy* | | |
| Why | *proč* | **Days of the week** | |
| How much is it? | *kolik stojí?* | Monday | *pondělí* |
| Are there any rooms available? | *máte volné pokoje?* | Tuesday | *uterý* |
| | | Wednesday | *středa* |
| I would like a double room | *chtěl bych dvou lůžkovy pokoj* | Thursday | *čtvrtek* |
| | | Friday | *pátek* |
| For one night | *na jednu noc* | Saturday | *sobota* |
| With shower | *se sprchou* | Sunday | *neděle* |
| Are these seats free? | *jsou tyto místa volná?* | Day | *den* |
| | | Week | *týden* |
| May we (sit down)? | *můžeme?* | Month | *měsíc* |
| The bill please | *zaplatím prosím* | Year | *rok* |
| Do you have . . .? | *máte . . .?* | | |
| We don't have | *nemáme* | | |
| We do have | *máme* | | |

**Months of the year**

Many Slav languages have their own highly individual systems in which the words for the names of the month are descriptive nouns – sometimes beautifully apt for the month in question.

**Some signs**

| | |
|---|---|
| Entrance | *vchod* |
| Exit | *východ* |
| Toilets | *záchod* |

| | |
|---|---|
| January | *leden* – ice |
| February | *únor* – hibernation |
| March | *březen* – birch |
| April | *duben* – oak |

| | |
|---|---|
| Men | *muži* |
| Women | *ženy* |
| Ladies | *dámy* |
| Gentlemen | *pánové* |
| Open | *otevřeno* |
| Closed | *zavřeno* |
| Danger! | *pozor!* |
| Hospital | *nemocnice* |
| No smoking | *kouření zakázáno* |
| No bathing | *koupání zakázáno* |
| No entry | *vstup zakázáno* |
| Arrival | *příjezd* |

| | |
|---|---|
| May | *květen* – blossom |
| June | *červen* – red |
| July | *červenec* – redder |
| August | *srpen* – sickle |
| September | *zaří* – blazing |
| October | *říjen* – rutting |
| November | *listopad* – leaves falling |
| December | *prosinec* – slaughter of pigs |

**Numbers**

| | | | | | |
|---|---|---|---|---|---|
| 1 | *jeden* | 14 | *čtrnáct* | 90 | *devadesát* |
| 2 | *dva* | 15 | *patnáct* | 100 | *sto* |
| 3 | *tří* | 16 | *šestnáct* | 101 | *sto jedna* |
| 4 | *čtyři* | 17 | *sedmnáct* | 155 | *sto padesát pět* |
| 5 | *pět* | 18 | *osumnáct* | 200 | *dvě stě* |
| 6 | *šest* | 19 | *devatenáct* | 300 | *tří sta* |
| 7 | *sedm* | 20 | *dvacet* | 400 | *čtyří sta* |
| 8 | *osum* | 21 | *dvacetjedna* | 500 | *pět set* |
| 9 | *devět* | 30 | *třicet* | 600 | *šest set* |
| 10 | *deset* | 40 | *čtyřicet* | 700 | *sedm set* |
| 11 | *jedenáct* | 50 | *padesát* | 800 | *osum set* |
| 12 | *dvanáct* | 60 | *šedesát* | 900 | *devět set* |
| 13 | *třináct* | 70 | *sedmdesát* | 1000 | *tisíc* |
| | | 80 | *osumdesát* | | |

# Prague's leading personalities – past and present

**Beneš, Edvard** (1884–1948). President from 1935 until the Munich Crisis and again from 1945 until the Communist coup in 1948. Making a stronger than expected comeback.

**Čapek, Karel** (1890–1938). Czech writer, journalist and unofficial spokesperson for the First Republic. His most famous works are *The Insect Play* and *R.U.R.*, which introduced the word *robot* into the English language.

**Dobrovský, Josef** (1753–1829). Jesuit-taught pioneer in Czech philology. Wrote the seminal text *The History of Czech Language and Literature*.

**Dubček, Alexander** Slovak Communist who became First Secretary in January 1968, at the beginning of the Prague Spring. Expelled from the Party in 1969, but returned to become speaker in the federal parliament after 1989.

**Dvořák, Antonín** (1841–1904). Perhaps the most famous of all Czech composers. His best-known work is the *New World Symphony*, inspired by an extensive sojourn in the USA.

**Fučik, Julius** (1903–1943). Communist journalist murdered by the Nazis, whose prison writings, *Notes from the Gallows*, were obligatory reading in the 1950s. Hundreds of streets were named after him, but doubts about the authenticity of the work, and general hostility towards the man have made him *persona non grata*.

**Gottwald, Klement** (1896–1953). One of the founders of the KSČ, General Secretary from 1927, Prime Minister from 1946 to 1948, and President from 1948 to 1953, Gottwald is universally abhorred for his role in the show trials of the 1950s.

**Hašek, Jaroslav** (1883–1923). Anarchist, dog-breeder, lab assistant, bigamist, cabaret artist and People's Commissar in the Red Army, Hašek was one of prewar Prague's most colourful characters, who wrote the famous *Good Soldier Švejk* and died from alcohol in 1923.

**Havel, Václav** (1936–). Absurdist playwright of the 1960s, who became a leading spokesperson of Charter 77 and, following the Velvet Revolution, the country's first post-Communist president.

**Havlíček-Borovský, Karel** (1821–56). Satirical poet, journalist and nationalist, exiled to the Tyrol by the Austrian authorities after 1848.

**Hrabal, Bohumil** Writer and bohemian, whose novels were banned under the Communists, but revered worldwide. Hrabal is a regular at Prague's *U zlatého tygra*.

**Hus, Jan** (1370–1415). Rector of Prague University and reformist preacher who was burnt at the stake as a heretic by the Council of Constance.

**Husák, Gustáv** (died 1991). Slovak Communist who was sentenced to life imprisonment in the show trials of the 1950s, released in 1960, and eventually became General Secretary and President following the Soviet invasion. Resigned in favour of Havel in December 1989.

**Jirásek, Alois** (1851–1930). Writer for both children and adults who popularised Czech legends and became a key figure in the *národní obrození*.

**Jungmann, Josef** (1773–1847). Prolific Czech translator and author of the seminal *History of Czech Literature* and the first Czech dictionary.

**Kafka, Franz** (1883–1924). German-Jewish Praguer who worked as an insurance clerk in Prague for most of his life, and also wrote some of the most influential novels of the twentieth century, most notably *The Trial*.

**Kelley, Edward** English occultist who was summoned to Prague by Rudolf II, but eventually incurred the wrath of the emperor and was imprisoned in Kokořín castle.

**Kepler, Johannes** (1571–1630). German Protestant forced to leave Linz for Denmark on account of the Counter-Reformation. Succeeded Tycho de Brahe as Rudolf II's chief astronomer. His observations of the planets became the basis of the laws of planetary motion.

**Kisch, Egon Erwin** (1885–1948). German-Jewish Praguer who became one of the city's most famous investigative journalists.

**Klaus, Václav.** Known somewhat bitterly as "Santa Klaus". The Finance Minister and driving force behind the country's present economic reforms.

**Komenský, Jan Amos** (1592–1670). Leader of the Protestant Czech Brethren. Forced to flee the country and settle in England during the Counter-Reformation. Better known to English-speakers as Comenius.

**Landovský, Pavel** Well-known Czech actor, long-time friend of Havel, and currently an MP.

**Mácha, Karel Hynek** (1810–36). Romantic nationalist poet, great admirer of Byron and Keats and, like them, died young. His most famous poem is *Maj*, published just months before his death.

**Masaryk, Jan** Son of the founder of the republic (see below), Foreign Minister in the postwar government and the only non-Communist in Gottwald's cabinet when the Communists took over in February 1948. Died ten days after the coup in mysterious circumstances.

**Masaryk, Tomáš Garrigue** (1850–1937). Professor of Philosophy at Prague University, President of the Republic from 1918 to 1935. His name is synonymous with the First Republic and was removed from all street signs after the 1948 coup. Now back with a vengeance.

**Mucha, Alfons** (1860–1939). Moravian graphic artist and designer whose Art-Nouveau posters and artwork for Sarah Bernhardt brought him international fame. After the founding of Czechoslovakia, he returned to the country to design stamps, bank notes, and complete a cycle of giant canvases on Czech nationalist themes.

**Němcová, Božena** (1820–1862). Highly popular writer who became involved with the nationalist movement and shocked many with her unorthodox behaviour. Her most famous book is *Grandmother*.

**Neruda, Jan** (1834–1891). Poet and journalist for the *Národní listy*. Wrote some famous short stories describing Prague's Malá Strana.

**Palacký, František** (1798–1876). Nationalist historian, Czech MP in Vienna and leading figure in the events of 1848.

**Purkyně, Jan Evangelista** (1787–1869). Czech doctor, natural scientist and pioneer in experimental physiology who became professor of physiology at Prague and then at Wrocław University.

**Rieger, Ladislav.** Nineteenth-century Czech politician and one of the leading figures in the events of 1848 and the aftermath.

**Rilke, Rainer Maria** (1876–1926). Despite having been brought up as a girl for the first six years of his life, Rilke ended up as an officer in the Austrian army, as well as writing some of the city's finest German *fin-de-siècle* poetry.

**Smetana, Bedřich** (1824–1884). Popular Czech composer and fervent nationalist whose *Má vlast* (My Homeland) traditionally opens the Prague Spring Music Festival.

**Svoboda, Ludvík.** Victorious Czech General from World War II, who acquiesced to the 1948 Communist coup and was Communist President from 1968 to 1975.

**Tycho de Brahe** (1546–1601). Groundbreaking Danish astronomer, who was summoned to Prague by Rudolf II in 1597, only to die from over-drinking in 1601.

**Tyl, Josef Kajetán** (1808–1856). Czech playwright and composer of the Czech half of the national anthem, *Where is my Home?*.

**Werfel, Franz** (1890–1945). One of the German-Jewish literary circle, which included Kafka, Kisch and Brod.

**Žižka, Jan** (died 1424). Brilliant, blind military leader of the Táborites, the radical faction of the Hussites.

# A glossary of Czech words and terms

**brána** Gate.
**český** Bohemian.
**chata** Chalet-type bungalow or country cottage.
**chrám** Large church.
**divadlo** Theatre.
**dóm** Cathedral.
**dům** House.
**dům kultury** Communal arts and social centre; literally "House of Culture".
**hrad** Castle.
**hranice** Border.
**hřbitov** Cemetery.
**hora** Mountain.
**hostinec** Local pub.
**jeskyně** Cave.
**jezero** Lake.
**kámen** Rock.
**kaple** Chapel.
**katedrála** Cathedral.
**kavárna** Coffee house.
**klášter** Monastery/convent.
**kostel** Church.
**koupaliště** Swimming pool.
**Labe** River Elbe.
**lanovka** Funicular or cable car.
**les** Forest.
**město** Town; *staré město* – Old Town, *nové město* – New Town, *dolní město* – Lower Town, *horní město* – Upper Town.
**most** Bridge.
**nádraží** Train station.
**náměstí** Square, as in *náměstí Svobody* – Freedom Square.
**národní výbor** Town council.
**ostrov** Island.
**památník** Memorial or monument.
**pivnice** Pub.
**prohlídka** Viewpoint.
**radnice** Town hall.

**Rathaus** Town hall (German).
**restaurace** Restaurant.
**sady** Park.
**sál** Room or hall (in a chateau or castle).
**skála** Crag/rock.
**skansen** An open-air folk museum, with reconstructed folk art and architecture.
**svatý** Saint. Abbreviated to sv.
**teplice** Spa.
**třída** Avenue.
**věž** Tower.
**vinárna** Wine bar or cellar.
**Vltava** River Moldau.
**vrchy** Hills.
**výstava** Exhibition.
**zahrada** Gardens.
**zámek** Chateau.

## An Architectural Glossary

**Ambulatory** Passage round the back of the altar, in continuation of the aisles.

**Art Nouveau** French term for the sinuous and stylised form of architecture dating from 1900 to 1910; known as the Secession in Czechoslovakia and as *Jugendstil* in Germany.

**Baroque** Expansive, exuberant architectural style of the seventeenth and mid-eighteenth centuries, characterised by ornate decoration, complex spatial arrangement and grand vistas.

**Beautiful Style** Also known as the Soft Style of painting. Developed in Bohemia in the fourteenth century, it became very popular in Germany.

**Chancel** The part of the church where the altar is placed, usually at the east end.

**Empire** Highly decorative Neoclassical style of architecture and decorative arts, practised in the early 1800s.

**Fresco** Mural painting applied to wet plaster, so that the colours immediately soak into the wall.

**Functionalism** Plain, boxy, modernist architectural style, prevalent in the late 1920s and 1930s in Czechoslovakia, often using plate-glass curtain walls and open-plan interiors.

**Gothic** Architectural style prevalent from the fourteenth to the sixteenth century, characterised by pointed arches and ribbed vaulting.

**Loggia** Covered area on the side of a building, often arcaded.

**Nave** Main body of a church, usually the western end.

**Neoclassical** Late eighteenth- and early nineteenth-century style of architecture and design returning to classical Greek and Roman models as a reaction against Baroque and Rococo excesses.

**Oriel** A bay window, usually projecting from an upper floor.

**Romanesque** Solid architectural style of the late tenth to thirteenth century, characterised by round-headed arches and geometrical precision.

**Rococo** Highly florid, fiddly though (occasionally) graceful style of architecture and interior design, forming the last phase of Baroque.

**Secession** Linear and stylised form of architecture and decorative arts imported from Vienna and a reaction against the academic establishment.

**Sgraffito** Monochrome plaster decoration effected by means of scraping back the first white layer to reveal the black underneath.

**Stucco** Plaster used for decorative effects.

**Trompe l'oeil** Painting designed to fool the onlooker into believing that it is actually three-dimensional.

# Index

# THE ROUGH GUIDES

The complete series of Rough Guides are available from all good bookshops but can be obtained directly from Penguin by writing to: *Penguin Direct, Penguin Books Ltd, Bath Road, Harmondsworth, West Drayton, Middlesex UB7 ODA; or telephone our credit line on 081 899 4036 (9am - 5pm)* and ask for Penguin Direct. Visa, Access and Amex accepted. Delivery will normally be within 14 working days.

| Title | ISBN | Price | Title | ISBN | Price |
|---|---|---|---|---|---|
| Amsterdam | 1858280184 | £6.99 | Mediterranean Wildlife | 0747100993 | £7.95 |
| Australia | 1858280354 | £12.99 | Mexico | 0747101493 | £6.95 |
| Barcelona and Catalunya | 0747102716 | £7.99 | Morocco | 1858280400 | £9.99 |
| Berlin | 1858280338 | £8.99 | Nepal | 185828046X | £8.99 |
| Brazil | 0747101272 | £7.95 | New York | 1858280737 | £6.99 |
| Brittany & Normandy | 1858280192 | £7.99 | Nothing Ventured | 0747102082 | £7.99 |
| Bulgaria | 1858280478 | £8.99 | Paris | 1858280389 | £7.99 |
| California | 1858280575 | £9.99 | Peru | 0747102546 | £7.95 |
| Canada | 185828001X | £10.99 | Poland | 1858280346 | £9.99 |
| Crete | 1858280494 | £6.99 | Portugal | 1858280222 | £7.99 |
| Cyprus | 185828032X | £8.99 | Prague | 185828015X | £7.99 |
| Czech and Slovak Republics | 185828029X | £8.99 | Provence/Cote d'Azur | 1858280230 | £8.99 |
| Egypt | 1858280753 | £10.99 | Pyrenees | 1858280524 | £7.99 |
| Europe | 1858280273 | £12.99 | St Petersburg | 1858280303 | £8.99 |
| Florida | 1858280109 | £7.99 | San Francisco | 0747102589 | £5.99 |
| France | 1858280508 | £9.99 | Scandinavia | 1858280397 | £10.99 |
| Germany | 1858280257 | £11.99 | Sicily | 1858280370 | £8.99 |
| Greece | 1858280206 | £9.99 | Spain | 1858280079 | £8.99 |
| Guatemala & Belize | 1858280451 | £9.99 | Thailand | 1858280168 | £8.99 |
| Holland, Belgium, Luxembourg | 1858280036 | £8.99 | Tunisia | 074710249X | £8.99 |
| Hong Kong & Macau | 1858280664 | £8.99 | Turkey | 1858280133 | £8.99 |
| Hungary | 1858280214 | £7.99 | Tuscany and Umbria | 1858280559 | £8.99 |
| Ireland | 1858280516 | £8.99 | U.S.A. | 1858280281 | £12.99 |
| Italy | 1858280311 | £12.99 | Venice | 1858280362 | £8.99 |
| Kenya | 1858280435 | £9.99 | West Africa | 1858280141 | £12.99 |
| | | | Women Travel | 1858280710 | £7.99 |
| | | | Zimbabwe & Botswana | 1858280419 | £10.99 |

The availability and published prices quoted are correct at the time of going to press but are subject to alteration without prior notice.
Penguin Direct ordering facilities are only available in the UK.

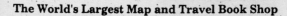

You are
A STUDENT

You travel
THE WORLD

You want
TO SAVE MONEY

Here's
how

The International
Student Identity Card

International Student Identity Card

ISIC

Family name/Nom de famille
Sian
First Name/Prénom
Sharovsh
Born/Geburtsdatum/Né le
20/8/1973
Nationality/Nationalité/Nationalité
French
Student of/University
University of Paris
STUDENT

Available at Student Travel Offices Worldwide.

Entitles you to discounts and special services worldwide.

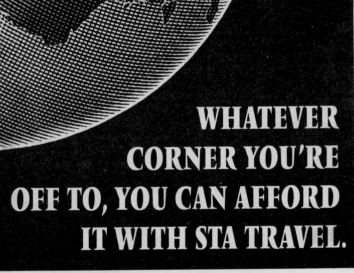